A HISTORY OF CONTEMPORARY KOREA

A HISTORY
OF
CONTEMPORARY KOREA

by

KANG, MAN-GIL

Korea University

GLOBAL
ORIENTAL

A HISTORY OF CONTEMPORARY KOREA

© Kang, Man-gil, 1994

Originally published in Korea by Changbi Publishers, Inc

First published in English 2005 by
GLOBAL ORIENTAL
PO Box 219
Folkestone
Kent CT20 2WP
UK

www.globaloriental.co.uk

© English translation Global Oriental Ltd, 2005

ISBN 1-905246-05-6

British Library Cataloguing in Publication Data
A CIP catalogue entry for this book is available
from the British Library

This book is published with the support of the
Korea Literature Translation Institute to
commemorate Korea as Guest of Honour
at the Frankfurt Book Fair 2005

Set in 9/10.5pt Stone Serif by Servis Filmsetting Ltd, Manchester
Printed and bound in England by Athenaeum Press, Gateshead, Tyne & Wear

Contents

Translator's Preface

There are two main reasons why I decided, despite an impossibly busy schedule, to translate Professor Kang, Man-gil's *Koch'yŏ ssŭn han'guk hyŏndaesa* or, as rendered here, *A History of Contemporary Korea*.

The first was my deep respect and affection for Professor Kang. During my years as an undergraduate student at Korea University in the early 1970s, Professor Kang's well organized, intellectually stimulating, and at times politically charged lectures were a source of inspiration for all of us fortunate enough to be in his classes. His determination and courage as a scholar and public intellectual to stand against the military dictatorships of Park Chung Hee and Chun Doo Hwan continued to inspire all of us who hoped for democracy and peace in Korea during the difficult years of the 1970s and 1980s.

The second was my belief in the importance of this book. Although there have been major situational and attitudinal changes since it was first written in 1984 and later revised in 1994, it still remains as a representative work of progressive south Korean historical scholarship. Conservatives will object to what they consider to be a leftist bias, while post-modernists, post-colonialists and advocates of colonial modernity will find fault with the oppression/resistance binary that forms the main interpretive thrust of the narrative. Nonetheless, the view of world and Korean history embodied in this book is characteristic of that which the new generation of south Koreans who have now emerged under the Roh Moo Hyun government as leaders of their society learned during their formative years in the 1980s. For that reason alone, it is vitally important that the rest of the world – and particularly the English-speaking world – be given access to the facts, concepts and interpretations contained here. It is also for that reason that I did my best, against the advice of some of my American colleagues, to produce a translation that renders, as faithfully as I can, Professor Kang's voice.

I would like to express my appreciation to the Korean Literature Translation Institute for their generosity in sponsoring this translation and for their tolerance of my inability to meet deadlines and to Global Oriental Ltd for their extraordinary efforts in publishing this translation under difficult circumstances. I would also like to recognize the efforts of Dr Hongjoon Jung, who laboured mightily to produce a rough draft of the first three chapters of this translation. Most of all, however, I wish to thank Kang sŏnsaengnim for being the man that he is and for doing the things he has done.

John B. Duncan
Somewhere between Seoul and Los Angeles
14 June 2005

Note on Korean Currency
Immediately after liberation, Koreans continud to use Japanese yen (read wŏn in Korean). The Syngman Rhee regime used the *hwan*, but that was replaced in the early 1960s with the wŏn at a conversion rate of 100 *hwan* = 1 wŏn. Professor Kang sometimes uses wŏn when discussing the 1950s economy.

Preface to the English Translation

This book was first published as *Han'guk hyŏndaesa* (Contemporary history of Korea) in 1984, revised and published again as *Koch'yŏ ssŭn han'guk hyŏndaesa* (Revised contemporary history of Korea), and now published in English translation as *A History of Contemporary Korea* in 2005.

When I wrote *Han'guk hyŏndaesa* in 1984, I had to be extremely careful in handling the history of the colonial period socialist movement and was able to include only a tiny portion. By 1994, however, the situation had turned for the better and I was able to write a comparatively more detailed history of the socialist movement. Furthermore, the growth of interest in and research on the left-right united front movement made it possible to include a more substantial treatment.

In the ten years since I wrote *Koch'yŏ ssŭn han'guk hyŏndaesa*, and particularly since the north-south joint statement of 15 June 2000, there have been great changes in the contemporary history of the entire Korean Peninsula. An association of northern and southern historians has been formed, many historians from both sides have met, and there have been several joint academic conferences. As I write this, preparations are underway for a joint conference on the 100th anniversary of the protectorate treaty of 1905, as are negotiations for the joint preservation of relics from the ancient kingdom of Koguryŏ.

I am fully aware of the need for writing and translating a new contemporary history of the Korean Peninsula that includes north Korea and the changes that have taken place in recent years. But much research remains to be done before such a book can be written and I regret that this translation is of the ten-year old *Koch'yŏ ssŭn han'guk hyŏndae* that covers only the history of south Korea.

I can only hope that a contemporary history of the entire Korean Peninsula will be written in the near future. I offer my thanks to Professor John Duncan who translated this book and to Dr Hong Joon Jung and the others who have helped him.

Kang, Man-gill
March 2005

Preface to the Second Edition

I remember starting to write *Han'guk Kŭndaesa* (*Modern History of Korea*) and *Han'guk hyŏndaesa* (*Contemporary History of Korea*) in January 1981. That was the time when, following the assassination of Park Chung Hee on 26 October 1979, the so-called 'new military' led by Chun Doo Hwan and Roh Tae Woo had come to power through the 12 December 1979 incident, the 17 May expansion of martial law and the suppression of the Kwangju *minjung* resistance, and was exerting immense tyranny against democratic forces in all sectors of society under the pretext of 'cleansing' south Korea. I was among those targeted by the regime and was forced out of my position at Korea University.

I decided to use my time in 'internal exile' to write books on the modern and contemporary history of Korea which I had been teaching during the previous twenty years. It was not to be an easy task. Even now I remember clearly how difficult it was to write under conditions so restrictive that I could not even use university libraries. At the time manuscripts were completed, I underwent another round of persecution from the authorities and experienced a great deal of difficulty in getting the books published. But the books received a much bigger response than I expected and that helped me to forget some of the pain.

The national democratic movement continued vigorously even under the tyranny of the military. The result was the lifting of the dark clouds of oppression as south Korea began to make some progress towards democracy. This progress towards democracy brought what can be called epoch-making results in scholarship, especially in research on our modern and contemporary history.

As an example, when I wrote *Han'guk hyŏndaesa* in the early 1980s, I had to be very careful in how I described the colonial period communist movement, and even that had to be limited to the 1920s. Nonetheless, I believe that that was the first time anyone had included the communist movement in either a general history of Korea or a history of the colonial period. At the time there were very few historians writing such histories who thought that the communist movement was part of the national liberation movement and even those few believed that any history included the communist movement could not be published because of government censorship. Furthermore, while there had been some research on the communist movement of the 1920s, virtually nothing had been done on the 1930s.

In the ten years following the publication of *Han'guk hyŏndaesa*, however, it became commonplace to include the communist movement in general history and history of the colonial period. Furthermore, rapid progress was being made in research on the revolutionary labour and peasant movements, the movement to reconstruct the Communist Party, the activities of the Northeastern Anti-Japanese Allied Army, the Fatherland Restoration Association and the united front movement. This research was done mostly by young scholars in their thirties who became the leaders of what might be called the 'group of progressive historians'. This must be considered a surprising change for the better.

Let me give one more example. In *Han'guk hyŏndaesa*, I depicted the 'liberation space' in terms of a national movement striving for the establishment of a unified nation state whose line went from the activities of the Committee for the Preparation of Korean Independence to the left-right coalition movement and then to the 1948 north-south meeting in P'yŏngyang. At that time, I had many colleagues who advised against it out of fear of repression by the government and the extreme right. In the ten years since then, a number of Ph.D. dissertations have appeared tracing the line of the national movement in the same way and the position occupied by the movement in our modern history is now widely recognized. Indeed, there has even been criticism that such a depiction of the movement is nothing but a kind of half-way measure. This has been a truly amazing transformation.

These changes led me to think that I needed to rewrite our modern and contemporary history and I seriously considered abandoning the idea of revising *Han'guk kŭndaesa* and *Han'guk hyŏndaesa* because I was pretty much satisfied that they had fulfilled a role in a dark time of our history and because I knew it would be difficult to incorporate all the productive new research that had become available since their publication. However, the view of history in those books, written on the basis of research up through the 1970s and reflecting late 1970s' historical consciousness, still had some life left in it. In fact, what had been a particular view of history in the early 1980s was on its way to becoming a universally accepted view of history in the 1980s. If anything, the changes occurring in both world history and our national history from the late 1980s confirmed and strengthened the historical view and historical direction laid out in *Han'guk kŭndaesa* and *Han'guk hyŏndaesa*. In the end, therefore, I decided to incorporate what I could of post-1980s' research into revisions of the two books.

In particular, the sections of *Koch'yŏ ssŭn han'guk hyŏndae* that deal with social and economic history of the time before and after liberation in 1945 not only incorporate new south Korean research but

also research by north Korean scholars, something that was very difficult to do ten years ago. In addition, I greatly expanded the treatment
of the post-1930 national liberation movement and rewrote the
entire section. I also added new sections on the movement to establish a
unified nation state and sections dealing with the politics, economy,
society and culture under the Chun Doo Hwan and Roh Tae Woo
regimes.

There is no denying that it is now somewhat easier, both academically
and politically, to add in treatment of the history of north Korea than it
was when I wrote *Han'guk hyŏndaesa*. Nonetheless, I decided to limit
Kochyŏ ssŭn han'guksa to south Korea. The reason is because I do not like
the current approaches of writing our post-liberation history either as a
south Korea-centred history to which a brief discussion of north Korea is
appended or as separate histories of south and north that are then
slapped together in one volume as 'histories of contemporary Korea'.
Rather, I believe that we must recognize that north and south each has
its own post-1945 historical development with its own specific historicity, that we should fuse the two into one national history that treats
north and south as equals and provides the same amount of coverage for
each. I do not believe that conditions are yet ready for that, either in
terms of scholarship or in terms of outside factors. Such historical consciousness also makes it difficult to call a book that treats both north and
south as '*Han'guk' hyŏndaesa*.

I must also touch on what some might consider a trivial matter. That
is the question of how to write the Chinese and Japanese proper nouns
that appear in this book. I believe that the principle should be, no matter
what country you are dealing with, to write proper nouns as they are
pronounced in their own countries, and in fact that is increasingly
becoming the practice. In the case of Chinese, however, the facts that we
are accustomed to reading Chinese characters in Korean pronunciation
and that the task of trying to verify Chinese language pronunciations is
daunting led me use Korean pronunciation and to add, when necessary,
Chinese pronunciation in parentheses. As for Japanese, in the case of
kunyomi, I simply used the original Japanese pronunciation without the
Chinese characters in recognition of the way in the Japanese have simply
borrowed those characters to write their own language. I also used the
Japanese pronunciation in the case of *onyomi*, although in some
instances I had no choice but to use Korean pronunciations of the characters. I crave the readers' indulgence.

Whereas I wrote *Han'guk hyŏndaesa* with the help of only a few
persons, I mobilized virtually all of the students in the Korea University
graduate programme, along with recent graduates of the programme specializing in modern and contemporary Korean history to accomplish this
revision. I could not have done this revision without their help. In addition, I received help from Kim Yongil in writing the sections on education and help from Chŏng Ihwan and Sin Tuwŏn in writing the sections
on the labour movement and culture. Despite all the help of many

people, I am responsible for any errors or omissions. I extend my thanks to those who helped me in the writing process and also to Chŏng Haeryŏm and Ko Sehyŏn of Ch'angjak kwa pip'yŏngsa.

Kang Man-gil
9 January 1994

Preface to the First Edition

Following the earlier publication of *Han'guk kŭndaesa*, which treated the history of the later period of the Chosŏn dynasty and the *Kaewha* period between the opening of the ports in 1876 and annexation by Japan in 1910, I am now publishing this book, *Han 'guk hyŏndaesa*, which covers the colonial period and the period of division after liberation in 1945.

The structure of this book and my intentions are the same as in *Han'guk kŭndaesa*. I have organized it as a kind of topical history in which I begin with the implementation of the Japanese policy of colonial rule and the development of the national liberation in opposition. I next discuss the evolution of Japanese colonial economic policy and Japanese colonial social and cultural policies and the national cultural movement. For the post-liberation period, I begin with the tragic process of the establishment of the division system and the development of the national reunification movement as an effort to overcome division, followed by the process of the reconstruction of a capitalist economy after the end of the colonial economic regime and its weaknesses, and treatments of the social and cultural systems and their limitations in the division era.

One of the reasons I chose to write this kind of topical history rather than a more conventional chronological history is to avoid the latter's focus on political and diplomatic history. Another reason is that it made me think carefully once again about the issue of what kinds of facts one chooses when writing history.

Research on colonial-period history still has a long way to go. There has been some progress in research on the independence movement, but it has not been systematized, and research on the colonial economy, society and culture has yet to reach the stage where it can provide a solid base for the writing of a general or a period history. That made it very difficult to write a history of the colonial period that the general educated public can read without too much effort. Indeed, we need a general history of the colonial period.

The post-liberation period of division occupies fully half of this book, which may seem like a lot for a history. Because there has been virtually no historical research on this period, I had to rely primarily on the research of social scientists. Not only do we historians in south Korea avoid researching the period in which we live, but we are also not able to fulfil the role of integrating social science research into a more comprehensive historical understanding of our period. This makes it truly difficult to write a history of post-1945 Korea. When we think, however, about how Pak Ŭnsik was able to write histories of his own time in the *Han'guk t'ongsa* (Painful history of Korea) and the *Han'guk tongnip undong ŭi hyŏlsa* (Blood history of the Korean independence movement), it becomes clear that we historians have been shirking our duty to research and write about our time, the division period.

The most important reason why the historians of today have to engage in researching and writing the history of the division period is because we have the duty to contribute to the overcoming of national division. Even as I point out this fact, I must admit to the embarrassment that I feel because this book, too, is not able to transcend the division system and stands simply as a history of the division period. I have striven to keep this book from becoming buried in the division system to the extent I can without avoiding the realities of the system, but I know that this shortcoming cannot be overcome by admitting to my embarrassment.

This book and the *Han'guk kŭndaesa* were written during the frustrating time after I was driven out of my university position, a time that still has not come to an end. I am not sure to what extent I have the ability to succeed in the historian's task of facing historical reality, objectifying that reality and writing it as a history. But I do have the heavy-hearted feeling, as the manuscript leaves my hands, that I should have done a better job.

As in the case of the *Han'guk kŭndaesa*, I included as references only those works which I actually used. I also wish to apologize for the duplication entailed in the writing of a topical history, for the excessively large number of statistical tables in the sections dealing with economic history. I also have not yet been able to digest fully modern economic theory. The reader will note some discrepancies in statistical data. Those are the cases I was unable to resolve because I was unable to access the original sources.

Publication has been delayed for over a year because of my personal situation. I offer my thanks to the Ch'angjak kwa pip'yŏngsa.

Kang, Man-gil
7 May 1984

PART 1

Colonial Rule and the National Liberation Movement

1

The Realities of Colonial Rule

INTRODUCTION

The thirty-five years of Japanese colonial rule over Korea can be generally broken down into three periods. The first is from 'annexation' in 1910 to the March First Movement of 1919, the second from the March First Movement to the 'Manchurian Incident' of 1931 and the third from the 'Manchurian Incident' to Japan's withdrawal after its defeat in 1945.

The first period is often called the period of military rule. This was the time when the Japanese, in order to suppress the Righteous Armies and the Patriotic Enlightenment Movement, prohibited all military, political and cultural activities, and laid down the administrative, economic, social and cultural foundations of colonial rule amid an atmosphere of fear. The Japanese military police controlled the Korean Peninsula so thoroughly that the residents could hardly breathe. However, even under such oppressive policies the national resistance movement continued, eventually exploding into the nationwide March First Movement for national liberation in 1919.

The second period, the time of the so-called 'Cultural Politics', was when Japan, surprised by the March First Movement and realizing that it could no longer control Korea by force alone, shifted to a policy of dividing the Korean nation through what was euphemistically called 'Cultural Politics'. Japan replaced its military police with regular police, permitted the publication of Korean language newspapers, and allowed some degree of public assembly and forming of associations. On the other hand, Japan also enjoyed some success in dividing the national liberation front by strengthening its efforts to promote the growth of pro-Japanese elements in the colony. One segment of the national liberation movement forces broke away from the line of absolute independence and armed struggle, instead advocating autonomy under colonial rule and transforming the national movement into a cultural movement. Of particular interest in this regard is the way in which the so-called system of local self-rule instituted at this time expanded the ranks of pro-Japanese Koreans, who had been limited to some members of the royal family and politicians at the time of 'annexation', to include landlords and intellectuals. This marked a further strengthening of the base of colonial rule.

The third period was the time after the end of the so-called Taisho democracy, when Japan began moving towards a fascist system. These were the years when Japan demanded wartime co-operation from its Korean colony in support of its growing military aggression in the Manchurian Incident (1931) the Sino-Japanese War (1937) and the Second World War. During the wartime years, the fascist regime was even stronger in the colony than in Japan itself. The Japanese implemented barbaric policies of a sort not seen in any other case of colonial rule, such as the Name Change Order and the eradication of the Korean language.

Although no political movement to overthrow monarchical rule had arisen in the years before Korea was colonized, there were political organizations, such as the New People's Association arising during the time of the Great Han Empire, that called for the establishment of a republic and showed signs of developing into a movement for popular sovereignty. Once Korea was colonized, however, no form of political activity was allowed and no political parties could exist. Thus, throughout the entire colonial period the people inside Korea were unable either to gain any training for democratic politics or to produce political leaders with democratic traits. The thirty-five years of colonial rule were the period when Korean history should have liquidated the old system of autocratic monarchy and established a democratic political system. But, under Japan's militaristic colonial rule, the Korean people were deprived of any opportunity to learn democratic politics.

Furthermore, Japan's colonial rule of Korea helped to set the stage for the north-south division of the Korean Peninsula after the end of the Second World War. Japanese colonial rule inhibited the growth of Korean capital and of the Korean bourgeoisie. The backwardness of capitalistic development and Japanese policies of suppression hindered the growth of an organized and trained proletariat. The Japanese strove prevent the development of a social class that would be capable of leading the national liberation movement while also seeking to intensify class differences through their policy of promoting internal divisions within Korean society.

As the Second World War was drawing to a close, Japan had already lost the ability to wage war. However, by refusing to surrender and girding itself for the 'final battle of Japan', the Japanese brought about the participation of the Soviet Union in the war and the advance of Soviet troops into Korea. The US, anxious to prevent the Soviets from occupying the whole peninsula, proposed the thirty-eighth parallel as the dividing line between Soviet and US forces in Korea. This divided occupation of the Korean Peninsula led to the territorial and national division of Korea.

The greatest political harm inflicted on Korea by Japanese colonial rule can be seen in two areas. One was the total denial of any opportunity for the Korean people to gain democratic political experience, thereby hampering the establishment of democratic forms of politics even after liberation in 1945. The other was creating the conditions that led to national division.

SECTION ONE
Oppression Under Military Rule

THE GOVERNMENT-GENERAL OF KOREA

'Annexation' in 1910 meant that the Great Han Empire had come to an end and Korea became simply one region, known as Chosen, within the Empire of Japan. The Japanese Residency-General of the protectorate period (1905–10) was reorganized as the Government-General of Korea as real and total colonial rule got underway. The Governor-General reported directly to the emperor and was almost completely free of control by the cabinet. He exercised absolute power in the colony, combining in his one office administrative, legislative and military authority. The men appointed as Governors-General of Korea were all army generals and navy admirals. The first Governor-General of Korea was Terauchi Masatake (1852–1919), who had been Resident-General at the time of 'annexation' and who stayed on as Governor-General. He was followed by a total of eight Governors-General through to 1945.

The euphemism of 'annexation' not withstanding, the Japanese constitution did not apply to Korea, whose people were denied even the most basic human rights. The Governor-Generalship of Korea, with its autocratic power, was an important position in Japan's military and political structures. In some cases, former prime ministers were appointed as Governors-General; in others, former Governors-General were appointed as prime ministers. Many of the Governors-General were politically ambitious men who implemented deceptive and harsh colonial policies in their pursuit of political achievements. There was even a case in which an incumbent Governor-General was dismissed on charges of fraud.

The administrative apparatus of the Government-General at the time of 'annexation' was basically a continuation of the old central bureaucratic structure of the Great Han Empire. On 20 August 1919, such ministries as the Finance, Home, Agriculture, Commerce and Industry, and Law were downgraded to bureaus. Throughout the colonial period, most of the men appointed bureau chiefs were Japanese although there were one or two exceptional cases where pro-Japanese Koreans were appointed.

Meantime, the Government-General of Korea reorganized the local administration system by dividing the whole country into 13 provinces, 12 prefectures, and 317 counties. During the protectorate, the Korean governors had Japanese assistant governors; nominally advisers, the Japanese assistant governors wielded actual power in the provines. After annexation, most of the governors appointed by the Government-General were Japanese, although pro-Japanese Koreans were also sometimes appointed. All of the post-annexation assistant governors, who were responsible for advising the governors on local conditions but had no real authority, were pro-Japanese Koreans. This was one way in which the Japanese rewarded collaborators.

Most positions, high and low, in the headquarters of the Government-General were filled with Japanese, and all the executive level posts in the provinces and prefectures were filled with Japanese. Although there were some Korean magistrates in the counties, real power usually belonged to Japanese directors of the bureaus of County Affairs and Financial Affairs. It was only at the township level that most officials were Koreans. Furthermore, there was a huge gap in remuneration between Japanese and Korean officials of the same rank.

The Government-General provided 'special treatment' for members of the former Korean imperial family and high-ranking pro-Japanese officials of the Great Han Empire. It established the Privy Council as a consultative body to the Governor-General, and appointed Koreans to the posts in the organ in order to legitimate the colonial rule by showing that Koreans were participating in government. The Government-General appointed fifteen pro-Japanese Koreans as first-class advisers, twenty as second-class councillors, and thirty-five others as vice-councillors of the Privy Council, which was headed by a Director-General of Political Affairs. In 1921, all of the vice-councillors were made councillors. Yi Wanyong (1858–1926) and Song Pyŏngjun (1858–1925), Koreans who had played important roles in facilitating annexation, were appointed advisers.

The Privy Council, however, was only for show. First, according to the rules of the Privy Council, the members were not allowed to speak without permission from the Director-General, nor were they allowed to speak more than one time on any single subject. Also, no one could speak about proceedings after the Director-General declared an end to discussion. Furthermore, not even a single meeting of the Privy Council was called until the after the March First Movement of 1919. These advisers and councillors, who received noble titles and financial rewards from the Government-General for helping with annexation and led lives of privilege while acting as window-dressing for colonial rule, were the most prominent national traitors of the entire colonial period.

THE MILITARY POLICE

The Japanese established their military police in Korea even before annexation. As part of their preparations for annexation, they made a 'Regulation for Military Police Stationed in Korea' on 7 October 1907, which prescribed that the 'military police stationed in Korea are mainly to take charge of affairs relating to security'. This was the beginning of the notorious 'Kempeitai' military police system.

With annexation, the Japanese promulgated a 'Government-General of Korea Police System' ordinance on 1 October 1910. This ordinance provided that the Provost Marshal of Japanese forces stationed in Korea would be the Director-General of Police Affairs and that the commanders of the military police in each province would concurrently serve as provincial police chiefs. Before annexation, the military police were concentrated in the cities, but after annexation they were dispersed throughout the country, with military police detachments and military police boxes being established even in farming villages. The Japanese also set up civilian patrol police offices and patrol police boxes everywhere throughout the country in order to suppress the widespread anti-Japanese movements that arose in opposition to 'annexation'.

As the whole country came under the rigid control of the military police, the number of military policemen and patrol officers increased rapidly. When Japan annexed Korea in 1910, the total number of the military police installations was 653 and the number of military policemen was 2,019, but in 1911, the number of military police officers increased more than three times: 7,749 officers in 935 police stations. In the case of patrol officers, in 1910 the number of installations was 481 and the number of officers was 5,881, but those increased in 1911 to 6,222 officers in 678 installations.

The ratio of civil patrol officers to military police officers was about 3:1 (74.4: 25.6) in 1910, but it changed significantly to 44.5: 55.5 in the following year. This shows the extent to which the strength of the military police was built up and the role of the military police was solidified.

The military police were involved directly or indirectly in every aspect of colonial rule, from the collection of intelligence to the extermination of anti-Japanese guerilla units, the summary disposition of criminal affairs, the mediation of civil suits, the serving of processes, the collection of taxes, the protection of forests, the compilation of population registers, the provision of escorts for postal officers, the enforcement of quarantines and the prevention of epidemics, the measuring of rainfall, the control of economic activities including smuggling, the oversight of labourers, and the diffusion of the Japanese languages, and projects for improving farming. Furthermore, the Higher Police expanded its surveillance and intelligence gathering activities beyond Korea to include Manchuria, Russia, China and the American continent.

It should not be overlooked that there were large numbers of Koreans in both the military and civil police forces. In 1910, for example, Koreans, at 1,012, made up almost half of the military police force. All of these Koreans were assigned as assistants at each military police installation, where they served the interests of the Japanese. Meanwhile, among 5,881 members of the civil patrol officers of the same year, Korean officers numbered 3,493. About 120 officers among them were in executive positions; others included 58 translators, 181 patrol officers and 3,131 assistant patrol officers. Koreans accounted for about half of the lower grade personnel in the military police organs that played the decisive role in suppressing the nationwide movement against the annexation and establishing the ruling system in the colony.

These military police and civil patrol officers, placed at outstations and police boxes even in mountainous areas of the country in units ranging from five or six to ten men, involved themselves in the everyday life of Koreans by managing about thirty kinds of affairs such as those mentioned above.

At the time of annexation, the Governor-General, despite the massive strength of the military police, went so far as to mobilize civil officials and school-teachers, who were forced to wear uniforms and hats with gold stripes and swords in order to intimidate the general populace and the students. The extent of the Governor-General's unease can be seen in the fact that he stationed large numbers of regular military forces at strategic locales throughout the country.

Although there was already one full division of regular Japanese military forces in Korea during the protectorate period, two additional regular divisions were dispatched in 1915. Army headquarters were established at Yongsan in Seoul and Nanam in the northeast, with regiments or battalions stationed in important cities, and naval bases were established in Chinhae on the southern coast and Yŏnghŭng on the northeastern coast. This enabled the Government-General to establish absolute military control over Korea.

That the Japanese could not maintain public order with the civil police alone and had to rely on an unprecedented military police system after they annexed Korea is evidence of the strength of Korean opposition to the Japanese takeover. Although the Japanese described their occupation of Korea as 'annexation', the simple fact that they had to rely to such a high degree on the military police indicates that it was a military occupation.

STRONGARM POLICY

At the time of the Japanese seizure of Korea, the most active opposition came from the righteous armies, which grew stronger after the Japanese dissolved the Korean army in 1907. Therefore, suppression of the righteous armies was the most urgent task for the Japanese in order to stabilize their system of colonial rule. To that end, the Japanese carried out their so-called 'Operation for the Subjugation of Southern Korea'.

The righteous armies in the northern areas of Korea moved to Manchuria or the Maritime Provinces of Russia around the time Japan annexed Korea. The Japanese began to execute an extensive and systematic operation to eliminate the remaining righteous armies in the southern regions, particularly in Mt Chiri in south central Korea and the coastal areas of Chŏlla Province in the southwest. In this operation, carried out from September through November 1909, two infantry regiments and naval vessels were mobilized. Hwang Hyŏn (1855–1910), who witnessed the operation, depicted the state of affairs in his memoir, *A Personal Account of Hwang Hyŏn* (*Maech'ŏn yarok*):

> The Japanese troops followed different courses in their search for the righteous armies in Chŏlla Province. They came from Chinsan, Kimje, and Man'gyŏng in the north, Chinju and Hadong in the east, and Mokp'o from the south, surrounding the righteous armies as though they had cast a net. They searched villages, ransacking each house and killing all the occupants on even the slightest suspicion. Because of this, there were no people on the streets and and no visiting among neighbours. The righteous armies scattered everywhere, but with no place to hide. Strong men lost their life during the fight and weak men were cut down while trying to escape.

The Japanese intention was to eradicate the righteous armies through the 'Operation for the Subjugation of Southern Korea' before annexation. However, the operation also provided a means for them to terrorize ordinary civilians, creating an atmosphere of fear throughout the country in preparation for colonial rule.

The occupation forces also suppressed the Patriotic Enlightenment Movement, whose members had sought to awaken their countrymen through the media and through educational activities. The Japanese Residency-General had already promulgated its 'Newspaper Law' in 1907 and its 'Publication Law' in 1908 to control the Patriotic Enlightenment Movement. As soon as the Japanese annexed Korea, they shut down both the *Capital Gazette* (*Hwangsŏng sinmun*) and the *Korea Daily News* (*Taehan maeil sinbo*), leaving only the Japanese language *Keijo Daily News* (*Keijo simpo*) and the Korean language edition of that paper, the *Daily News* (*Maeil sinbo*) as mouthpieces for the colonial administration.

Japanese controls on publications were not limited to newspapers. They also discontinued, confiscated and prohibited the sale of books and magazines. They banned the sale of some primary school textbooks such as the *Elementary Korean History* (*Ch'odŭng Taehan yŏksa*) and history books that were deemed dangerous, including the *History of Korea* (*Tonguk yŏksa*), *The Fall of Vietnam* (*Wŏllam mangguksa)*, the *Biography of Yi Sunsin* (*Yi Sunsin chŏn*), and the *History of the French Revolution* (*P'ŭrangsŭ hyŏngmyŏngsa*). They also shut down magazines related to the Patriotic Enlightenment Movement like the *Monthly Review of the North and West Educational Association* (*Sŏbukhakhoe wŏlbo*).

Furthermore, the Japanese broke up a variety of organizations like the Great Korea Association and the North and West Educational Association that had been deeply involved in the Patriotic Enlightenment Movement. The colonizers had already provided themselves with the legal tools for disestablishing organizations when they promulgated the 'Peace Preservation Law' in July 1907. At the time of annexation in August 1910, they promulgated their 'Regulations of Assembly' by which they outlawed political organizations. This meant the end of all the organizations of the Patriotic Enlightenment Movement.

The Government-General also thoroughly suppressed the national education boom that had arisen during the period of the Great Han Empire. During the period of the Residency-General, the Japanese had already sought to control free educational activities by enacting various school regulations while promoting government schools to which they posted Japanese instructors and enforced Japanese language education. The most decisive blows against nationalist education came in August 1908 with the promulgation of the 'Private School Law' and 'Village School Law' through which the Japanese controlled the establishment of private schools and the selection of textbooks. The 'Private School Law' authorized the Minister of Education to close schools that violated his orders or that were deemed to be injurious. The law also required that even those schools that had already been authorized had to seek new authorization within six months after the law went into effect. Of the 1,995 schools that applied for authorization by June 1909, only 820 received authorization – of those 778 were missionary schools, leaving only 42 schools run by Koreans. The end result was a dramatic decrease in the number of schools in Korea from 5,000 in 1908 to around 1,900 in August 1910.

In spite of these measures, the Japanese were not able to wipe out the Patriotic Enlightenment Movement. Thus, they fabricated such incidents as the 'Anak Conspiracy' and the 'Plot to Assassinate Governor-General' in 1911 as pretexts to arrest large numbers of movement members. The so-called 'Anak Conspiracy' was a case in which the Japanese arrested more than 160 influential Koreans in Hwanghae Province for complicity in An Myŏnggŭn's fund-raising campaign for the independence movement. The 'Plot to Assassinate the General-Governor' was an incident which the Japanese fabricated in order to suppress the 'New People's Association', a secret society that grew out of the Patriotic Enlightenment Movement. In this incident, the Japanese arrested about 600 Christians, 105 of whom they convicted.

The Japanese suppression of the righteous armies and the Patriotic Enlightenment Movement failed to extinguish the spirit of national resistance. The anti-Japanese movement related to the Patriotic Enlightenment Movement eventually resurfaced in the March First Movement of 1919 and the anti-Japanese movement of the righteous armies developed into armed independence struggles based in Manchuria.

REFERENCES

Kang Tŏksang, 'Kempo seijika no Chosen' (Korea under military police rule), *Rekishigaku kenkyu* 321, 1967.
Lew Youngick (Yu Yŏngik), 'Ch'ongdokpu ch'ogi ŭi kujo wa kinŭng' (Structure and functions of the early Government-General), *3.1 undong 50 chunyŏn kinyŏm nonjip*, Seoul: Tonga ilbosa, 1969.

Kim Yongdŏk, 'Hŏnbyŏng kyŏngch'al chedo ŭi sŏngnip' (Establishment of the Military Police System), *Kim Chaewŏn kinyŏm nonch'ong*, 1969.

Tsurumiya Yukiko, 'Iwayuru "Terauchi sotoku ansatsumisui jiken" nit suite' (On the so-called 'incident of the attempt to assassinate Governor-General Terauchi), *Chosenshi kenkyukai ronbunshu* 10, 1973.

Pak Kyŏngsik, 'Kempokeisatsu ni yoru "butan seiji"' ('Military rule' by the military police), *Nihon teikokushugi no Chosen jihai* jo, Aogi shuten, 1973.

SECTION TWO
The Realities of 'Cultural Politics'

STRENGTHENING OF POLICE ORGANS

After seizing Korea by force, the Japanese chose the method of military rule in order to govern Korea. This approach, however, proved to be ineffective because of the Koreans' strong sense of national cultural pride. Despite the harsh nature of Japanese military rule, the Korean people rose up in the nation-wide protest of the March First Movement of 1919, fewer than ten years after annexation. Japan, caught off guard, did succeed in suppressing the movement by mobilizing strong military forces, but the Japanese concluded that they would not be able to control the Koreans by military rule and decided to change their policy. The new policy was one of using appeasement to divide and weaken the national liberation movement front.

This new approach, known as 'Cultural Politics', included such features as administrative reforms that targeted bureaucratism and formalism, measures to reduce discrimination in the recruitment and treatment of Korean officials, and steps to allow some degree of the expression of the will of the people through freedom of speech, press and assembly. It also involved efforts to improve public welfare through reforms in education, industry, traffic, police and sanitation systems, moves to foster public morals and build civilian power through a system of local self-rule, and displays of respect for Korean culture and customs.

Moreover, the Japanese sought to downplay the military aspects of their control by revising the regulations of the Government-General's and abolishing the clause that required that: 'The position of Governor-General shall be filled by an army general or a navy admiral.' Nonetheless, all six subsequent Governors-General were former generals or admirals.

It has been said that the most obvious evidence of change from military rule to 'Cultural Politics' was that the Japanese replaced their military police with a civil police system. In fact, the military policemen of the military rule period were simply transferred to the civil police during the 'Cultural Politics' period, and the numbers of both army and police were greatly increased.

According to the law that abolished the military police system, the Director-General of Police Affairs was to hold concurrent appointment as head of the military police. Furthermore, when military policemen were transferred to the civilian police, they were retained as reserve military police without regard to their length of service. In addition, the Japanese trained many Koreans as assistant military police whom they assigned to both military police and regular police units. In effect, the Japanese had made provisions to maintain the military police system.

The national liberation movement became more active after the March First Movement and the formal abolition of the military police system. The Japanese military forces stationed in Korea, arguing that 'at least five divisions are required to rule Korea', requested an additional division of troops. They did not get the additional military troops, but the colonial police force was greatly strengthened. The number of police stations was increased from 751 in 1918 to 2,716 in 1920, an increase of nearly 300 percent in two years. (By contrast, the total number of civil and military police installations right after annexation in 1910 was only 1134.) There was also a similar three-fold increase in the total number of police officers, from 5,400 in 1918 to about 18,400 in 1920. The police budget also increased three times, from approximately 8 million yen to 24 million yen.

Even while proclaiming their 'Cultural Politics', the Japanese, in order to oppress the rising anti-Japanese and socialist movements, promulgated a new Peace Preservation Law in 1925. The law starts with the following clause: 'Those who constituted an organization for the purpose of changing the national polity or the denial of the private-ownership system or those who joined such an organization with knowledge of its purpose will be sentenced to up to ten years of imprisonment or confinement.' On the ground of 'controlling anarchists, communists, and other activists' the Japanese deprived Koreans of the freedom of assembly.

Teachers and civil officials took off their swords and enforcement by the military police did disappear for a while. But the three-fold increase of police organs within a two-year period meant that there was a police station in every county and a sub-station in every township throughout the country. A consequence of the Peace Preservation Law was a substantial increase in the numbers of special detectives, plainclothesmen and spies, and a corresponding increase in the surveillance and arrest of members of the national liberation movement, intellectuals and students.

While Japan pretended to pursue a policy of conciliation with the abolition of the military police system, it actually strengthened the colonial ruling system more by greatly increasing the number of civil police officers and tightening thought control and social movement suppression through the 1925 Peace Preservation Law. These facts show the deceitful nature of 'Cultural Politics'.

FOSTERING PRO-JAPANESE ELEMENTS

Another aspect of Japan's 'Cultural Politics' was the way in which the Japanese sought to divide the national liberation movement by increasing the number of pro-Japanese elements in the Korean population. Even before annexation, the Japanese had already converted some Korean students in Japan, political refugees and high-ranking officials into pro-Japanese elements through threats or bribery and made good use of them in the process of annexation. But, after annexation the Japanese allowed only a very small number of them to participate in colonial rule and relegated the rest to powerless positions.

When the March First Movement broke out, the Japanese tried to use pro-Japanese elements to save the situation. The activities of the pro-Japanese groups were totally ineffective. Furthermore, some of the pro-Japanese persons, caught up in the excitement of the Movement, broke with their colonial masters, resulting in an overall weakening of the pro-Japanese forces in Korea. Japan, realizing that the collaborators whom they used at the time of annexation would not be of value in ruling post-March-First Korea, set out to foster new pro-Japanese elements whom they could use to rule the colony and divide the national liberation movement front.

Saito Makoto (1858–1936), the new Governor-General appointed right after the March First Movement, devised a seven-part plan to cultivate pro-Japanese elements when he planned his 'measures to counter the Korean national movement':

(1) Strengthen the bureaucracy with persons totally loyal to Japan.
(2) Find pro-Japanese elements willing to die for Japan and have them infiltrate the nobility, the literati, the Confucian students, the wealthy, business persons, educators and religious leaders to form pro-Japanese organizations.
(3) Place pro-Japanese Koreans at the top of all religious organizations and appoint Japanese as their advisers in order to make them pro-Japanese organizations.
(4) Offer benefits and aid to pro-Japanese civilians and engage in the long-term plan of cultivating large numbers of pro-Japanese intellectuals under the guise of education for gifted children.
(5) Provide a means of living to jobless literati and Confucian students and use them for propaganda and intelligence purposes.
(6) Use labour and tenancy disputes to make the wealthy understand their position in confrontation with labourers and tenants, tie them to Japanese capital as comprador capitalists and thus bring them to Japan's side.
(7) In order to control the rural populace, establish pro-Japanese organizations to promote public morals and revive rural communities and recruit local notables to lead them by giving them the right to use national forest lands.

Saito's plan was carried out largely as he intended. First, the Japanese attained a measure of success in cultivating professional pro-Japanese elements that would lay down their life for Japan. Japan made use of them in a variety of ways, such as arousing public opinion in favour of Japan, forming pro-Japanese organizations, exposing independence movement activists, providing intelligence information, disrupting the independence movement, performing propaganda campaigns designed to present a positive image of colonial rule to the outside world and persuading independence activists to abandon their cause.

Organizations formed to promote pro-Japanese public opinion included the Association for Correcting Public Morals, the National Association and the Korean Companion Association. Other pro-Japanese organizations, such as the Taisho Friendship Association, were formed among large landlords and comprador capitalists, while such pro-Japanese organizations as the Korean Confucian Association and the Confucian Way Promotion Association were promoted among Confucian students. In order to weaken the peasant movement, a pro-Japanese organization called the Korean Tenants Mutual Aid Association was also created. The cultivation of pro-Japanese elements by the colonial government was an integral part of the policy of dividing the Korean nation.

Furthermore, with the introduction of socialist thought after the March First Movement, conflict and confrontation became acute between landlords and tenants, and between capitalists and labourers. The Government-General in Korea used this as an opportunity to suppress socialists, tenants and labourers. At the same time, by protecting landlords and capitalists, it sought to make them pro-Japanese and thus to weaken the national liberation front.

SUFFRAGE AND 'LOCAL SELF-GOVERNANCE'

Having succeeded in cooling the fever for national liberation after the March First Movement and in cultivating increasing numbers of pro-Japanese elements, the Government-General turned its attention to engaging a portion of the Korean bourgeoisie in a series of reform projects designed to further even more effectively the policy of dividing the national movement. These projects included the Campaign for the Promotion of Korean Products, the Cultural Movement and the Local Rule Campaign. The Government-General sought to give these projects greater credibility by suggesting that the Korean subjects of the Emperor might be given the same rights to suffrage and local autonomy enjoyed by his Japanese subjects.

The way in which Koreans could have been enfranchised under Japanese colonial rule was either in establishing a separate Korean assembly or in having Korean representatives in the Japanese Diet. However, the Japanese had no intention of allowing either of these to happen. Their purpose was to create the illusion of participation in local governance by creating advisory councils through which they sought to increase the numbers of pro-Japanese elements and create confusion in the ranks of the national liberation front, which had been holding fast to the line of complete and absolute independence.

As soon as the Government-General made public its policy of participatory governance, some pro-Japanese elements tried to divert anti-Japanese sentiment by launching the so-called the petition campaign for suffrage. The only result was the killing of the Korean prime mover, Min Wŏnsik, by another Korean, Yang Kŭnhwan, in 1921. Thereafter, the Government-General reverted to its original plan according to which local advisory committees were established at each level of government for the purported goal of training Koreans for local self-governance.

The advisory councils, which came into being when the Government-General reorganized the local administrative system after the March First Movement, consisted of four kinds. There were three types of administrative councils, prefectual municipality, township and provincial, along with educational councils for various schools. Of these, only the members of the municipality advisory councils, where many Japanese resided and the members of twenty-four specially designated urbanizing townships, where there were large numbers of Japanese and Korean landlords, were chosen by elections. All the members of the remaining 2,500 township councils were appointed by county supervisors.

In the case of the provincial councils, the governors appointed two-thirds of the members from among candidates selected by members of the municipal and township councils while the remaining one-third was also appointed by the governor as so-called learned persons of good reputation. School councils were established only in municipal and county districts. Municipal school council members were chosen by elections. County school council members were appointed by county magistrates from among candidates selected by township councils.

Needless to say, most of the appointed council members were pro-Japanese elements. Where there were elections, as in the municipal areas, the majority of the victors were Japanese. This was because the right to vote was limited to people who paid more than five yen per year in municipal or township taxes. Amost all such people were Japanese and Korean landlords, capitalists and wealthy merchants. The effects of this policy can been seen in the results of the 1920 elections: one of 45 Japanese residing in Korea was chosen to be a municipal or township council member, while only one of 2,800 Koreans was elected.

Even though these councils were not legislative bodies but simply advisory organs, the balance was sharply tipped towards Japanese or pro-Japanese Koreans by providing for more appointed members than elected ones. Furthermore, whereas the ballot tax in Japan was three yen, in Korea it was five yen, thus sharply limiting the number of Koreans who could vote. This was true even though Korea had been 'annexed' by Japan and was in theory a part of the Japanese polity. In the final analysis, the Japanese proposal to enfranchise Koreans, which they propagandized during the period of 'Cultural Politics' as 'training for self-governance', was nothing but a policy for the cultivation of pro-Japanese elements and the division of the Korean nation.

THE CULTURAL MOVEMENT AND THE THEORY OF SELF-RULE

Another aspect of the Japanese 'Cultural Politics' was to divert the post-March First Movement enthusiasm for absolute independence and armed struggle against Japan to the 'Cultural Movement'. The national independence movement front also included such groups as the movement for the preparation for independence, the movement for the cultivation of national ability and the diplomatic campaign for independence. Although the Japanese displayed some initial tolerance for all three, eventually they decided to try to use the first two and to link them up to the 'Cultural Movement'.

In the wake of the failure, at least within Korea, of the March First Movement and with the rise of the socialist movement, some nationalists inside Korea lost their bearings. The Japanese, under the rubric of 'Cultural Politics', did all they could to bring national movement leaders to their side. They actively encouraged such 'reform' movements as a religious movement, a campaign for self-cultivation, a project to promote harmonious social relations, a movement for the improvement of living conditions and a campaign for enlightening rural communities. For some conservative nationalists, who took a step backwards from the active independence movement front, there was no choice but to compromise with Japan and in the end to become pro-Japanese elements. They became pro-Japanese reformists with such slogans as 'the improvement of the national character', 'the cultivation of national ability', and 'self-rule' which shared the same logic as 'the Cultural Politics' and the Cultural Movement.

Yi Kwangsu (1892–1950), the renowned novelist who bolted from the Korean Provisional Government in Shanghai and returned to the colony, published an essay, 'A Treatise on National Reconstruction', in *The East Asia Daily News* (*Tonga ilbo*) in 1922. In the essay, he pointed out that one of reasons that the Independence Club of the 1890s failed was because the club had taken on strong political tendencies and suggested instead an a political concept of national reconstruction centred around the promotion of education, the development of industry and the inspiration of the people. Yi asserted that the contemporary Koreans: 'are false and lazy due to their inclination to enjoy fanciful ideas and impractical theories. Moreover, they are not faithful or brave and are very poor. In consideration of these realities, this reform proposes to transform the Korean national character in a totally new way.'

Yi reconciled national reconstruction with a 'self-rule theory' within the colonial rule. In another essay, 'A Statecraft of the Nation' (1924), published in a serial form of five editorials in *The East Asia Daily News*, he stated that the first reason that Koreans did not enjoy political life under the colonial rule was because the Japanese did not permit it. However, for the second reason he claimed: 'Because Koreans have had a strong sense of loyalty to the Chosŏn dynasty, they have rejected any political activities, including the campaigns for suffrage and self-rule, carried out by organizations authorized by Japan. Furthermore, they have even rejected the independence movement against the Japanese government.' Then, he suggested an alternative: 'Our position is that we must form, to the extent permitted, a large political organization inside Korea.'

Yi Kwangsu's theories of national reconstruction and self-rule appeared not as a product of his own statecraft, but as an elaboration of the theories of the preparation for independence and the cultivation of national ability that had already been part of the national liberation movement front both within and without Korea. Thus, his theories became a primary factor in the division of the front. The fact that Yi Kwangsu, a theorist of national reconstruction and the cultivation of national ability, converted into a hardcore pro-Japanese theorist and activist almost immediately indicates that he was not a theorist of the national liberation movement, but rather a Korean spokesman for the Japanese policy of national division during 'the Cultural Politics' period.

REFERENCES

Nakazuka Akira, 'Nihon teikokushugi to Chosen: 3.1undo to bunka seiji' (Japanese imperialism and Korea: the March First movement and cultural politics), *Nihonshi kenkyu* 83, 1966.

Yun Pyŏngsŏk, '3.1 undong e taehan Ilbon chŏngbu ŭi chŏnghch'aek' (Japanese government policy on the March First Movement), *3.1 undong 50 chunyŏn kinyŏm nonjip*, Seoul: Tonga ilbosa, 1969.

Pak Kyŏngsik, 'Kempokeisatsu ni yoru "butan seiji" ' ('Military rule' by the military police), *Nihon teikokushugi no Chosen jihai* jo, Aogi shuten, 1973.

Kang Tongjin, *Ilbon ŭi Han'guk ch'imnyak chŏngch'aeksa* (History of Japanese policy of aggression toward Korea), Seoul: Han'gilsa, 1980.

Kang Tongjin, 'Munhwajuŭi ŭi kibon sŏngkyŏk' (Basic nature of culturalism), *Han'guk sahoe yŏn'gu* 2, Seoul: Han'gilsa, 1984.

Pak Ch'ansŭng, *Han'guk kŭndae chŏngch'i sasang yŏn'gu* (Studies in modern Korean political thought), Seoul, Yŏksa pip'yŏngsa, 1992.

SECTION THREE

Ordeals of the Period of Japanese Military Aggression

THE COLONIAL FASCIST SYSTEM

Cultural Politics gave way to fascism in the early 1930s. This was the time when the so-called 'Taisho Democracy' came to an end and the home islands of Japan began to move toward fascism. This was also the time when the monopolistic capitalists of Japan, who were suffering the effects of the Great Depression, pushed for the invasion of mainland China in their search for a way to overcome their financial difficulties.

Emboldened by their success in the Manchurian Incident of 1931, the Japanese launched the Sino-Japanese War in 1937, which they eventually expanded into the Pacific War in 1941 with their attack on Pearl Harbor. The consequence was the rise of a military fascist system. As harsh as the fascist system was in Japan proper, it was even more so in the colony.

The intensification of the colonial fascist system began with the strengthening of Japan's military power and police force. Japan had two divisions of troops stationed in Korea during the 'Cultural Politics' period. One more division was added soon after the Manchurian Incident. By the end of the Pacific War, roughly 230,000 Japanese soldiers were in Korea, where they exercised control over the whole country. At the same time, the police force was also enhanced, from 22,229 police officers in 2,948 stations right after the Manchurian Incident to 35,239 officers in 3,212 stations when the Pacific War broke out in 1941.

Another way the Japanese sought to strengthen their fascist system was in thorough thought control. The Japanese colonial government promulgated their Korean Thought Criminal Protection and Surveillance Law in 1936 to watch violators of the Peace Preservation Law. The targets of this law were the national liberation movement activists who 'intended to change the national polity (*kokutai*) or the form of government or who denied the private property system'.

The colonial government established the Korean Central Intelligence Committee to collect individual information on intellectuals when the Japanese provoked the Sino-Japanese War in 1937. It also directed the Bureau of Police Affairs to organize a Korean Anti-Communist Association 'to exterminate communist thought and the communist movement, and to exalt the Japanese spirit' in August 1938. Moreover, in the same year the Government-General organized the All-Korea Patriotic Thought League to Cope with the Situation, an organization of former objectors who had been converted to a pro-Japanese position, and demanded that the members of the league 'become human bombs to smash and destroy anti-state thought in the front for the defence of national thought'.

While preparing for the Pacific War in 1941, the Japanese reorganized the Patriotic Thought League as the Yamato Institute, forced people identified as thought criminals to join, and compelled them to renounce their beliefs and become supporters of Japan and the war effort. The membership of the Yamato Institute in 1943 was 5,400 in 91 local chapters. In the meantime, the Japanese promulgated the Ordinance for the Prevention and Detention of Korean Thought Criminals in February 1941.

Thought control was further intensified during the Pacific War. In 1944 Japan implemented the Special Ordinance on Wartime Criminal Cases in Korea, by which penalties for such offences as advocating or plotting the overthrow of the national polity were raised significantly. In the same year, the Government-General in Korea also announced a Special Wartime Ordinance on Court Cases designed to speed up prosecutions by reducing the three-step trial system to a two-step system in both criminal and civil cases. Punishments for 'crimes of disturbing the national government' were particularly toughened.

Another way in which Japan strengthened its fascist system was to control all aspects of the people's life by emphasizing the 'wartime system'. The General Mobilization Order, issued after the Japanese provoked the Sino-Japanese War, was also applied to Korea in May 1938. In July of the same year, on the occasion of the first anniversary of the outbreak of the Sino-Japanese War, Japan organized the Korean League for General Mobilization of National Spirit. Various vocational leagues were subsumed in this new league. In addition, local leagues were established in each province, prefecture, county, township and village under the leadership of the heads of those local administrative units.

Each local league had 'Patriotic Circles' consisting of ten households, with household heads as circle representatives. In April 1942, there were more than 4,480,000 members in over 360,000 Patriotic Circles. Japan was able to control the Koreans so thoroughly through these Patriotic Circles that there was no space for the national liberation movement inside the colony.

Furthermore, these Patriotic Circles held regular community meetings where they compelled the people to hoist the Japanese flag, to attend Japanese Shinto shrines, to salute Japan's Imperial Palace, to use the Japanese language, to resist communists and spies, and to contribute to patriotic savings accounts. They also continuously carried out special campaigns, such as a 'Japanese Spirit Exaltation Week', 'Patriotic Labour Week' and 'Patriotic Saving Week', keeping the population in a high state of stress in support of their war of aggression.

THE POLICY TO DESTROY THE KOREAN NATION

After invading China in 1937, the Japanese, emphasizing the slogan 'Japan and Korea as One Body', began to pursue in earnest a policy of 'transforming the Korean people into subjects of the Japanese empire', with the ultimate goal of erasing Korean national identity. Japan made the so-called 'Pledge of Imperial Subjects', containing such phrases as: 'We are the subjects of the Great Japanese Empire' and 'We are fully loyal to the Emperor'. The Japanese not only forced Koreans to recite it in unison, but also coerced them to recite it in Japanese whenever they sought to receive food rations or purchase train tickets.

After annexation, the Japanese demanded that their Korean colonial subjects consider Japanese their national language and continually strengthened their programme of Japanese language education. They did offer some limited education in the Korean language, referred to as Chosengo (Chosŏn language), but even this was excluded from the school curriculum in April 1938. Furthermore, the Japanese forced their language upon the Koreans as their language of everyday business, and even punished elementary school students if they spoke Korean.

As the military situation grew more desperate, the Japanese became more forceful in their efforts to obliterate the Korean identity. An example is the so-called 'Name Change Order' by which Japan in effect forced its colonial subjects to take Japanese names. Some Koreans committed suicide in protest of this action; others, who simply chose to ignore the order, found themselves disadvantaged in many ways: they were not allowed to enroll at school, were refused service at government offices, were excluded from the lists for food rations and other supplies. The Japanese authorities even refused to ship freight addressed to Korean names. Faced with such compulsion, about 80% of the Korean populace complied with the Name Change Order.

At the same time, the Japanese mobilized government-patronized scholars to push a theory that 'Japanese and Koreans have the same ancestry', a notion that had first been put forth at the time of annexation in order to legitimize the takeover of Korea. This theory, which attempted to deny the very origins of the Korean nation, was revived near the end of the war in conjunction with the 'Japan and Korea as One Body' slogan as part of the effort to replace the Korean national consciousness with the 'Japanese spirit'. The Japanese contended that Koreans and Japanese had formed one ethnic nation in ancient times, forced some Korean intellectuals to support that notion, and compelled the Koreans to install and worship ancestral tablets of 'Amaterasu Oomikami', the ancestral god of Japan, in their homes.

This fanatical policy was born of Japanese determination to prevent resistance and to mobilize the Koreans for Japan's war effort. Despite being forced to use the Japanese language, to take Japanese names and to worship at Japanese shrines, many Koreans inside the colony continued to struggle against the Japanese, although their efforts were necessarily small and disorganized. On the other hand, a significant number of Koreans, particularly intellectuals, voluntarily presented themselves as subjects of imperial Japan and actively co-operated in the war of military aggression.

HUMAN EXPLOITATION

Japan, anticipating a manpower shortage after the Manchurian Incident in 1931, began to formulate a plan for conscripting Korean youth. It did not implement that plan because of concerns that it would be dangerous to arm young Koreans, many of whom had strong anti-Japanese sentiments. After invading China, however, the Japanese decided that the need outweighed the risk and promulgated a Special Army Volunteer Ordinance in February 1938 in order to mobilize young Koreans for the war as 'volunteers'.

From 1938 until 1943, when Japan executed a conscription order, roughly 18,000 Korean young men were mobilized as 'volunteers' to supplement the Japanese army. Although some were genuine volunteers who were caught up in the excitement of the moment, most were either deceived by Japanese enticements or simply joined in order to escape from the impoverished conditions of the rural communities in wartime. The so-called 'leading figures', who publicly supported the volunteer system and encouraged young men to volunteer, privately made sure that their own sons did not go. As a consequence, almost all the volunteers were the sons of impoverished tenant farmers.

The Japanese implemented a colonial conscription system near the end of the war and drafted about 200,000 young Korean men. In addition, the Japanese forced some 4,500 college students into uniform through a so-called 'student volunteer system' implemented in 1943.

Another way in which the Japanese forced Koreans to sacrifice themselves during the war was forced labour through such systems as recruitment, conscription, Patriotic Corps, labour mobilization and the Comfort Women. Even before the 1937 invasion of China, Japan had mobilized large numbers of impoverished Koreans who had been forced out of rural villages to work as 'cheap labour' in public works projects and mines in Japan. After 1937, the Japanese forcibly mobilized many Koreans to work in support of the war effort by promulgating a General Mobilization Law and subsequently a National Conscription Ordinance in 1939.

One source of statistical data indicates that from 1939 until the war ended in 1945 1,130,000 Koreans were forcibly mobilized. Another source shows 1,460,000. At any rate, both sources show that far more than one million Koreans were mobilized by force during the war years. They were most often put to work as labourers in coalmines, but also in mineral mines, construction sites and munitions factories. Many Koreans were injured or killed in those workplaces.

Furthermore, even middle and elementary school students were mobilized as labourers in the construction of military facilities. The Japanese also forcibly mobilized several thousand females between the ages of twelve and forty through its 1944 Female Volunteer Corps Service Ordinance. Japan put some of these women to work in munitions factories, but it also committed the atrocity of sending many of them to battlefields in China and the South Pacific as 'comfort women' to provide sexual services for Japanese soldiers.

In addition, the Japanese organized the conscripted Korean labourers in military fashion at the workplaces where they controlled them through military discipline. The workplaces where these forced labourers were held were surrounded with high voltage barbed wire in order to prevent escape. There were even instances when the Japanese massacred Korean workers after the completion of military facilities in order to maintain military secrecy. One such case was the massacre of eight hundred conscripts at the Mirim Airport in P'yŏngyang at the end of four years' hard work. Five thousand Korean conscripts are also said to have been massacred in the Kuril Islands in order to prevent the leakage of military secrets.

The atrocities committed against Korean workers by the Japanese military near the very end of the war when defeat became certain border on the insane. One example was leaving 1,700 Korean workers to die on a ship bound for Okinawa that had been bombed by US airplanes. Also, when US troops landed on Okinawa, the Japanese troops rounded up all the Korean workers in a cave and massacred them to prevent their escape or surrender.

The fourteen years from 1931 to 1945 were a time of unprecedented fascist madness in the home islands of Japan, but it was even worse in the colony of Korea. The colonial fascist regime not only drove individual Koreans to ruin, but it allowed absolutely no space, politically, economically, socially or culturally, for Koreans to prepare for the post-liberation construction of a nation state. Indeed, the Japanese war of military aggression prepared the way for the division of the Korean peninsula after liberation in 1945.

REFERENCES

Pak Kyŏngsik, 'Taiheiyo sensoji ni okeru Chosenjin kyoseirenko' (Forced mobilization of Koreans during the time of the Pacific War), *Rekishigaku kenkyu 297*, 1965.

Pak Kyŏngsik, *Nihon teikokushugi no Chosen jihai* ka (Rule of Korea by Japanese imperialism, vol. 2), Aoki shoten, 1973.

Kim Taesang, *Ilche ha kangje illyŏk sut'alsa* (History of forced labour under Japanese imperialism), Chŏngŭmsa, 1973.

Kimijima Kazuo, 'Chosen ni okeru sensotoentaisei no denkaikatei' (Development of wartime mobilization in Korea), *Nihon fashizumu to Toajia*, Aoki shoten, 1977.

Miyata Setsuko, 'Chosen ni okeru shikanbyo seido no denkai to sono igi' (Development of volunteer soldier system in Korea and its significance), *Hatada kinen Chosen rekishigaku ronshu* ka, Ryokei shosha, 1979.

2

The Development of the National Liberation Movement

INTRODUCTION

It is not easy to put in systematic order the events that occurred in the national liberation movement during the thirty-five years of colonial rule. The movement as a whole can be divided in various ways depending on the historian's point of view, but it can generally be broken down into three periods.

The first period, from the March First Movement of 1919 until the mid-1920s, featured the activities of the Korean Provisional Government and armed struggles in Manchuria and the Maritime Provinces of Siberia. The second period, from 1925 to 1930, witnessed the rise of a vigorous mass labour-peasant movement, a Korean Communist Party movement and efforts to form a national front as seen in a united national party movement overseas and the New Korea Association (Sin'ganhoe) movement inside Korea. The third period, starting in 1930, was characterized outside of Korea by new efforts to form a national united front in response to the rise of fascism in Japan and Comintern directives to dissolve and rebuild the Korean Communist Party, as well as by armed guerilla activities. Inside Korea, it was characterized by a movement to rebuild the communist party, by the development of revolutionary labour and peasant movements, and by the establishment of the National Independence League.

The national liberation movement after the March First Movement has conventionally been separated into two movements: a rightist movement typically referred to as the independence movement or the nationalist movement; and a leftist movement usually called the socialist or communist movement. In recent years, however, substantial new studies on the national liberation movement have appeared, deepening our understanding of the movement and giving rise to a historical consciousness. Historians now tend to regard the overall process of the liberation movement as a series of efforts to overcome divisions between

left and right and to establish a unified national front in preparation
for the establishment of a unified nation-state upon liberation from
Japanese rule.

At this time, no one disputes the understanding of the March First
Movement, which arose before the split between left and right, as a pan-
national movement led by a bourgeoisie oriented toward republicanism.
If, however, we take into consideration the Korean Socialist Party organized under Yi Tonghwi (1873–1935) in 1918, the Provisional Government of Korea founded as a result of the March First Movement can be
seen as the initial effort to reconcile and unify left and right.

The armed resistance in Manchuria, which became more active after
March First, was not under the direct control of the Ministry of Military
Affairs of the Provisional Government. It was, however, loosely connected with the Provisional Government via the Western Route Military
Administration located in southern Manchuria and the Northern
Route Military Administration located in north-eastern Manchuria. Also,
important members of the first Korean Communist Party (*Koryŏ kongsandang*), formed in the Maritime Provinces of the Soviet Union in 1919,
participated during the early days of the Provisional Government.
Hence, the Provisional Government movement can be as part of the
effort to form a left-right united front.

The Provisional Government movement in the early period was not
receptive to the leftist line or to the line of active struggle against Japan,
so those two elements soon broke away. Although an attempt was made
to reconstruct a unified government through the National Representative
Assembly, that effort failed, leaving the Provisional Government in a
weakened state. Nonetheless, the movement to unify left and right under
a national liberation front continued.

In response to the weakening of the Provisional Government movement overseas and the rise of the Cultural Movement inside Korea, the
national liberation movement front developed into the movement for a
united national party, which aimed to form a national co-operative front
in the second half of the 1920s, and its domestic extension in the New
Korea Society. It is important to note that the communist party movement also actively participated in united front tactics at this time.

This national co-operative front movement of the second half of the
1920s did fall apart for a while at the beginning of the 1930s due to
changes in various subjective and objective conditions. The rise of
Japanese fascism and its aggression in Manchuria, however, prompted
the movement's revival and development into a national united front
line, especially outside the country as seen in the establishment of the
Korean United Front League against Japan in China in 1932.

In response to the emergence of fascism, the international communist
movement developed an anti-fascist united front line in the mid-1930s.
After the Japanese invasion of China proper in 1937, all elements of the
Korean national liberation movement, including both left and right,
turned to a united front in the hope of national liberation.

The Korean activists of the overseas front, in particular those inside Chinese territory, who were free from the direct rule of Japanese imperialism took the progressive step in 1935 of dissolving the Korean United Front League against Japan and replacing it with the Korean National Revolutionary Party, an entity with no direct connections with the international communist movement's united front line.

By 1937, however, the Korean National Party, made up of faithful defenders of the Provisional Government formed, in league with elements that had broken away from the Korean National Revolutionary Party, a right-wing united front organization known as the Federation of Korean Restoration Movement Organizations. In the meantime, the leftists formed the Korean National Front League, a left-wing united front organization under the leadership of the National Revolutionary Party. Subsequently, a National United Front Association appeared in an effort to unify these two organizations.

The Association did not succeed in establishing itself as a national united front. By 1943, however, the Provisional National Assembly and the Provisional Government formed a united front government in Chinese territory from organizations such as the Korean Independence Party, the Korean National Revolutionary Party and anarchist groups. The Provisional Government did reach a tentative agreement for a united front government with the Korean Independence League founded in Yanan, a district under Chinese communist control, but the agreement failed to come to fruition due to the defeat of Japanese imperialism. Nonetheless, persons affiliated with this national united front movement continued campaigning for a unified nation-state during the immediate post-liberation years known as the 'Liberation Space' (1945–48).

On the other hand, the 1920s right-wing movement on the Manchurian front was replaced in the 1930s by right/left wing united front guerilla activities in the 1930s. These guerilla activities developed into the North-east Peoples' Revolutionary Armies and the North-east Anti-Japanese Allied Forces under the leadership of the Chinese Communist Party. Koreans played a major role in the armed struggles of these groups. By the second half of the 1930s, these armed struggles merged into a national united front movement. As a part of that movement, the Korean Association for the Restoration of Fatherland in Manchuria, established in 1936, initiated its own distinct national united front movement.

On the domestic front in the 1930s, the left-wing front pursued campaigns for the re-establishment of the communist party and revolutionary labour and peasant unions as part of the national front movement. The left continued to pursue these campaigns despite their designation as a 'left-wing deviationism' line by the Sixth Comintern Congress that dissolved the Korean Communist Party. After the Seventh Comintern Congress of 1935 adopted anti-fascist united front tactics, however, the Korean left shifted its line in part towards the establishment of an anti-Japanese, anti-fascist united front. Moreover, apart from the campaign to reconstruct the communist party, the left entered into a coalition with the right in the National Independence League in 1944 at the end of the colonial period, an organization that had some success in building links with overseas fronts, particularly that in inland China.

Despite differences of opinion and various other difficulties regarding the methods of forming a national united front, most notably the issue of hegemony, the overall process of the Korean national liberation movement after the March First Movement was oriented toward a national united front movement, striving to overcome the left-right confrontation and establishing a unified nation-state after liberation. Even in the 'Liberation Space' during the occupation and division of the country by US and Soviet troops, this movement for a national united front expressed itself in a number of important ways. Those included the left wing's united front activities for the Democratic National Front and the moderates' activities for a united front movement to form the Left-Right Cooperative Committee. Moreover, these two elements cooperated to support the North-South negotiations of 1948.

SECTION ONE

The March First Movement and the Early Activities of the Provisional Government

THE MARCH FIRST MOVEMENT

The national liberation movement started in earnest with the March First Movement. In the first half of the 1920s, it can be considered as a republican movement initiated by the national bourgeoisie. The March First Movement has often been understood as a consequence of the 'Tokyo Student Declaration' (8 February 1919) influenced by the concept of national self-determination that Woodrow Wilson, president of the USA, advocated as the First World War ended. Following this, according to the conventional interpretation, national representatives led by religious leaders declared the independence of Korea.

In fact, the concept of self-determination was a principle that was applied to the colonies of the defeated countries of Europe. As such, it was of no help to Korea, the colony of a Japan that had been on the winning side, even if it was late in joining the war. Some of the Korean representatives appear to have understood the situation but decided nonetheless to take advantage of the opportunity to voice their hopes for Korean independence.

The origins of, and the driving forces behind, the March First Movement should be sought in the pre-1910 national movement, and in the post-1910 growth of national consciousness and in changes in socio-economic circumstances. Furthermore, the success of the Russian

Revolution of 1917, just two years before the March First Movement, had an effect on Koreans as seen in particular in the young intellectuals who drafted the Tokyo Student Declaration.

While what remained of the Righteous Armies and the militant nationalists of the Patriotic Enlightenment Movement line were preparing a base for an independence movement centred in Manchuria, the surviving members of the Patriotic Enlightenment Movement still inside the country were waiting for an opportunity to carry out a large-scale independence movement. The Government-General of Korea was aware of this and fabricated the so-called Anak Conspiracy and Case of the One Hundred Five in order to suppress the nationalists. These were heavy blows to the national liberation movement activists, but they formed underground organizations, waited for their chance, and eventually took advantage of the proclamation of the doctrine of national self-determination after the First World War.

The reason that the entire Korean nation supported the independence declaration initiated by the domestic elements of the Patriotic Enlightenment Movement line led by the religious groups was because they felt a threat to their survival during the ten years of colonial rule. Korean capitalists had been among those hit hardest by Japanese policies.

After the Chosŏn government opened its ports in 1876, some progressive national capitalists emerged. However, they suffered badly from currency reforms before annexation and the Company Law after annexation. The Japanese land survey (1910–18) also dealt particularly heavy blows to medium and small landlords, as well as land-owning peasants. Those national capitalists and landlords who had not yet come to accept Japanese rule found themselves disadvantaged by the emerging colonial economic structure and were seeking a way out.

For peasants the situation was even more acute. The number of peasants owning their own land had been gradually increasing since the late Chosŏn dynasty, but – their strong opposition notwithstanding – they suffered badly from the post-annexation land survey pushed through by the Japanese. The upper stratum of peasants, a group who could have developed into capitalists, lost their lands and became tenant farmers labouring under conditions that were growing increasingly intolerable. The entire agrarian population of Korea, with the exception of a few landlords, found itself much worse off after ten years of colonial rule.

In the 1910s, Japanese monopoly capital had not yet made significant entry into Korea. The overwhelming majority of Japanese-owned enterprises in the colony were small-scale plants and factories. The consequence was a gradual increase in the number of workers but they had to work in extremely bad conditions. There was a huge difference between the wages of Korean and Japanese workers. In general, the wages of Korean workers were less than half or even one-third of those paid to Japanese workers. Because of low wages, long working hours, inhumane treatment and ethnic discrimination, Korean workers began to strike frequently in the 1910s.

During the first ten years of colonial rule, people from all strata, not only labourers and peasants, but also medium-and small-size landlords and national capitalists suffered direct and substantial damage. The consequence was a dramatic growth in their political and social consciousness. This made it possible for students, religious figures and intellectuals to fan the flames of anti-Japanese sentiment into a national liberation movement conflagration that spread rapidly throughout the whole country.

The developmental process of the March First Movement can be divided into three stages. The first stage was when the thirty-three or, by some counts, forty-eight 'representatives of the nation' – who were in fact the upper bourgeoisie – ignited the movement by declaring the independence of Korea. The representatives were largely made up of domestic elements of the Patriotic Enlightenment Movement line: new intellectuals, religious figures, and some national capitalists and landlords who had not made common interest with colonial rule.

As a general rule, colonial national movements in the initial stages arose under the leadership of the national bourgeoisie and intellectuals, and the March First Movement was no exception. Because the March First representatives still worked within the limits of the old Patriotic Enlightenment Movement, they were opposed to the use of arms and eschewed active resistance. Although they did issue a declaration of independence, they did not take to the streets to lead a mass movement.

In their declaration, these national representatives failed to point out the interests of the national capitalists, peasants and working classes under colonial rule, and also failed to take an active role in inducing a popular movement. They did eventually join in the plan formulated by young people and students, but withdrew at the decisive moment. Even so, we must recognize that they did play a decisive role in inciting a large-scale anti-Japanese movement in the difficult circumstances of military rule.

The second stage of the movement was when the movement was spread over the major cities of the country by intellectuals, including the youth, students, teachers, urban workers and merchants. It was the students and young intellectuals who called for a more active resistance and they found a receptive audience among urban workers and merchants. Merchants in major cities throughout the country closed their shops while the workers responded with great speed.

There were already more than twenty labour unions in the country at that time, but it does not appear that they had received advance notice of the declaration of independence. Nonetheless, when it happened, workers took to the streets almost instantaneously. On 2 March more than 400 workers rallied in Seoul, while other workers also demonstrated in P'yŏngyang and Kyŏmip'o. On 22 March roughly 800 workers gathered around a flag proclaiming a 'Workers' Convention'. Workers continued to demonstrate everywhere throughout the country.

The third stage was when this movement expanded from urban to rural areas. In the declaration of independence announced by the 'representatives', there was no mention about the exploitative nature of the Land Survey or other agrarian issues, and the writing was too difficult to understand for peasants. Nonetheless, the peasants, who had over the years fallen into tenancy, agricultural labour and even slash-and-burn cultivation, participated actively in the movement and continued to demonstrate in rural marketplaces throughout the country for over a year.

While the 'national representatives' who had signed the declaration were sentenced to three years at the most, and all of them were released before the end of their terms by the newly conciliatory Japanese authorities, the ordinary people who took part in the movement suffered seriously. Their peaceful demonstrations were met by Japanese military force and soon became riots. The outcome was heavy casualties. Among the roughly two million demonstrators, 7,500 were killed, 16,000 were injured, and more than 46,000 were arrested. Moreover, 49 churches and schools and 715 residences were put to the torch.

The March First Movement did not develop into a systematic and united movement as the massive Japanese military presence precluded any possibility of its development into an armed resistance movement. Even though it did not bring national liberation, it was historically significant in a number of ways.

First, externally, March First was an anti-Japanese movement while internally it was a republican movement. Republicanism had appeared in the Patriot Enlightenment Movement even before annexation and it continued to be part of the New People's Association in the early 1910s. Most of the representatives who signed the Declaration of Independence were oriented toward republicanism as were the young intellectuals who participated in the movement. The Korean Provisional Government established in the wake of the movement was the first republican government in Korean history. The post-March First period also saw the rise of restorationist elements seeking to reinstate the monarchy of the Great Han Empire, but they soon petered out without contributing to the development of the national liberation movement.

Second, the March First Movement became an occasion for the resurgence of armed struggle outside Korea. Before annexation, the national movement before 'annexation' had been divided into two lines: armed struggle by the Righteous Armies and the Patriotic Enlightenment Movement. After annexation, the righteous army line began to prepare for a war of independence while the Patriotic Enlightenment Movement was laying the groundwork for the cultivation of national abilities. The March First Movement provided the spark to ignite the armed struggle that had been in preparation in Manchuria. Many young Koreans, who had witnessed how the peaceful March First Movement turned into a fruitless bloodbath, decided that organized armed resistance was necessary. They went into exile in Manchuria and the Maritime Provinces in order to join the armed organizations already taking shape there. The result was an escalation in the armed struggle against Japan.

Third, the March First Movement intensified the popular movement. Before March First, the popular movement was led by bourgeoisie nationalists. However, participation in the March First Movement gave labourers and peasants a new socio-political consciousness that enabled them to develop their own distinct movement and line within the national liberation movement front. The labour and peasant movements grew remarkably during the 1920s. This set the stage for the emergence of a domestic socialist movement that subsequently played an important role in the national liberation movement front.

Fourth, March First marked a watershed in the direction of the national liberation movement. The national liberation movement front was now clearly divided over the issue of the best way to proceed. There were those, operating from bases in Manchuria and the Maritime Provinces, who argued for a war of independence and those who sought to gain independence through the diplomatic intervention of the great powers. There were those who called for unconditional and immediate independence and those who pursued a gradualist line of preparing for independence through the fostering of national abilities. The outcome was disarray in the independence movement front.

EARLY ACTIVITIES OF THE PROVISIONAL GOVERNMENT

Although suggestions had earlier been made to form a government to be the headquarters of the national liberation movement, concrete efforts began around the time of the March First Movement. Campaigns for forming a government arose in three places.

First, the Korean National Central Committee, which had already been formed in the Korean community in Vladivostok, was reorganized in February 1919 as the Korean Citizens' Assembly. This organization took the form of a government.

The second place where a government was formed was Shanghai. The New Korea Youth Party, an independence movement organization, had been organized in the city before the March First Movement and had engaged in such activities as dispatching Kim Kyusik (1881–1950) to the Paris Peace Conference. When the March First Movement occurred inside Korea, many patriots gathered in Shanghai and established the Provisional Office for Independence, after which more than a thousand nationalists came together to form the Provisional National Assembly on 10 April 1919. They promulgated a Provisional National Charter and chose ministers of state through an election. The government also adopted the democratic republic system. The Provisional National Assembly was made up of representatives of eleven districts, including Korea, the Maritime Provinces, China and the US, who were chosen through local election committees.

A third government, known as the Hansŏng (Seoul) government, was formed in Seoul. This government, which was planned right after the March First Movement, issued a proclamation in the name of the 'representatives of the thirteen provinces' that included a 'call for a citizens' convention' and six summary legal clauses. The Seoul government, like the other two, took the form of democracy.

The establishment of provisional governments in three places gave rise to the issue of forming a unified government. The government in Vladivostok put forth a plan for a unified government that would have placed the ministries of transportation and foreign affairs in Shanghai because of that city's geographic advantages and would have put the rest of the government and the legislature in either Jiandao (K. Kando, a region in Manchuria close to the Korean border) or the Maritime Provinces, the locales with the largest populations of Koreans.

In response, the Shanghai government entered negotiations with the Vladivostok government over the issue of unification with certain specific conditions. One was that the provisional government would be located in Shanghai, but could be moved in accord with a decision of the government or the opinion of the people. Another was that the national assembly would be formed by joining the Shanghai Provisional National Assembly and the Vladivostok Korean Citizens' Assembly. The Shanghai government also indicated a willingness to locate the national assembly in the Maritime Provinces if the Vladivostok group felt it to be absolutely necessary.

At about the same time, Syngman Rhee (Yi Sŭngman; 1875–1965), who was the chief executive of the Seoul Government, opened an office in Washington DC where he was proclaiming the legitimacy of his government. This meant that a truly unified government could not be formed by the Vladivostok and Shanghai groups alone. The result was negations for a unified government that included the Seoul group.

In the negotiating process, the following conditions were proposed and agreed upon. The governments formed in Shanghai and Vladivostok were to be dissolved in favour of the government in Seoul established by the representatives of the thirteen domestic provinces. The government was to be located, for the time being, in Shanghai. The administrative measures taken by the government in Shanghai were to be recognized. The name of the government was to be the 'Provisional Government of the Republic of Korea'. All cabinet ministers were to resign and be replaced by ministers selected by the Seoul government. In the end, the establishment of the Provisional Government of the Republic of Korea, widely known as the Shanghai Provisional Government, represented acknowledgement of the legitimacy of the Seoul government.

The unified government in Shanghai was formed with Syngman Rhee, former head of the Seoul government, as president and Yi Tonghwi (1872–1936), former leader of the Vladivostok government, as Prime Minister. The primary reason why a new unified government could be formed, in spite of the differing interests of the Shanghai, Vladivostok and Seoul groups, was the fervent national desire to form a new government to serve as the headquarters of the national liberation movement.

The Shanghai Provisional Government was launched as a united front headquarters of the liberation movement, bringing together the left- and right-wing fronts and the strands of armed struggle and diplomacy. The government's location in Shanghai, however, led to an emphasis on diplomatic efforts. The leftists, who preferred armed resistance, soon seceded, leaving the right wing in charge. Although there is some significance in the fact that the Shanghai Provisional Government was the first republican government in Korean history, it was not able to fulfil its role as the headquarters of the national liberation movement.

The most noteworthy activities of the Shanghai Provisional Government in its early years came in two areas, communications and diplomacy. The first directive of the new government ordered the implementation of a network of communication. This network, designed to establish communications between the Shanghai government and independence activists inside Korea and in Manchuria, had a co-ordinating office in Seoul, offices at the provincial, county and township levels inside Korea and a separate office in Jiandao. The primary purpose of this network was to raise money for the operations of the government, but because it was under the control of the Shanghai government's Minister of Home Affairs, it can be seen as a kind of local administrative system.

The Provisional Government's legislative body passed a measure issuing independence bonds, to be funded through a head tax of one yen on each Korean national inside Korea over the age of 20. The government sought to implement this through its communications network, but encountered severe difficulties. Japanese surveillance and oppression made if difficult to organize in large areas of the country, particularly at the township level. The limited network the Shanghai government was able to organize collapsed in 1921 when it was discovered by the Japanese police.

The Shanghai Provisional Government's diplomatic campaign for independence initially focused on the League of Nations. The Shanghai government sought to join the League and to gain the League's support for Korean independence. When this failed, the government shifted its efforts to gaining support from individual powers such as China, the US, Great Britain and the Soviet Union, setting up offices in Paris, Washington DC, London, Beijing and Ussuri. The only office able to engage in sustained activities, however, was the one in Washington DC which came to be called the Europe-America Office.

The Europe-America Office did not limit itself to diplomatic efforts. It also acted on behalf of the Provisional Government to obtain loans and to collect donations from Korean immigrants in the US. Its main activities focused on publicizing Korea's plight through publications and public lectures and lobbying the US Congress in hopes of gaining US support for Korean independence. Despite these efforts, it failed to gain American and European recognition.

On the other hand, the Provisional Government concluded a secret treaty with the Soviet Union in 1921. Disappointed at the indifference displayed by the great powers at the Versailles peace conference, the Shanghai government turned to the Soviet Union, which was advocating the liberation of weak and oppressed peoples throughout the world, to get help building an army of independence. The Soviets, on the other hand, were looking to use the Provisional Government to propagandize Communism in East Asia. The Soviet Union provided four hundred thousand rubles to the Provisional Government. Some of that money was reportedly arbitrarily appropriated by Prime Minister Yi Tonghwi, some was used to prepare for a Convention of National Representatives and some actually made its way inside Korea. But, the relations between the Provisional Government and the Soviet Government were broken off after the breakdown of the Convention of National Representatives, which was held in 1923.

Diplomatic negotiations with the Chinese began with the Canton government of Sun Yat-sen. The two governments agreed to recognize each other and to train Korean students at the Chinese military academy. But they failed to agree on Korean demands for loans and special funding for a Korean army of independence. Sun did promise, however, to 'help the Korean independence movement with all our efforts once we have completed our northern expedition'.

The Shanghai government subsequently maintained relations with Chiang Kai-shek's Republic of China. Chiang's government helped protect the Koreans living in Manchuria. The assassination of Japanese military officers in Shanghai by the Korean activist Yun Ponggil (1908–32) prompted Chiang to provide additional support. The Chiang government also helped the Provisional Government establish its Korean Restoration Army after the outbreak of war between Japan and China in 1937.

The Provisional Government, unable to exercise direct control over the many units of the independence army based in Manchuria and the Maritime Provinces, declared a war of independence was to be its 'last resort'. Although some members of the legislature made proposals for moving the Ministry of Military Affairs to Manchuria or the Maritime Provinces, for active efforts to raise an army and for the immediate declaration of a war of independence, the government rejected those proposals as financially unrealistic.

Having eschewed armed resistance to Japan, the Provisional Government soon became embroiled in factional strife. Much of the controversy arose out of President Syngman Rhee's proposal for entrusting rule over Korea to the League of Nations. Confrontation between the Kiho (Kyŏnggi and Ch'ungch'ŏng) Faction and the Northwestern Faction became particularly sharp after Beijing-based advocates of armed struggle such as Sin Suk (1885–1967) and Sin Ch'aeho (1880–1936) held a conference for the unification of the military affairs and declared their mistrust of Rhee. They also proposed to hold the afore-mentioned Convention of National Representatives for the purpose of changing the direction of Provisional Government activities and the independence movement as a whole. This proposal won the support of some members of the Shanghai Government as well as people in Manchuria and the Maritime Provinces.

More than a hundred people, representing over seventy ex-patriot Korean organizations overseas, attended the Convention of National Representatives in January 1923. The Convention saw a sharp confrontation between one group that argued for a reorganization of the Provisional Government based on an assessment of the entire national liberation movement and another group that argued for the dissolution of the Provisional Government and the creation of a new government. The two groups failed to find a compromise and the convention was disbanded. The group seeking the dissolution of the Provisional Government tried to establish a new government in the Maritime Provinces but that effort came to naught when the Soviet Union withheld support.

The Provisional Government, in an effort to recover from the damage it suffered at the Convention of National Representatives, impeached Syngman Rhee and amended its constitution. It abolished the post of president and replaced it with a system of collective leadership. It also sought to create a more realistic system by restricting the application of its constitution to those persons active in the independence movement. Despite these efforts, the Shanghai Provisional Government was unable to exert control over the whole national liberation movement and became simply one of many organizations engaged in the independence movement.

Although the March First Movement gave rise to a national liberation movement whose main forces were composed of workers, peasants and students, the Shanghai Provisional Government was unable to establish effective policies to mobilize, organize and train those forces. Its limits can be seen in its efforts to maintain itself as a government of elitist 'independence activists'. By contrast, Sin Ch'aeho, who left the Provisional Government, recognized the importance of the workers, peasants and students as a new popular force, which he referred to as the *minjung*. Sin, in his 'Declaration of Korean Independence', argued strongly that the national liberation movement must be a *minjung* revolution.

THE WAR FOR INDEPENDENCE IN MANCHURIA
AND THE MARITIME PROVINCES

The Righteous Armies, no longer able to operate inside Korea because of the pressure of Japanese troops, moved to Jiandao and the Maritime Provinces around the time of annexation. They were joined by some nationalists of the Patriotic Enlightenment Movement line who began preparations for a war of independence. The March First movement stimulated activities in this region, with over thirty national liberation organizations established in western Jiandao and over forty in northern Jiandao.

Although the Jiandao organizations included a few dedicated to the restoration of the monarchy, such as the Korean Independence Corps, most of the major organizations, including the Western Route Military Headquarters in western Jiandao and the Korean Citizens' Assembly or the Northern Route Military Headquarters in northern Jiandao, supported the republican line of the Shanghai Provisional Government.

The total colonization of Korea forced Korean migrants to organize their own ex-patriot communities. Koreans had been migrating to Jiandao and the Maritime Provinces since the 1860s, but the influx increased dramatically after annexation. These areas were considered appropriate for the establishment of bases for the war of independence. One such base was that at Sanyuanbao (K. Samwŏnbo) built by persons affiliated with the New People's Association of the Patriotic Enlightenment Movement.

Right after annexation, such men as Yi Tongnyŏng (1869–1940), Yi Sangnyong (1858–1932), Yi Hoeyŏng (1867–1932) and Yi Siyŏng (1868–1953) moved to Jiandao, where in 1911 they formed the Cultivation of Learning Society, an anti-Japanese organization. They also established a military school called the Sinhŭng Academy (renamed the Sinhŭng School in 1913). The Cultivation of Learning Society subsequently evolved into the People's Aid Corps and the Korean Association. In the meantime, the Sinhŭng School established an administration for military affairs that eventually became the Western Route Military Headquarters. The School also produced over 1,000 graduates prior to the March First Movement. After the Movement, the school changed its name to the Sinhŭng Military Academy and trained about 3,000 independence fighters before it was shut down in August 1920.

In addition, Yi Tonghwi, a nationalist from the line of the New People's Association, based himself in Hunchun County, where he trained more than 3,000 independence fighters whom he armed with weapons from the Soviet Union. Yi later collected donations from 6,500 Korean migrant households in the Mishan area, where he established a military school up in the mountains and employed former Korean army officers to train 1,500 young men in preparation for the war of independence. The Northern Route Military Headquarters under Sŏ Il (1881–1921) established an officer training school. The commander of that school, Kim Chwajin (1889–1930) trained more than four hundred independence fighters. The Korean Independence Army, led by the former Righteous Army leader Hong Pŏmdo (1868–1943), also trained independence fighters in Yanji County.

These Jiandao and Maritime Province war of independence bases, with their combination of civil and military offices, were not far removed from forming independent and autonomous governments. The Korean Association, for example, developed a government-like system of civil administration with a director-general supervising a group of directors in charge of education, finance, commerce, military affairs, foreign affairs and domestic affairs. The Association also had a local administrative system organized around units of 1,000 households, which were subdivided into units of 100 households, which in turn were further subdivided into units of ten households. The heads of all these units were appointed from the centre.

In short, the Korean community in Manchuria, which formed an important base for the national liberation movement in the 1910s, put into practice a republican form of self-rule. This indicates that the national liberation movement had reached the stage of the bourgeoisie movement to depose the monarchy and implement bourgeoisie democracy based on popular sovereignty.

With the outbreak of the March First Movement, the independence armies trained in Jiandao and the Maritime Provinces opened operations with the goal of advancing to the homeland. Beginning in 1919, independence fighters in Jiandao, such as Hong Pŏmdo's Korean Independence Army, frequently attacked Japanese border guards. Hong's troops attacked border posts such as Hyesanjin, Kapsan and Manp'ojin and once succeeded in occupying Hyesanjin for a short time. In the early 1920s, a force of more than two thousand soldiers drawn from the Korean Independence Army, the Northern Route Military Headquarters and a third group known as the Commandery Army crossed the border and killed three hundred Japanese soldiers.

There were many instances in which Japanese troops, pursuing Korean independence fighters, crossed the border into Manchuria where they ran into Korean counter-attacks and suffered heavy losses. For instance, in June 1920, Japanese troops of the 39th Division crossed the border while pursuing forces led by Hong Pŏmdo and Ch'oe Chindong (d. 1945) and were hit hard with a counter-attack by the independence fighters. In that incident, 120 Japanese soldiers were killed and more than 200 wounded. The Shanghai Provisional Government authorities verified that between March and early June of 1920, independence fighters and Japanese troops engaged in battle thirty-two times along the border, resulting in the destruction of thirty-four Japanese police and administrative buildings.

In May 1920, Japanese troops launched a raid on an independence army base in Fengwudong only to meet with a disastrous defeat. An allied independence force made up of elements of Hong Pŏmdo's Korean Independence Army, An Mu's (1883–1924) Korean Association Army and Ch'oe Chindong's Military Affairs Commandery Army, lured the Japanese into an ambush that resulted in 157 dead and over 300 wounded Japanese soldiers. This was the first major battle between the independence armies and the Japanese troops. It received major coverage in Chinese newspapers.

The Korean Independence Army under Hong Pŏmdo and the Northern Route Military Headquarters under Kim Chwajin moved to a safe area in the foothills of Changbai Mountain after receiving intelligence about a Japanese plan to negotiate with Zhang Zuolin (1875–1928; Chinese warlord who controlled eastern Manchuria) for permission to make a raid into Manchuria. The Japanese then fabricated the so-called Hunchun Incident as a pretext to send 15,000 troops across the border without Chinese permission to attack the independence forces gathered at Qingshanli (K. Ch'ŏngsanni) in October 1920. The independence armies engaged the Japanese troops in a number of locales and succeeded in killing more than 1,200 of the enemy, including one regimental commander, while suffering the loss of only 60 of their own number. This 'Chŏngsanni battle' was the greatest victory for the independence forces in the years following the March First Movement.

After this, the independence forces gathered at Mishan near the border between China and the Soviet Union. They did so not only to combine their forces, but also to avoid the damage that would certainly happen to the Korean community if the Japanese sent their troops into Manchuria. About 3,500 troops led by Sŏ Il, Hong Pŏmdo, Kim Chwajin, Cho Sŏnghwan (1875–1948), Ch'oe Chindong and Yi Ch'ŏngch'ŏn (1888–1959) established a united organization under the name of the Korean Independence Corps. Shortly thereafter, they moved across the border into Soviet territory because they did not consider Mishan to be an appropriate base.

After the independence forces moved north, Japanese troops, still smarting from their defeat at Ch'ŏngsanni, moved into Jiandao and took revenge against the Korean community. Over a period of two months, the Japanese, on the pretext of 'sweeping out' the independence forces, committed barbaric acts against noncombatants, including indiscriminate murder, rape, arrest and arson. According to the statistics of the Provisional Government, more than 3,000 Koreans were killed or arrested, and over 2,500 private residences and 30 schools were burned to the ground.

Later, when the Japanese sent an expedition to Siberia in support of the White Russians, the independence fighters who had moved into Soviet territory from Manchuria joined forces with the anti-Japanese armed resistance groups already formed among Korean migrants in the Soviet Union, and planned to carry out a large-scale war of independence with the support of the Red Army. However, power struggles among the various anti-Japanese groups erupted in the 'Free City Incident' of June 1921. Subsequently, the Soviet Union, hoping to improve relations with Japan, disarmed the independence forces. Some of the independence fighters then joined the Red Army while the rest relocated back to Manchuria or to the Maritime Provinces where they continued their anti-Japanese activities.

After the Japanese atrocities and the Free City Incident, the national liberation movement in Manchuria and the Maritime Provinces fell into disarray. Even so, the various independence movement organizations continued to seek ways to unify the movement. First, the Korean United Military Government was formed out of the 1922 union of the Western Route Military Headquarters and the Korean Independence Corps. It developed into the Korean United Righteous Government, an organization based in Tonghua and Jian counties, where it established its own government with both central and local administrative systems. It also had a military wing known as the Volunteer Army of the Korean United Righteous Government.

This government soon fell apart because of factional strife between republicans and monarchists. Some members, mostly from the Volunteer Army, formed the Administration of Army Councillors of the Provisional Government in Manchuria with the approval of the Shanghai Provisional Government in 1923. The Administration of Councillors developed into a sort of 'self-government' in the Korean communities in such counties as Jian, Fusong, Changbai, Antu, Tonghua and Liuhua. This organization comprised both civil and military administrative systems and provided military training for Korean youth in rural areas.

After the Administration of Councillors was formed, the Korean United Righteous Government and the Korean Independence Corps established a new Just Administration in 1925 as yet another effort to unify the independence movement. After the failure of the Convention of National Representatives, the Just Administration, under the leadership of Kim Tongsam (1878–1937), sought to establish a zone of Korean rule in the area south of Harbin and Emu County. It had about 1,500 Korean households under its control in 1926. It featured the separation of the three (legislative, executive, and adjudicative) powers and had a military force of about 700 men.

While the Councillors Administration and the Just Administration ruled the Korean communities in southern Manchuria, those independence fighters who came back into Manchuria from the Soviet Union after the Free City Incident formed a New People's Administration in northern Manchuria and part of northern Jiandao in 1925. The New People's Administration also had the separation of the three powers and had a military committee led by Kim Chwajin that established a military academy to train officers. It also had a force of about 500 soldiers who supported themselves by cultivating a garrison farm.

These three administrations, which came into being in the process of unifying the national liberation movement after the Ch'ŏngsanni battle, became *de facto* governments ruling the entire Korean population in Manchuria with the exception of the northern Jiandao area where Japanese influence was strong. The three administrations can be said to have further strengthened the independence movement bases that had already begun to develop before the March First Movement. The three administrations were governed by administrative, legislative and judicial offices chosen by the Korean community. The administrations ran their government and trained independence fighters with taxes collected from the Korean community. Unlike the Shanghai Provisional Government, which had neither people nor territory, these administrations can be considered as self-ruling republican governments in the sense that they had sovereignty, populations, territory and even military forces.

The Koreans in Manchuria bore the heavy burden of paying taxes to Chinese officials and also providing funds for these administrations on a regular basis. By the second half of the 1920s, some Koreans, dismayed at the lack of noticeable activity and internal factional fighting, began to leave the administrations. In 1928, one group of Koreans under the Just Administration seceded and declared the formation of their own autonomous organization, while others were suppressed by armed units when they began to discuss self-protective measures.

REFERENCES

Cho Chihun, 'Han'guk minjok undongsa' (History of the Korean National Movement), *Hang'uk munhwasa taegye* (An outline of Korean cultural history), vol. 1, Seoul: Kodae minjok munhwa yŏn'guso, 1964.

Kang Tŏksang, 'Nihon no Chosen sihai to san ichi dokuritsu undo' (Japanese rule over Korea and the March First Movement), *Iwanami koza seikei rekishi* (World History, Iwanami Lecture Series), vol. 25 (Gendai 2), Tokyo: Iwanami shoten, 1970.

Tongnip undongsa p'yŏnch'an wiwŏnhoe (ed.), *Tongnip undongsa* (History of the Independence Movement), vol. 4, 1975.

An Pyŏngjik, *Samil undong* (The March First Movement), Seoul: Han'guk ilbosa, 1975.

Pak Kyŏngsik, *Chosen sanichi dokuritsu undou* (The March First Independence Movement of Korea), Tokyo: Heibonsha, 1976.

Son Seil, 'Taehan minguk imsi chŏngbu ŭi chŏngch'i chido ch'eje' (The political leadership of the Korean Provisional Government), *Han'guk kŭndaesa ron* (Essays of Modern Korean History) II, Seoul: Chisik sanŏpsa, 1977.

Kang Mangil, 'Tongnip undong ŭi yŏksajŏk sŏngkyŏk' (Historical nature of the Independence Movement), *Pundan sidae ŭi yŏksa insik* (Historical views of the Division Period), Seoul: Ch'angjak kwa pip'yŏngsa, 1978.

Pak Yŏngsŏk, *Ilcheha tongnip undongsa yŏngu* (A study of history of the Independence Movement under the Japanese imperialism), Seoul: Ilchogak, 1984.

Sin Yongha, *Hanguk minjok tongnip undongsa yŏngu* (A study of history of the Korean National Independence Movement), Seoul: Ŭryu munhwasa, 1985.

Hanguk yŏksa yŏnguhoe (ed.), *Samil minjok haebang undong yŏngu* (Studies of the March First National Liberation Movement), Seoul: Ch'ŏngnyŏnsa, 1989.

Kang Mangil, 'Sin Ch'aeho ŭi yŏngung, kungmin, minjungjuŭi' (Hero, nation, and popularism of Sin Ch'aeho), *T'ongil undong sidae ŭi yŏksa insik* (Historical Views of the Unification Movement Period), Seoul: Ch'ŏngsa, 1990.

Pak Hwan, *Manju Hanin minjok undongsa yŏngu* (A study of history of the Korean National Movement in Manchuria), Seoul: Ilchogak, 1991.

SECTION TWO
Activation of Mass Movements

THE LABOUR MOVEMENT

Although some day labourers had appeared in the cities during the latter half of the Chosŏn dynasty, the number of wage labourers, such as dock-workers in the open ports and labourers in some of the more developed factories, gradually increased after the opening of the ports in 1876. Even so, the total number of factory workers at the time of colonization was no more than 2,500. After colonization, the introduction of Japanese capitalist colonial management led to some increase in the number of day labourers working at construction sites, but the increase in the number of factory workers was quite slow. The total number of factory workers in 1919 was about 42,000. By 1928 that number had increased to about 88,000. The progress of colonial industrialization in the 1930s brought a rapid increase. Statistical data from 1936 indicate a total of 190,000 male and female factory workers.

Colonial industrialization brought an increase in the number of workers, but the colonial working conditions were bad. For instances, Koreans were often paid less than half of what Japanese workers were paid for the same job. According to 1929 factory labourer statistics, Japanese adult workers' earnings averaged 2.32 yen per day, whereas Korean adult workers' earnings were only 1 yen per day. Koreans also worked longer hours: 46.9% of Korean workers laboured 12 or more hours per day, whereas only 0.3% of Japanese workers laboured more than 12 hours. These data reflect the conditions of the relatively small number of factory workers; the conditions for the many more Koreans working as day labourers at various constructions sites were undoubtedly even worse.

Bad working conditions and ethnic discrimination led to higher labour consciousness and increasing numbers of labour disputes. The 1920s in particular saw many labour disputes. Government-General statistics show 891 disputes involving 3,450 Korean labourers during the ten years from 1920 to 1930. The rapid increase in labour disputes can be attributed to a situation in which workers' social and national consciousness was greatly stimulated by the influx of socialist ideas after March First but there was virtually no improvement in working conditions. The most frequent cause of labour disputes was wages: Korean workers were seeking wage increases in 40.6% and opposing wage cuts in 25.4% of those disputes.

Labour organizations had started forming even before the colonial period. The 1890s saw the formation of a dockworkers' union in Sŏngjin and a joint labour union in Kunsan. The total number of labour organizations increased to over thirty between 1905 and 1919, and by the 1920s a nationwide labour organization known as the Korean Workers

Mutual Aid Society came into being. The Mutual Aid Society had over twenty local branches throughout the country with over 5,000 members. It published a magazine, and engaged in such activities as providing educational lectures, establishing consumer unions, and investigating and mediating labour disputes. In the end, however, the Mutual Aid Society disbanded in October 1922 because of conflict at its headquarters between conservative reformists and progressive labourers such as Ch'a Kŭmbong (1898–1929).

As soon as the Mutual Aid Society was dissolved, a new organization known as the Korean Labour Confederation was established. The Korean Labour Confederation, which called for 'the construction of a new society according to the necessary evolutionary principles of social history' and for 'solidarity based on class consciousness', displayed stronger and clearer class goals than had the Mutual Aid Society. This reflects influence from the spread of socialist ideas and the establishment of socialist organizations in Korean society. At the time of its founding, the Korean Labour Confederation had over 20,000 members. It focused its efforts on leading the peasant and worker movement and on organizing local unions.

After the founding of the Korean Labour Confederation, many worker and peasant organizations were established throughout Korea, including the Southern Korea Labour Alliance, the Chŏlla Labour Alliance, the P'yŏngyang Korean Labour Alliance, the Kyŏnggi Workers' Union, the Seoul Shoe Workers' Union, the Chinju Workers' Mutual Aid Society, the Ch'ŏngjin Workers' Mutual Aid Society, the Kwangju Tenant Farmers' Union and the Sunch'ŏn Peasants' Confederation. In April 1924, these various organizations were brought together, along with the Korean Labour Confederation, in the Korean Worker-Peasant League. The League, which set forth a programme of 'liberating the worker and peasant class and building a new society' and 'struggling with the great power of solidarity until the final victory over the capitalist class', presided over 260 some organizations and had over 53,000 members.

The founding of the League, which had a stronger class character than either the Mutual Aid Society or the Korean Labour Federation and which embraced almost all the worker and peasant organizations throughout the whole country, represented a significant step forward in the worker and peasant movement. But the movement of the early 1920s was centred on local organizations that included agricultural workers, factory workers and other free workers and had not yet arrived at the stage of differentiations between the peasant movement and the worker movement. Many of the peasants of that time toiled partly as farmers and partly as workers, while many of the urban workers were first generation workers who were still closely attached to the villages.

During the second half of the 1920s, discussion of the need to separate the peasant and worker movements arose as part of the debates about the future direction of the socialist movement. In December 1926, the League, acting under the guidance of the newly formed Korean Communist Party, published its 'New Policy for the Korean Peasant and Labour Movement'. The new policy had three major points. One, although the peasant and labour movement should be a mass co-operative movement centred on economic struggle, the movement's organizations to date had been nothing more than intellectual groups made up of a few men of foresight. Two, even though there were class distinctions between peasants and workers, they had been mixed together in the same unions, thus impeding the development of the movement; henceforth, they were to organized in separate alliances working together through a liaison office. Three, although the movement had rejected political activity in the past, it should now enhance the political consciousness of the labouring masses and carry out an active political struggle.

In September 1927, the Korean Worker-Peasant League split, with the overwhelming endorsement of its member organizations, into the General League of Korean Peasants and the General League of Korean Workers. At the time, the total population of Korea was 19 million. Workers, including 'free workers' numbered about 1 million, while peasant households accounted for 16 million persons. These 16 million, whose movement had been led by peasants' or tenant farmers' sections under the petit bourgeoisie- and intelligentsia-led Mutual Aid Society and the Korean Labour Federation, now had their own peasant movement organization.

The General League of Korean Workers, launched with Yi Nagyŏng as the chair of its central executive committee, continued the activities of the Korean Worker-Peasant League, organizing and leading many labour disputes. It suffered a major blow with the arrest of Yi Nagyŏng and many of its other leaders at the time of the third Communist Party incident in March 1928. After Ch'a Kŭmbong of the central committee of the General League of Korean Workers became responsible secretary of the fourth Korean Communist Party, the Party began to exercise active leadership of the labour movement. After suppression of the Fourth Communist Party began in July 1928, the General League of Korean Workers was severely crippled. It did manage to reorganize its central organs in July 1929, but it was unable to recover its former strength. At the time of the split between the workers' and peasants' alliances, the General League of Korean Workers had 156 organizations with over 26,000 members; in 1932, those numbers had shrunk to 56 organizations with about 18,000 members. Struggling against vicious Japanese oppression to create an alliance of labour unions and to guide labour disputes throughout the country, the General League of Korean Workers was transformed into a revolutionary labour union movement.

The largest and most organized struggle to come out of the active labour movement of the 1920s was the 1929 Wŏnsan general strike. Wŏnsan, one of the original three ports opened in 1876, developed one of the earliest labour movements. A Wŏnsan labour alliance was formed in 1925; at the time of the strike in 1929, it comprised 54 organizations with about 2,000 members. The strike arose as a protest against the beating of a Korean worker by a Japanese supervisor working for a British oil company.

The labour alliance demanded the dismissal of the Japanese supervisor, the establishment of a minimum wage system, arbitration for severance pay and compensation for the families of workers killed on the job. The Japanese police sought to disband the labour alliance and to replace it with a new pro-government union. Incensed at this, all the workers in Wŏnsan went on strike in support of the alliance. As the strike dragged on, labour unions, peasant unions, youth organizations and New Korea Society chapters throughout the country sent money to help the strikers. This meant that the labour movement had now become part of the national liberation movement.

The Wŏnsan general strike, which began as a labour action against one company and then developed into a general strike of all the workers in the city that received support from throughout the whole country, lasted about four months. After its strike funds began to dry up due to Japanese police oppression, the labour alliance decided, through a vote of the workers, to return to work. This strike was more than a major blow against the capitalists. It also raised the social consciousness of Korean workers and changed the colonial rulers' perception of the Korean working class.

THE PEASANT MOVEMENT

The 1894 Peasant War was not only an anti-foreign war but also an anti-feudal struggle in which the peasants sought to break up the holdings of the landlords and return the land to peasant ownership. This was also true, to some degree, of the anti-Japanese Righteous Armies struggles that followed the 1894 Peasant War. After suppressing the 1894 war and the Righteous Armies and pushing through annexation in 1910, Japan strengthened the landlord system through a land survey carried out between 1910 and 1918. The land survey blocked the growth of a rich peasant stratum by limiting peasant ownership of land and it also resulted in the dispossession of large numbers of peasants who were forced either to become tenants or to abandon their villages.

Peasant resistance against the colonial government's takeover of privately owned lands and postal station lands and against raises in tenancy rents erupted in various places during the time of the land survey. It was in the years after the March First Movement, however, when the real cost to the peasants of colonial agricultural policy became clear. The result was a rapid growth in the peasants' social and economic consciousness and the intensification of the peasant movement.

After solidifying the landlord system through the land survey of the 1910s and the Campaign to Increase Rice Production in the 1920s, the Japanese sought to pursue the development of Korean agriculture and rule rural society through the large landlords, a group that numbered about 5,000. Those two decades saw rapid changes. Land ownership became increasingly insecure, with many peasants losing their lands and becoming tenant farmers. Land rents also were raised to high levels, and peasants had to bear increasing costs associated with tenant supervisors. In addition, the peasants felt a national resistance to Japanese colonial agricultural policy and Japanese landlords. The consequence was the spread of tenancy disputes throughout the whole country after March First, with the numbers of disputes increasing each year.

In pursuing their disputes under colonial rule, the tenants formed their own resistance movements and developed a wide range of methods. In areas where large-scale, long-term disputes occurred, the tenants formed interim or even permanent peasant unions, tenant leader councils, and tenant alliances with fixed rules and regulations. Their methods of resistance included demonstrations, hunger strikes, refusal to pay rents, refusal to cultivate and refusal to harvest, as well as allying their struggles with the peasant movement and other social organizations.

According to the statistics of the Government-General, there were 15 tenancy disputes in 1920; 204 in 1925; 726 in 1930; 5,834 in 1935; 31,799 in 1937, the year with the highest number, and 16,452 in 1939. There was a total of 140,969 disputes over twenty years, for an annual average of 7,480. Not all of these were organized disputes; the figures include many instances where either individual tenants or landlords rejected the demands of the other side. Nonetheless, they indicate a sharpening of the contradictions in landlord-tenant relations and a growing resistance toward landlords among the tenants during the 1920s and 1930s.

The most common source of disputes was related to tenancy rights and tenant lands. The next most frequent type of dispute was related to rents. (See Table 1.) In particular, the numbers of disputes related to tenancy rights and tenant lands increased sharply during the second half of the 1930s, a sign that Korean peasants were finding it difficult even to find lands to rent. Rents were a secondary problem for the peasants whose most urgent problem was simply avoiding eviction from the land that was their livelihood.

Under colonial rural conditions where more and more peasants fell to tenancy and the conditions of tenancy continued to deteriorate, it was only natural that peasants would have turned increasingly to tenancy disputes as a means to protect themselves and that their disputes gradually developed into an organized peasant movement.

Table 1: Causes of tenancy disputes

Cause	1927–29	1930–32	1933–36	1937–39
Tenancy Rights, Tenant Lands	47.3%	58.2%	78.8%	82.8%
Rents	48.5%	30.5%	18.5%	16.1%
Other	4.2%	11.2%	2.7%	1.2%

Source: Han'guk kŭndae minjok undongsa (Seoul: Tolbegae, 1980) p. 587

Peasant organizations first arose spontaneously as isolated township tenant unions. By 1922, there were already thirty-some mass organization peasant organizations covering individual townships; by 1933, that number had grown to 1,301. These isolated tenant unions were first brought into a nation-wide organization by the Korean Workers Mutual Aid Association. The Mutual Aid Association was a labour movement organization, but it had tenant sections or peasant sections in its local branches through which it sought to organize the peasants. It also sponsored tenant meetings and led tenant disputes.

The Mutual Aid Association's Chinju branch, for example, held a cadre meeting in 1922 to discuss tenancy problems, after which it opened a tenant meeting. The meeting was attended by over 1,000 representatives from all the townships in the county who agreed on a set of demands to be presented to landlords. In order to achieve its goals, the Mutual Aid Association's Chinju branch established a temporary tenancy section and formed an executive committee of fifty members. The tenant unions of the early 1920s, however, were still operating within the principles of tenant-landlord coexistence and co-prosperity and class harmonization, so the resolutions of the tenant meeting were not much different from the resolutions of the county government-sponsored landlord association.

After the dissolution of the Korean Workers Mutual Aid Association, the tasks of supporting the formation of peasant organizations, such as the tenant unions, and of guiding tenancy disputes were taken up by the new nation-wide organization known as the Korean Workers-Peasants League. After the Korean Worker-Peasants League split into the General League of Korean Workers and the General League of Korean Peasants in 1927, the General League of Korean Peasants, led by In Tongch'ŏl and having thirty-two branches with over 24,000 members, became the central headquarters for the nation-wide peasant movement. Previously, peasant organizations had been mostly limited to the three southern provinces of Ch'ungch'ŏng, Chŏlla and Kyŏngsang, but after the founding of the General League of Korean Peasants they expanded into northern areas. This appears to have resulted in a rapid increase in the number of affiliate organizations – according to one record, the General League had over 200 affiliated organizations in 1928.

Another new development after the founding of the General League was the reorganization of tenant unions to include land-owning peasants. This was because even the land-owning peasants suffered badly from colonial policies, with many middle land-owning peasants falling to the status of poor peasants. The reorganization of the tenant unions into broader peasant unions including land-owning peasants was made necessary in order to expand and strengthen the peasant movement and to resist the oppression and divisive tactics of the Government-General of Korea.

Although the 1930s saw an increase in the number of tenancy disputes, the General League of Korean Peasants, like the General League of Korean Workers, found its activities greatly restricted as a result of

Government-General oppression. Furthermore, the General League's ability to organize effective struggles was hampered by a number of other factors, including arrests of cadre members involved in the Korean Communist Party affair, factional infighting, and reformist elements. Thus it was that this nation-wide peasant movement organization, despite having 33 branches and roughly 34,000 members in 1933, was on its way to extinction.

On the other hand, persons from the new faction of Ch'ŏndogyo (Religion of the Heavenly War; formerly Eastern Learning) such as Kim Kijŏn (1894–1948) and Yi Tonhwa (1884–?) organized the Institute of the Korean Peasant in 1925. Their programme called for 'securing livelihood rights for the peasant masses facing real insecurity' and 'pursuing a Korea-wide movement through the stout solidarity of the peasant masses'. The Institute, which published its own magazine called *The Korean Peasant*, developed into a large organization with 1,069 affiliated organizations and about 50,000 members in 1933. The Institute, which was largely controlled by Ch'ŏndogyo, was a reformist peasant organization with a strong religious nature. Dissatisfaction with this led some of its members, such as Yi Sŏnghwan, to break away in 1931 and form a new organization known as the All Korea Peasant Institute, but that, too, was unable to transcend the limits of reformism and soon collapsed.

One example of the continuous tenancy disputes carried out by tenant unions in the 1920s against vicious Japanese landlords was the case of Sŏsŏn farm owned by the Buni Kogyo Company. The Sŏsŏn farm, located in Yongch'ŏn County, North P'yŏngan Province, was a company-owned farm of 4,290 *chŏngbo* (1 *chŏngbo* equals 2.45 acres) cultivated by tenants. The company developed this farm from tidal flats by recruiting Korean peasants, promising to give them permanent tenancy rights, to compensate them for the costs of reclamation, and to give them a three-year exemption from rents once normal crop yields were attained. After the land was completely reclaimed in 1926, the peasants demanded compensation for their expenses. When the company-landlord refused, the peasants organized a tenant union for the purpose of collective bargaining.

Once crops reached a normal yield in 1929, the company-landlord went back on its promise to exempt rents and levied on the tenants excessively heavy rents and water taxes, and threatened to evict tenants who did not comply. Angered by this, the peasants adopted a resolution demanding recognition of permanent tenancy rights and compensation for reclamation expenses, and opposing forcible collection of rents. They also demanded the right to sell their tenancy rights, to have rents reduced from 80% to 50% and to have a moratorium on debt payments. When the company-landlord refused these demands, the peasants formed an alliance for the purpose of refusing to pay rents. The company-landlord then mobilized the police to collect rents by force. Under the leadership of the tenant union, the peasants attacked the farm office and seized the weapons of the police guarding the office. When the police arrested the leaders of the union, the peasants then attacked the police station.

The tenants continued to carry on their struggle to realize their demands by organizing hunger strikes. Also, in resistance to the forcible collection of rents by the police, 300 peasants surrounded an armed police unit in 1930 in an effort to press their demands – 150 of the peasants were arrested. Despite its tenacious struggle, the Yongch'ŏn tenant union – the largest in Korea at that time – eventually found it impossible to continue its activities in the face of police oppression and disbanded in 1932.

Taken as a whole, the peasant union movement of the 1920s had a number of limitations. First, most of the peasant unions did not have a strong mass base. They were led by young men of landlord or rich peasant backgrounds who were more interested in educational and enlightenment activities such as night schools and reading circles than in mass struggle. Second, as seen in the peasant unions' responses to clashes between new and old tenants and in the struggle in opposition to irrigation unions, they were not able to combine the economic struggle with the political struggle. Third, they were unable to carry out effective struggles against prohibitions of assembly or arrest and detention and by insisting on lawful struggle limited the sphere of the movement, leaving them unable to combine legal and illegal movement activities effectively.

THE YOUTH AND STUDENT MOVEMENT

After the opening of Korea in 1876, increasing numbers of youths and students received the new education and they gradually became more visibly active in the national movement of the open ports period. During the ten years of military rule after colonization in 1910, the youth and student movement was stifled, but it came back to life with the reactivation of various social movements after the March First Movement.

As early as 1920, there were 251 youth organizations formed for the purposes of training and enlightenment, a number than increased to 446 by 1921. The rapid increase in the number of youth organizations led to the need to form an alliance. In 1920, the All Korea Youth League, chaired by O Sanggǔn (1881–?) was formed. This alliance encompassed 116 organizations, including the Seoul Youth Association – a group that later became the 'Seoul Faction' of the communist movement. The central committee of the All Korean Youth League included both nationalists and socialists. Despite the appearance of a united front, its leadership was primarily reformist and its efforts were directly primarily toward promoting education, encouraging industry and providing ethical training.

Seoul Youth Association members of the central committee, such as Kim Saguk (1892–1926) and Yi Yŏng (1889–?), were discontented with the reformist leadership. Their unhappiness came to the surface over the issue of a public funeral service for Kim Yunsik (1835–1922), and the

Seoul Youth Association, which was opposed to the funeral service, left the League. After that, the Alliance, under Chŏng Nosik as chair, continued to pursue its reformist agenda. The Seoul Youth Association purged itself of reformist elements such as Chang Tŏksu (1895–1947), set forth such programmes as 'Charging towards the goal of constructing a new society, the requirement of historical evolution' and 'Resolving that the proletarian masses will, with class consciousness and class solidarity, become the advance guard of the liberation movement.' Thus the Seoul Youth Association made clear its nature as a socialist organization and purged the reformists.

The progressive youth forces centred on the Seoul Youth Association held an All Korea Youth Party Congress in 1923. This congress established subcommittees that discussed such issues as women's problems, educational problems, economic problems, labour problems, tenant problems and the national problem. In the process of their discussions, they declared that 'national self-determination and national liberation are useless today', and that the 'liberation of the proletariat is the first duty'.

This declaration revealed some confusion in the process of accepting socialism in that they believed that they had to choose between the liberation of the proletariat and the liberation of the nation. Of the total 488 youth groups of the time, 94 participated in this congress. The fact that only 35 groups participated in the Fourth general meeting of the All Korea Youth League held at the same time indicates the general orientation of the youth organizations of the early 1920s.

The All Korea Youth Party Congress was disbanded when the Government-General of Korea prevented it from meeting. Its key members then organized a Youth Party Company and published a journal called *Youth Party*, but it faded after experiencing internal ideological divisions. On the other hand, a New Youth Alliance, centred on the New Thought Study Society (later the Tuesday Society) and the North Star Society (domestically known as the North Wind Society), was formed in 1924. The New Youth Alliance's activities included publishing a journal called *New Youth* and organizing lectures on youth problems. Eventually such organizations as the Seoul Youth Association and the New Youth Alliance came together to form the General League of Korean Youth in 1924.

The forming of the General League came about in the same year as the formation of the General League of Korean Workers as part of a nationwide movement toward mass organization. The General League of Korean Youth included 223 organizations with over 37,000 members. It was founded at a meeting attended by 170 representatives to provide unified national leadership for the youth movement. Chaired by Yi Yŏng, the General League set forth a programme of 'striving to build a new society centred on the masses', and of 'resolving to become the vanguard of the Korean national liberation movement'.

The General League of Korean Youth subsequently suffered at the time of the first and second suppressions of the Korean Communist Party and the Koryŏ Communist Youth Association. In 1926, when the third Korean Communist Party and the Koryŏ Communist Youth Association issued their 'True Friend Society' proclamation, pushed for a national co-operative front movement and organized the New Korea Society, the General League of Korean Youth strengthened its central executive organs, established provincial leagues and actively participated in the New Korea Society-led national co-operative front movement. At the same time, General League of Korean Youth branches in China and Japan were also activated.

Even though the General League was a lawful organization, the Japanese prevented it from having central meetings and also disallowed provincial meetings when they sought to deal with the real problems of the Korean people. As in the case of the New Korea Society, in the 1930s the leadership was infiltrated by reformist elements and the organization began to slant towards the right. In response, the provincial leagues began to disband, denouncing the centre as a group of petit bourgeoisie. The loss of its mass base naturally brought the demise of the central General League of Korean Youth. Nonetheless, in later times the International Communist Youth League criticized the disbanding of the General League of Korean Youth as a 'serious political error brought about by a leftist tendency'.

On the other hand, the student movement, inspired by the 8 February declaration of Korean students in Tokyo, became even more active after the March First Movement. The first student organization formed after March First was the 1,000-plus member Congress of Korean Students. This organization, made up mostly of secondary school students, had a reformist orientation but is noteworthy for its creation of a unified nation-wide student movement. Even though this organization at one time had as many as 20,000 members, it was unable to carry out continuous activities because of the severe oppression by Japanese colonial authorities and school officials.

The next student organization was the Korean Student Association, organized in 1923 and made up only of students at two-year technical colleges. The Korean Student Association's activities included academic lectures, speech contests and music festivals. In 1925, the North Wind Society formed its Korean Mutual Student Association; this was followed by other socialist organizations such as the Seoul Youth Association's Kyŏngsŏng Student League, the North Wind Society's Seoul Student Club and the Tuesday Club's Korean Students' Social Science Research Society.

The latter was organized under the active leadership of the Korean Communist Party and the Koryŏ Communist Youth Association and was conspicuously active. It published a journal called the *Scientific Movement* and organized social science research groups in schools at all levels. It set forth a programme of propagating socialist thought, of the ideological unification of students and of resolving the problems of Korean students while striving to spread socialist theory through academic research, lectures and the establishment of libraries. It engaged in student strikes and provided leadership and assistance to the student movement, particularly in the case of the June 10th *mansei* movement of 1926. The June 10th *mansei* movement was prepared and organized by several different groups, but the fact that five of the six students targeted as organizers by the Japanese police were cadre or members of the Social Science Research Society indicates that this Korean Communist Party sponsored student organization played the major role.

The student strikes that arose continuously throughout the colonial period formed one of the most important parts of the student movement. These strikes also showed qualitative development over time. Whereas in the early 1920s most of the strikes arose over such issues as school facilities, improvement of school regulations and rejection of faculty, after the June 10th *mansei* movement, they developed into organized strikes with solid ideological foundations.

In particular, after the New Korea Society was organized and established its Student Department, frequent student strikes were carried out demanding such things as abolition of the system requiring licensing of private schools, Korea-centred education, using the Korean language for all educational terminology, freedom of research and academic autonomy. This in turn was linked to the Kwangju Student Movement.

The student movement, which in the early 1920s had been largely limited to campuses, moved beyond the campus and expanded into an organized national liberation movement after the June 10th *mansei* movement and the Kwangju Student Movement. Before the eruption of the student movement, in 1926 the South Chŏlla Province branch of Korean Communist Party had organized the Sŏngjin Association in the Kwangju area; it had also organized a 'Student Strike Central Headquarters' in support of the Kwangju High School student strike in 1928, and had established a 'Reading Club Headquarters' to lead the reading clubs organized at various schools. This provided the foundation for the 'Leadership Headquarters for the Student Struggle' that was established immediately after conflict arose between Korean and Japanese students in Kwangju and then developed into a nation-wide movement.

The student movement that erupted in Kwangju immediately spread to Seoul where high school and two-year technical college students engaged in student strikes and street demonstrations. These were led and supported by the New Korea Society, the General League of Korea Youth and the Korean Students' Social Science Research Society. Over the winter, this movement spread throughout the country as students used such slogans as 'Down with Japanese Imperialism', 'Long live the liberation of oppressed peoples' and 'Total opposition to Government-General politics'.

The Kwangju Student Movement, which can be seen as the turning point in the transformation of the student movement into a full-fledged national liberation movement, involved over 54,000 students in roughly 200 schools throughout the country. Over 1,600 students were arrested and jailed, while 600 were expelled and 13,000 were suspended indefinitely.

Table 2: Student 'thought crime' incidents, 1931–44

Year	1931	1932	1933	1934	1935	1939	1940	1941	1942	1943	1944
Incidents	6	22	24	8	5	6	16	48	57	46	16
Students	136	414	302	29	152	26	121	203	409	198	42

Source: Hong Sŏngnyul, 'Ilcheha ch'ŏngnyŏn haksaeng undong', *Han'guksa* vol. 15

With the intensification of Japanese oppression in the 1930s, the number of student strikes decreased while the movement transformed into a secret society movement centred on a small numbers of elites. Secret socialist student organizations such as the Red Attack Brigade, the Red Banner Society and the Red Light Society came into being. Their members, who learned socialist thought in reading clubs, joined in the revolutionary labour and peasant movements of the time. Small-scale non-socialist nationalist student movements also continued up until the end of the colonial period. One such example was the Korean Liberation Struggle League formed at Kyŏnggi Middle School in 1940, an organization which proclaimed its goal to be 'uniting socialists and nationalists in the common cause of struggling against Japanese imperialism for the liberation of the Korean nation'.

As can be seen in Table 2, from 1930 on there was a steady level of student 'thought crime' incidents.

Even as the student movement of the 1930s was moving in the direction of a secret organization socialist movement, there were other legal reformist movements that targeted the improvement of living conditions and the spread of literacy in poor rural areas led by the media, in which students participated. One was the 'Movement for Students to Return to their Villages and Spread Literacy' led by the *Korean Daily News*; another was the 'Vnarod Movement' sponsored by the *East Asia Daily News*. Many students joined in the Vnarod Movement during summer vacations from 1931 until 1934, when it was shut down by the Government-General of Korea.

REFERENCES

Han'guk noch'ong, *Han'guk nodong chohap undongsa ilche sidae p'yŏn* (Korean labour movement history, colonial period volume), 1979.

Cho Tonggŏl, *Ilcheha han'guk nongmin undongsa* (History of the Korean peasant movement under Japanese imperial rule), Han'gilsa, 1979.

Asada Hashinichi, '1920–30 nyŏndae hangil nongmin undong ŭi chiyŏkchŏk t'ŭkching' (Regional features of the anti-Japanese peasant movement of the 1920s and 1930s), *Han'guk kŭndae minjok undongsa*, Tolbaegae, 1980.

Kang Tongjin, 'Ilcheha ŭi han'guk sahoe undongsa' (The Korean social movement under Japanese imperial rule), op cit.

Kim Yunhwan, *Han'guk nodong undongsa* (The Korean labour movement), Ch'ŏngsa, 1980.

Kim Kyŏngil, *Ilcheha nodong undongsa* (History of the labour movement under Japanese imperial rule), Ch'angjak kwa pip'yŏngsa, 1992.

Hong Sŏngnyul, 'Ilcheha ch'ŏngnyŏn haksaeng undong' (The youth and student movement under Japanese Rule), *Han'guksa* vol. 15, Han'gilsa, 1994.

SECTION THREE
The Communist Movement

THE KORYŎ COMMUNIST PARTY IN RUSSIA

Koreans migrated to the Far East region of Russia before the colonial period, and the Korean communist movement started in the Korean community of the region. When the Russian Revolution broke out, about 250,000 Koreans lived there. The Koreans formed the Industry Encouragement Association and published a newspaper, the *Industry Encouragement News*. After the February Revolution in Russia, Koreans, who were already naturalized, formed the All Russia Korean Association Central Assembly (May 1917). They were later joined in the Assembly by such men as Yi Tonghwi who had gone into exile in after participating in the domestic national movement.

After the October Revolution in Russia, the political group who supported the Bolsheviks, including Yi Tonghwi, Pak Ae and Kim Ip, founded the first communist body – the Korean Socialist Party – but the leadership of the All Russia Korean Association did not join. Later, imperialist countries such as Japan sent troops in order to stop the Russian Revolution, leading to the collapse of the Far East People's Committee Government and the control of the Maritime Provinces by anti-revolutionary elements. As a consequence, the Korean Socialist Party was outlawed.

After the outbreak of the March First Movement, nationalists in Russia and Manchuria replaced the All Russia Korean Association with the Korean National Assembly, which was the assembly of the Korean community. The Korean Socialist Party became active again and in April 1919 set forth a programme for 'Organizing the proletariat and the agricultural workers and educating them with the revolutionary Marxist spirit' and 'Regarding the Soviet authority as the one best suited for our goals.'

Later, the leaders of the Korean Socialist Party, such as Yi Tonghwi and Kim Ip, severed their relations with the Korean National Assembly during the process of setting up the Provisional Government of the Republic of Korea. They relocated to Shanghai, where in August and September of 1920 they organized the Koryŏ Communist Party (August–September 1920) with Yŏ Unhyŏng (1886–1947) and An Pyŏngch'an (1854–1929), with the aim of forming a united front with the nationalists of the Provisional Government.

In the meantime, several communist organizations were formed in the wake of the March First Movement among Korean communities of Siberia, the Maritime Province and Manchuria, as well as in Korea itself. These included the First Generation Party in the Maritime Province (1919), the Maritime Province United Assembly of the Korean Communist Party (June 1920), the Amur Province Korean Communist Party (April 1920), the Chita Korean Communist Party (1920), the Moscow Korean Communist Party (March 1919), the Omsk Korean Communist Party (November 1919) and the Korea Bureau (*Korburo*) of the Russian Communist Party Irkutsk County Committee (January 1920). In addition, a Korean communist organization appears to have also been formed in Manchuria in the early 1920s and organizations like the Seoul Communist Group (October 1919) and the Social Revolutionary Party (1920) were established in Korea proper at about the same time.

In the early 1920s, Korean communist organizations formed in various regions gradually became engaged in the movement to form a united communist party embracing all Koreans, whether in Korea or overseas. As part of that process, under the leadership of the Korea Bureau of the Irkutsk Communist Party, the 'All Russia Koryŏ Communist Organization Central Committee', the so-called 'Irkutsk Faction', was established in July 1920. Also, the Shanghai Korean Communist Party and the Korean Department of the Far Eastern Bureau of the Russian Communist Party based in Chita formed the 'Shanghai Faction' in October 1920.

Efforts to form a united Korean national communist party continued, but when the Far Eastern Secretariat of the Comintern was established in Irkutsk centred on the Korea Bureau in January 1921, serious conflict arose between the Irkutsk Faction and the Shanghai Faction. This led to the dissolution of the Far Eastern Bureau's Korean Department, the power base of the Shanghai Faction. Under the leadership of the All Russia Koryŏ Communist Organization Central Committee, the Irkutsk Faction's Koryŏ Communist Party, led by Han Myŏngse, Ch'oe Koryŏ and Yi Hun (or Yi Kŭnt'ae), was organized (May 1921).

Meanwhile, Yi Tonghwi, who became prime minister of the Provisional Government as a leader of the Korean Socialist Party, sent a representative plenipotentiary, Han Hyŏnggwŏn, to Moscow to get 2 million rubles of aid funds. Han received 600,000 rubles, but brought only 400,000 to Shanghai. The issue of the missing 200,000 rubles led to a split in the Korean Communist Party in Shanghai between those belonging to the original Korean Socialist Party line and those belonging to the non-Socialist Party line, including Yŏ Unhyŏng and An Pyŏngch'an. The latter subsequently joined the Irkutsk Faction. The remainder of the Shanghai Faction communists joined together with other communist elements such as the representatives of the domestic Social Revolutionary Party and communists who were active in China and Japan in May 1921 to hold the 'Koryŏ Communist Party Assembly' and form the Shanghai Faction's Koryŏ Communist Party, with Yi Tonghwi as chair and Kim Ip as secretary.

Although the various communist groups formed both inside and outside Korea at the time of the March First Movement made efforts from the very beginning to form a united Korean communist party, the communist elements divided into two major groups: the Irkutsk Faction's Koryŏ Communist Party, led by Koreans who had become Russian citizens and who gave first priority to the socialist revolution and the Shanghai Faction's Koryŏ Communist Party, led by nationalists who went into exile with the colonization of Korea and who gave top priority to national liberation.

Earlier, when Japan sent troops to Siberia, Korean partisans became active guerilla fighters against the Japanese troops. One thousand Korean partisans fought against the Japanese troops in Nikolaesk in 1920. At the same time as armed units of Koreans in Siberia were gathering in the Amur region in order to unify their forces, the independence army, which had won a major victory at Ch'ongsanni and then had moved to the Far Eastern Republic region as a result of the dispatch of the Japanese troops to Jiandao, formed the Korean Independence Corps led by Sŏ Il.

The strength of the Korean forces in the Amur region at this time was about 4,500 men. The Far Eastern Republic formed the All Korea Military Committee in order to unify the Korean forces, which it then organized into the Korean Volunteer Army. At that time, in May 1921, the Far Eastern Secretariat of the Comintern and the All Russia Koryŏ Communist Organization Central Committee took the lead to form a separate Provisional Korean Revolutionary Military Administration Assembly with its own Korean Revolutionary Army in opposition to the Shanghai Faction's All Korea Military Committee and Korean Volunteer Army.

Command over the Korean troops in Russia moved from the Far Eastern Republic to the Comintern, and the Korean Bureau of the Far East Republic, the central body of the Shanghai communists, was dissolved. The Irkutsk Group then demanded that all Korean troops be assigned to the Provisional Korean Revolutionary Military Administration Assembly, but the Korean Volunteer Army did not comply. Efforts at mediation by leaders like Hong Pŏmdo and Ch'oe Chindong failed.

As the Korean Volunteer Army prepared to leave its base at Masanov for Manchuria, both sides reached an agreement by which the Korean Volunteer Army moved to nearby Alexeyevsk (now Svobodny). However, negotiations to unify the two sides broke off again. The Korean Revolutionary Army and the guard units of the Far Eastern Republic attacked the Korean Volunteer Army on 28 June 1921 on the pretext of disarmament. This was the so-called Free City Incident.

In this collision about 40 of the 1400 Korean Volunteer Army soldiers were killed, some 450 were missing, and the remaining 900 were taken prisoner. Among those 900, 364 joined the Korean Revolutionary Army. Another 428 were assigned to the 'prisoner units' of the Russian army where they were used for forced labour, while another 72 were jailed in Irkutsk. The Free City Incident was one of the crucial factors intensifying strife between the Irkutsk Faction's Koryŏ Communist Party and the Shanghai Faction's Koryŏ Communist Party.

Members of the post-March First Movement national liberation front inside and outside Korea were frustrated with the results of the principle of national self-determination and the Paris Peace Conference. They had hopes of a result from the August 1920 visit from a US congressional delegation and the November 1921 Washington Conference, but gained nothing. They then turned their expectations to the Congress of Far Eastern Nations held in Moscow in January 1922, in which the Irkutsk Faction and such nationalists as Kim Kyusik participated.

At the congress, the Irkutsk Faction argued, 'In Korea, industrial development is still weak and industrial labour has not yet developed as a class; the time is not yet ripe for class struggle,' while contending that 'We must pander to peasants, the overwhelming majority of the population, and must emphasize the national liberation movement in order to arouse their sympathies.' The Irkutsk Faction changed its line from class struggle to united front tactics and argued for reform of the Shanghai Provisional Government.

In the meantime, the Comintern adopted resolutions on the Korea problem in 1921 and again in 1922 intended to unite the Shanghai and the Irkutsk factions and also formed a provisional central cadre of the Korean Communist Party with equal numbers of representatives from each faction. Next the Comintern then held the October 1922 Koryŏ Communist Party Assembly in order to unite two parties, gathering almost equal number of representatives from the two factions in Verkhneudinsk (Ulan Ude). However, such issues as conflicts between naturalized Korean-Russians and non-naturalized Koreans, grudges from the Free City Incident and the use of the 400,000 rubles received from Moscow were not resolved, and the Verkhneudinsk assembly also ended in failure.

In December 1922, the Comintern dissolved both factions, after which it established the Korea Bureau (*Korburo*) in Vladivostok with committee members including Yi Tonghwi of the Shanghai Faction, Han Myŏngsŏ of the Irkutsk Faction, and Chŏng Chaedal (b. 1895) of the Domestic Faction, to direct the Korean communist movement. Nonetheless, antagonism between the Shanghai Faction and the Irkutsk Faction remained. In March 1924, the Comintern dissolved the Korean Bureau again and established the Organization Bureau (*Orgburo*) as a preparatory organ in order to organize the Korean communist party.

THE KOREAN COMMUNIST PARTY

There were socialist groups active inside Korea other than the Seoul communist organizations and the Social Revolutionary Party mentioned above. Intellectuals, youth, students and progressive labour led such ideological organizations as the Seoul Youth Association (1921), the Proletarian Comrades Association (1922), the New Thought Research

Society (1923), the Tuesday Society (1924) and the North Wind Society (1924). On 27 April 1925, the first Korean Communist Party was secretly organized with Kim Chaebong (1890–1944) who had been dispatched to Korea by the Comintern as secretary.

At that time, daily newspapers such as the *East Asia Daily News* and the *Korean Daily News* published in serial form such essays as the 'Outline of Marxism' and the 'Materialistic Concept of History'. Publications such as *New Life*, *New World*, *Creation* and *Light of Korea* introduced socialist thought. The organization by 1926 of over 3,380 organizations devoted to the study of thought formed the backdrop for the establishment of the Korean Communist Party inside Korea.

Seoul-based elements were excluded from the organization of the first Korean Communist Party, which was led by the Tuesday Society and the North Wind society. With the rise of the Koryŏ Communist Youth Association under secretary Pak Hŏnyŏng (1900–55), which was centred on Tuesday Society elements, the movement lost its unity. Although the first party was not able to adopt a party programme before the members of its central committee were arrested, it did promulgate party rules made up of 12 chapters and 95 clauses. According to those rules, the highest organization was the party congress. The central executive members were elected by the party congress, and the party membership consisted of full members of a party and candidate members. The basic party organization was the cell (*yacheika*).

The organization put up various struggle slogans: 'Smash Japanese imperialism completely'; 'Achieve the independence of Korea completely'; 'Put an eight-hour day into effect'; 'Establish the legal minimum wage system'; 'Relieve the unemployed'; 'Practise the social welfare system'; 'Guarantee the freedom of press, publication, assembly and association'; 'Exterminate the colonial enslavement education'; 'Turn the imperialist aggression to the anti-imperialist revolutionary war'; 'Reject Japanese products'; 'All Korean officials, retire from office'; 'Workers in Japanese owned factories, go on a general strike'; 'Do not pay farm rents to Japanese landlords'; 'Do not learn from Japanese teachers'; 'Disconnect the relationship with Japanese merchants'.

The Korean Communist Party and the Koryŏ Communist Youth Association both gained recognition from the Comintern after dispatching representatives to Moscow. The Koryŏ Communist Youth Association was able to organize twenty-seven county leagues and nine provincial leagues after joining the General League of Korean Youth, which was a legal organization. It also sent twenty-one students to communist universities in Moscow to study. The Association also planned to take over the *Light of Korea*, and to publish *New Youth*. However, the Association's communist affiliations were soon revealed in an incident in Sinŭiju in which a young member of the organization assaulted a lawyer. One hundred and one members out of 220 arrested went on trial, and 83 were convicted of crimes. This November 1925 incident, the so-called 'First Communist Party Incident', destroyed most of the organization.

Immediately after the Sinŭiju incident, Kim Chaebong and other leaders who were in hiding entrusted Kang Taryŏng (1887–1942), Director of Chinju Branch of the *Korean Daily News*, with the re-establishment of the party. The Second Korean Communist Party, with Kang as secretary was formed in December 1925. The Koryŏ Communist Youth Association was also reconstructed with Kwŏn Osŏl (1899–1930) as secretary.

The Second Korean Communist Party selected cadre and dispatched cadre to each province, as well as to the Seoul District Executive Committee and organized cells in all districts and workplaces. It also established liaison offices in Manchuria, Shanghai and Japan. Furthermore, the Communist Youth Association sent students to Moscow Communist University with funds it received from the International Communist Youth Association.

The Second Party was a continuation of the First Party which had been mostly organized around the Tuesday Society, but the Communist Youth Association made efforts to establish a unified front with the Koryŏ Communist Youth League made up mostly of members of the Seoul faction. In addition, there was also a political goal of building a 'national party' through a co-operative front between nationalists and socialists. Although these plans to unite the socialist forces and create a united front with the nationalists were not realized under the Second Party, they exerted substantial influence on the Third Party.

The organization of the Second Party came to light with the June 10th *mansei* movement at the time of the funeral of Emperor Sunjong (r. 1907–10) in 1926. Secretary Kwŏn Osŏl of the Koryŏ Communist Youth Association was detected attempting to disseminate proclamations and leaflets printed by the party. This became the occasion for the arrest of over 100 party members throughout the whole country, including Kwŏn and Kang Taryŏng, and the sentencing of 82. This meant the effective demise of the Second Party. The First and Second Communist Party incidents also resulted in the arrest or exile of almost all the major cadre of the Tuesday Society. As a result, the Third Party was formed by new forces and became more of a united party.

The Third Korean Communist Party, the so-called ML Party, was formed in September 1926 under secretary Kim Ch'ŏlsu (1893–1986), an organization committee member of the Second Party who had managed to escape arrest. After its founding congress, it held a second congress in December 1926 at which it chose An Kwangch'on of the Japan-based January Society to be secretary and brought in elements of the Tuesday Society, the Seoul Faction and socialists without factional affiliations to create a 'unified Communist Party'. It also got Comintern recognition after it dispatched Kim Ch'ŏlsu to Moscow.

The True Friend Society, an ideological organization led by An Kwangch'ŏn during the time of Second Party, issued its 'True Friend Society Declaration' in August 1926, in which it argued for the formation of a national co-operative front. It also advocated the extermination of factional strife within the Communist movement, the organization of

a national co-operative front with national bourgeoisie who did not col-
laborate with the Japanese and the change from the class struggle line to
the national independence political struggle line. After An Kwangch'ŏn
became secretary of the Third Party, the Korean Communist Party participated actively in organizing the New Korea Association as a 'mediator
of the united national co-operative front party'.

Meanwhile, the Koryŏ Communist Youth Association, with Ko
Kwangsu (1900–30) as secretary, joined with the Seoul Faction Koryŏ
Communist Youth League and gained recognition from the second
congress of the Korean Communist Party, the Comintern and the
Communist Youth International. The Comintern highly praised the
'revolutionary co-operation' of the two communist youth groups.

The Third Korean Communist Party appointed provincial cadre in all
provinces except Kangwŏn, and established about 40 cells with over 200
party members. Moreover, the party reconstructed the defunct Manchuria
General Bureau and the Shanghai branch. It also reactivated the Japan
branch through which it issued such publications as the *Mass Newspaper,
Theoretical Struggle* and the *Present Phase.* The Third Communist Party's
Koryŏ Communist Youth Association, formed out of the Tuesday Society
and the Seoul Faction, had 18 cells with over 50 members inside Korea,
two cells with over 20 members in Japan and 50 cells with over 400
members in Manchuria and Shanghai.

The Third Party underwent a number of changes in its secretary from
Kim Ch'ŏlsu, to An Kwangch'ŏn, Kim Chunyŏn (1895–1971) and Kim
Seyŏn (1899–1928) as it maintained itself for over one year. It, too,
however, was dissolved after it was discovered in February 1928 and more
than 200 members, including members of the Koryŏ Communist Youth
Association, were arrested. In relation to this 'Third Korean Communist
Party Incident', various mass organizations, General Alliance of Korean
Labour, the General Alliance of Korean Peasants, the New Korea
Association and its women's auxiliary, the Friends of the Rose of Sharon,
suffered badly and were forced into temporary inactivity.

Even as the Japanese police were proceeding to arrest Third Party
members, the Korean Communist Party held a third party congress to
amend parts of the party rules in February 1928. It also accepted the
'Comintern resolution' that ordered the extermination of factional strife,
the promotion of men of working class origins to party leadership positions, the organization of labour unions by industry and the organization of a national revolutionary mass party. In addition, in March 1923,
the members approved a 'report of the domestic political affairs to the
Comintern', and formed the Fourth Korean Communist Party, with the
progressive labourer Ch'a Kŭmbong as secretary.

The Fourth Party immediately made clear its revolutionary line by
adopting the 'Thesis on the Korean National Liberation Movement'. The
party set up organizations in both the centre and the provinces and
became active outside Korea in such places as Manchuria, Shanghai,
Beijing and Japan. The Fourth Party had especially close relations with

the New Korea Society to the extent that party members were engaged in activities in 32 different branches of the Society. Furthermore, the Fourth Party revived its domestic publication, *Light of Korea*, and the publications of its Japan Bureau, *Mass News* and *Present Phase*, and published *Revolution* out of its Manchuria Bureau. The Manchuria branch of the fourth Koryŏ Communist Youth Association also put out a publication called *Flames*.

The Fourth Party received funds from the Comintern, which it used to send representatives to the Comintern, Communist Youth International and Profintern (Red International of Labour Unions) congresses. This organization, too, was also soon exposed. Over 170 of its members were arrested and its leaders like Ch'a Kŭmbong and Kim Chaemyŏng were tortured to death. With the Fourth Party collapsing, the Comintern directed its dissolution and the construction of a new party in its 1928 'December Thesis'.

Although the Korean Communist Party collapsed four times within three years after its formation in 1925 due to the arrests of large numbers of its members, it continued to reconstruct itself. This shows how thoroughly the Japanese oppressed the Communist movement. At the same time, it also shows how the Communist Party could endure because it did not limit itself solely to the Communist movement, but also actively engaged in the national liberation movement. In particular, the Korean Communist Party made significant contributions to enhancing the political character of the popular movement during a time of severe oppression by effectively leading the activities of such popular movement organizations as the General Alliance of Korean Labour, the General Alliance of Korean Peasants and the General League of Korean Youth.

Nonetheless, the Korean Communist Party movement of the second half of the 1920s had many problems. As the Comintern indicated: 'It was a narrow-minded combination of intellectuals and students that included only a relatively small number of workers and peasants.' Even if Korea still lacked sizeable numbers of industrial workers, the vast majority of its population was made up of peasants. But the party was an 'intellectuals' communist party' which was not rooted in the peasants. For that reason, the party had been embroiled in severe factional strife since the initial Korean Communist Party was formed in Irkutsk. Although the severe oppression by the Japanese was the primary source of the Korean Communist Party movement's difficulties, internal strife within the party formed another important source of trouble.

The Comintern pointed out in its 'December Thesis' that 'The difficulties in organizing a communist party were the result not only of objective conditions, but also the result of the internal strife that has tormented the Korean communist movement for several years', and ordered the dissolution of the intellectual-led party and the construction of a new party organized around labourers and peasants. Nonetheless, a successor party to the Fourth Party was not established. Furthermore, even the Manchuria and Japan bureaus were dissolved. The re-establishment movement continued as directed by the Comintern, but all it produced was large numbers of victims due to the tenacious oppression of the Japanese. The Korean Communist Party could not be reconstructed until liberation in 1945.

REFERENCES

Kim Chunyŏp and Kim Ch'angsun, *Han'guk kongsanjuŭi undongsa* (History of the Korean Communist Movement), vols 1–5, Seoul: Asea munje yŏn'guso at Korea University, 1967–75.
Ko Chunsŏk, *Chosen kakumei undou shi* (History of the revolutionary movement in Korea), Tokyo: Shakai hyoronsha, 1983.
Suh Dae-Sook, *The Korean Communist Movement: 1918–1948*, New Jersey: Princeton University Press, 1967; Hyŏndaesa yŏn'guhoe trans. *Han'guk kongsanjuŭi undongsa yŏn'gu*, Seoul: Hwada, 1985.
Scalapino, Robert A. and Chong-Sik Lee, *Communism in Korea, Part I: The Movement*, Berkeley, California: University of California Press, 1972.
Im Kyŏngsŏk, 'Koryŏ kongsandang yŏn'gu' (A study of the Koryŏ Communist Party), Ph.D. Dissertation from Sŏnggyun'gwan University, Seoul, 1993.

SECTION FOUR

The National Co-operative Front Movement

BACKGROUND OF THE CO-OPERATIVE FRONT MOVEMENT

The split in the Korean national liberation movement front became quite clear after the March First Movement as one group linked to the Japanese policy of national division began to follow a line of collaboration with the Japanese while, on the other hand, the socialist movement began to spread and develop both inside and outside Korea. Furthermore, after the failure of the 1923 Convention of National Representatives, the Provisional Government movement became inactive and the entire national liberation movement front became fragmented. Thus activists in the national liberation front of the mid-1920s found it necessary to search for a new methodology. On the overseas front, this methodological search went beyond the movement to establish an interim government of the early-1920s and manifested itself in movements based on the principle of 'rule the country through the party' such as a united national party or the Grand Independence Party.

It was in the mid-1920s that a movement arose on the overseas front to establish a united national party to take the place of the Provisional Government as the main headquarters of the national liberation movement. This movement grew out of the recognition, following the lapse into inactivity of the Provisional Government, of the need to bring together the fragmented elements of the national liberation front and to unify the left- and right-wing fronts in order to strengthen the front. It also provided the moment for the transition of the national liberation movement to the next stage: the political party movement.

On the overseas front, activities in the national liberation movement of the first half of the 1920s in mainland China focused on the campaign for the foundation of the provisional government. At the same time, the movement in Manchuria, while maintaining a certain connection with the provisional government movement, developed as armed struggles, followed by the forming of the three administrations (Councillors, Just and Free People's administrations). In the second half of the 1920s, the movement developed into a campaign for the establishment of a united national party as a means to create a united front in the Maritime Provinces and China proper, while a movement to unify the three administrations and the left and right fronts arose in Manchuria.

On the domestic front, in 1923, landlords, capitalists and some intellectuals initiated the Campaign for the Promotion of Korean Products and the Campaign for the Foundation of the Korean University, but they met with little success. After Yi Kwangsu published his 1923 essay, 'A Statecraft for the Nation', the right-wing camp split into those who collaborated with the Japanese and those who did not. The latter then joined with socialist elements to form a national co-operative front in opposition to the collaborators.

The socialist North Wind Society issued a 1924 programme that said: 'Even though we reject a simple national movement that ignores class relations, we call for interim co-operation between the socialist movement and national movement because they both arise from the same unavoidable realities of the current situation in Korea'. The nationalists responded in like tone: 'Even though the national movement and the socialist movement are essentially different, they should not split until after liberation.' Some nationalists even believed that: 'The national movement is part of the course of realizing the social movement.' The desire for a national co-operative front was further stimulated in 1925 by the Japanese imperialists' implementation of the Security Maintenance Law.

Preparation for the unification of the national co-operative front gained even further impetus in September of that year when non-collaborationist nationalists formed the Korean Situation Research Society. In the same year, the newly formed Korean Communist Party put forth the slogan: 'Complete overthrow of Japanese imperialist rule and compete recovery of Korean independence.' Moreover, the Party argued: 'We must mobilize all Korean forces to make a United National Party front in order to prepare a total attack against the enemy.' In August 1926, the True Friend Society, founded in January 1926 as the Party's mouthpiece, issued its declaration calling for the foundation of a national co-operative front in concert with non-collabourationist nationalists.

Furthermore, in February 1926, the thirteenth central executive committee meeting of the Korean Communist Party adopted a resolution calling for 'using the Religion of the Heavenly Way as preliminary foundation for the establishment of a national party to unify nationalists and communists.' Kang Taryŏng, secretary of the Second Party, then contacted such non-collaborationist nationalists as An Chaehong (1891–1965) and Kwŏn Tongjin (1861–1947). Negotiations stopped, however, after concerns arose that the co-operative front movement might fall under the leadership of collaborationist Heavenly Way figures such as Ch'oe Rin (b. 1878).

These domestic activities towards the creation of a national united front, along with the overseas National Unified Party movement and the change in the Comintern's line, formed the backdrop for an alliance between socialists from the Seoul Youth Association group and the nationalists of the Association for the Promotion of the Korean Products. This led to the July 1926 formation of the Korean People's Prosperity Society, whose participants included religious and educational figures along with some national movement activists who had recently returned from overseas. This limited-scope organization then took a major step towards the formation of a full-fledged domestic national co-operative front when it decided that all its members must participate in the New Korea Association.

THE OVERSEAS MOVEMENT FOR A UNITED NATIONAL PARTY

In the wake of the failure of the Convention of National Representatives and the subsequent deactivation of the provisional government movement, a non-collaborationist national movement organization known as the Preparatory Committee for the National Party was formed in Vladivostok in March 1926 as a forerunner to the movement for a united national party. The Preparatory Committee, in which leaders of the Irkutsk Group Koryŏ Communist Party like Ch'oe Koryŏ and Kim Sŏkha joined hands with the Creation Faction of the Shanghai Provisional Government and the Seoul group of the domestic socialist movement, received authorization from the Comintern to form a 'national communist organ'. Its members 'infiltrated into Seoul and urged both nationalists and communists to join the organization'. This activity was also connected with the foundation of the Korean People's Prosperity Society.

The campaign for the formation of a united national party in China proper began first in Beijing. The Bejing Association for the Promotion of the United Korean Independence Party, led by Chang Kŏnsang (1883–1974), Wŏn Sehun (b. 1887), and Cho Sŏnghwan, was organized in October 1926. The Association argued that: 'It is needless to say that revolutionaries who are engaged in the movement and the struggle for accomplishing the same goals, must gather under one flag and one command in order to attain success.' Moreover, the organization set forth slogans such as 'Exterminate Japanese imperialism', 'Uphold the absolute independence of Korea', 'Make a single front for a national revolution', and 'Unite the oppressed peoples of the whole world'. The establishment of this association in Beijing sparked the spread of a united national party movement in such locales throughout China as Shanghai, Wuhan and Guangdong, where similar associations were established.

At the same time, such organizations as the three administrations in Manchuria also became actively involved in the movement to establish a United National Party. Thirty-nine representatives of eighteen independence movement organizations in Manchuria gathered in 1928 to discuss the promotion of a united national party, but were not able to come to an agreement. The groups in Manchuria did, however, coalesce into two larger organizations. One was the All Korea United National Party Organization Promotion Association, led by such organs as the General League of Youth in North Manchuria, the League of Youth in South Manchuria and League of Peasants in Manchuria. The other was the All Korea United National Party Organization Council, in which the Justice Administration, the Tamul Corps, the General League of Korean Youth in North Manchuria and the Alliance of Youth in South Manchuria participated with the agreement of the Councillors Administration and the New People's Administration.

The Justice Administration, the main force of the 'Council', strove to unite with the other two administrations, but failed to attain complete unity. When the Justice Administration in 1929 formed a new National Administration by bringing in the civil government faction of the New People's Administration along with some members of the Councilors Administration, the three administrations were dissolved. On the other hand, the Promotion Association created a rival organization in the Association for Planning the Foundation of a United National Party in Manchuria, the so-called Revolutionary Assembly, by bringing together elements from the New People's Administration and the Justice Administration.

Socialist elements in China and Manchuria also participated actively in the campaign for a united national party. Eight youth bodies, including the China Headquarters Youth League, that existed throughout mainland China, came together in 1928 to form the League of Korean Youth in China. This League resolved to participate in the campaign for a united national party and became a part of the Revolutionary Assembly by joining the military administration faction of the New People's Administration. In addition, six youth groups, including the Alliance of Youth in South Manchuria, came together to form the General League of Korean Youth in Manchuria in support of the National Administration. In the end, a united national party Movement in Manchuria was unable to create a single unified front and resulted only in the reorganization of the three administrations, which had been the leading organs of the national liberation movement in Manchuria of the first half of the 1920s, into the National Administration and the Revolutionary Assembly.

In the early-1930s, the Revolutionary Assembly group formed the Korean General Federation under Kim Chwajin. After he was assassinated, it founded the Korean Independence Party with the leadership of Hong Chin (1877–1946) and Yi Ch'ŏngch'ŏn. Its military organ, the Korean Independence Party Army, was active in northeastern Manchuria before moving south into China proper sometime around 1933.

The National Administration group organized the Korean Revolutionary Party and the Korean Revolutionary Army with Hyŏn Chŏnggyŏng (1886–1941) and Hyŏn Ikch'ŏl (1890–1938) as leaders and was active in the southern Manchuria region. Over 10,000 Korean independence fighters, led by Commander-in-Chief Yang Sŏbong (1894–1934) of the Korean Revolutionary Army, joined with Chinese forces to engage in regular warfare against the troops of Japan and Manchukuo in the first half of the 1930s. After Yang Sŏbong died, Ko Ihŏ (1902–36) created the Korean Revolutionary Military Government, joined with the Chinese anti-Manchu anti-Japanese force to organize the Korean-Chinese Anti-Japanese League and remained active until 1936.

The foundation of the Revolutionary Assembly and the National Administration, and of their successors in the Korean Independence Party and the Korean Revolutionary Party, as a consequence of the united national party movement in Manchuria indicates the establishment of the principle of 'rule the state through the party' in the national liberation movement front. The Korean Independence Party, as a coalition of local resident associations, formed the Korean Self-Governing Federation and guided it while being engaged in military activities through its Korean Independence Party Army. The Korean Revolutionary Party showed a similar character, operating the National Administration as a government and involving itself in military activities by organizing the Korean Revolutionary Army.

The campaign for a united national party that arose in the national liberation movement front overseas during the second half of the 1920s faced conflicts over the method for organizing the party. One side argued for creating the party as an alliance of the various scattered movement organizations already in existence. Another side contended that it would be virtually impossible to form a united national party based on all the pre-existing organizations and called for the party to be led by a small number of powerful organizations that had 'revolutionary authority' and 'histories of accomplishments' to which all other organizations would be subordinated. A third side asserted that powerful organizations were in fact little more than regional and factional groupings, that there was no effective and authoritative central organization, and that a united national party had to be organized around individuals rather than groups. Ultimately, movement activists were unable to overcome these differences.

After the Shanghai Provisional Government lost its leadership over the overall national liberation movement front, the foundation of a united national party emerged as the biggest issue across the entire national liberation movement front. The proponents of a united national party, however, were not able to overcome the same problems of localism and factionalism and the confrontations over ideology and method that had also plagued the Provisional Government. In the end, the overseas movement for a united national party did not succeed.

THE NEW KOREA ASSOCIATION MOVEMENT

Although the campaign for the foundation of a united national party overseas did not succeed at the final stage, it did produce an important domestic offshoot in the New Korea Association (Sin'ganhoe) movement that attained some important successes as the representative organization of the national unified front movement of the late-1920s. The national liberation movement of the first half of the 1920s focused on the foundation of the provisional government and making it the headquarters of the movement while after 1925 it focused on forming a united front by organizing a united national party. Unlike the failed campaign for a united national party overseas, the New Korea Association movement developed as a national united front movement that represented the direction of the domestic national liberation movement in the second half of the 1920s.

The Association was formed on 5 February 1927, with Yi Sangjhae (1850–1927) as President and Hong Myŏnghŭi (1888–1968) as Vice-President, at the suggestion of twenty-eight non-collaborationist representatives from both the left and the right, including journalists Sin Sŏgu (1894–1953) and An Chaehong, the Christian Yi Sŭnghun (1864–1930), the Religion of the Heavenly Way's Kwŏn Tongjin, the Buddhist Han Yongun (1879–1944), and the Communist Han Wigŏn for the Communist Party. As seen in its programme of 'complete rejection of opportunism', the New Korea Society was formed as a national united front organization opposed to the theory of self-governance put forth by the likes of the Politics Research Society.

The New Korea Association, considered as a united national party or a mediator for a united national party when it was formed, was an association of individuals, not organizations. However, the active participation of such mass-movement organizations as the General League of Korean Workers and the General League of Korean Youth brought a dramatic increase in the number of branches and members. By the end of 1927, the total number of branches, including both those is Korea and local branches in Tokyo and Osaka, was 104. The number of branches subsequently increased to 149 before declining to 124 at the time of its dissolution in 1931. The number of members was 20,000 at the first anniversary and reached about 40,000 at the time it was dissolved.

Under the circumstances where the Korean Communist Party was oppressed thoroughly and such organizations as the general leagues for labour, peasants and youth were barred from assembly, the New Korea Association directed labour strikes, tenancy disputes and student strikes, while taking positions against the exploitation of Koreans by Japanese entities, Japanese migration to Korea, collaborationist political movements and colonial education policies, and speaking out in favour of a Korea-centred educational system, and freedom of research in social science and thought. Also, the Tokyo branch issued demands for the basic rights of the working class such as the right to organize, strike and enter into collective bargaining, the protection of child and women workers, the implementation of an eight-hour workday, and amendments of the Factory Law, the Mines Act and the Seamen's Law.

Non-collaborationist nationalists dominated the Association's central body, while socialist elements had the upper hand in the local branches. Local branch members pointed out such problems as the concentration of power at the centre, the marginalization of workers and peasants, and the ways in which the organization's programme inhibited concrete activity. The branch members demanded such things as changing from a presidential system to one headed by the chair of an executive committee, creating an organization for inter-branch co-ordination and providing a concrete programme of action for the anti-Japanese struggle.

When Government-General oppression made it impossible for the Association to hold regular general assemblies, small numbers of branches in each district took the desperate countermeasure of joining together to elect representatives. Those representatives then held a June 1929 Double Representative Convention where they enacted 'the program and regulations of the New Korea Association' (June 1929).

The Double Representative Convention changed the existing executive secretary system to a central executive committee and expanded the authority of local branches, thus increasing their ability to constrain the central headquarters. The local branches' demand for inter-branch co-ordination was realized in the establishment of provincial federation assemblies, and the Association was transformed into a bottom-up organization with the subdivision of the local branches into occupational and district sub-branches. On the other hand, the convention was unable to attain the shift from an individual-based to an organization-based structure as argued by the local branches, the Korean Communist Party and the Comintern, nor was it able to amend the Association's programme.

The Double Representative Convention elected Ho Hŏn (b. 1884) as the executive committee chairman. It also chose fifty-seven executive members including Hong Myŏnghŭi, eight candidates for the executive council member including Cho Pyŏngok (1894–1960) and thirteen central audit committee members including Kwŏn Tongjin. Socialists accounted for 46% of the men chosen. The fact that 27 out of 74 activists who were arrested in April 1930 by the Japanese police of the Kyŏnggi Province Police Station on suspicion of participation in the Korean Communist Party re-establishment movement were members of the New Korea Association gives some indication of the extent to which socialists were active in the Association. Furthermore, the Double Representative

Conventions reorganization of the Association facilitated the entry of large numbers of socialists into the headquarters executive ranks.

After the dissolution of the Korean Communist Party with the 'December Thesis', the socialist camp, which considered the re-establishment of the Communist Party as its most urgent task, began to recruit Association members, especially those from local branches into the re-establishment movement while engaging in a much more active struggle against Japanese colonial rule than had been the case earlier. When it was banned from holding a meeting to report on the July 1929 Kapsan Slash and Burn Peasant Incident, the central standing executive committee fought back by publishing a statement and by establishing a 'resolution on the guidelines for real struggle', which included plans to publish a bulletin, to enhance local branch activities, to acquire financing and to conduct provincial inspections.

The New Korea Association became involved in the Kwangju Student Movement, sending a team to investigate the incident in order to link it with the mass movement. When the Association was banned in December 1929 from holding a 'Lecture meeting to report on the Kwangju Student Incident', it then joined hands with such groups as the Religion of the Heavenly Way, Christians, Buddhists, as well as with such movement organizations as the General League of Korean Youth, the General League of Korean Labour and the Friends of the Rose of Sharon to hold a 'People's Congress' in order to spread the student movement throughout the rest of the country. However, the plan was stopped when executive committee chair Ho Hŏn and some 90 other members were arrested.

The 'People's Congress Incident' was a major blow to the New Korea Association. After Kim Pyŏngno (1887–1964), who had charge over the Association's finances, became the new leader, the Association gradually assumed a more rightist and collaborationist line. The New Korea Association headquarters issued only muted responses to such incidents as the June 1930 *North Chŏlla Daily News* 'Insult to Koreans', the July 1930 'Campaign against the Tanch'ŏn Forestry Union' and the September 1930 shooting of a Korean suspected of being a Communist in Manchuria's Tunhua County.

At this time, the New Korea Association began to co-operate with the campaign for self-rule initiated by Ch'oe Rin of the Religion of Heavenly Way and advocated that the Association limit its movement to such activities as were permitted under colonial law. Moreover, the Association linked up with the General League of Korean Youth which argued for 'a legal movement in accordance with the principles of social democracy theory'. As a result, the persons who actively supported the legal-struggle line became central standing executive members and took charge of each of the Association's offices. The conversion of the Association headquarters to the legal-struggle line led the socialist-dominated branches to raise the issue of dissolution.

The first branch to call for dissolution was the Pusan branch in December 1930. Consequently, branches in Iwŏn, P'yŏngyang, Kyŏngsŏ,

Inch'ŏn, Tanch'ŏn, Hongwŏn, Sŏngjin, Ch'ilgok and Seoul also voted to dissolve. The proponents of dissolution argued: ' "Dissolution" is different from "dismantling" which means break-up of an organization, rather it means dialectic self-development of transformation from one movement form to another.' They gave a number of reasons why the New Korea Association should be dissolved.

First, they pointed out the collaborationist line of the Association leaders. For example, the Pusan branch asserted: 'The headquarters has ignored the fundamental spirit of no compromise because of the national reformists who seek to pursue a legal movement.'

Second, they brought up the issue of the Association's organization, arguing it was organized like a political party. For instance, Tanch'ŏn branch pointed out: 'The serious contradictions in the organization and its petit bourgeoisie style leadership have resulted in the total inability to mount active struggle, in the destruction of the working masses' desire for struggle and in hindering the great class advance that is required by objective conditions.'

Third, they raised the issue of the Association's programme, arguing that the main principles were abstract and lacked concrete movement guidelines. As the P'yŏngyang branch indicated: 'The present programme of the New Korea Association has no guidelines for action and only dampens the members' desire for struggle.'

Fourth, they cited the conditions for subjective response to changes in the objective situation. Changes in the objective situation referred to the Great Depression and Japanese intervention in the Manchurian issue, and the conditions for subjective response meant the militarization and revolutionization of the working masses.

Even as the local branches were raising the issue of dissolution, the international Communist movement also changed the way in which it defined the New Korean Association. The 'December Thesis' of the Comintern had maintained recognition of the significance of anti-imperialist united front tactics in dealing with colonial issues. This position, however, was reversed in the September 1930 'September Thesis' of the Profintern that defined the New Korea Association as a national reformist organization.

There were some arguments against dissolution in the early period of the Korean Communist Party re-establishment movement. Some persons such as Han Wigŏn thought that 'the New Korea Association could function to some degree as a mediator', and men such as Im Wŏn'gŭn contended that the New Korea Association was not completely dominated by the petit bourgeoisie, nor was it an organization that destroyed the worker and peasant masses' capacities for struggle.

By contrast, men such as Ko Kyŏnghŭm (b. 1910) asserted: 'The anti-imperialist co-operative front should not be developed within the New Korea Association, by the Association, or through the Association, but outside the Association by the Communist Party.' Moreover, Kim Kyŏngjae criticized the New Korea Association as being nothing but a social gathering of petit bourgeoisie, totally lacking in any capacity for struggle, that destroyed class consciousness.

Non-collaborationist nationalists who had joined the New Korea Association movement were against the dissolution. Representative of this group was An Chaehong, who argued: 'The situation of the movement in Korea is one that requires the greatest comradely co-operation of the two great camps, not their antagonistic confrontation.' Such arguments notwithstanding, the dissolution issue was raised in May 1931 at the second general congress session held since the founding of the Association. Even though the Japanese police forbade arguments for and against, the measure was to put to a vote. The motion for dissolution was approved by a vote of 43 for and 5 against, with 30 abstentions.

The New Korea Association movement took root in the popular movement as a 'surface organization' that led the national liberation movement in both Korea and Japan during the second half of the 1920s. The Japanese, who initially were content merely to watch the situation, became alarmed at the development of the movement and began to apply cunning and tenacious oppression, restricting the activities of the headquarters and striving to dismantle local branches throughout the whole country.

At the same time, the socialist dominated local branches were raising the issue of dissolution against the rightist and collaborationist tendencies of the centre and the Comintern changed its attitude toward the Association. The 1930 Decision of the International Party Executive Committee asked: 'What kind of organization is the New Korea Association? Is it a single party of the entire nation, or its mediator?' The Decision concluded: 'Ignorant Communists have held up the sign of a unitary front and have advocated a united national party or have lent their abilities to the support of the slogan of national unification while burying the Third International and independent action. It is needless to say that these are definitely acts of betrayal against the elementary truths of Communism.' This change in the Comintern's attitude was yet another factor in the dissolution of the New Korea Association.

REFERENCES

Yun Pyŏngsŏk, '1928–29 nyŏn ŭi Chŏngŭi, Ch'amŭi, Sinmin pu ŭi t'onghap undong' (The Movement for the Unification of the Three Administrations of Justice, Councillors, and New People, 1928–29), *Sahak yŏn'gu* (Journal of Historical Studies), 21, Seoul: Sahak yŏn'guhoe, 1969.

Chŏng Wŏn'gak, 'Chaeman hangil tongnip undong tanch'e ŭi chŏn minjok yuiltang undong' (The campaign for a United National Party by the Anti-Japanese Movement Bodies in Manchuria), *Paeksan hakpo* (Journal of the White Mountain), 19, Seoul: Paeksan hakhoe, 1975.

Song Kŏnho, 'Sin'ganhoe undong' (The New Korea Association Movement), *Han'guk kŭndae saron II* (Essays on Modern Korean History II), Seoul: Chisik sanŏpsa, 1977.

Mizuno Naoki, 'Shinkankai undo ni kansuru jatsukan no mondai' (Some Issues on the New Korea Association Movement), *Chosenshi kenkyukai ronbunshu* (Bulletin of the Society for Korean Historical Study), 14, 1977.

Kang Man-gil, 'Tongnip undong ŭi yŏksajŏk sŏngkyŏk' (Historical Character of the Independence Movement), *Pundan sidae ŭi yŏksa insik* (Historical Perception in the Division Period), Seoul: Ch'angjak kwa pip'yŏngsa, 1978.

Yi Kyunyŏng. *Sin'ganhoe yŏn'gu* (A Study of the New Korea Association), Seoul: Yŏksa pip'yŏngsa, 1990.

SECTION FIVE

The United National Front Movement in China

THE KOREAN NATIONAL FRONT LEAGUE AND THE KOREAN VOLUNTEER CORPS

The failure of the campaign for a united national party front overseas and the dissolution of the New Korea Association in Korea marked the end of the late-1920s stage of the movement to establish a national co-operative front. The 1930s saw new efforts overseas – particularly in China – to form a united front in response to Japanese aggression in Manchuria. This effort was led by a number of organizations including the Korean Independence Party, the Korean Righteous Fighters' Corps, the Korean Revolutionary Party and the Korean Restoration Comrades' Association.

The leaders of those organizations, such as Kim Kyusik, Kim Tubong (b. 1889), Pak Kŏnung, Sin Ikhi (1894–1956), and Ch'oe Tongho (b. 1892), gathered in Shanghai and formed the Korean Anti-Japanese United Front League on 10 November 1931. The League's programme included such goals as 'achieving Korean independence through revolutionary means' and 'extending and strengthening the front against Japan by concentrating our revolutionary capacities and unifying our leadership'.

The representative bodies of the League were the Korean Righteous Fighters' Corps and the Korean Independence Party. The Righteous Fighters' Corps, organized after the March First Movement, pursued the independence movement by means of individual acts of violence both inside and outside Korea throughout the 1920s. From the second half of the 1920s, however, the organization had participated in the movement for a united national party. It also began to assume a leftist nature as seen in the principles it announced at its 4 October 1928 Third National Representative Assembly: 'Confiscation of property of the great landlords'; 'Provision of land, housing and implements to peasants'; 'State administration of large-scale production facilities and monopoly enterprises'. At the beginning of the 1930s, the leader of the Righteous Fighters'

Corps, Kim Wŏnbong (1898–1958), joined hands with An Kwangch'ŏn, who had just escaped from Korea, to form the Alliance to Reconstruct the Communist Party. This Alliance established the Leninist Politics School in 1930. Two years later they established another school, the Korean Revolutionary Leader School, emphasizing that 'a genuine revolution in Korea cannot be accomplished without a proletariat government'.

The other core organization of the Korean United Front Alliance against Japan, the Korean Independence Party, was formed in Shanghai under the leadership of such men as Yi Tongnyŏng, An Ch'angho (1878–1938) and Kim Tubong. This organization was formed in order to 'unite the nationalist movement front by exterminating regionally-based factional strife and to form a basic political party for the Provisional Government'. At that time, the Korean Righteous Fighters' Corps represented the left wing in the national liberation movement front in China, while the Korean Independence Party stood for the right wing. Therefore, the formation of the Korean United Front Alliance against Japan meant the formation of a left-right united front.

On 5 July 1935, the Korean United Front Alliance against Japan, which was declared to be little more than a form of 'co-operation among revolutionary organizations', was replaced by a united front party known as the Korean National Revolutionary Party. The plan was to dismantle all existing organizations, including the Righteous Fighters' Corps, the Korean Independence Party and the Korean Revolutionary Party, and even the Provisional Government in order to make the Korean National Revolutionary Party a truly united front party. The National Revolutionary Party criticized aspects of the past national movement front through its bulletin, the *National Revolution*. They attacked the left for its failure to understand the particularity of the Korean situation, for its leftist infantilism that led to purges and its preoccupation with the struggle for hegemony. They attacked the right for its fragmentation, factional strife and chauvinism. The Korean National Revolutionary Party presented itself as a united front party that aimed to overcome those limitations, build a strong central party armed with scientific theory, analyse the particular situation of Korea in relation to trends of international development in order to indicate the line for national survival and to present a new revolutionary current for the nation as a whole.

The Korean National Revolutionary Party's claim to be a truly united front part was weakened, however, when the so-called Provisional Government Defenders' Faction under the leadership of Kim Ku (1876–1949) refused to join the Korean National Revolutionary Party. The Party's position deteriorated even further when the Korean Independence Party under Cho Soang (1887–1959) and the Korean Revolutionary Party under Yi Ch'ŏngch'ŏn seceded.

The 1937 outbreak of war between China and Japan, however, prompted a new surge of activity in the national liberation movement and led to new efforts to construct a united front. In December 1937, the National Revolutionary Party took the lead in forming the Korean

National Front League in Hankou, bringing in such organizations as the Korean National Liberation Activist League led by Kim Kyugwang (alias Kim Sŏngsuk, 1898–1969), the Korean Youth Vanguard League led by Ch'oe Ch'angik (1896–1957) and the anarchist Korean Revolutionist League led by Yu Chamyŏng (1891–1985). This represented the formation of a leftist united front in China.

The Korean National Front League declared that the united front should not be a class front or a European style people's front, but a national front in its inaugural manifesto. 'The only way for the Korean nation to survive is by using the capacities of the entire nation to overthrow Japanese imperialism and attain national independence. Therefore, the Korean revolution is a national revolution, and our front is a national front as well'. The League adopted a programme that included the foundation of a genuine democratic and independent state, guarantees of the freedom of speech, publication, assembly, association and religion, complete confiscation of the property of Japanese imperialists and traitors, improvement of the livelihood of the labouring masses and equality of the sexes.

The Korean National Front League created a military arm in the Korean Volunteer Corps on 10 October 1938. The Volunteer Corps was formed with the help of funds from the Nationalist Chinese Guomindang government and had a nucleus of graduates from the three classes produced by the Korean Revolutionary Leader School of the Korean Righteous Fighters' Corps. It began with 150 men divided into two units; a third unit was added in 1939. The Volunteer Corps troops were split up and dispatched to the Nationalist Chinese government's six war districts in thirteen provinces, where they engaged in such activities as gathering intelligence, conducting anti-war propaganda, urging Japanese troops to surrender, interrogating prisoners of war and harassing the Japanese rear.

The Volunteer Corps headquarters worked together with Chinese central forces in such places as Guilin and Chongqing. The Corps' first unit was attached to the headquarters of the Chinese seventh war district and participated in the scorched-earth resistance at Changsha, Hunan Province, after which it operated in such places as Tongcheng County, Wutongshan, and Hongshan. The Second Detachment was active in Laohekou before joining the battle at Ebei. It then engaged in guerilla warfare in such places as Nanchang. The Third Detachment was active in the third war district throughout Jiangxi Province. In early 1941, about 80% of the members of the Volunteer Corps moved to the zone where the Chinese communist troops dominated and participated in the battle at Taixing Mountain.

THE PROVISIONAL GOVERNMENT AND THE KOREAN
RESTORATION ARMY

The right wing elements that had defended the Provisional Government under the leadership of Yi Tongnyŏng and Kim Ku formed the Korean National Party in November 1935, championing the Three Equalities

Theory of equal opportunities in politics, economy and education. They put up a party platform featuring the nationalization of land and large-scale production facilities and the equalization of the people's right to live. After the outbreak of Sino-Japanese War in 1937, they began to push for the unification of the right wing front in China. The Korean National Party formed the Korean Restoration Movement Federation in 17 August 1937 with Cho Soang's Korean Independence Party and Yi Ch'ŏngch'ŏn's Korean Revolutionary Party, two groups that had earlier participated in the Korean National Revolutionary Party.

Before long, members of both united fronts, the left-wing Korean National Front League and the right-wing Federation of Korean Restoration Movement Organizations, began to push for unification. The result was the foundation of the United National Battle Line Association. In July 1939, representatives of the two fronts, the rightist Kim Ku and the leftist Kim Wŏnbong, put out an 'Open Letter to Our Comrades and Compatriots' in which they said: 'Feeling pain over the mistakes that have been made frequently in the past, these two persons promise to co-operate with one mind in order to accomplish the great task of the sacred liberation of the Korean nation.'

The 'Open Letter' also set forth a political programme that called for 'purging feudal and anti-revolutionary elements and founding a democratic republic', and 'confiscating both public and private property of the Japanese imperialists in Korea and all the property of the betraying collaborationists'. Nonetheless, the United National Battle Line Association was not able to establish itself as a united front organization. In an effort to bolster the Battle Line Association, four organizations from the National Front League and three organizations from the Restoration Movement Federation held the Conference of Seven Organizations for Unification of the Korean Revolutionary Movement in August 1939. This effort, too, floundered because of differing views over such issues as the continuation of the Provisional Government and command of the Korean Volunteer Corps.

Although the Conference of Seven Organizations failed, it did produce a new Korean Independence Party formed on 8 May 1940 out of the union of the old Korean Independence Party, the Korean National Party and the Korean Revolutionary Party. This new Korean Independence Party developed as the political party of the right-wing front Federation of Korean Restoration Movement Organizations. Its political programme was centred on the Three Equalities Theory of political equality through popular vote, economic equality through the nationalization of land and big business, and educational equality through free compulsory education.

The Provisional Government under the leadership of the Korean Independence Party announced in 1941 a general plan for the foundation of the state in anticipation of Japan's defeat in the Second World War. The general plan included such features as the 'nationalization of large-scale production facilities, land, fisheries, mines, banks, telegraph service and transportation, prohibiting inheritance and sale of land, and raising farmers' and workers' living and cultural standards by establishing and expanding such organs as farmers' cooperatives, state-run factories, and joint systems of production, consumption, and trade'.

The approaching defeat of Japanese imperialism increased the necessity of uniting the political and military forces in the national liberation movement. Thus, the campaign for the united front of the national liberation movement continued, and resulted in the unification of military forces with the May 1942 incorporation into the Provisional Government's Korean Restoration Army by including the roughly 20% of the Korean Volunteer Corps who did not relocate to Chinese Communist territory.

The political sphere also saw progress toward unification. Kim Wŏnbong, Wang T'ong, Yu Chamyŏng and Kim Sangdŏk of the left-wing Korean National Front League were elected as members of the Provisional Assembly in October 1942. Another major step in that direction occurred in April 1944 when members of the Korean National Front League were appointed to key posts, including Kim Kyusik as Vice-President and Kim Wŏnbong, Chang Kŏnsang, Yu Rim (1894–1961) and Kim Sŏngsuk as state councillors. The Provisional Government had finally become a strong united front government.

As the Provisional Government started to function as a real united front government, it emphasized a united front armed struggle embracing all the elements in the national liberation movement. In its 9 August 1944 'Announcement to Our Compatriots at Home and Overseas', the Provisional Government proclaimed: 'We are determined to do our best to carry out an aggressive full-scale armed struggle against the Japanese imperialists and to strengthen and expand our united front to include all revolutionary organizations, military units, fighters, and all our compatriots at home and overseas.'

At the time of its initial founding, the Shanghai Provisional Government established a military academy under its Secretary of Military Affairs. That academy trained 43 army officers in two sixthmonth classes, but it soon closed in 1920. Subsequent efforts were made to bring the Western Route Military Headquarters and the Southern Route Military Headquarters, both in Manchuria, under the Provisional Government but the paralysis of the Provisional Government after the failure of the National Representative Conference left it unable to engage in any military activities until the outbreak of the Sino-Japanese war. At that time, the Provisional Government returned to an armed struggle line by establishing a military affairs committee under its Secretary of Military Affairs and organizing the Korean Restoration Army.

Although the Provisional Government proclaimed the foundation of the Korean Restoration Army on 15 September 1940 and activated its General Headquarters of the Korean Restoration Army under the commander of Yi Ch'ŏngch'ŏn, it was unable to get recognition from the Nationalist Chinese government. Later, on 15 November 1941 the

Restoration Army gained recognition on the conditions that it would be under the control of China's Military Affairs Committee according to the nine-clause Fixed Rules of Conduct. More than half of its officers were Chinese, its officers and men had to wear specially-marked Chinese uniforms and were unable to have their own code of conduct until the Fixed Rules of Conduct were finally cancelled on 23 August 1944,

The Restoration Army started with a headquarters and three units, and added one more unit in 1941. The first unit was founded with nine members, including Yi Chunsik (1900–66) of the military mission dispatched to Xian by the Provisional Government. The second unit was established around a nucleus of cadre from the General Headquarters, including Ko Ungi (alias Kong Chinwŏn; 1907–43). At the time the third unit was created, the only member was its commander, Kim Hakkyu (1900–67). Another unit, known as the fifth unit, was made up of members of the Korean Youth Field Manoeuvre Corps in Xian. In addition, there were five local recruiting offices.

After the assassination of the fifth unit's commander, Na Wŏrhwan (1912–42), the Restoration Army underwent a reorganization that merged the first and fifth units into the second unit under the command of Yi Pŏmsŏk (1900–72), by merging the First, Second and Fifth Detachment'. A new first unit under the command of Kim Wŏnbong, who was also the headquarters vice-commander, was created in 1942 when the roughly forty members of the Korean Volunteer Army who remained behind in Chongqing were brought in to Restoration Army. The total strength of the Restoration Army is estimated to have been about 700 men at the time of Japan's surrender in 1945.

Before the annulment of the Fixed Rules of Conduct, the Korean National Revolutionary Party concluded an agreement with the British troops in India and Burma regarding the dispatch of a Korean National Army Propaganda and Liaison Unit in 1943. The Restoration Army headquarters then dispatched, with Chinese approval, a nine-member operational detachment. They were attached to the 201st and the 204th Units of the British Army where they engaged in such activities as broadcasts towards the Japanese troops, translation of documents, interrogation of war prisoners and making leaflets. After the annulment of the Fixed Rules, there was some discussion about renaming the detachment the Korean Restoration Army Liaison Unit in India and sending more soldiers, but nothing came of it.

Meanwhile, the troops of the second and third units trained guerillas to infiltrate Korea as a joint operation between the Provisional Government and the OSS, an intelligence organization of the US. The second unit trained two classes of 50 soldiers each in May 1945 at Duqu near Xian and the third unit trained 21 selected members at Lihuang in July 1945. The 94 soldiers who finished the second unit's training were organized into eight 'Homeland Vanguard Squads' for the purpose of infiltrating Korea, but the Japanese surrendered before the squads could be dispatched. Some members including Captain Yi Pŏmsŏk, Chang

Chunha (1915–75), Kim Chunyŏp and No Nŭngsŏ, entered Seoul on a US military airplane on 18 August 1945, but were forced to return to China because of the obstinate rejection by the Japanese military.

THE KOREAN INDEPENDENCE LEAGUE AND THE KOREAN VOLUNTEER ARMY

There were Koreans in China, such as Kim Mujŏng (b. 1905), who participated in such things as the National Government's northern expedition of 1926, the Guangdong Commune of 1927, the foundation of the Provisional Government of the Chinese Soviet in 1931 and the Long March of 1934. Furthermore, after the Chinese communist army settled in Yanan, there were Koreans, like Ch'oe Ch'angik and Han Pin (b. 1904) who come to Yanan from Nationalist controlled territory. They organized the North China Korean Youth Federation, including the members of the Korean Volunteer Army who moved to north China, on 10 January 1941.

The Youth Federation's programme included such principles as, 'Uniting Korean youth in all of north China to participate in the great task of the independence of our homeland' and 'Overthrowing Japanese imperialist rule in Korea and establishing an independent and free republic for the Korean nation.' It also called for the 'formation of a united front with Koreans in China and making them the vanguard of the Korean liberation movement'.

The Youth Federation actively supported the unification of the entire national liberation movement front actively by 'paying out boundless respects to the heroic struggles displayed by all the revolutionary bodies, including the Provisional Government of Korea, the North-east China Youth Volunteer Army, the Korean Independence Party, the Korean National Revolutionary Party, the National Liberation Struggle Alliance and the various revolutionary organizations in the United States.'

After the foundation of the Youth Federation, activists continuously flowed into north China, including men from Nationalist Chinese controlled territory such as Kim Tubong and members and leaders of the Korean Volunteer Corps, such as Pak Hyosam (d. 1952) and Yi Ch'unam. As a result, on 15 August 1942, the Youth Federation was dissolved and replaced by the Korean Independence League as a full-fledged national liberation organization with about 300 members and Kim Tubong as its president.

The Korean Independence League's stated goal was to 'overthrow Japanese imperialist rule in Korea and establish an independent and free democratic republic in Korea.' Moreover, the Alliance called for 'establishing a democratic regime through the popular vote of the entire nation' and 'confiscating all the property, including land, of Japanese imperialists in Korea, nationalizing big businesses closely linked to Japanese imperialism and carrying out land redistribution'.

The Korean Independence League set up local branches in north-west and south-east Jin in Shanxi Province, Taixing in Hebei Province, central

Shandong and the border district of Jinlu City in Shandong Province, Huaibei in Anhui Province, Taiyue in Henan Province, and Jixi and Jinchaji in Hubei Province. In addition, the League sent Yi Sangjo to set up a provisional district committee in north Manchuria. .

The League also secretly dispatched Yi Kŭk to Korea to contact Yi Yŏng and Yŏ Unhyŏng and investigate such issues as the re-establishment of the Korean Communist Party and the possibility of armed struggle in Manchuria. The League's domestic operations linked up with Yŏ Unhyŏng's National Foundation League and reached an agreement to hold an All Korean National Congress in Yanan on 29 August 1945, but it did not materialize due to the defeat of the Japanese.

The Independence League pursued both international and national united front movements. In the 'Anti-Fascist Representative Congress of Oriental Nations', held in Yanan in 1941, Provisional Government President Kim Ku was included in the Honorary Presidium of the Congress, and his portrait was displayed alongside those of Sun Yatsen and Mao Zedong at the founding meeting of the League's northwest Jin branch. Provisional Government Minister Chang Kŏnsang went to Yanan and came to an agreement about the formation of a united front between the Provisional Government and the Independence Alliance. Kim Tubong made plans to go Chongqing to sign the agreement, but did not follow through because of the defeat of the Japanese imperialists. The North-South negotiations held in 1948 in an effort to avoid national division can be seen as a continuation of this united front movement.

In the meantime, about 300 members (roughly 80%) of the Korean Volunteer Crops who had moved into Chinese Communist territory were organized as the North China Detachment of the Korean Volunteer Army. Afterwards, when the Korean Independence League was formed, they were reorganized as its military force known as the Korean Volunteer Army. They engaged in joint operations with the Chinese Communist Eighth Route Army against Japanese forces. The Korean Volunteer Army distinguished itself in the battle at Hujiazhuang Battle, a counter-offensive in which the Eighth Route Army fought against 400,000 Japanese troops. It was also engaged in such activities as propaganda against the enemy and harassing the enemy in the rear.

Most of the fighters of the Korean Volunteer Army were intellectuals who were educated in such Chinese institutes as the Huangpu Military Academy, Nanjing Central Military Academy and Zhongshan College. Their numbers also included some Japanese soldiers who changed sides after being captured. They enjoyed great success at the front lines with their anti-war propaganda aimed at Japanese soldiers and in inducing Korean conscripts to desert from the Japanese army. The Korean Volunteer Army later moved to Yanan where in 1943 it established its Korean Youth Revolutionary Military Administration School to train its members. After the Japanese were defeated, members who had been engaged in various locales gathered in Shenyang. They were reorganized into four units that participated in the civil war between the

Chinese Communists and the Chinese Nationalists. Most of them eventually went to North Korea where they were incorporated into the People's Army.

REFERENCES

Han Honggu (ed.), *Hangjŏn pyŏlgok* (Song of Resistance), Seoul: Kŏrŭm, 1986.

Han Honggu, 'Hwabuk Chosŏn Tongnip Tongmaeng ŭi chojik kwa hwaltong' (Organization and activities of the North China Korean Independence League), Master's thesis, Seoul National University, 1988.

Kim Hakchun (ed.), *Hyŏngmyŏngga tŭrŭi hangil hoesang* (Revolutionaries' recollections of anti-Japanese activities), Seoul: Minŭmsa, 1988.

Kang Man-gil, 'Chosŏn minjok hyŏngmyŏngdang kwa t'ongil chŏnsŏn' (The Korean National Revolutionary Party and the United Front Tactics), Seoul: Hwap'yŏngsa, 1991.

Han Sijun, 'Hanguk Kwangbokkun yŏn'gu' (A study of the Korean Independence Army), Ph.D. dissertation, Inha University, 1993.

SECTION SIX

Guerilla Struggles in Manchuria and the Fatherland Restoration Association

THE NORTH-EASTERN PEOPLE'S REVOLUTIONARY ARMY AND KOREANS

The socialist movement in Korean community in the Manchuria region began in the first half of the 1920s and grew rapidly after 1925. In North Jiandao, which includes Yanji, Helong, Wangqing and Hunchun, Koreans accounted for more than 76% of the total population in 1930. According to a March 1931 report from the Manchurian Provincial Committee of the Chinese Communist Party, Koreans totalled 618 of 636 party members in east Manchuria and 193 of 200 in south Manchuria.

After the Japanese imperialists provoked the Manchuria Incident, the Chinese Communist Party ordered the formation of guerila units and opened guerila districts through its 12 October 1931 'Directive on Military Operations in Manchuria'. This led to the establishment of guerila districts and the formation of guerila units in east, south and north Manchuria. For example, according to the decision of the Mingyuegou Conference of December 1931, soviets were established in such east Manchuria locales as Yanji, Wangqing, and Hunchun counties, while a small number of revolutionary committees were also formed in such places as Yulang. In south Manchuria, the Red Guards, who had been organized in Panshi, provided the foundations for a guerila unit.

Members of the Panshi Labour-Peasant Volunteer Army, formed in south Manchuria after the Manchuria Incident, were mostly Koreans including their commander Yi Honggwang (1910–35). The 'Volunteer Army' joined with the Chinese in the struggle against the Japanese and the so-called Manchukuo Army and by 1933 developed into the South Manchuria Guerilla Corps of the Thirty-second Labour-Peasant Red Army of China. In the autumn of that year, the strength of the South Manchuria Guerilla Corps increased to 2,000. It was then reorganized as the First Independent Division of the North-eastern People's Revolutionary Army and then reorganized again as the First North-eastern People's Revolutionary Army when its forces increased to two independent divisions in 1934.

A Yanbian-based guerilla unit was formed out of the Red Guards in Yanji County of east Manchuria in 1932. In the same year, a Helong guerilla unit, made up mostly of Red Guards and Pingkang guerillas, was organized with its base at Yulang in Helong County. Another guerilla unit with a nucleus of eighteen shock attack troops was formed in Wangqing County in 1932. This unit later incorporated the Peitong and Antu units. The Lingnan and Lingbei guerilla units arose in Hunchun in September 1932 and merged as the Hunchun county guerilla unit in 1933.

These four guerilla units, the majority of whose members were Koreans, were reorganized as the East Manchuria Guerilla Corps of the Thirty-Second Labour-Peasant Red Army of China in 1933. When their strength reached approximately 900 men, they were reorganized again into the Second Independent Division of the North-eastern People's Revolutionary Army under Korean Commander Chu Chin (1906–45). The Second Independent Division opened bases for guerilla activities in Antu and Wangqing counties while engaging in 900 battles in the one year of 1934 alone. After overcoming the Japanese Army's 'Third Security Enforcement Plan' (September 1934 to January 1935), the Division had over 1,200 men with over 980 guns. Two-thirds of its strength was Korean.

In north Manchuria, the Zhuhe anti-Japanese guerilla unit, most of whose members were also Koreans, was formed and became active in 1933. The Zhuhe unit was reorganized as a unit of the North-eastern Anti-Japanese Guerilla Corps in June 1934 before being restructured as the Third North-eastern People's Revolutionary Army in January 1935. The Mishan County Committee of the Chinese Communist Party was formed with seven Koreans in 1932, while the Mishan anti-Japanese guerilla unit was organized in March of 1934 with over forty Korean members. The guerilla unit achieved brilliant results in the Mishan County fortress battle in concert with the Chinese National Salvation Army and was combined with the National Salvation Army to form the Fourth North-eastern Anti-Japanese Allied Force in September 1934.

Moreover, in Dangyuan, a locale where many Koreans moved in the 1920s, the Chinese Communist Party formed a Dangyuan County Committee with Koreans as key members in 1929. The Dangyuan guerilla unit started off with about 20 members in 1932, but after going through many battles, its membership increased to over 600. In 1935, in accordance with the united front tactics of the Chinese Communist Party, it was merged with the self-defence corps and the constabulary unit to form the Sixth North-eastern People's Revolutionary Army. The commander of its First Division was a Korean named Ma Tŏksan.

Some Koreans such as Ch'oe Sŏkch'ŏn (alias Ch'oe Yonggŏn; 1925–76), who graduated from Huangbu Military Academy and then joined the Guangdong Commune, moved to Liaohe where they organized a Military Administration Training Class in which over a hundred Korean youths participated. These youths became the nucleus of the Liaohe anti-Japanese guerilla unit led by Ch'oe Sŏkch'ŏn in 1933. Somewhat later the Liaohe guerilla unit, under the leadership of Yi Hakpok, struck major blows against Japanese troops on the left bank of the Ussuri River and on the lower Sunghua River. It was reorganized in 1935 as the Fourth North-eastern People's Revolutionary Army.

These guerilla units operating throughout south, east and north Manchuria, were reorganized as part of People's Revolutionary Army according to the 1933 'January Letter' adopted by the Chinese Communist Party. The Letter emphasized strengthening the national united front and ensuring the leadership of the working classes by revising the 'Directive on Military Operations in Manchuria'. Moreover, the Party ordered such things as the confiscation of the property of the Japanese imperialists and their stooges, guarantee of the rights and interests of minority ethnic groups, the dissolution of the soviets, the establishment of a people's revolutionary government, and the reorganization of the guerilla bands as the People's Revolutionary Army.

According to the directives of the Letter, the soviets and revolutionary committees were replaced by the People's Revolutionary Government and its Peasant Committee. Both were formed through direct election by people 16 years or older, with the exclusion of the stooges of the Japanese and anti-revolutionary elements. The People's Revolutionary Government avoided confrontation with anti-Japanese landlords by abandoning its policy of land confiscation in favour of the enforcement of a 20% tenant fee.

Meanwhile, the anti-Japanese troops engaged in joint operations in accordance with the Letter's directive on the strengthening of the united front. For example, 1,500 men, including over one hundred partisans from Hunchun and Wangqing in concert with the National Salvation Army, attacked the Dongning County fortress, killing or wounding over 105 Japanese troops in September 1933.

THE NORTH-EASTERN ANTI-JAPANESE ALLIED FORCES AND KOREANS

The People's Livelihood Corps, a pro-Japanese organization under the control of the Japanese Consul in Jiandao, was formed in February 1932 and advocated Korean self-rule in Jiandao. It was unable to achieve any particular results and was soon disbanded. However, the tendency of the

Chinese communists to exclude other ethnic groups and their tendency toward leftist adventurism resulted in the victimization of many of the Korean fighters in the anti-Japanese front on suspicion of being members of the People's Livelihood Corps. This was the so-called 'Anti-People's Livelihood Corps Struggle'.

Through four years of the struggle, about 560 members were arrested. Among that number some 430 Korean activists, including over 40 cadre, were punished. After the 'Anti-People's Livelihood Corps Struggle' was stopped in obedience to a February 1936 Comintern directive, the strength of the North-eastern People's Revolutionary Army, and of the Second Army in particular, recovered quickly. In this period, too, Koreans accounted for much of the Second Army's strength: 60% of its military officers, 70% of its political officers and 50–60% of its ordinary soldiers were Koreans. Two of its four divisions were 80% Korean.

After the Seventh Congress in 1935, the Comintern ordered the establishment of an anti-Japanese united front government, and the establishment of a North-eastern Anti-Japanese Allied Army in order to strengthen the anti-Japanese national united front. The Comintern presented its 'Declaration on the Unification of the North-eastern Anti-Japanese Allied Army' on 20 February 1936. Accordingly, the North-eastern Anti-Japanese Allied Army made up of eleven armies was organized as an armed united front organization that included the North-eastern People's Revolutionary Army, the North-eastern Anti-Japanese United Army, the North-eastern Revolutionary Army and a variety of guerilla bands in 1936 and 1937. This included, for example, the formation in Jiandao of the Second North-eastern People's Revolutionary Army with a core of four Korean-dominated guerilla units. When it was subsequently reorganized as the Second North-eastern Anti-Japanese Allied Army in March 1936, it had over 2,000 men in three divisions and one training unit. Of those 2,000 men, roughly 50% were Korean. The Third Division, in particular, was made up mostly of Koreans and was commanded by Kim Il Sung (Kim Ilsŏng). The Third Division later advanced into Linjiang and Fusong counties in the area of Mount Paektu where it engaged in numerous battles including the 'Russian Territory Battle', 'Xijiang Battle' and the 'Dongjiang Battle'.

In the meantime, the First and Second Armies, whose combined force was over 6,000, were reorganized in July 1936 as the First Route Army of the Regional North-eastern Anti-Japanese Allied Army under Commander-in-Chief Yang Jingyu (1905–40). At that time, the First, Second and Third Divisions of the Second Army were designated as the Fourth, Fifth and Sixth Divisions of the First Route Army. The Sixth Division, under the command of Kim Il Sung, acting in concert with the Fourth Division, which had as many Korean partisans as the Sixth Division, decided to build a guerilla district in the Mount Paektu area. From that time, the Mount Paektu area became the focal point of the Korean anti-Japanese struggle in Manchuria and a battlefield between the guerilla units and the Japanese and so-called Manchukuo armies. It was also the place where the Korean Fatherland Restoration Association in Manchuria was founded, as well as the base for advance operations into the homeland of Korea.

The Sixth Division of the First Route Army had as its mission the conduct of anti-Japanese struggles in the border area between Korea and China. In order to create a guerilla district in the Mount Paektu region and establish branch organizations of the Fatherland Restoration Association inside Korea, the Division crossed the Amnok (Yalu) River and carried out a successful attack on the Japanese military base at Poch'ŏnbo in Kapsan in June 1937. This raid inspired people inside Korea, who thus came to know of the activities of the Korean partisans of the North-eastern Anti-Japanese Allied Army Forces and the name Kim Il Sung.

After the outbreak of the Sino-Japanese War, the North-eastern Anti-Japanese Allied Army was ordered to harass the Japanese rear in order to hinder the advance of the Japanese forces into Chinese territory. Afterwards, the Army moved to the Rehe area in order to link up with the Eighth Route Army in China proper and build a new guerilla district. The First and Third Divisions of the First Army left for the Maritime Provinces in July 1937 while the Sixth Division left the Mount Paektu region for Mengjiang and Huinan counties. This plan was disrupted by pressure from Japanese troops. After the disastrous surrender of commander Chŏng Pin in 1938, the First Route Army was reorganized into a guard brigade and three directional armies.

At this time, the strength of the Anti-Japanese Allied Army was about 1,850 men. Nearly 60% of the men in the Third Directional Army, which was formed out of the Third and Fourth Divisions, were Koreans. The Korean-dominated former Sixth Division, now known as the Second Directional Army, returned to the Mount Paektu area under the command of Kim Il Sung.

The directional army troops continuously launched heavy attacks on the enemy. Those attacks included the Musan Battle in North Hamgyŏng Province as an advance operation by the Second Directional Army, the Dashahe Battle in Antu County of Manchuria, in which the Second Directional Army joined with the Thirteenth Unit of the Third Directional Army, led by Ch'oe Hyŏn, to kill more than a hundred Japanese and Manchukuo soldiers, and the battle in Hualong County, where the Second Directional Army killed over 120 Japanese soldiers of the Maeda Punitive Corps. Despite these setbacks, the Japanese troops put heavy pressure on the First Route Army and killed the Commander-in-Chief Wang Jingyu in February 1940.

Subsequently, the North-eastern Anti-Japanese Allied Army, facing difficulties in mounting organized military activity in Manchuria, suspended large-scale operations after the first Khabarovsk Conference of January 1940, eventually crossing the border into the Soviet Union in October of that year. The forces, which consisted of the Second and Third Directional Armies and part of the Second Route Army's Fifth Army, built the South Camp (B Camp) near Vladivostok.

Other forces, which consisted of much of the Second Route Army and all of the Third Route Army, made the North Camp (A Camp). In July 1942, the South Camp joined with the North Camp to form the Training Brigade of the North-eastern Anti-Japanese Allied Army under the command of Zhou Baozhong. The Training Brigade also included Koreans who resided in Russia and other ethnic minority soldiers. The Brigade thus came to be known as the as the Eighty-Eighth Special Brigade of the International Red Army.

The Training Brigade had four training camps. Korean leaders in the Brigade included Vice Chief of Staff Ch'oe Yonggŏn and camp commanders Kim Il Sung, Hŏ Hyŏngsik (1909–42) and Kang Sint'ae (a.k.a. Kang Kŏn). When the South and North Camps were built, the Brigade had about 1,700 men, but by 1944 the number decreased to about 1,000, of which the number of Koreans is estimated to have been between 100 and 200. Even after they moved to the Russian territory, the North-eastern Anti-Japanese Allied Army continued to be engaged in combat-related activities, such as dispatching small squads to Manchuria on reconnaissance missions and destroying transport routes such as railroads and main roads.

Small squad operations became more active after the outbreak of war between the Soviet Union and Germany in June 1941. In July 1945, after Germany had surrendered and Japan was nearing defeat, the Soviet Union was preparing to join the war against Japan. A 'Korean Operations Corps' was formed in the Eighty-Eighth Bridge to further liberation activities and the foundation of a Communist Party in Korea. When the Soviet Union declared war against Japan on 9 August, Korean members of the Training Brigade participated in the operations against Japan, advancing into Manchuria and the Korean Peninsula. Meanwhile, the main force of Koreans, led by Kim Il Sung, returned to Korea through Wŏnsan without having an opportunity to engage in war against Japan and became the core group in the establishment of the north Korean regime.

THE KOREAN FATHERLAND RESTORATION ASSOCIATION IN MANCHURIA

After the dissolution of the Korean Communist Party at the direction of the Comitern, even the Korean communists in Manchuria could not continue being active unless they joined the Chinese Communist Party according to the Comintern's principle of 'one country-one party'. Even though the activities of the Korean Communists in the North-eastern People's Revolutionary Army or the Northeastern Anti-Japanese Allied Army followed the Comintern's directive, their ultimate goal was still the attainment of Korean independence.

The Chinese Communist Party and the Comintern began to show some changes in their policy towards ethnic minorities in China around the time of the Seventh Comintern Congress. The Seventh Congress decided to allow the Koreans to form the Fatherland Restoration

Association in Manchuria and to organize a separate Korean People's Revolutionary Army within the North-eastern People's Revolutionary Army. In November 1935, even as it was arguing for the formation of a northeastern people's united front, the Chinese Communist Party suggested in the Comintern bulletin the formation of a 'national revolutionary party' as a Korean anti-Japanese united front party in Jiandao. In the military sphere, however, the judgment was that independent activities by Korean might present problems of strategy and the Korean troops were not allowed to be completely independent but required to take the form of an alliance. That is the reason why the Manchurian forces were called an Allied Army.

Although Korean troops in the North-eastern Anti-Japanese Allied Army as well as in the North-eastern People's Revolutionary Army were not allowed complete separation, the Second Anti-Japanese Allied Army, which was made up primarily of Koreans, advanced to Chinese border with Korea and the Mount Paektu area where it prepared the base for the 'Fatherland Restoration Association'. Later, following the decision of the Dongjiang Conference of top-rank military officers in May 1936, a meeting among the high-ranking executive members of the Second Army and the Korean Fatherland Restoration Association in Manchuria was convened at the suggestion of O Sŏngnyun (alias Chŏn Kwang; 1900–47), Yi Sangjun (alias Yi Tonggwang; 1904–1935) and Ôm Sumyŏng. The Association declared: 'Regardless of class, sex, position, party, age or religion, Koreans, should rise up in unison against the bitter Japanese enemy and achieve the restoration of the fatherland.'

The Fatherland Restoration Association announced a 'Ten-Point Programme'.

(1) Establish a genuine independent Korean people's government by realizing a broad national united anti-Japanese front.
(2) Realize genuine autonomy for Korean residents in Chinese territory.
(3) Form a military body that will fight for the genuine independence of Korea.
(4) Confiscate property and land from the Japanese colonial government and the Japanese individuals as well as the traitorous pro-Japanese elements to pay the costs of the independence movement.
(5) Develop national industry, agriculture and commerce.
(6) Achieve the freedoms of speech, press, assembly and association, and release all political criminals.
(7) Ensure equality irrespective of sex, nation or religion, and enhance the social status of women.
(8) Implement free compulsory education.
(9) Improve labour conditions and implement a worker's insurance act.
(10) Maintain friendship with those states and nations that are favourable or neutral towards the Korean national liberation movement.

The Fatherland Restoration Association, which was promoted with the leadership of the Third Division of the Second North-eastern Anti-Japanese Allied Force (the Sixth Division of the First Regional Army after July 1936), formed an extensive network throughout such locales as Changbai County in Manchuria, the northern regions of North Hamgyŏng and North P'yŏngan provinces, and the cities of Hŭngnam, Hamhŭng and Wŏnsan. Its lowest unit, the local branch, had to have at least three members. The Association placed district offices in places where there were three or more local branches, metropolitan or county offices in places where there were three or more district offices and provincial offices in places where there were three or more county offices.

The local branches elected executive committees at a meeting of representatives that were then charged with the leadership of the branches' entire operations. Each local organization with over 30 members established eight departments responsible for organization, propaganda, general affairs, armament, economy, justice, youth and women. In February 1932, the Changbai County operations committee established three district offices, eleven local branches, forty-one sub-branches, ten teams and four production guerilla units in Manchuria while also creating one Korean National Liberation League, three local branches, three sub-branches, one True Friend Society, one Anti-Japanese Society and fourteen anti-Japanese groups across the border in Korea.

Inside Korea, the Korean National Liberation League's organization at Unhŭng Township in Kapsan County consisted of twenty-six different bodies, including the Anti-Japanese Youth League, the Anti-Japanese Group, the Anti-Japanese Women's Group, the Anti-Japanese Society, the Do-or-Die Squad, the Peasant Union and the Evening Class Club. The local organization in Poch'ŏn Township had nine groups, including the Anti-Japanese Youth League and the Anti-Japanese True Friend Society. Local branches and operations committees were also formed in Pyŏltong and Sinp'a townships in Hamgyŏng Province's Samsu County. In 1937, the Association also sent political operations agents to such places as Wŏnsan City, Hamhŭng City, P'ungsan County and Tanch'ŏn County in South Hamgyŏng Province; Musan County, Sŏngjin County and Kilchu County in North Hamgyŏng Province; and Sinŭiju City and Huch'ang County in North Py'ŏngan Province.

In order to realize a national united front, the Fatherland Restoration Association contacted the religious leader Pak Injin, who had jurisdiction over temples of the Religion of Heavenly Way in Changbai County and the three counties of Kapsan, Samsu and P'ungsan inside Korea and persuaded him to join the Association. Although a plan to contact Ch'oe Rin, the leader of the Religion of the Heavenly Way's central organization, did not materialize, his followers in P'ungsan County joined the North-eastern Anti-Japanese Allied Army and were assigned to the production guerilla units. In 1937 and 1938, however, the Japanese authorities – in what has come to be known as the Hyesanjin Incident – conducted two sweeps in which they arrested 739 persons suspected of being Fatherland Restoration Association partisans, including Kwŏn Yŏngbyŏk (1907–43), Yi Chesun (1908–43), Pak Tal (1910–60) and Pak Kŭmch'ŏl (b. 1911). This brought about the collapse of most of the Association's organizations inside Korea.

REFERENCES

Kim Chunyŏp and Kim Ch'angsun, *Han'guk kongsanjuŭi undongsa* (History of the Korean Communist Movement), vol. 5, Seoul: Asea munje yŏnguso at Korea University, 1976.

Im Ûn, *Puk Chosŏn wangjo sŏngnip pisa* (A secret history of the establishment of north Korean dynasty), Chayusa, 1982.

Dongbei kangri lianjun shiliao (Historical materials of the Northeastern Anti-Japanese Allied Forces), 2 vols, Beijing: Zhonggong dangshi shiliao chubanshe, 1987.

Yi Chaehwa, *Han'guk kŭnhyŏndae minjok haebang undongsa- hangil mujang t'ujaengsa p'yŏn* (History of the Modern Korean National Liberation Movement-History of the Anti-Japanese Armed Struggle), Seoul: Paeksan sŏdang, 1988.

Yi Chongsŏk, 'Pukhan chido chiptan kwa hangil mujang t'ujaeng' (The Ruling Group of north Korea and the Anti-Japanese Armed Struggle), *Haebang chŏnhusa ŭi insik* (Perceptions of history before and after liberation), vol. 5, Seoul: Han'gilsa, 1989.

Wada Haruki, *Kim Ilsŏng kwa Manju hangil chŏnjaeng* (Kim Il Sung and the Anti-Japanese War in Manchuria), Seoul: Ch'angjak kwa pip'yŏngsa, 1992.

Kang Chaeŏn. *Manshuu no Chosenjin paruchisan* (Korean partisans in Manchuria), Tokyo: Aoki shoten, 1993.

Sin Chubaek, '1930 nyŏndae 'Manju' hangIl mujang t'ujaeng' (The Anti-Japanese Armed Struggle in Manchuria of 1930s), *Han'guksa* (History of Korea), vol. 15, Seoul: Han'gilsa, 1994.

SECTION SEVEN

The Domestic National United Front Movement

THE REVOLUTIONARY LABOUR-PEASANT UNION MOVEMENT

In the second half of the 1920s, labour strikes and tenancy disputes became more active. This was due to the enhanced struggle for consciousness of the workers and also of the peasants, who were suffering from an agricultural recession. This, along with the student movement that arose out of the Kwangju Student Incident, contributed to the popular spread of socialism. The outcome was a dramatic increase in the number of social movements as shown in Table 3 below.

Table 3: Yearly trend in the formation of social movement organizations

Year	Peasant movements	Labour movements	Youth movements
1920	0	33	251
1921	3	90	446
1922	23	81	488
1923	107	111	58
1924	112	91	742
1925	126	128	847
1926	119	182	1,092
1927	160	352	1,127
1928	307	432	1,320
1929	564	465	1,433
1930	943	561	1,509
1931	1,759	511	1,482
1932	1,380	404	863
1933	1,301	374	1,004

Source: Saikin no Chosen chian joko (The Recent Security Situation in Korea), 1933 ed., pp. 168–69.

The Government-General of Korea's response to the increasing activity was to allow a limited activation of the national reformist and cultural movements while at the same time seeking to keep the popular movement from becoming leftist by intensifying its oppression through broad application of its Security Maintenance Law. The Vnarod Movement and the Movement to Revive Korean Studies of the 1930s were the products of this atmosphere.

This change led to the gradual reformist transformation of the leaders of various legal movement organizations including the New Korea Association. Inspired by the rising mass movement and the Comintern's various directives such as the December Thesis of 1928, the September Thesis of 1930 and the October Letter of 1931, the socialists parted with those nationalists who were becoming reformists. This resulted in the dissolution of such organizations as the New Korea Association, the General League of Korean Youth, the General League of Korean Labour and the General League of Korean Peasants.

After the demise of those legal organizations, the socialist activists either attempted to infiltrate the working class or the peasant class directly, or else tried to bring students, intellectuals infiltrate and petit bourgeoisie together. The socialists now rejected the top-down type of united front movement such as the New Korea Association and sought to organize a bottom-up movement based in workers, peasants, and students. They were continuously engaged in such activities as forming labour and peasant unions and anti-imperialists leagues that provided a foundation for a movement to reconstruct the Korean Communist Party.

The revolutionary labour union movement was promoted both in older industrial centres and in the areas where new industries were developed in the 1930s as part of the Japanese policy to turn Korea into a logistical base. The activists established branch associations based on cell-like entities such as teams or factory groups. Above the branch associations they organized factory committees, which in turn belonged to regional industry unions. They then sought to bring the regional industry unions into nationwide industry unions, which they planned to use as the foundation for the re-establishment of the Party.

During the years 1931 through 1935, 1,759 persons were involved in 70 cases related to the revolutionary labour union movement while 4,121 persons were implicated in 103 cases related to the peasant union movement. One of the most noteworthy revolutionary labour union movements was the 1931 Leftist Labour Union National Council, which was based in Hamhŭng and had branches in such industrial cities as Ch'ŏngjin, Wŏnsan, Seoul, P'yŏngyang, Sinŭiju, Kwangju, Mokp'o and Pusan. Another was the series of four incidents between 1930 and 1935 involving the Pan Pacific Labour Union in which such men as Kim Hoban (b. 1902) and Yi Munhong (b. 1905) were active.

In addition, there were such activities as the 'Sinŭiju Illegal Factory Labour Union Incident' led by Kye Kyŏngsun, the first and second 'P'yŏngyang Red Labour Union Incidents' directed by Kim T'aesŏk (1875–1953) and Chŏng Tarhŏn (b. 1899), the 'Kyŏmip'o Iron Plant Red Labour Union Incident' led by Chu Yŏngha (b. 1908), the 'Yŏsu Red Labour Union Incident' led by Kim Yonghwan (1912–48), and the 'Masan Red Labour Union Incident' of Chang Kyugyŏng and Yi Sŭngyŏp (1905–53). There were also numerous activities throughout the country in relation to the movement for re-establishment of the communist party.

Taking Seoul as an example, the group led by Yi Chaeyu (1905–44) was quite active between1932 and 1936. They organized factory teams and directed strikes in over thirty workplaces and factories from a variety of sectors, including such metalworking plants as the Railroad Bureau Factory and the Yongsan Machinery Cooperation, chemical plants such as the Continental Rubber and the Keijo Rubber factories, the textile industry such as the Tongsŏng Spinning and Showa Spinning plants, the electrical industry's Keijo Electric Company, as well as enterprises in other sectors including the Korea Printing plant, the Monopoly Bureau Factory and the Hwasin Commercial Company. Furthermore, they guided revolutionary peasant union movements in such places as Yŏju and Yangp'yŏng and organized students at all levels, including Keijo Imperial University. These activities were intended to build a base for the re-establishment of the Communist Party.

The revolutionary peasant union movement was more extensive and more active than the revolutionary labour union movement. The fact that the revolutionary peasant union movement arose in over 80 of the country's 220 counties shows that it was not simply a localized movement. South Hamgyŏng Province had the highest proportion, with revolutionary peasant movements occurring in 81% of its counties, followed by North Hamgyŏng Province at 46%.

Somewhere between 15,000 to 20,000 peasants were arrested for their involvement in the union movement during those years. Approximately 6,200 of those were referred for prosecution, with roughly 1,770 actually brought to trial. The provinces with the most active revolutionary peasant union movements were, in addition to North and South Hamgyŏng, South Chŏlla, North Kyŏngsang and Kangwŏn Provinces. The most active counties included Myŏngch'ŏn, Sŏngjin, Hongwŏn, Chŏngp'yŏng, Yŏnghǔng, Munch'ŏn and Tanch'ŏn.

The revolutionary peasant movement can be seen as having developed in three stages. The first came in 1930 and 1931, when many legal peasant unions were reorganized as illegal unions. The second was the years from 1932 to 1937, a time of the expansion and reconstruction of the revolutionary peasant movement. The third came after 1937, after the movement adopted the anti-fascist people's front tactics.

The revolutionary peasant union movement organized village peasant union teams that typically had three to seven members. Those were then used as the base for township union branches which in turn formed county unions. At the beginning, revolutionary peasant union activists typically called for land redistribution and the establishment of the labour-peasant soviets while emphasizing the principle of giving first priority to poor peasants. Over time, they began to argue for the exclusion of rich peasants. The goals of the revolutionary peasant movement included: the progressive organization of the peasant masses in a bottom-up united front; the promotion of revolutionary mass struggle combining economic and political struggles and legal and illegal struggles; and establishing an organizational foundation for the re-establishment of the Communist Party.

The leadership of the revolutionary labour and peasant union movements was made up of a broad range of elements. Those included Communists of the 1920s who remained faithful to the Party and persons who came into Korea under Comintern sponsorship, along with socialists of various regions who were inspired by the transformation of the social movement into an illegal movement, and students who left their schools to work in the villages or factories after the Kwangju Student Movement. But it also included leaders of the existing legal labour and peasant union movements, and labourers and peasants who developed as leaders during the late-1920s and early-1930s.

The revolutionary labour and peasant union activists developed their propaganda skills through a variety of bulletins and illegal publications. They also developed such tactics as organizing night schools, dramas and sporting events. They strengthened their ability to protect their organization by strengthening the education and training of their members. However, because they rejected top-down united front tactics and used united front tactics from below, they sometimes displayed left-wing deviation or adventurism in their lines and activities.

The 1935 Comintern's Seventh Congress' concrete guidelines for people's front tactics and the intensification of Japanese fascism after the 1937 outbreak of war between Japan and China substantially weakened the domestic revolutionary labour and peasant movements. Nonetheless, activists in a few locales continued reconstructing labour unions and peasant unions while looking for ways to transform their tactics.

In the second half of the 1930s, some of the movements, mostly in the northern part of Korea, developed into riots or even armed movements. There were also localized incidences between 1936 and 1940 of activists attempting to realize the people's united front tactics within the mass movement. One such case was that of the labour movement led by Yi Chuha (1905–50) in the Wŏnsan area and the related activities led by Han Pongjŏk, in Ch'ŏngp'yŏng and Ch'ŏngjin.

In the mid-1930s, under the leadership of Yi Chuha and Chŏn T'aebŏm, the Wŏnsan area labour union movement, in order to form a Wŏnsan left-wing committee of the Red Labour Union, began to organize red labour teams as the base for industry union committees in each of three major sectors: railroad, metalworking and chemicals. The members of the railroad committee's red labour team were particularly active. In 1938 they applied the guidline of people's front tactics to the railroad, chemical and metalworking sectors and formed such social organizations as the Railroad Friends' Society.

In the beginning, the activists in the revolutionary labour union movement in Wŏnsan area defined the Korean revolution as a bourgeoisie democratic revolution and sought instead to establish a labour-peasant soviet that would have confiscated large-scale production facilities and implemented land reform. In 1937, however, the leaders, such as Yi Chuha, Ch'oe Yongdal (b. 1902) and Yi Kangguk (1906–53), met to form a new organization and accepted the Seventh Comintern's directive on united front tactics. They now contended: 'We must not underestimate the intelligentsia and petit bourgeoisie or look down upon left-wing nationalist bourgeoisie. Let us organize the entire people's united front against the Japanese imperialism and fascism'.

In spite of this effort, the revolutionary labour-peasant union movement during the 1930s collapsed due to the arrest of the majority of the activists. It was not able to develop into an entity that could guide the spontaneously generated popular struggle that arose under the wartime regime of the 1940s.

THE MOVEMENT TO RE-ESTABLISH THE KOREAN COMMUNIST PARTY

The 'December Thesis' of the Comintern had determined that the character of the Korean revolution was to be a bourgeoisie democratic revolution against Japanese fascism and the Korean feudal system. It thereby ordered the dissolution of the Korean Communist Party and the formation of a new Party. Moreover, it emphasized a revolutionary resolution of land issue and the establishment of the democratic dictatorship by the proletariat and the peasant through the soviet form. It directed the firm rejection of factional strife in the party re-establishment movement, and that the workers and farmers, instead of a small number of intellectuals and students, should be the basis for the re-establishment movement.

Activists in the early party re-establishment movement (1929–31), right after the 'December Thesis', believed that they would quickly be able to utilize the existing capacities of the Korean Communist Party to reconstruct a united Bolshevik party. The method they chose was to form a Korea Communist Party Re-establishment Preparation Association, which they then planned to expand and strengthen.

This movement was pushed by the leadership of already existing factions. The Korea Communist Party Re-establishment Preparation Association came into being in Jilin, Manchuria in February 1929, under the leadership of such Shanghai faction members as Kim Ch'ŏlsu and Yun Chayŏng (b. 1894), published a bulletin called the *Bolshevik*, and dispatched political operatives to main cities inside Korea, including P'yŏngyang, Hamhŭng, Hŭngnam, Seoul, Ch'ŏngjin, Kwangju and Chinju to form party, communist youth organization and red labour union cells. The Marxist-Leninist faction also met in Chilin in May 1929 to form a Central Committee for the Reorganization of the Korean Communist Party whose members included Yi Kyŏngho, Han Pin and Han Wigŏn, and began to build its organizations in each province and county of the country while publishing its own bulletin, the *Class Struggle*. The Tuesday Society also secretly formed a Committee to Prepare for the Organization of the Korean Communist Party Organization November 1929 and selected Kim Tanya (b. 1900), Pak Minyŏng (b. 1904) and Ch'ae Kyuhang (b. 1897) as central committee members. The Tuesday Society tried to reestablish the Party by sending graduates of communist universities in Moscow to organize new cells of workers and farmers in various locales throughout the country.

The activists in the early period of the party re-establishment movement sought to exterminate the intelligentsia nature of the Party and to go to the masses and re-establish the party under the leadership of poor farmers and industrial workers under the slogan of 'organization through struggle'. They had a strong tendency, however, to promote the re-establishment movement on the basis of old factional affiliations. They were also unable to realize the directives of the 'December Thesis' in that they followed a top-down approach by first forming a central organization to guide the re-establishment of the party.

Moreover, due to the circumstance where the activists based in Manchuria and Japan could not easily engage in the re-establishment movement due to the principle of one country-one party of the Comintern, many of them were victimized by the Japanese' harsh suppression. On the other hand, however, the re-establishment movement began to build connections with the mass movement.

The party re-establishment movement in the early period developed by the method of forming preparatory committees for the nation-wide party re-establishment movement first and then building cell organizations in industrial areas and agrarian communities. Sometime around 1932, however, the activists changed their approach. They now considered the formation of the revolutionary peasant unions in agrarian communities and the revolutionary labour unions in urban areas as their main priorities and gradually organized regional industrial councils and nation-wide labour and peasant union committees. In the process, élite members were chosen to form 'communist groups' in each locale. Their method was to reorganize the communist party over the long term through a representative assembly drawn from those groups. In other words, they intended to re-establish the Party by cultivating new types of communists produced out of a revolutionary mass movement.

With this change in approach, the Seoul-Shanghai faction dissolved the Korean Communist Party Re-establishment Preparation Association on the grounds that it was a factional organization, and formed the 'Left-Wing Labour Union National Council' in order to re-establish the party through revolutionary labour and peasant unions. The communists who belonged to the Marxist-Leninist faction also shifted their methodology from first forming a communist party and a communist youth association to first organizing revolutionary labour and peasant unions. The Comintern also sent numerous graduates of communist universities in Moscow as political operatives to help form new communist groups in various locales. Because of changing circumstances and regional differences, the party re-establishment movement of the 1930s was not able to establish regular linkages between the local groups and the revolutionary labour and peasant movements, although the two did have some influence on each other.

The party re-establishment movement gradually collapsed after the mid-1930s because the majority of the activists were arrested by the Japanese imperialists who had begun even more severe suppression of anti-Japanese thought after they provoked war with China in 1937. Moreover, the re-establishment movement was also influenced by the inactivity of the domestic mass movement and the change in the Comintern's line after the Seventh Congress.

The Seventh Comintern Congress adopted the anti-fascist people's front tactics and confirmed the need for the formation of the national united front with anti-imperialistic bourgeoisie nationalists in the revolutionary movements of colonized countries. Kim Hail, who participated in the Congress, divided the national bourgeoisie into those who had anti-Japanese sentiments and those who did not. He emphasized the need of drawing the anti-Japanese bourgeoisie into the national revolutionary front. Later, the Comintern also dispatched political operatives, such as Pak Ch'angsun in Waegwan, North Kyŏngsang Province and Yi Sun in Ch'ŏngjin, North Hamgyŏng Province, to Korea in order to support the change in tactics.

After the Comintern's directive to change tactics, the party re-establishment movement was unable to resolve the question of whether power should be exercised by the dictatorship of workers and peasants or of the people as a whole. However, there were instances in which activists, considering united front tactics inevitable, sought to dissolve the revolutionary labour and peasant unions to form extensive anti-Japanese mass organizations. One such case was the revolutionary movement organization of the Fatherland Restoration Association in Kapsan where the existing Operations Committee was transformed into a national united front organ known as the Anti-Japanese National Liberation League.

There were other cases, such as in Wŏnsan and Ch'ŏngjin, where activists sought to develop both the revolutionary labour union movements and anti-Japanese united front organizations at the same time. Moreover, there were other examples where communist groups, such as the 'Yi Chaeyu Group' around 1936 and the 'Kyŏngsŏng Com Group' under Yi Kwansul (b. 1900) and Pak Hŏnyŏng established separate people's front departments in 1939 and 1941.

Even though the Korean Communist Party re-establishment movement suffered from some degree of confusion in its tactics, it continuously developed its local communist group movement. During the first eighteen months after the outbreak of the Sino-Japanese war, there were twenty-one incidents in which ten or more communist group members were arrested, and a grand total of 1,355 persons taken into custody in connection with these incidents. Although these local communist groups existed all over the country, there were particularly large numbers in the northern areas where new industrial facilities were being developed, such as Hŭngnam, Hamhŭng, Wŏnsan, Ch'ŏngjin, Myŏngju, Kilchu, Tanch'ŏn and Chŏngp'yŏng.

Meanwhile, factional strife almost disappeared from the party re-establishment movement after the mid-1930s. After 1939, when most of reconstruction movement in the country had collapsed as the Japanese imperialism turned to the fascist war system, Kim Tanya, Yi Kwansul and Pak Hŏnyŏng, who returned from Moscow, took the lead to form the Kyŏngsŏng Com Group. They prepared for last-ditch resistance while gathering the remainder of the party re-establishment movement and the revolutionary labour and peasant union movement in the country up until they were arrested in 1941. Low-level organizations continued to exist in the Seoul-Kyŏnggi area and also in Hamgyŏng and Kyŏngsang provinces. There were also some activities in the labour unions and street sectors, as well as in the people's front sector. The activists, who were greatly interested in guerilla activities, made efforts to find various types of tactics while watching the changing world situation. Some activists who managed to escape arrest participated in the Communist Assembly or the National Foundation League of 1944.

Even after the outbreak of war between Japan and the United State, the party re-establishment movement continued in the face of the desperate suppression by the Japanese imperialists. Sŏ Chungsŏk (b. 1904), Yi Chŏngyun and Kim T'aejun (1905–50) formed the 'Communist Assembly' in Seoul in November 1944, the 'Im Ch'ungsŏk Group' was active in Changjin County, South Hamgyŏng Province and the 'Yun Il Group' was active in Pusan and Kŏje Island, South Kyŏngsang Province. Over 70 activists, including men evading conscription, formed an anti-Japanese guerilla band, the Diffusion of Lights Party (*Pogwang tang*) in Mount Chiri under the leadership of Ha Chunsu (alias Nam Tobu, 1921–54). The re-establishment movement continued throughout the country, but in the end the activists greeted the liberation without forming a united Korean Communist Party.

THE NATIONAL FOUNDATION LEAGUE

Yŏ Unhyŏng was arrested by the Japanese police while he was involved in the Shanghai Provisional Government and stayed inside Korea after finishing his prison term. In 1940, the Japanese government, which hoped to send him as an emissary to seek peace with Chiang Kai-shek, invited him to Tokyo. Although the mission never came about, he did get a chance to grasp the situation in Japan through his contacts with Japanese leaders. Furthermore, he was able to anticipate the defeat of Japan through communication with such comrades as Yi Yŏngsŏn and Ch'oe Kŭnu in such locales throughout China as Yanan, Beijing and Manchuria.

Yŏ Unhyŏng planed to form the Korean National Liberation League for the preparation of liberation of Korea when he was imprisoned again (December 1942 to June 1943). After being released, he discussed the formation of a people's front with Yi Kisŏk and Kim T'aejun, while also suggesting the formation of a people's front, a national liberation league and people's assembly to such communist groups as the Freedom and Independence Group of Yi Sŭngyŏp and the Communist Assembly of Kil Ilsu and Kim T'aejun. Subsequently on 10 August 1944, he formed his National Foundation Union in the hope of attaining some unity with the Korean Independence League in Yanan and in anticipation of the defeat of the Japanese.

The National Foundation League's programme had three main principles. One was to attain national solidarity to expel the Japanese imperialists and recover the freedom and independence of the Korean nation. A second was to form an anti-Japanese united front in co-operation with countries that opposed the hegemonic powers and to exterminate all the reactionary elements that hindered the complete independence of Korea. The third was the foundation of the nation to be based on democratic principles with particular attention to the liberation of the labouring masses.

The leading members of the central organ of the National Foundation League were: Yŏ Unhyŏng, chairman; Cho Tongho (1892–1954) and Hyŏn Uhyŏn in the Department of Home Affairs and in charge of mustering men of the same mind inside Korea; Yi Kŏlso, Yi Sŏkku and Hwang Un in the Department of Foreign Affairs in charge of communication with national liberation movement organizations overseas; and Kim Chinu and Yi Sumok in the Department of Finance in charge of raising and controlling funds. In addition, there were many other men from both the right and left, such Yi Mangyu (1882–1978), Kim Seyong (1907–66), Yi Yŏsŏng (b. 1901), Pak Sŭnghwan and Yi Sangbaek (1904–66) who joined the League.

The League established local organizations by appointing persons to be responsible for ten provinces, including North and South Ch'ungch'ŏng, throughout the country while also organizing a peasant union at Mount Yongmun in Kyŏnggi Province on 8 October 1944. The resistance policies of the peasant union called for burning census registers in order to interfere with conscription, developing the anti-Japanese struggle through the whole country, destroying railroads in order to hinder the transport of war materials and helping Koreans evade conscription. There were a number of other organizations linked with the National Foundation League, including the Diffusion of Light Party in Mount Chiri, the Korean National Liberation Cooperative Corps of Yŏm Yun'gu, organized in the mountains of P'och'ŏn County, Kyŏnggi Province, and the Mountaineering Band of Yi Hyŏkki, formed in Mount Sŏrak, Kangwŏn Province.

The National Foundation League planned to disturb the Japanese rear and organize a labour-peasant army. To that end, it formed a military committee in connection with the Communist Assembly in March 1945. The military committee, whose goals were to spark an armed uprising and destroy railroads, gathered men of like mind by sending agents to such areas as Kyŏnggi, Hwanghae and Kangwŏn Provinces while also making efforts to expand the organization to such places as Taegu, Pusan, Mokp'o, Hŭngnam, Ch'ŏngjin, P'yŏngyang and Chinnamp'o. The League planned to launch offensive operations inside Korea by winning over Korean soldiers serving under Pak Sŭnghwan (a graduate of the Manchukuo Military Academy) in the Manchukuo Army, and also tried to seize weapons from Japanese armouries.

The National Foundation League, which had a sense that national liberation was near, not only set out to realize the formation of a united front among the various liberation movement forces in the homeland, but also succeeded partly in forming a united front with liberation movement forces overseas. Kim T'aejun, who had links with Yŏ Unhyŏng, and Pak Chinjong of the Communist Assembly managed to evade the Japanese and make their way to Yanan at the order of the Assembly's Military Affairs Forum in order to meet Kim Mujŏng, while the novelist Kim Saryang (1914–50) escaped to Yanan through with the help of Yi Yŏngsŏn, Yŏ Unhyŏng's representative in Beijing. Even under the severe control and surveillance of the Japanese imperialists, ways were found to negotiate with the overseas front about the formation of a united front.

The National Foundation League dispatched members to link up with the front overseas in various places in China: Ch'oe Kŭnu in north Manchuria; Yi Yŏngsŏn, Yi Sangbaek, Pak Sŭnghwan and Ôm T'aesŏp in Beijing; and Yi Yŏngsŏn, Pak Sŭnghwan and Yi Sangbaek in Yanan. The plan for forming a united front with the Yanan Independence League included such things as the organization of a military force and of guerilla bands, communications with Kim Mujŏng of the Korean Volunteer Army for in preparation for its advance into Korea, and the provision of hiding-places and food for guerilla bands after they advanced to the homeland.

The National Foundation League and the Independence Union reached an agreement on holding an all Korea national convention in Yanan on the anniversary of the National Humiliation Day (29 August) in 1945, and the Foundation League sent delegates Kim Myŏngsi and Yi Yŏngsŏn to Yanan. Meanwhile, the Foundation League also sent Ch'oe Kŭnu to Chongqing to form a united front with the Provisional Government which had followed Chiang Kai-shek to that city. Before those plans could be actualized, however, the Japanese imperialists were defeated. The efforts of the Foundation League were a continuation of the united front movement that had been pursued throughout the entire national liberation movement since mid-1930s.

Japanese imperialism developed into fascism after the outbreak of the Manchurian Incident in 1931. The Japanese extended their military aggression to bring on war with China in 1937 and with the United States in 1941. That brought the likelihood of war with the Soviet Union also, a war that would mean the end for Japan. In order to prepare for that eventuality, activists in the entire national liberation movement front came to consider the formation of a military and political united front as the most urgent task.

The formation of a united front movement began the establishment of the Korean Anti-Japanese United Front League and developed into a united front party movement in the Korean National Revolutionary Party. After that, Korean militants in Manchuria were reorganized as the Northeastern Anti-Japanese Allied Army, which aimed to form a military united front. The Allied Army then formed the basis for the Korean Fatherland Restoration Association in Manchuria. Moreover, this trend developed in many different ways as seen in the formation of such organs as the Korean National Front League, the Federation of Korean Restoration Movement Organizations, the transformation of the Provisional Government to the united front government through forming the United National United Battle-Line Association, agreement on formation of the united front between the Provisional Government and the Yanan Independence Union, and the change over to a united front line in the movement to re-establish the Korean Communist Party.

The united front movement of the National Foundation League developed as part of the larger effort to form a united national liberation front. The movement continued to develop in the form of co-operation between the 'Provisional Government' and the 'People's Republic' when the danger of national division became apparent after liberation, in the co-operation movement between the Left and the Right, and in the North-South negotiations of 1948.

REFERENCES

Yi Man'gyu, *Yŏ Unhyŏng sŏnsaeng t'ujaengsa* (History of Mr Yŏ Unhyŏng's struggle), Minju munhwasa, 1946.

Hanguk yŏksa yŏn'guhoe (ed.), *Ilcheha sahoejuŭi undongsa* (Socialist movement under Japanese imperialism), Seoul: Hangilsa, 1991.

Han'guk kŭnhyŏndae sahoe yŏn'guhoe (ed.), *Ilche mal Chosŏn sahoe wa minjok haebang undong* (Korean society and the National Liberation Movement at the end of the Japanese imperialist period), Seoul: Ilsongjŏng, 1991.

Chi Sugŏl, *Ilcheha nongmin chohap undong yŏngu* (A study of the Peasant Union Movement under Japanese imperialism), Seoul: Yŏksa pip'yŏngsa, 1993.

Chŏng Pyŏngjun, 'Chosŏn Kŏn'guk tongmaeng ŭi chojik kwa hwaltong' (The organization and activities of the Korean National Foundation League), *Han'guksa yŏn'gu* (Journal of Korean History), 80, Seoul: Han'guksa yŏn'guhoe, 1993.

Im Kyŏngsŏk, 'Chosŏn kongsandang chaegŏn undong' (The re-establishment movement of the Korean Communist Party), *Han'guksa* (History of Korea) 15, Seoul: Hangilsa, 1994.

3

The Realities of Colonial Economic Exploitation

INTRODUCTION

Understanding the structure of the colonial Korean economy is one of the most important keys for grasping the historical nature of the period as a whole. The nature of the colonial economy can generally be summarized in the following five points.

First, the most important goal of colonial agrarian policy was to make Korea a granary for Japan. The first economic policy the Japanese carried out after annexation was the 1910–18 Land Survey. The Land Survey transferred large tracts of agricultural land to Japanese individuals and Japanese institutions. It also established the capitalist principle of exclusive rights to land ownership as a means to facilitate the accumulation of large landholdings. The Japanese, whose agricultural villages had been sacrificed to capitalist progress, thus laid the foundation for Korea to fill the role of Japan's rice bowl. Once they completed the Land Survey, the Japanese next implemented a 'Programme to Increase Rice Production' in the 1920s. The Government-General encouraged Japanese individuals and companies to amass large landholdings while guaranteeing high profits from rice production, thus increasing the production of rice for export to Japan. In the 1930s, the Japanese, responding to the devastation of Korea's rural communities and the rise of the revolutionary peasant movement, sponsored the so-called Rural Revitalization Campaign in hopes of mollifying the peasants and preventing problems in food supplies. After they provoked war with China in 1937 and with the US in 1941, the Japanese forced Koreans to supply foodstuffs to the Government-General through their Rice Collection system.

Second, colonial agrarian policy maintained and strengthened the landlord system, thereby transforming owner-cultivator peasants and part-owner/part-tenant peasants to pure tenants and even forcing large numbers of peasants off the land. The demise of owner-cultivators and part-owner part-tenants led to the division of the agrarian population into two classes, landlords and tenants, and hindered the growth of an agrarian middle class. Furthermore, the strengthening of the landlord system and the forcing of peasants off the land created a large pool of cheap labour for use in Japan's wars of aggression. The continuous and dramatic internal social differentiation of the peasant class and the limited development of commercial agriculture did not, however, result in the growth of an agrarian bourgeoisie. On the contrary, it constituted a process of the strengthening of the old landlord-tenant system. This reveals the true nature of colonial economic history and, indeed, of the history of the colonial period as a whole.

Third, from 1930 onwards, the colonial economy began to move beyond the agriculture-centred system of the 1910s and 1920s as the Government-General pursued a policy of developing Korea as a logistics base for Japan's military aggression against Manchuria and China. This industrial development, however, was limited by the structural defects inherent to the colonial economy. At the time of annexation, Japan's *zaibatsu* (conglomerates) were not in a position to penetrate Korea. This was partly because the *zaibatsu* had not yet reached the stage where they could export significant amounts of capital, but also because Korea still did not have the kind of infrastructure needed for industrial development. As a consequence, in its early years the Government-General devoted a large portion of its budget to the development of such facilities as railroads, roads and harbours. By the 1930s, Japanese monopolistic capital, seeking a way to overcome the depression, began to penetrate the colony to take advantage of Korea's cheap labour and natural resources. The consequent industrial development in Korea was centred on war industries, completely controlled by Japanese monopoly capital and almost totally unrelated to the development of native Korean capital and technology. In short, it showed the typical colonial features of concentration, uneven development and maldistribution.

Fourth, despite constant hindrance from Japanese policies, Korean capital experienced a limited degree of growth in small and medium businesses in the 1920s. The fascist economic policies of the 1930s, however, resulted in the total subjugation of what few Korean large capitalists there were. Furthermore, even small and medium Korean capitalists were incorporated into the wartime economic regime in the late 1930s and early 1940s. By the end of the colonial period, there was no national capital to provide financial support for the national liberation movement – indeed there was no way for Korean capital to survive without compromising with colonial rule.

Fifth, the colonial period, especially in the earlier years, featured a process of primitive accumulation in which the Korean peasants were dispossessed of the land that was their means of production. The resulting accumulation of capital, however, was not linked to the formation of national capital. On the contrary, it provided the underpinnings for the development of Japanese capitalism. The people who were victimized in the process of primitive accumulation were Korean peasants. Those who profited were the Japanese imperialists who gained huge profits from the Land Survey, the building of railways, and the development of mining and fishery resources. Because these resources were not available for the formation of national capital, Korean capitalism after liberation had to start with virtually no capital or technology.

SECTION ONE

Colonial Agricultural Policies and the Ruin of the Peasant Economy

THE LAND SURVEY

Once they had gained complete colonial rule over Korea, the Japanese conducted their cadastral Land Survey as one of the first steps in establishing a colonial economic system. The Government-General of Korea established the Provisional Land Survey Bureau and promulgated the Land Survey Ordinance in September 1910, one month after 'annexation'. On the pretext of establishing a modern land ownership system, the Japanese spent over twenty million yen on an eight-year survey of land ownership, land prices, land forms and land classification.

The Government-General claimed that the purpose of the survey was to establish exclusive capitalist ownership rights that recognized only one owner for one piece of land. However, private ownership of land had already existed before Korea was opened up to the outside world in 1876. Furthermore, during the open port years from 1876 to colonization in 1910, the Chosŏn court took steps to set up a system of 'modern' ownership rights based on pre-existing private ownership as a means to establish a landlord-centred capitalist system.

The Land Survey by the Government-General of Korea can perhaps be understood as the completion of the 'modern' legal process. The Japanese, however, did not engage in a thorough examination of traditional private ownership. In particular, they did not recognize or provide any compensation for such things as the permanent tenancy rights that had constituted a form of partial ownership. Moreover, the Government-General seized the lands of the old Korean royal household along with other land, such as the post station fields, that had been used to support Korean government agencies. The Government-General also took possession of some formerly royal land that had passed into private ownership, along with land that had been commended to the court or land that was mixed in with royal land. At the same time, influential persons took advantage of the situation to establish private ownership of lands that had been held in common by villages or clans. The 'Land Survey' produced intense ownership disputes, particularly in relation to state-owned lands. There was a total of roughly 100,000 disputes, 99.7% of which were disputes in ownership; 65% of those related to lands that had been appropriated by the Government-General. Such disputes notwithstanding, about 135,000 *chŏngbo* (1 *chŏngbo* = 2.45 acres = 1 hectare) of post station lands and over 46,000 *chŏngbo* of privately held land reverted to the Government-General.

The Government-General's Land Survey had a variety of effects. It enabled the Government-General to seize large amounts of land and dealt a devastating blow to Korean peasants. But most importantly, it produced a great increase in revenue from land taxes, thus providing the financial basis for colonial rule. The revenue from land taxes nearly doubled between 1910 and 1918, from 6,000,000 to 11,569,000 yen. The increase in land tax revenues represented a newly heavy burden on the peasants of Korea who also had to pay other new taxes, such as a special household tax and a residency tax.

The Land Survey resulted in a rapid increase in Japanese landholdings in Korea. As seen in Table 1 below, the number of Japanese landowners and the amount of Japanese investments in Korean land more than tripled during the first six years of the Land Survey while the amount of land they owned more than doubled. The acquisition of land by the Government-General, the Oriental Development Company and Japanese individuals meant a corresponding loss of land by Koreans. The main victims of the Japanese land grab were not Korean landlords, but small owner-cultivators and part-owner/part-tenant peasants.

Table 2 shows the effects of colonial land policy on the rural population. The percentage of landlords increased somewhat during the years of the Land Survey, then held steady thereafter. On the other hand, the percentage of small holder owner-cultivators and part-owner/part-tenants declined steadily. This tells us that the landlords continued to increase their holdings at the expense of self-cultivators and part-owner/part-tenants who were forced into pure tenancy.

The development of commercial agriculture in Korea after the opening of the ports in 1876 had allowed some degree of growth in the numbers of self-cultivators and the upper stratum of part-owner/part tenants. The possibility that they might have developed into a rural bourgeoisie, however, was forestalled by the way in which the Land Survey resulted in owner-cultivators and part-owner-tenants being forced into tenancy.

THE PROGRAMME TO INCREASE RICE PRODUCTION

Having completed their Land Survey during the period of military rule in the 1910s, the Japanese imperialists implemented a new colonial agricultural policy in the 1920s. This was their 'Programme to Increase Rice Production'. This programme, coming on the heels of the Land Survey, represented the concrete realization of Japan's original plan to make Korea a permanent base of food supplies.

The Japanese domestic situation forced the colonial authorities to move quickly. The rapid growth of Japanese monopoly capitalism during

Table 1: Japanese agrarian management (Investment, 1000 yen; land, *chŏngbo*)

Year	Owners	Investment	Paddies	Dry Fields	Forest	Undeveloped	Other	Total
1910	2,254	13,737	42,584	26,727	13,867		3,773	86,951
1911	3,839	12,473	58,004	35,377	10,278	8,918	13,573	126,110
1912	4,938	29,662	68,376	39,605	8,254	9,407	5,156	130,798
1913	5,916	36,671	89,624	60,403	17,870	6,415	9,933	184,245
1914	6,049	38,820	96,345	63,517	19,414	9,213	9,446	197,935
1915	6,949	45,587	108,742	62,311	17,499	8,958	8,027	205,537

Source: Kobayakawa Kuro, ed. *Chosen nogyo hattatsu shi, Hattatsu hen* (History of Korean Agricultural Development, Development Volume), p. 592.

Table 2: Change in ratios of agrarian household types, 1916–1932

Year	Landlords	Owner-cultivators	Part-owner/ Part-tenants	Tenants
1916	2.5	20.1	40.6	36.8
1917	2.8	19.6	40.2	37.4
1918	3.4	19.6	39.3	37.7
1919	3.4	19.7	39.3	37.6
1920	3.3	19.5	37.4	39.8
1921	3.6	19.6	36.6	40.2
1922	3.7	19.7	35.8	40.8
1923	3.7	19.5	35.2	41.6
1924	3.8	19.5	34.5	42.2
1925	3.8	19.9	33.2	43.1
1926	3.8	19.1	32.5	43.4
1927	3.8	18.7	32.7	43.8
1928	3.7	18.3	32.0	44.9
1929	3.8	18.0	31.4	45.6
1930	3.6	17.6	31.0	46.5
1931	3.6	17.0	29.6	48.4
1932	3.5	16.3	25.4	52.7

Source: Chosen sotokufu norinkyoku ed. *Chosen kosaku nenbo* (An Annual Report of Tenant Farming in Korea) vol. 1, pp. 148–49 (excludes slash and burn peasants).

the years of the First World War brought destitution to the Japanese masses, particularly in rural areas. This resulted in a sharp drop in agricultural production which in turn led to large-scale food riots. The urgency of the situation meant that the Japanese imperialists had to force increased production of foodstuffs in Korea in order to secure a reliable source of foodstuff supplies. The foundation for making Korea a base for Japan's foodstuffs was laid with the Land Survey.

In the 1920s, the Japanese imperialists faced a number of problems, including the needs to secure foodstuffs, to maintain low wages and to win over Korean landlords in order to deal with the crisis in colonial rule resulting from the March First Movement. Furthermore, they needed to invest the excess capital accumulated during the war. Rather than investing in the Korean industrial sector, which still did not meet basic conditions for investment, the Japanese chose to invest in the agricultural sector, primarily in large-scale irrigation projects and regularization of arable land. This allowed them to rake in greater profits through high-interest loans to rural credit unions and irrigation co-operatives.

The Programme to Increase Rice Production called for the improvement, over a period of thirty years, of a total of 800,000 *chŏngbo* of land: irrigation improvements for 400,000 *chŏngbo* of paddies; conversion of 200,000 *chŏngbo* of dry fields to paddies; and the creation of 200,000 *chŏngbo* of new paddies. For the first fifteen years, the Japanese planned to invest 168 million yen to improve approximately 427,000 *chŏngbo* of land and to increase rice production by 9.2 million *sŏm* (5.12 bushels), of which 7 million was to be taken to Japan.

The plan was not carried out as envisioned. The plan called for work to begin on a total of 165,000 *chŏngbo* and to be completed on 123,100 *chŏngbo* by 1925. By that year, however, work had begun on only 97,500 *chŏngbo* (59% of the target) and had been completed on only 76,000 *chŏngbo* (62% of the target). This forced the Japanese to revise their plan. The new plan called for the improvement of 350,000 *chŏngbo* between the years of 1926 and 1934, but work was completed on only 165,000 *chŏngbo* (47% of the target). One important reason for the slow progress was the cost of funds. Nearly 42% of the budget came from funds borrowed at high interest rates from private businesses.

The Government-General attributed the slow progress of the Programme to a number of problems, including the lack of a general survey for irrigation construction, the weakness of the agricultural financial system and difficulties in borrowing funds. The most fundamental reason, however, was that it was far more profitable to purchase existing farmland and rent it out at high rates than it was to improve marginal land or reclaim new land. Japanese capitalists showed little interest in the plan – they were much more concerned with accumulating farmlands. Even in 1924, a year that saw a fall in grain prices, rice farming, with an annual return of 13%, was more profitable than certificates of deposit which returned only 7.9%. Furthermore, even the irrigation work that was the central project of the Programme to Increase Rice Production, resulted in accelerating landholding by the Japanese rather than increasing rice production through land improvements.

Another reason why the Programme did not progress as planned was that the programme itself was not established on the basis of a full understanding of the agrarian situation in Korea. It was planned around the interests of the Government-General and Japanese capitalists and landlords without the participation of Korean peasants. Thus it ran into strong opposition from the peasants. The land improvement work focused on large-scale irrigation projects, and little was done to provide the kind of small-scale land improvements that might have helped the peasants. The irrigation co-operatives benefited a few large landlords, but damaged all other peasants. That led to the rise of a broad movement in opposition to the irrigation cooperatives.

The main reason why the Programme to Increase Rice Production was completely stopped in 1934 was that imported Korean rice was driving the Japanese rural economy to ruin during the depression. Other reasons included increasing numbers of defunct irrigation co-operatives and strong opposition movements by the Korean peasants.

Although the Programme to Increase Rice Production was not implemented as originally planned, the Japanese did enjoy considerable success in their original goal of securing food supplies for Japan. The amount of rice production increased 36% between 1920 and 1928, the highest year, as shown in Table 3 below. In the same time frame, the

Table 3: Production, export, and per capita consumption of korean rice (Unit: *sŏm*)

Year	Yield	Export	Per capita Korean	Per capita Japanese
1920	12,708,000	1,750,000	0.63	1.12
1921	14,882,000	3,080,000	0.67	1.15
1922	14,324,000	3,316,000	0.63	1.10
1923	15,014,000	3,624,000	0.65	1.15
1924	15,174,000	4,722,000	0.60	1.12
1925	13,219,000	4,619,000	0.52	1.13
1926	14,773,000	5,429,000	0.53	1.13
1927	15,300,000	6,136,000	0.52	1.09
1928	17,298,000	7,405,000	0.54	1.13
1929	13,511,000	5,609,000	0.45	1.11
1930	13,511,000	5,426,000	0.45	1.18

Source: Chosen beikoku yoran (An Outline of Korean Rice)

amount of rice exported to Japan increased by more than 400%, from 1.75 million *sŏm* to 7.405 million *sŏm*.

The Programme to Increase Rice Production resulted in a rate of increase in Korean rice exports to Japan that was higher than the rate of increase of rice production. The consequence was a decrease in the consumption of rice and an increase of the consumption of other, less-favoured grains by Korean peasants. The per capita consumption of rice by Koreans decreased more than 28% from 0.63 *sŏm* to 0.45 *sŏm* during the first ten years of the programme, falling to less than half the consumption by Japanese. What the Koreans ate instead was hulled millet, imported from Manchuria in increasing amounts.

The Programme not only increased the export of Korean rice to Japan, it also accelerated the accumulation of large landholdings by Japanese and some Korean landlords. This led to the demise of many Korean small-to-medium landlords, owner-cultivators and poor peasants. The irrigation co-operatives that were the centrepiece of the Programme were dominated by a small number of great landlords (over 53% of Korea's total farmland was controlled by the 2% of landlords who owned over 10 *chŏngbo*). Those great landlords managed the irrigation co-operatives for their own benefit and rarely took into consideration the interests of ordinary peasants. The consequence was that small-to-medium landlords, owner-cultivators and poor peasants lost their lands because of excessive irrigation co-operative fees and because of the pressure or fraudulent actions of co-operative leaders. An example of this is the change in landholdings in five irrigation associations in North Chŏlla Province between 1920 and 1931: the number of Japanese landlords doubled and their holdings increased nearly 250% while the number of Korean landholders, including owner-cultivators, decreased 5.8%, and their holdings shrank by 15.2%.

The Programme to Increase Rice Production had a number of negative effects for the Korean rural economy. First, although the Programme did result in some increase in the production of rice, all of the increase, plus more, went to Japan, leaving Koreans to eat less favoured grains, mostly millet brought in from Manchuria. Second, large numbers of Koreans, including small-scale landlords and owner-cultivators, lost their lands because of the high fees of the Programme's irrigation co-operatives. Third, the Japanese demand for rice transformed Korean agriculture into a single-crop economy. The consequence was that Korea's villages, having been incorporated by Japan into a regional north-east Asian economy, were hit particularly hard by the world-wide agrarian depression that set in at the end of 1920s. The ensuing years saw the majority of Korean peasants reduced to absolute penury.

THE REALITIES OF PEASANT DESTITUTION

Colonial agrarian policies and the agrarian depression beginning at the end of the 1920s brought disaster to the Korean rural population. The concrete course of this process was downward. Owner-cultivators and part-owners/part-tenants became pure tenants, pure tenants became slash-and-burn or poor peasants, and those latter unfortunates became wanderers or were reduced to beggary.

According to the statistics of the Government-General of Korea in 1925, 46.6% of all peasant households had incomes of less than 12 yen per year and were falling into debt. According to 1926 statistics, poor peasants totaled about 2.15 million, or 11% of the total population, while beggars numbered about 10,000. Statistics from 1931 show that poor peasants increased to about 5.2 million, or 25% of the total population, while the number of beggars increased to 160,000. Three-quarters of tenants were in debt, with the average amount of debt per household about 65 yen.

The majority of peasants who were reduced to absolute poverty as a result of colonial policies had no choice but to leave their villages. In 1925, for example, the number of peasants who left their homes was over 150,000, and the rural exodus accelerated thereafter. Many of the peasants forced off their lands fled deep into the mountains to engage in slash-and-burn agriculture or, in the worst case, became beggars. Others flowed into labour markets in Japan, Manchuria and Siberia, or gathered in cities inside Korea in search of jobs where they came to be known as dugout dwellers.

In the Chosŏn period, there had also been slash-and-burn fields, but those were generally found only in limited areas near villages. After colonization, however, rapidly increasing numbers of persons victimized by the agrarian policies of the Japanese imperialists became slash-and-burn peasants, many of who went deep into the mountains. Statistics from the end of 1928 indicate that the total number of slash-and-burn peasants, including both those who cultivated only slash-and-burn fields and those who cultivated both slash-and-burn and regular fields was

1.2 million. That number represented 8% of Korea's 15 million peasants and 6.3% of the country's entire population. The slash-and-burn peasants, particularly those living deep in the mountains, led a very primitive life. After the Government-General prohibited slash-and-burn farming on the grounds of forest conservancy, many of those unfortunates left Korea for Manchuria.

The population that departed villages because of the absolute poverty and flowed into labour markets in Japan and Manchuria increased year by year. In the 1930s, over 100,000 persons went to Japan each year. Although no small number of those migrants failed to find jobs and returned to Korea, the overall numbers of cheap Korean workers continued to increase in Japan. Among the Koreans who were in Japan in 1932, 48% were employed, 35% were jobless, and 5% were merchants. Among those with jobs, menial construction labourers accounted for one-third and factory workers another third. Very few of those employed in factories were skilled workers – the vast majority worked at odd jobs.

Wage levels of the Korean workers were very low compared to those of Japanese workers. According to Osaka City statistics, the maximum wage of Japanese miners was three yen per day while that of Korean miners was two yen and thirty sen. In the case of textile workers, the maximum wage of Japanese workers was two yen and eighty sen while that of Korean workers was two yen. Most Koreans in Japan barely managed to survive, engaging in physical labour and suffering severe discrimination.

Even before the colonial period, indigent Koreans had been flowing into Manchuria and the Maritime Provinces, but their numbers increased sharply after colonization. In the 1930s, it is estimated that there were roughly one million Koreans in Manchuria and another half-million in the Maritime Provinces. Nine out ten were tenant farmers. Farm rents there were somewhat cheaper than in Korea, ranging generally from 25% to 50% of harvests. The Koreans in Manchuria, however, were subject to a variety of special taxes levied by Chinese prefectural governments, including special household and per capita taxes imposed only on Koreans. Despite these burdens, the Korean community in Manchuria provided an economic base for armed struggle by contributing money to such national liberation movement organizations as the Just Administration, the New People's Administrations and the Administration of Councillors.

Not all Koreans who lost their land went overseas. A substantial number gathered in urban areas inside Korea in hopes of finding a way to make a living. Because of the limited capacity of colonial industry to absorb labour power, the vast majority ended up as day labourers, finding shelter in dugouts they made on the outskirts of cities. Most of the dugout dwellers struggled to earn money as A-frame porters or ragpickers. They were barely able to keep themselves and their families alive. The typical family of four or five lived in a dugout slightly bigger than one *p'yŏng* (about 3.3m^2) with no furniture or bedding and only the barest of clothing. Seoul City statistics indicate that in 1931 there were about 5,000 dugout dwellers in over 1,500 households, but by 1939 the number had increased to over 20,000 in 4,200 households. The numbers of dugout dwellers also increased continuously in other cities, such as Pusan, Inch'ŏn, P'yŏngyang and Chinnamp'o.

Although Korea's peasants were continuously forced off the land by the colonial agrarian policies of the Japanese imperialists, colonial industry did not develop the capacity to absorb them as industrial workers. The result was the making of the so-called Three Poor Classes: impoverished peasants, slash-and-burn peasants and dugout dwellers. These people were the true products of Japan's colonial policies.

THE RURAL REVITALIZATION CAMPAIGN AND POLICIES TO PLACATE THE PEASANTS

The 1920s' implementation of the Programme to Increase Rice Production, which resulted in the concentration of lands in a few great landlords and the absolute impoverishment of many middle and poor peasants, induced the impoverished peasants to engage in struggles against the colonial agricultural administrations. In the 1930s, therefore, the Government-General of Korea found it necessary to pursue conciliatory policies in order to drag the middle and poor peasants into the colonial ruling system.

The early-1930s saw frequent tenancy disputes and the spread of the revolutionary peasant union movement, developments that posed a threat to the colonial ruling system. The Japanese imperialists had no choice but to try to correct the irrationality of the landlord-tenant system. Because of the connection between tenancy disputes and the socialist movement, the Japanese launched their Rural Revitalization Campaign in 1932 as an anti-communist agrarian policy. Features of the Campaign included elimination of springtime hunger, forgiveness of debts and prevention of indebtedness. Another factor behind the Campaign was that the 1920s policy of agricultural-centred exploitation had reached its limits. By the early-1930s Japanese capital began to move away from agricultural land in pursuit of more profitable investments and more marketable commodities. Therefore, the Japanese had no choice but to abandon the landlord-based, agriculture-centred development policy of the 1920s.

The main themes of the revitalization policy were to curb, to some degree, the spread of landlordism and to stabilize the smallholder system. The Japanese had already begun moving in that direction in the home islands, enacting the so-called 'Regulations for the Establishment of Owner-Cultivators' and a 'Tenant Ordinance' in the second half of the 1920s. In Korea, however, the Government-General was forced into action by the devastation of the peninsula's rural villages by the Great Depression that set in in 1929 and the subsequent spread of the revolutionary peasant union movement.

In order to contain the peasant movement, the Japanese promulgated the 1932 Korean Tenancy Arbitration Ordinance aimed at preventing tenancy disputes through judicial mediation. Two years later, in 1934, the Japanese enacted the Agricultural Lands Ordinance with the objective of 'stabilizing the position of tenants and improving productivity of tenant lands in the spirit of harmony between landlords and tenants'. This ordinance established some degree of control over high rents and also provided legal means for tenants to seek reductions in rents in times of crop failure. With this, the Government-General planned to provide security of tenancy and to increase agricultural production as means to placate the peasants and control rural communities at a time when Japan was expanding its aggression on the East Asian continent.

The Government-General also began a 'Project for the Creation and Maintenance of Owner-Cultivators' as a more active policy of fostering self-cultivating peasants. The Project provided loans for peasants to buy land through loans from the Government-General, from credit unions and from peasant associations. The goals were 'to revitalize agrarian communities, which were in need of ideological and economic stability, and to prevent peasants from abandoning their villages and becoming vagrants'.

The average loan amount was 660 yen, with a maximum of 1,000 yen for a standard area of 4 *tanbo* (1 *tanbo* = 0.245 acres) of paddies and 1 *tanbo* of dry fields per household. But continuous increases in land prices, along with tax increases, kept the Project from progressing as planned. Furthermore, the landlords were not in financial distress and had no incentive to sell land to the peasants.

The devastation that swept Korea's rural villages in the 1930s threatened the colonial ruling system. This forced the Japanese imperialists to take measures to provide political, ideological and economic stability for villagers and landlords. This was also in accord with the demands of Japanese monopoly capital's industrialization of colonial Korea and who promoted the industrialization of colonial Korea and the invasion of the continent.

THE RICE COLLECTION SYSTEM

After their military aggression extended to wars with China and the US, the Japanese found it necessary to intensify their appropriation of the Korean peasants' agricultural products. This eventually took the concrete form of the Rice Collection System. The Japanese, under a wartime regime after the outbreak of hostilities with China in 1937, revived the Programme to Increase Rice Production in 1939 in response to increased food demand, but failed to achieve the expected results. The Japanese then implemented a number of more aggressive long-term measures in order to increase food supplies, including the 1940 Plan to Renew Increased Rice Production in Korea and the 1941 Provisional Farmland Management Ordinance through which they secured the absolute quantity of land.

The Government-General began to carry out a full-scale food-control policy in 1939, when it promulgated the Korean Rice Market Stock Company Ordinance and the Korean Rice Rationing Mediation Ordinance. In 1940 the Japanese adopted the Rice Collection System which compelled each farm household to sell rice to the Government-General at a set 'fair price'. The Japanese also implemented a food-rationing system by establishing Food Rationing Co-operatives and applying Provisional Rice Rationing Regulations.

The Japanese proclaimed that the Rice Collection System was to be based on the principle that rice collection would be done on a voluntary basis for a fair price in regions that produced surplus rice. In the beginning, it was applied to rents collected by landlords. After the outbreak of war with the US, however, worsening financial and food supply situations led the Government-General to promulgate the 1943 Korean Food Management Ordinance that forced all peasants to deliver all the rice they produced except what they needed for their own households. Furthermore, the Collection System was also applied to other grains, making it impossible for the direct producers to find any way to survive outside the Collection System.

In order to counter strong peasant resistance to the forced collection of grains, the Government-General used subsidies and price guarantees to establish a dual price system for rice by which it fixed producer costs at a higher rate than consumer costs. It also tried to placate the peasants through such strategies as special distributions of daily necessities. Wartime inflation, however, diluted the value of the subsidy. Furthermore, the Government-General forced the peasants to save part of the payments and subsidies they received, leading them to rebel against the system. In order to suppress peasant resistance and secure food supplies, the Government-General resorted to such coercive measures as the Village Collection Responsibility System the Prearranged Quota System and the Agricultural Production Responsibility System.

The Government-General gave broad authority to the peasant associations, organizations that were intimately familiar with peasant household situations. The associations assigned a quota to each household which they then extracted by mobilizing administrative and police authority and by forcing peasants to report on each other. Because of this, by the end of war the Korean peasants were on the verge of starvation.

Table 4 below shows the percentages of total harvests seized by the Government-General through its Rice Collection System, put into practice in 1940 and subsequently expanded to include other grains.

The basic agrarian policy that the Japanese planned while colonizing Korea was to set up Korea as a permanent base of food supplies for Japan. It was for that purpose that the Japanese reinforced the landlord system in the colony. In general, both the Land Survey and the Programme for Increased Rice Production were policies designed to accomplish this goal. Although the Japanese proclaimed that the Rural Revitalization Campaign and the Agricultural Lands Ordinance were actions taken to protect the livelihoods of the tenants, in reality they were measures taken to secure Korean villages as a stable base of food supplies. In addition, those policies were put into operation in order to check the revolutionary peasant union movement. Even these policies of the early 1930s were

Table 4: Production and collection of rice and barley (unit: thousand *sŏm*)

Year	Harvest		Quota		Collection		Collection as % of yield
	Rice	Barley	Rice	Barley	Rice	Barley	
1940	21,527	8,565	–	2,674	9,208	1,699	42.8
1941	24,886	7,305	–	2,853	11,255	1,329	45.2
1942	15,687	6,323	9,119	1,638	8,750	1,593	55.8
1943	18,719	8,142	11,956	3,221	11,957	3,067	63.9
1944	16,051	–	10,541	–	9,634	–	60.0

Source: Pak Kyŏngsik. *Nihon teikokushugi no Chosen sihai* (Imperial Japan's Rule over Korea), Vol. II, Tokyo: Aoki shoten, 1973, p. 193.

all but discarded during the war years when such exploitative policies as the Rice Collection System were enforced.

REFERENCES

Miyada Sekko, '1930 nendai Niteika Chosen ni okeru "noson shinko undo" no tenkai' (Development of the rural Revitalization campaign in Korea of the 1930s under Japanese imperialism), *Rekishigaku kenkyu* (Journal of Historical Studies), 297, 1965.

Saijo Akira, '1920 nendai Chosen ni okeru mizuri kumiai hantai undo' (Struggles against the Irrigation Association in Korea of the 1920s), *Chosenshi kenkyukai ronbunshu* (Bulletin of the Society for Korean Historical Study), 8, 1971.

Kim Yongsŏp, *Hanguk kŭndae nongŏpsa yŏngu* (A study of the agrarian history of modern Korea), Seoul: Ilchogak, 1975.

Miyajima Hiroshi, '"Tochi chosa jigyo" no rekishiteki zentei joken no keisei' (Formation of historical preconditions of the 'Land Survey'), *Chosenshi kenkyukai ronbunshu* (Bulletin of the Society for Korean Historical Study), 12, 1975.

Sin Yongha, *Hanguk Toji josa saŏp yŏngu* (A study of the Land Survey in Korea), Seoul: Hanguk yŏnguwŏn, 1979.

Kang Man-gil, *Ilche sidae pinmin saenghwalsa yŏn'gu* (Studies in the lives of the poor during the period of Japanese imperialism), Seoul: Ch'angjak kwa pip'yŏngsa, 1987.

Ch'oe Yuri, 'Ilche malgi 'Chosŏn chŭngmi kyehoek' e taehan yŏngu' (A study of the 'Programme to Increase Rice Production in Korea'), *Hanguksa yŏngu* (Studies of Korean History), volume 61–62, Seoul: Hanguksa yŏn'guhoe, 1988.

Chŏn Kangsu, 'Chŏnsi ch'ejeha Chosŏn e issŏsŏŭi migok chŏngch'aek e kwanhan Yŏn'gu' (A study of rice policy in Korea under the wartime system), *Kyŏngjesahak* (Economic History), 14, 1990.

Chi Sugŏl, '1932–35 nyŏn ŭi Chosŏn nongch'on chinhŭng undong' (The rural revitalization campaign in Korea between 1932 and 1935), *Hanguksa yŏngu* (Studies of Korean History), 46, Seoul: Hanguksa yŏnguhoe, 1984.

Chŏng Yŏnt'ae, '1930 nyŏndae Chosŏn nongjiryŏng kwa Ilche ŭi nongch'on t'ongje' (The Korean Agricultural Lands Ordinance and the Japanese imperialists' control over agrarian communities), *Yŏksa wa hyŏnsil* (History and Reality), 4, Seoul: Hanguk yŏksa yŏn'guhoe, 1990.

Chŏng Yŏnt'ae, '1930 nyŏndae 'Chajangnong ch'angjŏng saŏp e kwanhan yŏngu' (A study of the 'Project of Creating Self-Cultivators' in the 1930s), *Han'guksa ron* (Korean History), 26, 1991.

Chŏng T'aehŏn, '1930 nyŏndae singminji nongŏp chŏngch'aek ŭi sŏngkyŏk chŏnhwan e kwanhan yŏn'gu' (A study of changes in the nature of colonial agrarian policies during the 1930s), *Ilchemal Chosŏn sahoe wa minjok haebang undong* (Korean society and the National Liberation Movement at the End of Japanese imperialism), Seoul: Ilsongjŏng, 1991.

Yi Songsun, 'Ilche malgi chŏnsi ch'ejeha Chosŏn esŏŭi migok kongch'ul kwa nongch'on kyŏngje ŭi pyŏnhwa' (Rice collection and change in the agrarian economy in Korea under the wartime regime system at the end of Japanese imperialism), M.A. Thesis, Korea University, Seoul, 1992.

SECTION TWO

Colonial Government Finances and the Reality of Financial Policies

EXPLOITATIVE FINANCES

After colonizing Korea, the Japanese abolished the old Chosŏn dynasty system of taxation and replaced it with a capitalist system. They established two main categories of taxes: national taxes and local taxes. The national taxes that the Government-General collected included direct and indirect taxes. The direct taxes were taxes on income and on profits. The indirect taxes were transportation taxes and consumption taxes. The local taxes that were collected by provinces, prefectures and townships included not only a surtax on national taxes, but also school fees and school association dues.

Government-General revenues mainly consisted of taxes, income from government enterprises and government-owned properties, taxes, and government bonds, along with subsidies provided by the Japanese government to support colonial rule. Income from government enterprises and government-owned properties came primarily from railroads and government monopoly enterprises and accounted for 20 to 30% of total revenue at the beginning of the colonial period. After the tobacco business, which was quite lucrative, became a government monopoly in 1921, the importance of income from government enterprises and government owned properties increased. Once the Government-General cancelled the arrangement through which the South Manchuria Railroad Company managed railroads in Korea in 1925, the income from government enterprises and government-owned properties increased to about 50% of total revenues.

Government bonds and borrowed money formed 10 to 20% of the annual revenue throughout the colonial period. The Government-General borrowed 140 million yen up through 1918, including 45.59 million yen in foreign loans prior to annexation; over 300 million yen between 1919 and 1933; and 2.5 billion yen after 1933. One particular cause of the dramatic increase in government borrowing was the excessive issuing of war bonds after 1933. Most of the 3 billion yen borrowed after 1933 came from capital markets in Japan or through the Savings Section of the Treasury Ministry.

The funds obtained from bonds and loans were used to lay the foundations for the management of the colony and for the penetration of Korea by Japanese capital. Over 70% of those funds went to the railroads while another 10% went to the construction of roads, harbours, and telegraph and telephone lines. Profits from the railroads along totalled over three billion yen, more than enough to cover both principal and interest.

Over 469 million yen of subsidies were brought in from the home government in Japan throughout the colonial period. Although subsidies accounted for more than 20% of total annual revenue in the early years, they gradually declined to the point where they had little significance. They were primarily to provide colonial-duty allowances for Japanese officials in Korea, an amount that was 40% greater than their counterparts in Japan received. Other uses included general expenses, iron manufacture, increased coal production and recovery from flood damages.

The amount of subsidies paled in significance in comparison with the amount of compulsory savings enforced by the Government-General after the outbreak of war with China – compulsory savings between 1938 and 1940 totalled approximately 650 million yen. Although the total value of public and private bonds held by Korean financial organs was at least ten billion yen, the bonds turned to worthless scraps of paper when the Second World War came to an end.

Throughout the colonial period, pure tax income formed 20% of total revenue, but the amount of taxes collected increased 42.3 times between 1911 and 1943 in Korea while increasing 36.2 times during the same time frame in Japan. The total revenue of the colonial government increased from 5.2 million yen to 1.88 billion yen between 1911 and 1943.

The colony was no exception to the general trend of development-tax systems, which meant institutional changes resulting in increasingly effective tax exploitation following the developmental stages of capitalism. In the 1910s, taxes on profits, mostly the land tax, formed the main source of tax revenues. In the 1920s, consumption taxes, particularly on such items as liquor, tobacco and sugar, became the mainstay. From the mid-1930s, income taxes, including taxes on corporations, interest earnings and individual incomes constituted a major source of revenue.

The 1910s, up to the time of the 1919 March First Movement can be understood as a transitional period in the formation of a capitalist financial structure. The revenue from land taxes decreased from 64% to 33% of the total internal revenue between 1910 and 1918. The promulgation of the Korean Land Tax Ordinance in 1914 and the revision of the Land Tax Ordinance in 1918 represented important steps in establishing a system of taxation based on the capitalist principle of exclusive ownership. The liquor and tobacco taxes, consumption taxes that the Japanese imposed in 1909, were less important. However, once the Japanese prohibited small-scale production, including production for self-consumption, of tobacco and liquor in order to promote their production by large-scale capital interests, taxable consumption of those commodities increased.

The period from the occurrence of the March First Movement to the second revision of the tax system in 1934 can be seen as the formation period of capitalist finance. Land taxes shrank to the range of 20% to 32% of total revenues, much lower than it the 1910s. Export duties were annulled in 1919 and import duties were either abolished or reduced in accordance with the interests of Japanese capital.

While land-tax revenue was decreasing in importance, consumption-tax receipts, primarily those on liquor and sugar, increased rapidly while tobacco, a lucrative source, was converted to a state monopoly in 1921. Liquor taxes accounted for 11% of pure tax receipts in 1920 and increased to over 30% by the mid-1930s. Consumption taxes were a product of the development of a capitalist economy and a typical form of regressive taxation which imposed a heavy burden on the proletariat masses.

The Japanese, through their First Tax Reform of 1927, put the implementation of a general income tax system on hold, and instead improved their collection of taxes on profits. The essential elements of the reform were the development of new tax sources, the creation of a business tax, the levying of taxes on interest income and raising the tax on liquor. There were two main reasons why the Government-General decided to delay the implementation of a general income tax. One was that the colonial economic system had not yet developed to the point where the Government-General could ascertain individual incomes. The other was a reluctance to impose an income tax on the propertied classes, especially the landlords, at a time when the Government-General was pushing its Programme to Increase Rice Production.

The time from the implementation of the Second Tax Reform in 1934 to the defeat of Japanese imperialism in 1945 was the 'period of development' of the capitalist financial system in order to lay down the foundations for long-term colonial exploitation. This period saw the reduction of land taxes from 20.2% in 1933 to 3.5% in 1942. The wartime restrictions on consumption also resulted in a downward trend in consumption-tax receipts. The difference was made up by an income tax that was mainly imposed on landlords and capitalists.

The years between the late-1920s and the Second Tax Reform of 1934 that implemented a general income tax system, was a complex transitional period that saw such developments as the spread of the labour and peasant movements inside Korea, the rise of a united front movement and of armed struggle in the national liberation front overseas, and the invasion of Manchuria as an effort to resolve the contradictions in Japanese capitalism. At the time, Japanese capitalism felt the urgent need to wean the Korean masses away from the influence of the national liberation movement front. Thus, when they reached the limits of exploitation through such sources as the land tax and consumption taxes, they turned instead to an income tax system as a means of dealing with such issues as the gap between rich and poor and the intensification of class antagonisms. That explains why they allowed the Koreans to exclude a relatively high amount of their income from taxes (800 yen versus 1,200 for Japanese) even though the average Korean income was less than one-fifth of that of the average Japanese.

Statistics on tax revenues are available for only the years from 1934 to 1942, but what we have shows that tax exploitation increased six-fold during those eight years. This increase can be attributed to the collection of income taxes which increased nearly 29 times during those years. Increases in income taxes on individuals and income taxes on corporations rose at almost the same rate until 1936. But after Japan invaded China, corporate taxes rose much more sharply than did taxes on individuals. Because the Japanese capitalists in Korea were given special funding and tax exemptions under the wartime regime, the burden fell almost entirely on Korean capitalists.

Another feature of the Second Tax Reform was the independence of the tax administrative organs. Before the introduction of the income tax system, the tax offices were under general administration. The Second Tax Reform brought about the establishment of an independent tax administration because dealing with the complex sources of income taxes required the development of substantial expertise in tax collection and business accounting. Supervisory tax bureaus were established in five locales, including Seoul and P'yŏngyang, while ninety-nine tax offices were set up throughout the rest of the country.

Annual expenditures of the Government-General increased 33.3 times from over 46 million yen to 1,532 million yen between 1911 and 1943 while gross domestic consumption grew only 14.9 times during the same period. General administration and judicial and police expenditures accounted for an average 18.1% of total expenditures throughout the colonial period, but gradually declined over time from 30–40% in the 1910s, to 20–30% between 1920 and 1937, and about 10% after the outbreak of war with China. After the establishment of the wartime regime, expenditures on provisional economic controls and the movement to mobilize the populace increased. The annual expenditures to support the Yi Royal House were 1.5 million yen per year between 1910 and 1920, after which they increased to 1.8 million yen.

The bulk of Government-General expenditures throughout the colonial period went to government enterprises. Those included transportation and communication facilities such as railroads, roads and harbours, as well as monopoly enterprises, forestry and construction. Throughout the colonial period, expenditures on transportation and communication accounted for an average 38.5% of the total annual expenditures of the Government-General, while monopoly enterprises accounted for 7.7%, forestry 1.8% and construction 6.9%. Together, these government enterprises took an average of 55% of total annual Government-General expenses.

During the years from 1917 to 1925, expenditures on government enterprises shrank to between 38% and 44%. This was because railroad management in Korea was consigned to the South Manchuria Railroad Company since 1917. But once the railroads were put back under the direct management of the Government-General of Korea in 1925, expenditures on government enterprises began to grow again. After the outbreak of war with China, the Japanese raised expenditures on government enterprises up to 60%.

Expenditures on the economy averaged 7.4% throughout the colonial period. Major items were expenditures on agriculture such as the Land

Survey, the improvement and expansion of arable land, the Rural Revitalization Campaign, the opening of new lands in northern Korea and measures to increase foodstuff production along with subsidies for private railroads and mining subsidies to encourage the increased production of minerals. During the period from 1910 to 1918, expenditures on the Land Survey accounted for as much as 50% to 60% of total expenditures on the economy. In the early of 1930s, expenditures on farmland improvement reached 30%, and during the1930s before the outbreak of war with China, expenditures on land reclamation projects in northern Korea ranged from 10% to 14% of total expenditures. By 1943, expenditures on farmland improvement and expansion along with various measures to increase foodstuff production swelled to 43%. Grand slogans notwithstanding, expenditures for the Rural Revitalization Campaign were a mere 5.1% of total expenditures in 1942.

Subsidies for the private railroad lines, intended to induce Japanese capital to invest in Korea, constituted, along with investments in farmland improvement and expansion, the major form of expenditures on the economy in the 1920s. Following the promulgation of the Korean Non-Governmental Railroad Line Ordinance in 1920 and the Korean Non-Governmental Railroad Line Support Law in 1921, subsidies for private railroad lines came to form 40% of expenditures on the economy, and continued to account for approximately 30% until the first half of the 1930s. Following the 1937 promulgation of the Korean Gold Mining Ordinance as part of a Five Year Plan for Gold Mining and the 1938 Ordinance for Increased Yields of Major Products in Korea, expenditures to encourage gold mining and to provide price guarantees increased from 37% to 51% of total expenditures on the economy between the years of 1938 and 1940. Government-General support mostly took the forms of subsidies and preferential tax exemptions to such Japanese monopoly enterprises as Mitsui, Mitsubishi and Sumitomo that had been mobilized to develop war materials.

Expenditures on public bonds that were to be paid from internal tax revenues formed and consumed an average 25% of internal revenue throughout the colonial period: 20% in the 1910s, 41% between 1920 and the outbreak of war with China in 1937 and 17.2% thereafter. Meanwhile, expenditures on education averaged only 3% of total outlays throughout the colonial period. It is not clear how much of that money was spent for the Koreans, who numbered over 20 million, and for the Japanese, whose population in Korea was only slightly over 600,000.

The Japanese imperialists even shifted the burden for their war expenses onto the Koreans. Expenditures on military affairs averaged 4.9% of total expenditures throughout the colonial period, but the budget in 1945 called for transferring 23.1% of the total annual expenditures to special accounts for provisional military expenses, an amount that equaled 111.1% of tax revenues.

The Government-General of Korea's financial system had several important features. First, it was centred on government enterprises.

Second, huge expenditures on police, justice and prisons formed about 12% of annual expenditures and increased every year. Third, expenditures on subsidies were immense, particularly for construction projects to provide basic facilities for colonial industries and for the building of private railroad lines in order to attract Japanese monopoly capital to Korea. Fourth, public debts including loans, public bonds and treasury bonds increased continuously. Finally, expenditure on education was very low and expenditure on social welfare was almost nonexistent.

COLONIAL BANKING

After colonizing Korea, the Japanese imperialists sought to subjugate industry in Korea to Japan by creating an industrial finance system centred on a central bank and by attracting capital from Japan. Accordingly, they founded the Bank of Korea as the central bank right before annexation which they then reorganized as the Bank of Chosen (Japanese pronunciation of Chosŏn) immediately after annexation.

This brought Korea completely under the currency system of Japan. Because the colonial monetary system was the yen standard system, which was based not on the gold reserve system but on the yen reserve system, the supply of currency of the Bank of Chosen was totally under the control of the Bank of Japan.

The first step toward the systemization of industrial finance organs in the colony actually came with the foundation of the Bank of Agriculture and Industry in 1906. That bank was established in six cities throughout the country for the purpose of 'loaning money in order to improve and develop agriculture and industry'. At the end of 1908, lending for agricultural capital and industrial capital formed only 7.7% and 4.4% each, while lending for commercial capital totaled 83%. Even ten years later, there was still a strong tendency to concentrate on commercial lending. At the end of June 1918, the proportions of loans were agricultural capital 28.1%, industrial capital 3.2%, and commercial capital 58.0%. In the early years of colonial management, the Japanese focused on controlling the supply of funds in order to exploit Korean merchants through usury, to exploit resources and to gain control over networks of distribution. The Japanese also established regional credit unions in 1907 as subsidiaries to the Bank of Agriculture and Industry. Those credit unions were charged with such duties as investigating debtors, collecting loans and acting as agents for loans using real estate as security.

It was not possible, however, to meet the increasing demand for loans with just those two organizations. Hence the Oriental Development Company established a financial section and began to engage in banking operations using funds gathered from foreign loans on the Japanese money market. The Bank of Agriculture and Industry acted as the Oriental Development Company's agent in loaning money. This development furthered the systematization of colonial banking and made it possible for the Japanese to intensify their exploitation by expanding beyond the distribution networks to which they had been making most of their loans and infiltrating their capital into the production sector, primarily agriculture. Having begun to infiltrate the production sector, the Japanese imperialists then reorganized the six-branch Bank of Agriculture and Industry into the Industrial Bank of Korea in 1918. The Industrial Bank expanded its business by actively bringing in new financial capital which it got either from the Japanese Treasury Ministry or from bonds issued in Japan.

At the time of the foundation of the Industrial Bank, the Japanese also established Urban Credit Unions and also organized provincial Credit Union Associations in order to facilitate commercial and industrial investment. The Industrial Bank provided funds for each credit union while the credit unions put their savings accounts on deposit at the Industrial Bank. By making the Industrial Bank the central depository, the Japanese were able to systemize the infiltration of their capital into Korea's agrarian communities.

Because the Bank of Chosen, even while maintaining its role of regulating currency in the colony, had already begun by the mid-1910s to focus on advancing into Manchuria, the management of colonial banking in Korea was left largely to the Industrial Bank and its subsidiary credit unions. The Industrial Bank, which was supplied with Japanese capital through such means as assuming debentures, acting as agent for loans and receiving low interest funds, made loans on its own but also invested funds in a variety of industries in Korea through the provincial credit union associations and urban credit unions that primarily serviced medium and small landlords and businessmen, most notably through the provision of funds to buy land and oxen. The profits created from the Industrial Bank's loans and investments flowed back to Japan. The Industrial Bank fulfilled its role as a centre of colonial banking.

The Industrial Bank combined the roles of ordinary commercial banks, savings banks, and banks for the encouragement and promotion of industry. It also issued bonds the proceeds of which were used to provide funds to large landlords and agricultural management companies, as well as to the farmland improvement projects and the irrigation associations related to the Programme to Increase Rice Production. The Industrial Bank had the privilege to issue bonds up to fifteen times of paid-up capital. The amount of bonds issued during the bank's first ten years was 264.53 million yen.

Using 1930 as an example of the bank's operations, its authorized capital was 30 million yen, its paid-up capital was 20 million yen, its amounts on deposit totalled 51.06 million yen and its net profits were 3,023,448 yen. The bank's net profit was 15.12% and it paid dividends at a rate of 9% for a total amount of 885,154 yen in paid dividends.

The Oriental Development Company emerged as a major financial institution in the early-1920s. It collaborated with the Bank of Chosen to promote the campaign for a Japan-Korea-Manchuria banking block. It also engaged, along with the Industrial Bank, in the supply of funds to landlords and agricultural organizations for the irrigation and farmland improvement projects of the Programme to Increase Rice Production as well as for agricultural management. The Oriental Development Company was initially established for the purposes of the so-called development projects. However, the company extended its influence to the banking business and became, along with the Bank of Chosen and the Industrial Bank, one of the so-called Three Great Banking Organizations of colonial Korea. This company, which enjoyed special protection from the Japanese government, had nine branches in Korea alone through which in 1930 it collected approximately 400,000 *sŏm* of rice in rents from the tenants working its 110,000 *chŏngbo* of land. It also issued bonds worth approximately 370 million yen.

The amount of loans extended by the Oriental Development Company reached about 138 million yen, and the interest from those loans totalled 9.06 million yen which amounted to 53% of its annual net profit of 17.24 million yen. The company offered its loans mostly to Korean landlords and owner-cultivator peasants, taking real estate as security. Most of the interest it collected came from those Koreans.

The credit unions that had been local agrarian financial organs were formed into a regular commercial bank when they were brought together in one single central organization as the Korean Credit Union Association in 1928, an entity that later developed into the Korean Credit Union Federation in 1933. At the same time, the Industrial Bank also expanded and reorganized its savings department as the Korean Savings Bank in 1929, with the goal of bringing ordinary Koreans into the network of colonial banking. Furthermore, the laws and regulations regarding trust funds and mutual loan businesses were amended to allow the establishment of large-size trust and mutual loan businesses. Together, these developments represented the shrinking of the base on which Korean-owned banks could be founded.

Earlier, following the 1912 Korean Bank Ordinance, twelve Korean banks, including the Haedong Bank, the Kyŏngsang Mutual Foundation Bank, the Kyŏngil Bank and the Honam Bank, with capital sizes between one-half million and two million yen, had been established before 1920. These banks fulfilled the role of marginal banking organizations in the colony.

However, undercapitalized Korean banks were gradually being acquired by Japanese capital following the 1928 Bank Ordinance Amendment which stipulated that new banks could only be established by corporations with over two million yen of capital, and that already existing banks had to secure at least one million yen of capital within five years.

The Japanese capitalist-owned Korean Commercial Bank bought the Samnam Bank, while the Japanese capitalist-owned Kanjo Bank also bought the Kyŏngsang Mutual Foundation Bank, the Kyŏngil Bank, the Bank of Southern Korea, the Bank of Commerce and Industry in Taegu, the Haedong Bank and the Kyŏngsang Unified Bank. The Korean capitalist-owned Tongil bank acquired the Tongnae Bank, the Hosŏ Bank, and Honam Bank. The consequence was that by the 1940s, only three ordinary commercial banks were left: the Japanese-owned Korean Commercial and Kanjo banks and the Korean-owned Tongil Bank.

With the forced combination of banking organizations under the wartime regime, in 1943 the Kanjo Bank absorbed the Tongil Bank and changed its name to the Chohŭng Bank. This marked the final disappearance of Korean-owned banks.

The withering of commercial banks, which had been the source of capital for small and medium merchants and industrialists, and limitations on borrowers imposed by the colony's special financial organs resulted in the spread of usurious private money-lenders and pawn shops. Usurers preyed on small producers and poor people who were excluded from access to colonial banking organizations which favoured large capital. The consequence was the bankruptcy of small producers and acceleration of the subjugation of the Koreans to Japanese banks.

According to research by the *East Asian Daily News* in 1931, the amount of loans that Korean peasants borrowed from the Government-General, banks and credit unions was 345.45 million yen, of which loans from credit unions accounted for 29.2% of the total, or 101 million yen. The amount of loans that the peasants borrowed from private financial organs such as individuals or mutual loan companies was 435.45 million yen, far more than amounts borrowed from banks and credit unions.

After provoking war with China, the Japanese imperialists promulgated the Provisional Fund Regulation Law in September 1937 to restrict nonessential industries and control the limit of loans in order to secure war resources and ensure the smooth provision of war supplies. The result was the dismantling and absorption by Japanese capital of small and medium Korean capital in non-war and non-major industries.

Moreover, in accordance with the November 1940 implementation of the Ordinance on the Use of Funds by Banks and Other Financial Organs, the Government-General required banks to invest in government bonds. The National Mobilization Law established controls over operational and equipment funds and also required banking institutions to make mandatory loans. Once Japanese military aggression led to armed conflict with the United States, banking organizations in Korea had to provide funds for the conduct of the war.

After the outbreak of war with China, the Government-General issued huge amounts of war bonds the proceeds from which were used to support the Japanese monopoly capitalists' acquisition of excess profits in the colony. At the same time, the Government-General also enforced a savings movement to finance war expenditures. 'Tenbiki savings', a mandatory savings plan that required buyers to deposit a fixed percentage of the purchase amount for such commodities as agricultural products, reached as much as 30% of purchase amounts in 1943. The implementation of the Savings Union Law, which was designed to force workers to save money, resulted in the establishment of some 94,000 savings unions with over 447,000 members – roughly 19% of the Korean population. The total amount of forced savings in those unions was 332 million yen.

The Bank of Chosen purchased war bonds with notes from the Bank of Japan that it held temporarily in the process of transferring funds for military expenses to Manchuria. It sought to underwrite those purchases through the excessive issuance of Bank of Chosen notes. Furthermore, because the Bank used its own notes, rather than notes from the Bank of Japan, to pay military expenses into the Special Account for Provisional Military Expenditure, it aggravated inflation in Korea.

The amount of notes issued by the Bank of Chosen increased almost three times, from 1,466 million yen to 4,339 million yen, in the two years from 1943 to June 1945. The rate of increase was much higher than that of the Bank of Japan. If we set the index of the year 1936 at 100, the index figure of Bank of Chosen notes rose to 208 by June 1945, while that of the Bank of Japan was no more than 140.

REFERENCES

Kim Tujong, 'Shokuminchi Chosen ni okeru 1920 nendai no nogyo kinyu ni tsuite' (On agrarian finance during the 1920s in colonial Korea), *Keizaigaku kenkyu* (Studies of Economics) 5, Tokyo: Tokyo University Press, 1965.

Akisada Yoshikazu, 'Chosen kinyu kumiai no kozo to kino' (Structure and functions of the Korean credit unions), *Chosenshi kenkukai ronbunshu* (Bulletin of the Society for Korean Historical Study), 5, 1968.

Hanejima Toshihiko, 'Senjika (1937–1945) Chosen ni okeru tsuka to *infureishon*' (Currency and inflation in Korea during the war (1937–1945)), *Shokuminchi Chosen no shakai to teiko* (Society and struggle in colonial Korea), Tokyo: Miraisha, 1981.

Hori Kazusei, 'Shokuminchi sangyo kinyu to keizai kozo: Shokugin no bunseki o toshite' (Industrial finance and economic structure in the colony: an analysis of the Industrial Bank), *Chosenshi kenkukai ronbunshu* (Bulletin of the Society for Korean Historical Study), 20, 1983.

Hori Kazusei, 'Chosen ni okeru futsuu ginko no senritsu to tenkai' (Origins and development of commercial banks in Korea), *Shakai keizaishi gaku* (Journal of Socio-Economic History), 49–1, 1984.

U Tongmyŏng, 'Ilcheha Chosŏn chaejŏng ŭi kujo wa sŏngkyŏk' (Structure and nature of finance in Korea under Japanese imperialism), Dissertation at Korea University, Seoul, 1987.

Chŏng T'aehŏn, 'Singminji sidae Chosŏn ŭi chabonjejŏk chose chedo sŏngnip e kwanhan yŏn'gu' (A study of existence of a capitalist tax system in Korea during the colonial period), *Kyŏngjesahak* (Journal of Economic History), 11, 1987.

Pae Yŏngmok, 'Singminji Chosŏn ŭi t'onghwa kŭmyung e kwanhan yŏn'gu' (A study of currency and finance in colonial Korea), Ph.D. Dissertation, Seoul National University, 1990.

Chŏng Pyŏnguk, '1918–1937 Siksan ŭnhaeng ŭi chabon hyŏngsŏng kwa kŭmnyung hwaltong' (Capital formation and financial activities of the Industrial Bank between 1918 and 1937), M.A. Thesis, Korea University, Seoul, 1991.

Chŏng T'aehŏn, 'Singminji sidae che ilchong (pŏbin) sodŭkse ŭi toip kwa sihaeng kwajŏng' (Introduction and operation of the First Class (Corporate) Income Tax), *Hanguksa yŏn'gu* (Studies of Korean History), 79, 1992.

Kim Poyŏng, 'Ilcheha chŏnsi kukch'ae wa Chosŏn kyŏngje' (War bonds and the Korean economy under Japanese imperialism), *Ilche mal Chosŏn sahoe wa minjok haebang undong* (Korean society and national liberation movement at the end of Japanese imperialism), Seoul: Ilsongjŏng, 1991.

SECTION THREE

The Realities of Colonial Industry

THE REALITIES OF KOREAN OWNED INDUSTRIES

During the years between the opening of the ports in 1876 and colonization in 1910, such problems as the lack of government policies, the weakness of the indigenous economic base and the influx of foreign capital precluded the possibility that the Korean economy could achieve its own industrial revolution. What little modern industry that began to develop in those years encountered greater adversities because of the impediments presented by colonial policies.

In December 1910, just two months after they colonized Korea, the Japanese promulgated the Company Law which stipulated that corporations, both public and private, could not be established without licences from the Governor-General. Moreover, it contained provisions that allowed the Governor-General to suspend or prohibit operations, shut down branch offices, or even cancel licences for corporations that violated his orders or the conditions he established for licensing or corporations that engaged in activities injurious to public order and proper morals.

The Company Law was intended to impede the development of Korean capital and the growth of an industrial bourgeoisie by limiting the establishment and management of Korean corporations. Even as the Government-General strictly limited the establishment of corporations by Koreans and shut down a number of Korean corporations that had been established before annexation, it brought in such established Japanese corporations as Osha Paper and Dai Nippon Sugar while also issuing new business licences to Japanese applicants. A 1914 amendment of the Company Law made it somewhat easier to establish new corporations.

During the years of the enforcement of the Company Law, the growth of Japanese industrial corporations was higher than that of Koreans, allowing the Japanese to seize control of industrial management in the colony. Table 5 shows that the Japanese corporations' share of total authorized capital increased from 26.4% in 1911 to 77.2% in 1917 while the share of Korean corporations decreased from 18.6% to 15.0% during the same period. Furthermore, the bulk of the capital in unlimited partnerships was owned by Japanese.

Table 5: Capital of industrial corporations by ethnicity (unit: thousand yen)

	Authorized capital				Paid-Up capital			
	Korean	Japanese	Partnerships	Total	Korean	Japanese	Partnerships	Total
1911	7,400	10,500	21,900	39,800	2,700	5,100	8,100	15,900
	18.6%	26.4%	55.0%	100%	17.0%	32.0%	51.0%	100%
1917	11,500	59,200	6,000	76,700	5,800	38,000	1,900	45,700
	15.0%	77.2%	7.8%	100%	12.7%	83.2%	4.1%	100%

Source: Chosen sotokufu tokei nenbo (Statistical Yearbook of the Government-General of Korea).

Table 6: Korean factory capital (unit: thousand yen)

	1911		1919	
	Factories	Capital	Factories	Capital
Industrial Corporations (Korean-owned)	4	79	13	808
Industrial Corporations (Joint Korean/Japanese)	3	117	3	28
Factories (Mostly private individuals)	66	637	958	7,589

Source: Yi Yŏsŏng & Kim Seyong, ed., *Suji Chosen kenkyu* (A Numerical Study of Korea) vol. 2, 1932, pp. 397–98.

Korean capital responded to this situation in a variety of ways. Some of the larger Korean capitalists resorted to partnerships with Japanese capitalists to establish jointly-operated factories while most medium and small Korean capitalists postponed the establishment of corporations, seeking instead to accumulate capital through individual private management. These changes in modes of management were the methods by which the Korean capitalists, who had little capital or productive capacity, strove to overcome the Company Law and compete with Japanese capitalists.

As seen in Table 6, in 1911 there were only four Korean-owned industrial corporations with a total capital of 79,000 yen while there were 66 privately managed factories with a total capital of 637,000 yen. By 1919, the number of privately managed factories 1919 increased to 958 with 7,589,000 yen. The privately managed factories outnumbered the Korean-owned industrial corporations by a factor of 73, while their combined capital was nine times greater than that of the Korean industrial corporations. On the other hand there were three jointly-owned Korean/Japanese corporations with combined capital of 117,000 yen. After the 1914 relaxation of the Company Law, the number of Korean-owned industrial corporations increased from four to thirteen and their combined total capital increased over ten times. By contrast, the capital of the joint Korean/Japanese-owned companies shrank from 117,000 to 28,000 yen.

The Korean-owned factories of the early colonial period were limited to cloth dyeing, paper manufacturing, leather tanning, ceramics and grain milling. Although the number of Korean-owned factories increased from 26% of the total number of factories in 1911 to 46% in 1921, the total output of Korean-owned factories increased only 15%. This is a good indicator of the poverty of Korean factories.

Even though Korean capitalists faced great obstacles to incorporating and developing into industrial capitalists in the 1910s, after the abolition of the Company Law in 1920, they began to achieve some degree of growth through industrial corporations. One such example is the brewing industry, which had a relatively large market. The brewers who had been in existence since the end of the nineteenth century were weeded out and replaced by a new generation of owners as Korean-owned breweries came to account for nearly half of the total production of liquor. There was also some growth in Korean-owned factories producing cloth, knitted goods and rubber shoes in such major urban areas as Seoul, P'yŏngyang, Taegu and Pusan.

In the case of P'yŏngyang, the hosiery industry, which began as small knitting operations producing socks before colonization, survived through the 1910s in the form of small-scale management by petty merchants or handicraft workers who had only one or two knitting machines. In the 1920s, however, these small shops began to grow rapidly into full-fledged industrial concerns.

Table 7 shows the extent of development of this industry in P'yŏngyang with the emergence of factories that had as many as 200 or more workers. P'yŏngyang had approximately 750 weaving machines in 30 factories in 1922. In 1925, there were 18 factories with five or more weaving machines and 300 manufacturers with two or three machines. By 1927, the total number of machines increased to 1,531, the output reached 60% of the total national production, and there were four factories with over 200 machines. The products of these P'yŏngyang factories were sold throughout a broad area extending from Cheju Island in the southwest to the Jiandao region of Manchuria.

The Korean people discarded their traditional straw sandals for rubber shoes as they entered the modern era. Koreans began to operate rubber shoe factories sometime around 1920. Korean-owned rubber shoe factories included such large-scale operations as the Taeryuk Rubber Company which was launched with capital of 500,000 yen by a man who had once been a noble before colonization and the Tonga Rubber Industries Company which was established by a landlord and a wealthy merchant from Mokp'o with 300,000 yen. There were also factories established with 50,000 yen in capital, such as the Pando Rubber Industries, started by a shoemaker, and the Chosŏn Rubber Factory, launched by merchants who were of the Paejae School. Although the Japanese did invest some money in the rubber shoe industry, Koreans prevailed as seen in statistics from 1930, when Koreans ran 30 rubber shoe factories compared to only 17 owned by Japanese. This can be at least partly explained by the fact that the overwhelming majority of consumers of rubber shoes were Koreans.

Because knitting and rubber were the two fields in which Korean capitalists invested most heavily throughout the colonial period, later researchers looking to demonstrate the existence of 'national capital' have focused on these industries. The reality, however, was that it was impossible for national capital to survive under Japanese colonial rule.

Although the knitting industry was able to meet some of the conditions for industrial capitalization in the 1920s, it was faced with two difficult tasks. One was to win over the newly active labour movement

Table 7: Major hosiery factories in P'yŏngyang (yield in pairs of socks)

Owner	Classification	1921	1922	1923	1924	1925	1926
Yi Chinsun	Workers	104	250	72	168	103	60
(Kongsin)	Yield	45,000	104,500	7,000	20,000	75,000	75,000
No Tŏkkyu	Workers	60	12	–	–	–	–
	Yield	26,000	4,000	–	–	–	–
Pak Ch'ihong	Workers	70	50	70	40	50	55
(Sech'ang)	Yield	15,000	30,000	6,000	10,000	55,000	30,000
Son Ch'angyun	Workers	20	50	90	150	250	165
(Samgong)	Yield	5,000	10,000	20,000	30,000	250,000	150,000
Pang Yun	Workers	?	?	60	180	120	40
(Taewŏn)	Yield	?	?	20,000	70,000	80,000	60,000
Yi Ch'angyŏn	Workers	–	40	70	105	80	60
(Taedong)	Yield	–	18,000	24,000	60,000	80,000	50,000
Yi Kisun	Workers	20	23	50	–	–	–
(Pando)	Yield	3,000	20,000	10,000	–	–	–
Ch'a Hyŏngp'il	Workers	–	–	14	35	30	55
(P'yŏngsin)	Yield	–	–	3,500	5,000	15,000	15,000

Source: Kajimura Hideki. *Chosen ni okeru shihon shugi no keisei to tenkai* (Formation and Development of Capitalism in Korea), p. 167.

while beginning to accumulate capital. The other was to accelerate the accumulation of capital through greater productivity by making the change from manual to automatic machines. This situation meant that after the onset of the Great Depression in the late 1920s, Korean-owned industries had no option but to build ties with the Government-General.

The Government-General helped them by mobilizing its police force to suppress the labour movement. After the Manchurian Incident of 1931, it also gave Korean capitalists, including medium and small capitalists, the opportunity to accumulate capital by allowing them to penetrate the Manchurian economy. In the case of the knitting industry in P'yŏngyang, 'there was a boom in plant building in China as over twenty industry owners moved their operations to mainland China and Manchuria.' The active penetration of Manchuria by Korean business interests alarmed the Japanese imperialists, who responded by having their Manchukuo puppet state levy heavy duties on Korean products while allowing unrestricted duty-free imports from Japan. Nonetheless, Korean capitalists benefited to some degree from the post-1931 war industry inflation policy. The beneficiaries included the P'yŏngyang knitting industry, some of whose companies developed into substantial corporations.

After Japan provoked war with China in the late-1930s, the colonial economy was brought under the wartime economic regime and the so-called national mobilization system. The brought the reorganization of Korean capital. The Government-General of Korea began the process when it implemented the Laws for Control of Major Industries in 1936 in order to make the shift from the existing policy of promoting both light and heavy industries to a new policy that emphasized war industries and the introduction of large-scale Japanese capital.

At the same time, in anticipation of a shortage of consumer goods as a result of the mobilization of resources for war, including the state-led development of military heavy chemical industries in Japan proper, the Japanese prepared a series of laws designed to promote and regulate small- and medium-size industries. The Industrial Association Law of August 1938 established industrial associations as corporate bodies designed to consolidate, control and maintain the productivity of widely dispersed small and medium industries, many of which were managed by private individuals. The Japanese actively pursued the establishment of such industrial associations until 1940. After that time, the Japanese enacted several new laws and regulations relating to the merger of small and medium industries, including the January 1941 Principles for the Regularization of Small and Medium Industries, the Enterprise Authorization Ordinance of December 1941 and the Enterprise Consolidation Ordinance of June 1942. Japan's first goal was to: 'develop the sectors in need of expansion and strengthening in order to produce and process war supplies and other war-related resources and to secure a minimum standard of living for the people in wartime.' An additional goal was the 'disposition of industrial enterprises which are unable to increase productivity or improve quality because of insufficient management facilities, or which are difficult to utilize because of poor management techniques.' Although the first goal might have applied to some of the Korean-owned medium and small industries that experienced growth in the 1940s, many were in danger of being shut down by the Government-General pursuant to the second goal.

These ordinances dealt fatal blows to some firms in the knitting industry. For example, hosiery factories in P'yŏngyang were taken over by the Korean Knitting Corporation which was dominated by such Japanese conglomerates as Mitsubishi. At the same time, Japanese monopoly capital made extensive inroads into the knitting industry through such textile firms as Chuo Spinning and Weaving and Chosen Spinning and Weaving. On the other hand, most Korean-owned small and medium industrial enterprises managed to persist, despite their low levels of capitalization, through the wartime regulation and maintenance policies of the Government-General.

The Principles for the Regularization of Small and Medium Industries called for 'Minimizing change to existing firms while encouraging and utilizing individual creativity and research, while striving to organize them by incorporating them into industrial associations.' This approach of simultaneous regulation and maintenance reveals the practical principles of Japanese colonial economic management which aimed to absorb the productivity of even the lowest levels of Korean industry.

This policy was different from that applied in the home islands of Japan, where medium and small industries were either consolidated or transformed into subcontractors for big enterprises. The difference can be attributed to Japanese concern that such consolidation in Korea, where the vast majority of enterprises were medium or small industries, would result in a decline in productivity. One sector in which the Japanese policy of regulation and maintenance paid off was the colonial machine tool sector, which was made up mostly of medium and small industries with a Korean capital investment proportion of 42%. This sector saw a doubling in the number of factories and the value of production over a four-year period, from 613 factories and 53,225,000 yen in 1939 to 1,354 factories and 115,000,000 yen in 1943.

In short, during the 1940s there was a division of labour in Korea through which the Japanese *zaibatsu* took charge of heavy, chemical and munitions industries while a large number of small and medium factories under some control companies were responsible for consumer goods and primary and simple processed goods. The consequence was that, after all, the small and medium enterprises of that time in Korea were being subjugated to a part of the wartime economy while being forced to co-operate with Japanese imperialists who conducted war. Therefore, it was simply impossible for true national capital that was not subjugated to, or compromised by, the colonial control economy and that could provide financial support for the national liberation movement to exist as long as the Japanese imperialists controlled Korea.

JAPANESE MONOPOLY CAPITAL

Although the Japanese managed far more industries than did Koreans during the early colonial period, the entire industrial output was not particularly significant at that time. Even as late as 1920, industrial output lagged far behind agricultural production, accounting for only 13.5% of the colony's gross domestic product.

Early Japanese industrial management in Korea, which was generally limited to silk reeling, cotton ginning, brewing, printing, tobacco processing, salt production and confections, remained at a minimal level of capitalization until the outbreak of the First World War. According to 1913 statistics, factories with capital of less than 10,000 yen accounted for 68.2% of all Japanese factories, factories with fewer than ten employees accounted for 50.4%, factories with outputs of less than 10,000 yen accounted for 47.2%, and factories without electric power accounted for 53% of all Japanese-owned factories.

There were two major reasons why early Japanese industrial management was so poor. One was that Japanese accumulation of capital was still too weak for significant investment in Korea. The other was that in the 1910s, Korea's Japanese rulers focused their investments on such basic projects as the Land Survey and the construction of railroads, roads and harbours in order to build the basic infrastructure for the colonial economic system. The outbreak of the First World War, however, brought the penetration of Korea by large amounts of Japanese monopoly capital.

The wartime economy made possible the rapid growth of Japanese monopoly capital at the same time as conditions inside Korea were readying for penetration. The Company Law, which the Government-General had enacted because it was still too early for large Japanese capital to infiltrate Korea and because it wished to check the growth of Korean national industries and protect small Japanese capitalist in Korea, was abolished in April 1920. The Government-General repealed the Company Law in order to allow the penetration of Korea by the Japanese monopoly capital that had grown during the First World War.

The removal of the Company Law was followed by full-scale penetration of Korea by Japanese *zaibatsu* capital in the 1920s. Some of the *zaibatsu* that moved into Korea in those years were Mitsui, Mitsubishi and Noguchi. Mitsui established seven companies in Korea, including the Mitsunari Mining Corporation with five million yen in capital. Mitsubishi founded the Korean Anthracite Coal Corporation with 10 million yen of capital and Noguchi established four companies, including the Korean Nitrogen Fertilizer Corporation with sixty million yen in capital. In addition, Japanese capital extensively penetrated such industries as chemicals, electricity, textiles, mining and railroads. The amount invested by Japanese in colonies and semi-colonies, such as Korea, Taiwan, China and Mongolia, reached 7.159 billion yen. The amount invested to Korea was 1.627 billion yen, second only to China.

Another feature of industry in Korea during the 1920s was the growing gap between Japanese and Korean owned firms as a consequence of the aggressive penetration of the colony by Japanese capital. The total of 341 Japanese-owned industrial corporations in 1929 was more than double the 143 Korean-owned corporations. Even more telling, however, the total investment, or paid-up capital, of Japanese-owned corporations was fifteen times greater than that of Korean firms and the per-corporation average of investment or paid-up capital for Japanese corporations was seven times that of their Korean counterparts.

In spite of the dramatic increase in the penetration of Japanese capital through the 1920s, light industries, and the food processing industry in particular, surpassed any other sector in industrial output. The food industry formed 63.5% of total industrial output, but was engaged mostly in the business of milling and polishing grain. The textile industry placed second at 10.9%, primarily as a result of the rapid growth of Japanese textiles during the First World War. Japanese textile firms enjoyed control over Korea as a market for their commodities and also established factories in the colony to take advantage of Korea's cheap labour and abundant resources.

By contrast, the metallurgical, chemical and machine tool industries accounted for only 5.8%, 5.0% and 1.3% each of total colonial industrial output. The bulk of metallurgical industry was made up of mere blacksmith shops except for the Japan Steel Company's Kyomip'o plant and the Japan Mining Corporation's Chinnamp'o smelter, two large plants whose output was sent mostly to the home islands. The largest portion of the chemical industry was made up by the processing of fish oil. Finally, the machine tool industry, with the exception of one or two larger plants such as the Yongsan Engineering Corporation, accounted for nothing except the production of simple tools or repair shops.

Although the 1920s saw the establishment of some large-scale Japanese *zaibatsu*-owned factories, on the whole small-size shops predominated. According to 1932 statistics, factories with fewer than 50 employees totaled 4,277 of the total number of 4,525 factories. The number of factories with between 50 and 99 workers was 151, or 3.3% of the total, while factories with between 100 and 199 workers numbered only 46, or 1% and large factories with more than 200 employees totaled 51, or 1.1% of all factories. These statistics shows how underdeveloped industry ,was in Korea prior to the onset of Japanese military aggression in the 1930s.

INDUSTRIALIZATION POLICY AND THE WARTIME INDUSTRIES IN KOREA

Although a small number of large-scale industrial plants were established by Japanese monopoly capital in Korea during the 1920s, those plants were nothing but subsidiaries for industries in Japan. Even though some factories run by Koreans experienced a limited degree of development, nearly all Korean-owned factories were limited to small-scale management.

After the 1930s, the Japanese monopolistic capitalists, driven out by depression in the homeland, penetrated Korea more aggressively. Moreover, as the Japanese imperialists initiated their full-scale invasion of the continent in 1937, Korea became a military supply base, resulting in the transformation of the overall colonial industrial structure into a system for the production of war materials. This process increased the overall industrial productivity of Korea.

The amount of capital introduced from Japan to Korea increased from 1.8–2.1 billion yen in the years preceding 1931 to 7.2–7.5 billion yen between 1931 and 1936 before reaching approximately 10 billion yen by 1945. Japanese monopoly capital, having enforced the accumulation and concentration of capital after the onset of the Great Depression in the late-1920s, sought to find a breakthrough in its Korean colony where labour was cheap and resources were abundant. Whereas the enactment of the Laws to Control Major Industries and the Factory Act presented obstacles to corporate operations in Japan, there was no legislation for protecting workers in colonial Korea where the Government-General helped Japanese monopoly capital penetrate Korea by suppressing the labour movement.

With the increasing emphasis on the Japan, Korea and Manchuria Economic Block, Japanese monopoly capital began to invest in Korea in order to secure a bridgehead for its penetration of markets in Manchuria and China. Relying on Korea's hydroelectric power, the Japanese put large amounts of money in such heavy industry sectors as chemicals, fertilizers and cement. In addition, they also invested in textile industries targeted on the Manchurian market. In the second half of the 1930s, the negative balance of Japan's foreign trade was more than offset by profits from the 'Yen Block'. After the outbreak of war with China, Japanese monopoly capital concentrated its investments in war industries in order to preserve and expand the 'Yen Block'.

To put it in concrete terms, at the beginning of the 1930s, Mitsui established more companies, including three chemical industry companies such as the Kita Chosen Paper and the Chemical Industry Company that had 20 million yen in capital and six other new companies in such areas as textiles, brewing and milling. Noguchi founded two electrical companies, the Changjin River Hydroelectricity Co-operation with 20 million yen and the Korea Electric Supply Cooperation with 15 million yen in capital, two chemical industry companies, and one railroad company. Other new companies continued to be established by Japanese capital in such industries as chemicals, electric machinery, iron and textiles.

Japan's active policy of military industrialization brought significant change in the structure of industry in Korea. As seen in Table 8 below, in 1930, the food industry was the largest, accounting for 57.7% of total output, followed by textiles at 12.8% and chemicals at 9.4%. In 1936, the food industry was still the largest, but its share of total output had dropped to 45.2% while the rapidly growing chemical industry was now in second place at 22.9% and the textile industry dropped to third at

Table 8: The movement of industry in korea during the 1930s (unit: thousand yen)

	1930			1936		
	Yield (%)	Factories	Workers	Yield (%)	Factories	Workers
Metals	15,263 (5.8)	231	4,542	28,365 (4.0)	259	6,787
Machinery	3,328 (1.3)	224	2,854	7,398 (1.0)	344	7,939
Chemicals	24,676 (9.4)	515	14,720	162,462 (22.9)	1,425	41,972
Gas & Electricity	6,432 (2.4)	35	525	39,988 (5.6)	50	812
Ceramics	8,348 (3.2)	314	5,366	19,032 (2.7)	336	8,269
Textiles	33,674 (12.8)	270	19,011	90,378 (12.7)	402	33,830
Food	152,054 (57.8)	2,088	27,055	320,580 (45.2)	2,258	32,617
Lumbering	7,037 (2.7)	163	2,629	19,230 (2.7)	271	4,906
Printing	8,184 (3.1)	215	4,146	12,426 (1.8)	286	6,273
Others	4,068 (1.5)	206	3,052	10,002 (1.4)	296	5,394
Totals	263,064 (100)	4,261	83,900	709,861 (100)	5,927	148,799

Source: Zenkoku keizai chosa kikan rengokai Chosen shibu (The Korean Branch of the National Federation of Economic Research Institutes). *Chosen keizai nenbo* (The Annual Report of Korean Economy), 1939 edition.

12.7%. During those same six years, the number of food-processing factories increased by 170 and the number of textile factories by 132, while the number of new chemical plants increased by no fewer than 910 facilities.

Table 8 also reflects the effects of the 1931 enactment of the Law to Control Major Industries. Large-scale capital engaged in civilian industries in Japan suffered heavy blows, leading to the large-scale flight of capital to Korea in the 1930s. The amount of capital of industrial companies in Korea that were branches of Japan-based corporations, increased dramatically from 290 million yen to 1,050 million yen between 1932 and 1936. As a consequence, Korean capitalists suffered the loss of marketshare, while the export to Japan of low-price commodities produced by cheap Korean labour threatened industries in Japan.

This led Japan to extend the Law to Control Major Industries to Korea in 1936 in order to convert civilian industries into munitions and heavy-chemical operations as part of a plan to put industry in the colony on a wartime footing. But the law had only limited application because most industrial enterprises in Korea were medium- and small-size concerns. In the end, the Government-General of Korea took into consideration the particular situation of Korea in its application of the Japanese principles of wartime economic control, organizing medium- and small-industrial firms and mobilizing capital to promote wartime industrialization through such laws as the Industrial Association Act, the Enterprise Consolidation Ordinance, the Industrial Readjustment Act and the Responsibility System for Munitions Production.

In 1937, after the Japanese invaded China, they enacted the Interim Funding Adjustment Law which they also applied to Korea in order to control financial markets and establish a framework for planned finance. At the same time, they restricted the production of civilian goods in order to ensure the smooth provision of war supplies and also established the Korean Finance Self-Adjustment Corps to control lending.

The Law to Control Major Industries as applied in Korea had the goals of improving the productivity of light industry, a sector with a substantial proportion of Korean-owned companies, and of incorporating Korean-owned industries into the wartime economic system. After the implementation of the National Mobilization Law in March 1938, the Japanese strengthened their control of manpower, goods and resources in Korea. At the same time, they reduced ethnic discrimination that had been applied to loans and interest rates for Korean-owned companies, while allowing Korean companies subcontracting rights. In particular, they aimed at increasing production by organizing small- and medium-size factories in industrial associations.

Although the Japanese policy of making Korea a base for munitions production did allow some degree of development in such fields of industry as chemicals and electric machinery, in the final analysis that policy ended up intensifying the colonial features of industry in Korea in several ways, as shown in Table 9 below.

Table 9: Capitalization of Korea-based companies at the end of 1944 (unit: 1,000 yen) (Includes only companies with capital exceeding one million yen)

	Numbers of companies			Paid-Up capital (% of totals)		
	Korean	Japanese	Total	Korean	Japanese	Total
Metal	3	30	33	3,975 (1.8)	202,330 (98.2)	206,125 (5.1)
Machine	3	30	33	1,500 (15.1)	64,530 (84.9)	76,030 (5.6)
Chemical	1	36	37	250 (0.1)	252,925 (99.9)	253,175 (5.6)
Gas & Electricity	–	7	7	– (0)	506,262 (100)	506,262 (100)
Ceramic	–	10	10	– (0)	40,908 (100)	40,908 (3.0)
Textile	2	18	21	1,250 (15.6)	90,975 (84.4)	72,225 (5.3)
Lumbering	1	6	7	5,500 (15.3)	30,350 (84.7)	35,850 (2.5)
Food	3	32	35	1,314 (2.2)	59,152 (97.8)	60,466 (4.4)
Printing	1	1	2	1,500 (68.2)	500 (31.8)	2,000 (.15)
Construction	4	13	17	2,760 (10.1)	24,385 (89.9)	27,145 (2.0)
Others	–	11	11	– (0)	30,750 (100)	30,750 (2.8)
Totals	18	196	214	37,869 (2.8)	1,273,067 (93.6)	1,360,936 (100)

Source: Chosen shoko kaigisho (The Chamber of Commerce and Industry of Korea). *Chosen Keizai yokei yoran* (A Statistical Handbook of Korean Economy), 1949, p. 73.

First, Japanese monopoly capital came to dominate Korean industry much more thoroughly than before as it accounted for the overwhelming majority of capital in every sector except the smallest – printing. As Table 9 shows, the Japanese owned almost 94% of the capital invested in Korean industries in the early 1940s. This indicates the extent to which Japanese capital managed industries in Korea.

Second, there was a significant, if limited, development of heavy industry in Korea. In 1936, production from such major heavy industries as metallurgy, machinery and chemicals was only 27.9% of total economic production. The bulk (22.9%) of that came from chemical plants which mostly produced fertilizer for the increased rice production. The combined total for the metallurgical and machinery industries was a mere 5%.

The imposition of wartime controls in 1937, however, brought major change, particularly in the penetration of Korean heavy industry by Japanese *zaibatsu* capital. Japanese *zaibatsu* devoted as much as 74% of their total capital investments in Korea to industrial facilities, whereas companies based in Korea invested only 27% of their total 1944 capital of 536 billion yen in that area. Furthermore, Japanese *zaibatsu* branches in Korea concentrated 70 to 80% of their investments in the heavy-chemicals industry. The result of such movement by Japanese monopoly capital was that the investment in heavy chemicals in 1943 was 1.01 billion yen, accounting for 49% of total industrial investment at that time.

In the case of the metallurgical industry, there were no factories with over 200 employees prior to 1935, an indication of the poor productive capacity of Korean basic industries in the pre-war era. After the enactment of the Law to Control Major Industries, however, the Japanese invested heavily in metallurgical and machine industries. The single year of 1942 saw the construction of such major metallurgical plants as the Nippon Steel Corporation's Kyŏmip'o Steel Works and Ch'ŏngjin Steel Works along with plants owned by Mitsubishi Heavy Industry, the Chosen Metallurgy Company, the Sŏngjin plant of the Industrial Bank's Nippon Takazoha Heavy Industries and the Chosen Steel Mill run by the Oriental Development Company. Japanese *zaibatsu* such as Nichitsu, Mori, Mitsui and Sumimoto also established plants for the production of such light metals such as aluminum and magnesium. There was a total of thirty-three metallurgical plants with one million yen or more in capital, of which three were operated by Koreans. Despite the active development of the metallurgical industry in Korea in the final years of colonial rule, the vast bulk of their production was taken out to Japan for use in the munitions industry. Statistics from 1944 indicate, for example, that 89.4% of the pig iron produced in Korea went to Japan. In other words, the late-colonial development of heavy industry made virtually no contribution to the growth of Korean industrial capacity – it was almost entirely a matter of production by Japanese capital for consumption by Japanese war industries.

The machine industry in Korea was mostly limited to repair rather than manufacturing. As the war was drawing to close, machine production in railroad cars, vessel machinery and shipbuilding increased somewhat, but the machine industry still formed only 6% of total industrial output even as late as 1943. What increased demand for machinery in the metallurgical, machine, electrical and chemical sectors was completely dependent on the machine industry in Japan. This meant that it was next to impossible for Korean owners to improve their technological capacities, especially in the machine industry itself. In the early 1940s, Japanese *zaibatsu* monopolists did build some major machine factories such as Chosen Heavy Machinery and Chosen Sumitomo Steel. They also built or expanded other large-scale machinery factories such as the Chosen Electrolytic Steel Plant and Sunan Steel with the stated purpose of tying colonial technology with that of the home islands of Japan.

Third, the development of heavy industries during the war years had almost no effect on the livelihood of the vast majority of the Korean people. Statistics from 1939 show that only nine of 295 metallurgical plants had 200 or more workers but those nine plants accounted for 88.4% of total metallurgical output. In the case of the chemical industry, only 33 of 618 plants had 200 or more workers, but those 33 plants produced no less than 76% of total chemical output. The same trend prevailed in the machine industry, where only 20 factories with 200 or more workers accounted for 52.7% of total production. The reason for the relatively low figure for the machine industry is that that sector saw the development of medium- and small-scale factories as subsidiaries of large-scale factories.

Fourth, light industry in the 1930s and early 1940s did not develop sufficiently to meet the needs of Koreans. This was because the Japanese developed only those sectors that produced excess profits. Even though the food processing and textile industries did not experience the kind of spectacular growth in the 1930s that they enjoyed in the 1920s, they continued to expand and to outweigh other light industry sectors.

The proportion of total industrial output occupied by textiles increased from 12.8% in 1930 to 14% in 1937 and 17% in 1943. One important factor behind this early and continuing growth was that the Japanese could earn surplus value from the colony in this sector by taking advantage of abundant cheap materials and labour. But this did not represent some sort of overall development in response to Korean demand, but rather development centring on certain fields, primarily cotton spinning and weaving, that were advantageous for Japan's textile industry.

The food-processing industry, and particularly rice polishing, grew in order to supply food to the home islands of Japan and to meet the demand from Japanese residents and Japanese troops in Korea. Even as late as 1940, rice mills accounted for 1,700, or roughly 81%, of the total 2,100 food-processing factories in Korea. Other minor food-processing industries included flour milling, brewing and soy sauce production, primarily to meet the needs of Japanese living in Korea. After 1942, the food-processing industry was regularized and consolidated according to the provisions of the Enterprise Consolidation Ordinance and came under the control of the Food Management Corps.

Light industry in Korea, dominated as it was by textile and foodstuff production, was closely linked to the agricultural sector that provided it with cheap materials and did not have an organic production relationship with heavy industry. This was because the Law to Control Major Industries as applied in Korea was centred on the promotion of heavy-chemicals production, while the Law as applied in Japan also fostered growth in other sectors experiencing shortages such as textiles.

Finally, during the years when the Japanese were reorganizing Korea as a supply base of munitions, there was an imbalance between industry and agriculture and severe regional maldistribution of industrial facilities. Even in the 1930s, Korea's rural population was heavily dependent on

Table 10: Industrial production in Southern and Northern Korea (1940)

	Southern Korea	Northern Korea
Metals	9.1	90.9
Machines	71.6	28.4
Ceramics	26.8	73.2
Chemicals	14.0	86.0
Wood Products	63.4	36.6
Printing	88.5	11.5
Foodstuffs	61.1	38.9
Textiles	83.2	16.8
Gas & Electricity	20.4	79.6
Others	77.8	22.2
Totals	44.3	55.7

Source: Kawai Akitake, *Chosen kogyo no gen dankai* (Present Stage of Korean Industry)

domestic handicraft production for daily necessities. The small amounts of machine industry products they used were mostly produced in Japan. Statistics from 1937 indicate that even in the textile sector, only 50.3% of textiles consumed in Korea was produced in Korea, including 11.5% produced in peasant households by traditional spinning and weaving methods. The remaining 49.7% were produced outside Korea, almost all in Japan.

According to the statistics of 1937, even in the case of the products of the spinning industry, among the amount of consumption in Korea, only 50.3% was domestic products and 11.5% was product of the domestic industry. Accordingly, the rest, 49.7%, was foreign products, among them, 44.7% was products of Japan.

The location of industrial facilities in colonial Korea was not for the development of the Korean economy as a whole, but to support the goals of Japanese colonial rule and to facilitate the exploitation of resources. The rice-milling industry was concentrated in ports such as Inch'ŏn and Kunsan that were located close to major rice-producing regions. Metallurgical and chemical plants were concentrated close to ports in the northern parts of Korea where there were abundant raw materials and electric power. The reason that the textile industries were concentrated in and around Seoul was because that area was the centre of colonial political power and urban consumption.

Table 10 shows the severity of industrial maldistribution in colonial Korea. Heavy industries such as metallurgy, chemicals, and gas and electricity were concentrated in the northern half of the country, while light industries such as textiles were concentrated in the southern half. The colonial maldistribution of industrial capacities had an even more negative effect on the national economy when Korea was divided after liberation.

REFERENCES

Kobayashi Hideo, '1930 nendai Chosen Kogyoka seisaku no tenkai katei' (Developmental process of industrialization of Korea in the 1930s), *Chosenshi kenkyukai ronbunshu* (Bulletin of the Society for Korean Historical Study), 3, 1967.

An Pyŏngjik, '1930 nyŏn ihu Chosŏn e ch'imiphan Ilbon tokchŏmjabon ŭi chŏngch'e' (True nature of the Japanese monopoly capital that penetrated Korea 1930), *Kyŏngje nonjip* (Journal of Economy), vol. 10, no. 4, Seoul Sangdae, 1971.

Cho Kijun, *Hanguk chabonjuŭi sŏngnipsa ron* (Essays on history of the establishment of Korean capitalism), Seoul: Korea University Press, 1973.

Kobayashi Hideo, '1930 nendai shokuminchi kogyoka no sho tokucho' (Features of industrialization in the colony in the 1930s), *Tochi seido shigaku* (Journal of Land System History), 71, 1976.

Kajimura Hideki, *Chosen ni okeru shihonshugi no keisei to tenkai* (Origins and development of capitalism in Korea), Ryukei shosha, 1978.

Hashitani Hiroi, 'Ryo taisen kikan no Nihon teikokushugi to Chosen keizai' (Japanese imperialism and Korean economy during the two world wars), *Chosenshi kenkyukai ronbunshu* (Bulletin of the Society for Korean Historical Study), 20, 1983.

Hŏ Suyŏl, 'Ilcheha Hanguk e issŏsŏŭi singminji kongŏp ŭi sŏngkyŏk e kwanhan yŏngu' (A study of nature of the colonial industries in Korea under Japanese imperialism), Ph. D. Dissertation, Seoul National University, 1983.

Son Chŏngmok, 'Hoesaryŏng yŏngu' (A study of the company law), *Hanguksa yŏn'gu* (Journal of Korean History), 45, 1984.

Hŏ Suyŏl, '1930 nyŏndae kunsu kongŏphwa chŏngch'aek kwa Ilbon tokchŏmjabon ŭi chinch'ul' (The policy of military industrialization and the penetration of Korea by Japanese monopoly capital), *Ilche ŭi Hanguk singmin t'ongch'i* (Colonial Rule of Korea by Japanese Imperialists), Seoul: Chŏngŭmsa, 1985.

Kang Chaeŏn (ed.) *Chosen ni okeru Nissho kontserun* (The Nitrogen Industry Concern in Korea), Tokyo: Huji shuppan, 1985.

Hori Kazusei, 'Chosen minzoku shihon ron' (An Essay on national capital in Korea), *Kindai Chosen no rekishi zo* (Historical images of modern Korea), Tokyo: Nippon hyoronsha, 1988.

Yi Hangu, *Ilcheha Hanguk kiŏp sŏllip undongsa* (History of the movement for the foundation of Korean enterprises under Japanese imperialism), Seoul: Ch'ŏngsa, 1989.

Kim Inho, 'Chŏnsi t'ongjegi (1937–45) chungso kongjang sŏngjang ŭi yŏksajŏk sŏngkyŏk' (Historical nature of the growth of small and medium factories during the period of wartime control), *Howŏn nonjip*, 1993.

SECTION FOUR

The Plunder of Resources and Control over Traffic, Communication and Trade

PLUNDERING RESOURCES

The Japanese plundering of Korean resources was not limited to the acquisition of land through the Land Survey of 1910–18. After colonization, the Japanese began to plunder a variety of resources in order to support the capitalist development of Japan. The Japanese, who had been eyeing Korea's abundant mineral resources before colonization, ascertained mineral deposits through a survey of Korean mines from 1911 to 1917.

The Japanese promulgated the Korean Mining Ordinance in 1915 and rules for implementation of the Ordinance in 1916 in order to limit Korean mining operations and facilitate penetration by Japanese interests. The promulgation of the Ordinance allowed Japanese mining capital to penetrate Korea on a large scale, as such Japanese corporations as Mitsui Mining and Furukawa Mining Unlimited seized all the mines in Korea that had significant ore deposits, including the mines at Kaech'ŏn and Kapsan. The Ordinance also resulted in a reduction in the proportion of mining permits given to Koreans, from 51% of the total in 1911 to 37% in 1919 and an increase in the proportion of permits given to Japanese, from 47% in 1911 to 63% in 1919.

Table 11 below shows the extent to which Japanese interests came to dominate mining in Korea during the first ten years after colonization. In 1911, Koreans accounted for 4.8% of total mining production, the Japanese 22.6%, and foreigners, including Americans and British, 72.6%. By 1920, however, the percentages of production accounted for by Koreans and foreigners fell to 0.4% and 19.7% while the percentage of production owned by Japanese climbed to 79.9%.

The table also shows that the bulk of the transfer of mining assets into Japanese hands occurred after the implementation of the Korean Mining Ordinance in 1915. The Japanese maintained their domination of the mining sector in the following years. In 1931, for example, Japanese-owned mines accounted for 79% of production, Korean-owned-mines 9.4%, and foreign-owned mines only 11%.

Once the Japanese began full-scale military aggression in the 1930s, they intensified their plunder of Korean mineral resources. The Government-General's 1932 budget set aside 200,000 yen to subsidize gold mining. Gold production increased threefold between 1931 and 1939, with 55% of the production sent to Japan via the Bank of Chosen. After the outbreak of war with China, the Japanese promulgated the Korean Gold Mining Act of September 1937 in order to increase the production of gold to pay for the war. The Japanese sought to subjugate

Table 11: Mine ownership and production in Korea, 1911–1920 (unit: 1,000 yen)

	Korean		Japanese		Foreign	
	Mines	Production	Mines	Production	Mines	Production
1911	90	296 (4.8)	103	1,401 (22.6)	14	4,488 (72.6)
1915	108	384 (3.7)	182	2,820 (26.8)	19	7,311 (69.5)
1920	23	89 (0.4)	150	19,337 (79.9)	5	4,777 (19.7)

Source: Chosen sotokufu tokei nenbo (Statistical Yearbook of the Government-General of Korea).

the mining industry to the munitions industry and to increase the production of twenty-five minerals, including gold, silver, iron, tungsten and graphite, that were deemed 'particularly essential to national defense' by ordering mine operators to open new mines, expand existing mines and upgrade their mining equipment. Moreover, in May 1938 they promulgated the Law to Increase the Production of Major Minerals in Korea, a measure that allowed the Government-General to order mine operators to surrender ownership of their mines, and established the Korean Mining Industry Promotion Corporation in 1940 to control the flow of funds to gold mine operators.

In the meantime, the Government-General used revenue from public bonds to provide exclusive mineral-production subsidies to such major *zaibatsu* as Mitsui, Mitsubishi and Sumitomo in order to promote the consolidation of the mining industry. Table 12 below shows the extent to which Japanese businesses dominated mineral production during the war years. Production by Korean-owned mines was limited to a few metals such as gold, silver and lead and even there Korean firms accounted for barely 10% to 20% of total production. The rest was produced by Japanese-owned corporations.

The Japanese also dominated the fishing industry. In 1909, the year before annexation, there were 75,063 Korean fishermen working on 12,567 boats with a total catch worth 3,690,300 yen, which breaks down to a per fisherman average of 49 yen. In the same year, there were 15,749 Japanese fishermen on 3,755 boats with a total catch of 3,076,800 yen, an average of 195 yen per fisherman. This shows that the Japanese had already begun to plunder Korean waters even before annexation.

As soon as the Japanese colonized Korea, they nullified existing fishing rights and compelled Korean fishermen to apply for new licences through the Government-General's June 1911 Korean Fisheries Law. Licences were approved only for those fishermen, predominantly Japanese, who used modern technology such as dragnets and diving suits. This law also transferred some Korean fishing grounds, including those belonging to the old Korean imperial family, to Japanese ownership. Furthermore, the Government-General established fishing associations under Japanese

Table 12: Percentages of Korean and Japanese mining production, 1937–1944

	1937		1941		1944	
	Korean	Japanese	Korean	Japanese	Korean	Japanese
Gold	25	65*	20	80	10	90
Copper	20	80	20	80	20	80
Zinc	5	95	5	95	5	95
Lead	10	90	10	90	10	90
Iron	–	100	–	100	1	99
Manganese	–	–	–	100	–	100
Tungsten	–	100	–	100	2	98
Molybdenum	–	100	–	100	–	100
Nickel	–	–	–	–	–	100
Cobalt	–	–	–	–	–	100
Fluorspar	–	100	10	90	10	90
Mica	–	100	–	100	3	97
Asbestos	–	100	–	100	–	–
Graphite	–	100	1	99	1	99
Iron Sulfide	–	100	–	100	–	100
Magnesium	–	100	–	100	–	100
Phosphorus	–	100	–	100	–	100

Source: the Bank of Chosen. *Chosen keizai nenbo*, 1948 edition.
* Other foreign mining operators accounted for 10% of gold production in 1937.

management. In short, the Government-General pursued a policy of transferring fishing rights from Koreans to Japanese.

During the first decade after annexation, the amount of catch by Japanese increased six-fold, while that of Koreans increased only four-fold. The value of Japanese per capita catch increased substantially to 245 yen while that of Koreans barely increased at all, creeping up to 54 yen. The Japanese also dominated fish farming through large-scale operations. Whereas 25,290 Koreans had roughly 4.04 million *p'yŏng* (*p'yŏng* is about 3.3 square metres) of fish farms, a mere 86 Japanese fish farmers had approximately 16.5 million *p'yŏng*.

The Japanese had already implemented a bold policy of plundering Korean forests even before annexation. The Japanese, who coveted the streamside forests in the valleys of the Amnok (Yalu) and Tuman (Tumen) rivers, in October 1906 forced the Chosŏn government to accept the Agreement of Co-operation in the Management of the Amnok and Tuman Riverside Forests, an agreement that facilitated their broad exploitation of the forests in those areas. Less than two years later, in January 1908, the Japanese Director-General in Korea established the Forest Law to provide the legal foundation for plundering the forests of the entire country which the law classified as Imperial Household forests, state-owned forests, publicly-owned forests and privately-owned forests.

During the first three years of the annexation of Korea, the Government-General earned about one billion yen through extensive lumbering operations in the so-called 'forest yards' it established in the Amnok and Tuman river valleys. That amount was nearly 18 times the 58 million yen annual budget of the Government-General at that time. Once it completed the Land Survey in 1918, the Government-General immediately implemented a Forest Survey that classified the entire country's woodlands into two major categories, state-owned and privately-owned forests and further sub-classified state-owned forests into forests to be preserved and forests to be used. That latter sub-category included about one million *chŏngbo* of forests that had previously been held by peasants for village common use along with about three million *chŏngbo* of mountainside lands that had been used by villages for gravesites. All of these lands now belonged to the Government-General.

The Government-General, along with Japanese individuals and companies established monopoly rule of all types of resources in Korea, in effect robbing the Korean people of their resources. The consequence was that the Japanese imperialists were able to secure resources to finance their colonial rule while preventing the growth of Korean national capital.

TRADE IN THE COLONY

After Korea opened its ports in 1876, the Japanese enjoyed an almost total monopoly on the rapidly growing trade between Korea and Japan. Such trade consisted of exchange of Korean raw materials for Japanese manufactured goods. This situation was intensified after Japan established full-scale colonial rule over Korea in 1910. There were two consistent features of trade throughout the colonial period. One was that the Japanese continued to enjoy a monopoly over the continuously increasing trade with Korea. The other was the transformation of Korea into a materials supply base and a market for Japanese products.

Korea's foreign trade increased rapidly in the early years after colonization, but Japanese domination of that trade also intensified. The total value of exports from Korea in 1910 was 19,914,000 yen, of which 15,379,000 yen, or 77.2%, went to Japan. By 1919, the total value of exports had grown rapidly to 221,948,000 yen, of which 199,849,000 yen, or 90%, went to Japan. The total value of imports in 1910 was 39,783,000 yen, of which 25,348,000 yen, or 63.7%, came from Japan. In 1919, the total value of imports increased to 283,077,000 yen, of which 184,918,000 yen, or 65.3%, came from Japan. There is no need to emphasize that both exports and imports were dominated by Japan.

At that time, the bulk of exports were made up of raw materials and crude foodstuffs while the bulk of imports were manufactured goods. This indicates the transformation of Korea into a source of raw materials for Japanese industries and a market for Japanese products.

Table 13: Trade amounts by commodity, 1910–1919 (unit: thousand yen)

	Exports		Imports	
	1910 (%)	1919 (%)	1910 (%)	1919 (%)
Raw materials	3,818 (19.2)	29,040 (13.1)	4,162 (10.5)	37,473 (13.2)
Goods as materials	110 (0.6)	20,043 (9.1)	4,064 (10.2)	23,554 (8.3)
Crude food articles	13,229 (66.4)	150,522 (67.8)	1,336 (3.4)	23,353 (8.2)
Refined food products	24 (0.1)	4,111 (1.9)	4,427 (11.1)	17,633 (6.2)
Finished Products	659 (3.3)	2,022 (0.9)	22,400 (56.3)	146,093 (51.6)
Re-export and re-import goods	213 (1.1)	1,502 (0.7)	42 (0.1)	34,936 (12.3)
Totals	19,909 (100)	221,939 (100)	39,789 (100)	283,070 (100)

Source: Chosen boeki kyokai (The Trade Association of Korea). *Chosen boeki shi* (History of Korean Trade)

As seen in Table 13 above, crude foodstuffs accounted for 66.4% of exports in 1910 and 67.8% in 1919, while manufactured goods accounted for 56.3% of imports in 1910 and 51.6% in 1919. The most significant foodstuff exports were rice, other grains, marine products, and tobacco leaf, while the most important imports were finished products from such light industries as textiles.

In the early-1920s the proportion of Japan's total trade accounted for by Korea rose even more. Japan's total exports had expanded greatly during the First World War, from 590 million yen in 1914 to over 2 billion yen in 1919. In the post-war years, however, Japanese exports decreased sharply, falling to 1.2 billion yen in 1921. In the midst of this dramatic drop in Japan's overall exports, however, exports to Korea continued to grow. They jumped from 72,690,000 yen in 1917 to 234,230,000 yen in 1925, after which they increased to 315,325,000 yen by 1929. The proportion of exports accounted for by finished products also increased during this time frame, from 51.9% in 1919 to 75.6% 1921. There was something of a decrease to 63.5% in 1931, but finished products still accounted for the bulk of exports from Japan to the colony. It is significant that while the import of textiles increased by only 1.5%, the import of finished machine products increased 220%. This was both a reflection of the strengthening of Japan's industries in Korea and of the growing significance of Korea as a captive colonial market.

As discussed earlier, in the 1920s, Japanese policies such as the Programme to Increase Rice Production, further strengthened the role of Korea as a food supply base for Japan. Table 14 below shows that Korean rice exports to Japan increased substantially between 1917 and 1933,

Table 14: Rice exports from Korea, 1917–1933 (unit: thousand *sŏm*)

Average yearly output	Exports to Japan (%)	Exports to other countries (%)	Totals (%)
1917–21: 14,100	2,196 (15.57)	247 (1.76)	2,443 (17.33)
1922–26: 14,500	4,343 (29.95)	34 (0.24)	4,377 (30.19)
1927–31: 15,798	6,607 (41.82)	9 (0.06)	6,616 (41.88)
1932–33: 16,108	7,770 (48.24)	59 (0.36)	7,829 (48.60)

Source: Chosen beigoku yoran (A Handbook of Korean Rice), 1934 edition.

more than doubling between 1917 and 1926. At the same time, the amount of rice exported to other countries, never very high, shrank to almost nothing in the second half of the 1920s.

After the Japanese turned to military aggression in the 1930s, the position occupied by Korea in Japan's overall trade picture rapidly grew more prominent and raw materials, especially raw materials for war industries, formed a larger proportion of exports from Korea to Japan. Using 1939 as an example, Korea was the largest recipient of Japan's total exports at 23.7%, followed by the Guandong district in the Liaodong Peninsula, where large numbers of Japanese troops were stationed, at 14.6%, the US at 12.4% and Manchuria at 10.3%. Imports from the US were the highest at 23.8%, followed by Taiwan at 21.1% and Korea at 17.5%.

In 1930, there was some parity between exports and imports, with the total value of exports from Korea to Japan at 240 million yen while the value of imports from Japan was 278 million yen. By 1940, however, while the value of exports to Japan increased to 741 million yen, the value of imports from Japan skyrocketed to 1.336 billion yen, nearly double the value of exports. In the wake of Japan's launching of its wars of aggression, the significance of Korea as a market for Japanese products grew even greater than before.

During that time, the bulk of exports to Japan was made up by materials for the munitions industry such as lumber, coal, cotton, oils, minerals, raw silk and metals. These materials formed 65% of total exports to Japan in 1940 while agricultural products and marine products formed 27% in 1941. Thus Korea played a role not only as a food-supply base, but also as a materials-supply base for the munitions industry.

On the other hand, the proportion of finished goods, most notably machinery, but also including textiles, metal products, vehicles and ships, among imports from Japan increased sharply to account for as much as 71% of the total in 1942. The increase in machinery imports was related to the expansion of munitions industries to Korea during the war years. In these years, too, Korea functioned both as an important source of supplies for Japanese industry and an important market for Japanese products.

CONTROL OVER TRANSPORTATION AND COMMUNICATION

The Japanese made huge profits through the construction of railways such as the Seoul-Pusan line and the Seoul-Ûiju line before annexation and laid more railways after the annexation, including the Honam (Seoul-Mokp'o) line, the Seoul-Wŏnsan line, and Hamhŭng-Kyŏngwŏn line. The total length of railroads was over 1,000 kilometers before 1910 and extended to about 2,200 kilometers by the end of 1919. Although the home government in Japan raised the funds for railroad construction by issuing bonds, in reality it was the Government-General of Korea that was responsible for redeeming those bonds according to the provisions of the Korean Project Bond Law.

The railroads were constructed at the expense of Koreans, but it was the Japanese who made high profits through their monopoly operations. Net profits from railroad management increased from 3,843,000 yen to 16,681,000 yen between 1910 and 1930. Not only did the Japanese strengthen the foundation of their military and political rule over Korea through extension and control of railroads, but the railroads, which allowed greater efficiency in turnaround, also facilitated the plunder of the Korean economy. Furthermore, the railroads became a primary factor in the development of the colonial commercial economy in Korea.

With the expansion of railroad lines, the volume of freight traffic increased dramatically from about 390,000 tons in 1907 to about 3,640,000 tons in 1919. There was a tendency toward even greater increases in freight from 1920 onwards. Many of the railway stations the Japanese established along the expanding railroads developed into significant commercial and industrial cities.

Japanese capital monopolized maritime transport as well. After the Chosŏn government opened its ports in 1876, Japanese shipping agents controlled coastal routes and kept traditional Korean transport operators from developing into modern shipping agents. After the Japanese annexed Korea, they dissolved most of the Korean maritime transport companies that had developed between 1876 and 1910 and founded instead the Korean Postal Ship Corporation to monopolize maritime transport and to prepare for the provision of military transport in times of need.

Japanese capital also invested in the expansion of harbour facilities. Before 1910, the Japanese Residency-General in Korea had already started building harbours in Pusan, Inch'ŏn, Chinnamp'o and Wŏnsan. After annexation, the harbours were linked with the expanding railway system and came to have great economic and military significance for the Japanese. The expanded harbours not only formed strategic points for Japanese economic exploitation, but also became important centres of industrial development. Moreover, the harbours provided bases for the growth of modern labour such as stevedores.

Although foreign investors began to build telegraph and telephone facilities in Korea in the 1880s, those facilities fell under complete

Japanese control after the protectorate was established in 1905. After annexation, the Government-General increased budgets continuously to expand telegraph and telephone lines, completing the construction of basic blocks by 1919. Telegraph lines were extended from 5,454 km to 8,030 km between 1910 and 1921, while telephone lines were extended from 486 km to 7,056 km during the same time span. The extension of telegraph and telephone lines meant the establishment of networks for Japanese rule over colonial Korea. The networks, of course, were linked to military purposes and contributed greatly to maintenance of security. Moreover, communications were Government-General monopoly enterprises that yielded high profits, ranging from 10% to 40% per year.

The Japanese also actively promoted road construction as a part of building their network for colonial rule. During the Residency-General period from 1907 to 1910, a total of over 800 kilometers in automobile roads were constructed in the sections between Taegu and Kyŏngju, and Chŏnju and Kunsan. An additional 2,600 kilometers of roads were built between 1911 and 1917. The Japanese then set up a six-year plan by which they completed the construction of main roads in 1923. All the funds used for road construction came from the Government-General's budget. Farmlands were condemned for road construction without compensation to the owner, while most of the work was done as compulsory labour by peasants who were subject to mobilization at any time. The road between Haenam and Hadong in south-western Korea was built by the forced labour of former righteous army fighters, who had been arrested during the armed struggle against Japan. The Japanese constructed roads in order to take resources and agrarian products out of Korea and facilitate the infiltration of Japanese manufactured goods into Korea's rural communities in areas where they had not yet been able to lay down railroad lines.

The colonial period did see increases in mining production, fisheries production, and forestry production, as well as the expansion of railroads, roads, and telegraph and telephone lines. However, the production of these resources, including minerals, was not done by or for the Korean people. Rather these resources were monopolized by the Japanese colonial government or Japanese corporations and thus supported the development of capitalism in Japan. Transportation and communications networks were built with taxes paid to the Government-General by Koreans, but were used mainly to solidify colonial rule.

REFERENCES

Mun Chŏngch'ang, *Kunguk Ilbon Chosŏn kangjŏm 36 nyŏnsa* (The thirty-six year history of the Japanese militarist occupation of Korea), vol. II, Seoul: Paekmundang, 1966.
Kobayashi Hideo, 'Chosen sankin shorei seisaku ni tsuite' (On the policy of gold mining promotion in Korea), *Rekishigaku kenkyu* (Journal of Historical Study), 321, 1967.

Pak Kyŏngsik, *Nihon teikokushugi no Chosen sihai* (Imperial Japan's rule over Korea), vols. I, II, Tokyo: Aoki shoten, 1973.

Cho Kijun. *Hanguk chabonjuŭi sŏngnip saron* (Essays on the capitalist development in Korea), Seoul: Korea University Press, 1973.

Chŏn Sŏktam and Ch'oe Yungyu, trans. by Kajimura Hideki. *Chosen kindai shakai keizai shi* (Socio-economic history of modern Korea), Ryukei shosha, 1978.

Pak Kiju, '1930 nyŏndae Chosŏn sangŭm chŏngch'aek e kwanhan yŏn'gu' (A study on the policy of gold mining promotion in Korea during the 1930s), *Kyŏngjesahak* (Economic History), 12, 1988.

4

Colonial Cultural Policy and the Resistance Movement

INTRODUCTION

Japan's position in the East Asian cultural sphere throughout the pre-modern era had been that of a backwards region receiving advanced civilization from China and Korea. In the process of moving towards a modern society, however, Japan was the first country in East Asia to accept Western civilization and followed the model of Western imperialism to colonize Korea. Although the Japanese were able to establish military and economic dominance over Korea in the late-nineteenth and early-twentieth centuries, they still had not overcome their pre-modern sense of cultural inferiority. Some scholars contend that this feeling of cultural inferiority was a major factor behind the atrocities the Japanese perpetrated in Korea and China. At any rate, during the first ten years after their annexation of Korea, the Japanese had their civil officials, and even teachers, wear swords in order to create an atmosphere of terror while not hesitating to put to death Koreans who resisted colonial rule.

Once their system of military rule and their specious arguments such as the theory of Japanese-Korean common ancestry (*Nissen dosoron*) proved useless in the face of the March First Movement, the Japanese revised their method of rule and pursued a policy of national division under the slogan of cultural politics. This new policy of national division sought to foster the growth of pro-Japanese elements in cultural, religious and economic circles, and to channel Korean passions away from politics to culture.

During the era of military aggression after 1930, the Japanese demanded co-operation in the war effort from the Korean people and vigorously strove to convert all Korean cultural leaders and intellectuals into pro-Japanese elements. Near the end, the Japanese tried to eradicate the Korean language, the Korean script and even Korean names. In the process, many Korean cultural leaders and intellectuals, including both those who had retreated from the line of absolute independence and those who had sought to lead the resistance movement in the direction of a strong cultural movement, ended up collaborating with the Japanese.

Under colonial rule, some elements of the national cultural movement lost their resistance and their critical sense and turned towards apolitical 'pure' cultural movements or cultural preservationist movements. Those elements ended up either falling into the snares of colonial rule or trying hopelessly to restore pre-modern culture. On the other hand there were those who steadily persisted in scholarly and cultural movements opposed to Japanese colonial cultural policy. There were nationalist historians, both inside and outside of Korea, who stood up in opposition to the distorted historical views propagated by the apologists for imperial Japan. There were also historians who sought to find the principles of universal historical development in Korea's past and attempted to grasp Korean history as part of world historical processes. Furthermore, colonial era research into the Korean language by Korean scholars produced a uniform spelling system and the editing of a comprehensive Korean language dictionary. Cultural resistance to Japanese rule continued all the way to liberation in August 1945.

Genuine national cultural movements under colonial rule shared a number of common features. One was facing, either in research or creative activities, the difficulties experienced by the Korean people as a result of colonial rule. A second was the way in which dealing directly with those difficulties led to resistance. A third was the way in which facing those difficulties led to the development of cultural activities as an integral part of the national liberation movement, as represented by such persons as Pak Ŭnsik, Sin Ch'aeho, Han Yongun and Yi Yuksa. On the other hand, 'purists' who removed themselves from the realities of the sufferings of the Korean nation could only engage themselves in the simple accumulation of knowledge or indulge themselves in asceticism or escapism, while those who were concerned about the national problem but lacked a spirit of resistance or a sense of criticism could only call for the preservation and restoration of traditional culture.

SECTION ONE
Colonial Cultural Policy

EDUCATIONAL POLICY

The sector in which the Japanese most vigorously pursued their policy of making Korea a permanent colony was education. Having succeeded in depriving Koreans of their political and economic autonomy, the Japanese set forth a colonial educational policy designed to destroy the cultural and spiritual independence of the inhabitants of the Korean Peninsula and to make them accept permanently their situation as an oppressed colonial people. It was for those purposes that the Japanese promulgated their first Educational Ordinance for Korea in August 1911.

The Educational Ordinance for Korea had as its first goal the creation in Korea of loyal subjects of the kind called for in the Meiji emperor's Rescript on Education promulgated somewhat earlier in Japan while limiting education in Korea to 'common' (elementary) schools, vocational schools and technical schools. This meant the diffusion of the Japanese language through common school education, the creation of semi-skilled employees in the agricultural, commercial and industrial sectors through vocational education and the training of persons with a limited degree of technical skills in two-year technical colleges. There was no provision for university education for the oppressed residents of colonial Korea.

The school system itself was different from that of Japan. Unlike the six-year elementary schools of Japan, the common schools in Korea provided only four or five years of schooling. Also, whereas Japan's secondary schools, the 'middle schools', offered five years of training, Korea's secondary schools, which were known as 'higher common schools', offered only four years for boys and three years for girls. With regard to the curriculum, the common schools of the colony gave five to six hours per week of instruction in the Korean language as opposed to ten hours per week of instruction in the Japanese language, while higher common schools gave a combined three hours per week to Korean and classical Chinese and seven hours to Japanese. Furthermore, all schools in Korea required students to take ethics courses that taught the 'concept of loyalty to the Emperor and the state' in order to turn Koreans into loyal subjects of the Japanese empire.

Even though the curriculum after annexation emphasized the benefits of colonization, educational facilities were extremely lacking. The number of private schools for Koreans was reduced from 1,362 in 1912 to 742 in 1919, while the number of Korean students decreased from 57,377 to 38,204 during the same period.

By contrast, the educational facilities established for Japanese residents in Korea were far superior. Whereas there was a total of 484 elementary schools for 17 million plus Koreans, there were no fewer than 393 elementary schools for the 330,000 Japanese residing in the colony. In contrast to the Korean school attendance rate of 3.7%, the attendance rate of Japanese children in Korean was 91.5%.

The gap was even greater at the secondary school level. The higher common schools and vocational schools established for Korean students numbered twenty-eight, with total enrolment of 3,800 students. The middle schools and vocational schools established for Japanese students living in Korea numbered 19, with total enrolment of 4,700 students. A small number of two-year technical schools established before 1910 received official recognition from the Government-General after colonization, including four government-established schools, such as a legal school founded in 1902, a medical school founded in 1899 and an industrial school founded in 1906, along with two private schools. These six schools had a total enrolment of 801 students, of which 625 were Koreans.

Japanese colonial education policy sought to suppress nationalistic private schools while fostering the development of government and public schools. The August 1911 Education Law for Korea was immediately followed by an October 1911 promulgation of Rules for Private Schools that greatly strengthened the requirements for the licensing of private schools and resulted in the above noted significant decrease in the total number of private schools. It also featured a strengthening of control over the contents of textbooks so that the vast majority of textbooks produced before 1910 were prohibited from use in schools. The Japanese abolished the college courses at Sungshil and Ewha that had been approved by the old Korean government and denied the requests for the establishment of colleges by Pak Ûnsik and Yang Kit'aek, who hoped to use for that purpose the six million yen they had gathered during the movement to repay the national debt in the late-1900s.

The Japanese, rattled by the eruption of the March First Movement in 1919, modified their policy of suppressing private schools, allowed some degree of foreign language training in the higher common schools and modified somewhat their heavy emphasis on vocational education. They revised their Education Law for Korea in 1922 to provide six years of education in the common schools, five years in boys' higher common schools and four years in girls' higher common schools. They also established a normal school and set up regulations for university education, thus clearing the way to establish a university in Korea. This revision of the Education Ordinance resulted in increasing the total years of education in Korea from the previous 11 or 12 years to 17, thus making the education system in Korea similar to that of Japan.

These changes in the educational system were an integral part of the Japanese cultural policy implemented in the wake of the March First Movement to soothe the nationalistic feelings of the Korean people and to draw them more deeply into the system of colonial rule. The Japanese subsequently engaged in a limited expansion of educational facilities in Korea so that by 1933 there were 680,000 students in 2271 elementary schools. They expanded vocational education from 21 schools with 1,872 students in 1919 to 52 schools with 9,220 students in 1935. They also set up 579 rudimentary village schools for 35,000 students in rural areas.

The expansion of elementary and vocation school education during the years of cultural politics was intended to produce workers who understood Japanese and who had basic technical skills, but the Japanese continued to restrict the expansion of liberal arts secondary schools. In 1935, there were 21 state-run boys' and girls' higher common schools with slightly over 10,000 students, a ratio of one student for every 2,200 Koreans. In the same year, there were 21 private boys' and girls' higher common schools with fewer than 10,000 students. There was also a total of 406 various irregular schools with roughly 70,000 students.

After the revision of the Educational Law for Korea to allow for a college in Korea, a group led by Yi Sangjae formed the Society for the Establishment of a National University in November 1922 and launched a campaign to raise 10 million yen, setting up local branches in over 100 places throughout the country. This movement envisioned the initial creation of departments of law, liberal arts, economics and science to be followed by a department of engineering and eventually departments of medicine and agriculture. The combination of interference from the Japanese, nation-wide floods in 1923 and severe drought in 1924 made it impossible to raise the funds and the movement foundered. This was followed by continuous efforts to elevate the Osan School and the two-year Yŏnhŭi and Posŏng technical colleges to university status, efforts that also failed because of Japanese interference.

In response to the Korean movement to establish a national university, in 1924 the Japanese set up Keijo Imperial University as a state-run university. At the beginning of the colonial period, the Japanese judged that the establishment of post-secondary educational institutions in Korea would not benefit their policy of colonial rule. In the years following the March First Movement, they realized that they could not suppress the Koreans' desire for college educations, so they created Keijo Imperial University with a college of law and humanities and a college of medicine. A college of engineering was added in 1938 in response to the need for greater numbers of persons with advanced technical skills after the outbreak of war with China. Although Keijo Imperial University was the only four-year institute of higher education in the colony, it was not a university just for Koreans. On the contrary, Japanese students significantly outnumbered Korean students. In the university's preparatory department, for example, there were 204 Japanese students and 104 Korean students in 1927, and 479 Japanese and 200 Korean students in 1943. Regular undergraduate enrolments were composed of 407 Japanese and 200 Koreans in 1933 and 407 Japanese and 335 Koreans in 1943.

Although there was some gradual expansion of educational institutions in colonial Korea, the expansion was limited to that necessary for the Japanese to carry out their policies of colonial rule, while the curricular content, too, was subjugated to that same goal. It can thus be said that the increase in the educated population represented the increase in population that was being assimilated to Japanese rule. This was particularly true after the outbreak of war in the late-1930s, when Japanese education in Korea emphasized the transformation of Koreans into 'subjects of the Emperor' (*kominka*).

After provoking war with China, the Japanese revised their Educational Law again in March 1938 as part of the process of strengthening their fascist system. The revised Educational Law set forth three major programmes. The first called for 'clarifying the national polity' (*kokutai*) in order to make Koreans subjects of the Empire. The second proclaimed 'Japan and Korea as one body' (*naisen ittai*) in order to eradicate Korean national identity. The third called for 'growing stronger by overcoming hardships' in order to inure the colonial population to wartime deprivation. These were expressed in the 'oath of imperial subjects' that the Japanese forced students to memorize and recite in unison.

For the institutional implementation of *naisen ittai*, the Government-General expanded elementary schools with the goal of one for each township. It also changed the higher common schools to middle schools like those of the home islands and established middle schools attended by both Korean and Japanese students in each region. These changes in the educational system came about because the Japanese needed the co-operation of the Koreans in carrying out their war of aggression. In the field of higher education, however, the only thing that changed was the intensification of demands for co-operation from the students; there was no change in the principle of discrimination against Koreans in higher education. In the case of the state-run two year technical colleges, the number of schools increased from seven in 1936 to nine in 1943. Whereas the number of Korean students in those schools increased somewhat from 605 to 805 during those years, the number of Japanese students jumped sharply from 1,202 to 2,281. In the case of private technical colleges, most of whose students were Korean, the number of schools increased from eight in 1936 to eleven in 1943 while the number of students increased from 2,440 to 4,025. But the total number of Korean students in both types of technical college did not even total 5,000. If we add in the Korean students at Keijo Imperial University, the total reaches slightly over 5,000. In other words, only two of every 10,000 Koreans were receiving any form of higher education.

After Japan attacked the United States, Japan's colonial education all but ground to a halt. Technical college and middle school students were mobilized as labour for all sorts of public works projects, and even elementary school students were mobilized to collect pine tar. Near the end, technical college and university students were forced to volunteer as 'student soldiers' (*hakto pyŏng*). On the other hand, Korean Christian schools that rejected demands to worship at Shinto shrines were shut down. Posŏng Technical College was renamed the Keijo Industrial Economics School, Yŏnhŭi Technical College the Keijo Industrial Management School and Ewha Women's Technical College the Keijo Women's Technical School. Furthermore, Korean teachers were replaced by Japanese teachers even in private schools.

Modern education was just beginning to take off in Korea at the beginning of the twentieth century. But that development was closed off by the Japanese imperialists who instead pursued a colonial education policy whose basic goal was the Japanization of Koreans. The intent, however, was not to put Koreans on an equal footing with the Japanese but rather to keep the Koreans in a permanent position of colonial inferiority. Thus Japanese colonial policy restricted higher educational opportunities for Koreans and sought instead to foster the growth of a labour force with the minimal skills needed to maintain colonial rule.

RELIGIOUS POLICY

The years of the Great Han Empire at the turn of the century also saw major changes in the field of religion. It was a time when Confucianism was turning away from its medieval focus on Nature and Principle Learning and seeking new directions and when Buddhism finally escaped from centuries of suppression to seek a new more prominent position for itself. It was also the time when Christianity became very active in transmitting modern civilization while old popular beliefs were struggling to transform themselves into higher modern religions, as Eastern Learning had done. After Korea was colonized, however, these religions were used to support colonial policy, or, if they refused, were suppressed.

Throughout the Chosŏn dynasty, Confucian scholars had played a strong role in forming public opinion. For that reason, after annexation the Japanese made efforts to mollify and win over Korean Confucians, many of who were not happy with colonization. The first step was to select 9,700 Confucians over the age of 60 to receive special 'gifts of money for the elderly' ranging from 15 to 120 yen. Despite pressure from the Japanese to accept the money, many refused – some even committing suicide in protest. But in the end 3,100 men took the payments. In 1911, the Japanese reorganized the Sŏnggyun'gwan (Royal Confucian College) as the Keigakuen (Confucian Academy), with the Governor-General himself as director. From that time on, the Government-General provided the funds to maintain the Academy. The Japanese also recognized the property rights of the traditional county schools in order to assuage the protests of rural Confucians.

There was not one single Confucian among the signers of the March First Declaration of Independence, although 137 Confucians did sign a petition calling for Korean independence that was sent to the Paris peace conference. In response, immediately after the March First Movement, the Japanese organized a number of pro-Japanese Confucian groups such as the Great Eastern Confucian Society (Taedong samunhoe) and the Society for the Promotion of the Confucian Way (Yudo chinhŭnghoe) in the hope of establishing firm control over all of Korea's Confucians. The Society for the Promotion of the Confucian Way, which proclaimed its founding goals to be 'respect the state system, obey the state's laws and work for the welfare of the people', established provincial organizations and co-operated actively with the Japanese.

The Japanese, who were aware of the harsh suppression Buddhists had endured from Confucians and from the government throughout the Chosŏn dynasty, actively pushed the entry of Japanese Buddhism into Korea immediately after the opening of the ports in 1876. Such Japanese Buddhist sects as Jodo, Jingen, Soto and Nichren came into port areas where they sought to win converts and to join with Korean Buddhists. The Soto sect, in particular, sought to use pro-Japanese Buddhist groups such as the Wŏn Buddhists to make a secret alliance, but was stymied when Korean monks learned of the plan and erupted in protest in 1910.

In 1911, right after annexation, the Government-General issued its Monastery Law in order to control Korea's Buddhists and to make them pro-Japanese. The Monastery Law restructured Buddhists into two major schools, Meditational and Scholastic, and established 30 major monasteries throughout the country with jurisdiction over some 1,300 minor monasteries. The Law established the Government-General's authority over the consolidation, relocation, disestablishment, and name changes of monasteries as well as over rules and regulations concerning monks. Sales of monastic property, including land, forests, buildings, statues, and old documents and paintings also required authorization from the Government-General. The abbots of the 30 major temples, who were appointed by the Government-General, established a joint office in 1914. Several years later, in 1922, they established two central organizations to control monasteries throughout the whole country. Those two organizations were merged into the Central Institute for Korean Buddhism (Chosŏn pulgyo chungang kyomuwŏn) in 1925. They also designated T'aego Monastery to control the now 31 major temples throughout Korea and called their unified body the Chogye school.

In spite of the Government-General's efforts to control the Buddhists, there were three monks, including Han Yongun, who signed the March First Declaration of Independence. Monks continued to participate in the national liberation movement in the post-March First years. Most monks, however, responded positively to Japan's colonial Buddhism policy and Korean Buddhist was becoming more pro-Japanese.

Abbots had originally been chosen by their fellow monks, but colonial policy required that they be appointed by the Government-General. The Government-General gave a broad range of powers to the abbots they appointed to head major monasteries, including the power to manage and dispose of monastery property and the power to control personnel affairs. The Government-General also gave them special privileges, such as audiences with the Japanese Emperor, congratulatory new year visits to the Governor-General and tours of Japan. The Government-General's policy of protecting their assets also enabled them to become major landowners. These powers and privileges soon made Korea's Buddhists, who had long suffered under the Chosŏn dynasty, into pro-Japanese elements. Those Korean monks who opposed the pro-Japanese Buddhist establishment organized the Korean Buddhism Restoration Association in December 1921 to move for the separation of church and state and for monastic autonomy. They also organized the a group known as the Mandang under the leadership of Han Yongun in 1930 to fight for the separation of church and state and for the abolition of the Monastery Law but the Monastery Law remained in effect until liberation in 1945.

The Protestant Christians of the Great Han Empire years were very active in establishing schools and hospitals, but their churches were still run mostly by foreign missionaries. Some of those foreign missionaries welcomed Korea's annexation by Japan. The General-Secretary of the Foreign Mission Committee of the US Presbyterian Church said: 'It is better for Korea to be ruled by Japan than by any other country, and far better than for Korea to be ruled by the Koreans themselves.' He also reported that foreign missionaries in Korea, who could be opposed to, indifferent to, co-operative with, or loyal to Japanese rule all agreed to be loyal to the Japanese. This pro-Japanese attitude of the missionaries can be attributed to the friendly relations that existed between the US and Japan at that time and to the Japanese Residency-General's policy of appeasement towards missionaries in the years leading up to annexation.

The Case of the One Hundred Five that arose right after annexation, however, marked the beginning of the Government-General's oppression of Protestants. This case, which was fabricated by the Japanese in order to suppress the New People's Association group of the Patriotic Enlightenment Movement, resulted in the arrest of large numbers of Protestant believers. Christians, both Catholic and Protestant, formed the nucleus of the March First Movement in its early stages. Protestants played a major role in the spread of the Movement throughout the country, with the result that they also suffered major sacrifices such as the Cheamni Church incident. Some foreign missionaries also became targets of Japanese oppression.

Once Japan shifted over to cultural politics, however, it began to pursue a policy of reconciliation toward foreign missionaries. The Government-General created a new Religion Section and changed its policy of requiring authorization for the establishment of churches and other religious facilities to one of merely requiring the establishment of facilities to be reported to the Religion Section, while warning that their 'use will be prohibited if they cause disruption of peace and order'. The Government-General also revised its regulations for private schools to allow Protestant schools to study the Bible. It also gave corporate status to property held by religious organizations, thus facilitating the activities of missionaries. The result was the rise of a number of strongly pro-Japanese missionaries.

The Japanese also brought in a government-controlled Japanese Protestant church organization to which they tried to make Korean Protestant Churches join. This ploy to separate Korean Christians from foreign missionaries and to bring them under the control of pro-Japanese Koreans had some success as some Protestants came together to form the Korean Congregational Church in September 1921, but that organization was unable to expand and soon fell apart. Despite the failure of the Japanese to bring Korean Protestants into a government-controlled organization, Korean lay Protestants thereafter maintained some distance from the national liberation movement and devoted themselves to a pure religious movement that did enjoy some success in converting new members. On the other hand, church leaders were becoming more clearly pro-Japanese.

It was under these circumstances that the Korean Protestant churches had to undergo their most severe trial yet: the issue of worshiping at

Shinto shrines. Shinto had originally been a popular religion but was elevated to become official state religion after the Meiji Restoration. In August 1915 the Government-General of Korea promulgated its Rules for Shinto Shrines. It established a main Chosen Shrine in Seoul and additional shrines in the provinces. The Japanese initially required Koreans to worship at Shinto shrines in 1935, starting with students in all levels of school. Protestant schools opposed this on the grounds that it was not a state ceremony but a religious ritual. The Japanese, however, were insistent in their demands. At that point, many Protestant schools throughout the country, including the Sungsil and Sungŭi schools in P'yŏngyang (October 1936), chose to close their doors rather than comply with the Government-General's orders, while others were forced to shut down by the Japanese.

After the Government-General closed schools that refused to worship at Shinto shrines, it next turned its attention to churches. The Roman Catholic pope in 1936 declared: 'Shinto rites are simple expressions of patriotism that show affection for the Emperor and persons who have made contributions to the state. Therefore, these rituals have value for citizens and I authorize Catholics to participate.' In 1937, the Protestant Methodist Church, which also had a system of centralized control, also accepted participation in Shinto rites. The only Christian group that held out, for a while, against the Shinto rituals was the Presbyterian Church. The Presbyterians, however, eventually decided to allow participation in the Shinto rites at the suggestion of a number of pro-Japanese ministers during its 27th General Assembly of Presbyters, held in P'yŏngyang at the insistence of the Government-General and surrounded by several hundred policemen. Nonetheless, the movement in opposition to the Shinto rites continued among some students, missionaries and ministers. There were even some ministers such as Chu Kich'ŏl (1897–1944) whose active opposition resulted in jail terms and martyrdom.

After annexation in 1910, when political organizations and political activities of any form were prohibited, the only organized social activity allowed for Koreans was religious activity. That was the reason why religious circles could take the lead in the March First Movement. But post-March First Japanese policies of oppression and appeasement led most religious organizations to pursue pure religious movements. The result was that, with the exception of a few religious leaders who pursued religious activities in connection with the realities of the national situation, religious organizations and leaders in Korea did not follow an anti-Japanese line.

THE DISTORTION OF KOREA'S HISTORY

The Japanese, having established colonial rule over a Korea which had enjoyed a high cultural position and a long tradition in the East Asian cultural sphere, felt the need to buttress their political and military control over the Korean Peninsula by demonstrating that Japan was culturally and historically superior to Korea. This was necessary to weaken Korean resistance to colonial rule and also to enhance the cultural pride of the Japanese people who had long suffered from a sense of cultural inferiority to China and Korea.

Research on Korea in Japan began during the Edo period of the Tokugawa shogunate. It began with Confucian scholars who were studying the works of such Korean Nature and Principle Learning scholars as Yi Hwang (T'oegye), and with some Japanese scholars who dealt with Korea as part of their research into such early Japanese histories as the *Kojiki* and the *Nihonshoki*. It was in the second half of the nineteenth century, after the Meiji Restoration, that Japanese research on Korea became suddenly very active. It was at that time that Hayashi Taisuke published his *Chosenshi*, the first Japanese general history of Korea. Around the time of annexation, government-sponsored Japanese scholars began to advance the idea of Japanese/Korean common ancestry and to fabricate arguments about the backwardness and stagnation of Korea.

After annexation, the Government-General plundered all sorts of Korean cultural treasures through excavations and surveys of historical remains, while looking the other way as Japanese civilians robbed graves and other sites. The Government-General also engaged in distortions of Korean history to support its political goals. Perhaps the most egregious example of this was the Government-General's establishment of the Society for the Compilation of Korean History that compiled the 37-volume *Chosenshi* (*History of Korea*). The Society's aims of severing pre-annexation historical scholarship and of stamping out the self-aware and autonomous historical scholarship coming from the national liberation movement front are stated quite clearly in the following summary it put out at time of the publication of the *Chosenshi*:

> The Koreans are not like the barbarian or half-civilized peoples of other colonies in that they have a literate culture as good as that of civilized peoples. Therefore, they have many histories from ancient times and also many new historical writings. The former, however, are from the time before Korea became independent of China and before colonization and have no relationship with current times, while the latter are marred by empty and abstract old dreams of an independent country. The latter also write of the rights and wrongs of Korea in the midst of power struggles between Japan and China and Japan and Russia or, as in the case of histories written overseas such as Pak Ûnsik's *Painful History of Korea* (*Han'guk t'ongsa*), fail to examine the real situation and engage in baseless hyperbole. The noxious effects of these histories on the minds of the people are beyond calculation.

Histories such as the *Chosenshi*, which the Government-General compiled by mobilizing government flunkies, generally depicted the flow of Korean history in terms of two negative features: heteronomy and stagnation.

Simply put, the heteronomy theory refused to recognize the autonomous development and historical and cultural independence of the Korean Peninsula. The essence of that argument was that Korean history was not something that developed through the self-generated activities of its inhabitants but rather was something that was simply maintained by the stimulation and rule that the Korean people received from neighbouring peoples in China, Manchuria and Japan. In the case of Korea's ancient history, the Japanese invented such notions as the 'theory of Japanese management of southern Korea' and the 'theory of the Mimana (Imna) Japanese Government' to argue that part of the Korean Peninsula had been under Japanese control. For medieval history, the Japanese contended that Korea had been under the consecutive rule of such Chinese dynasties as the Tang, the Yuan, the Ming and the Qing. Hence, the Japanese contended, annexation simply meant the return to Japanese control of a Korea that had never been truly independent. In other words, the Japanese sought to rationalize the colonization of Korea in terms of the restoration of ancient Japanese-Korean relations.

The grounds for the refusal to recognize the historical and cultural independence of Korea can be summarized in the historical views of the advocates of 'Manchurian/Korean history'. According to those scholars, the Korean Peninsula had never had its own independent political system; rather it was an area controlled by political forces that relocated there after failing to gain control on the continent. The Korean Peninsula also never developed its own unique culture; rather it was simply the recipient of continuous cultural influences from the continent. The only way to understand Korea's history and culture was to grasp it as part of continental and, particularly, Manchurian history. The discourse on 'Manchurian/Korean history' was nothing more than a way for the Japanese imperialists to rationalize their occupation of Korea and to prepare the theoretical basis for their aggression against Manchuria by lumping Korea and Manchuria together. While some of this fabrication was done by government-controlled scholars mobilized by the Government-General, an important role was also played by the Manchuria/Korea Geography and History Research Office of the South Manchuria Railway, a company that facilitated Japanese aggression in Manchuria.

The stagnation or backwardness theory was put forth primarily by government-controlled economists. Those stooges contended that unlike Japan and other regions that had gone through continuous stages of historical development in accordance with the world historical process, Korea experienced no process of historical development, failed to develop into a medieval society and was still at the level of ancient society when it was opened up to the outside world in 1876. In concrete terms, they argued that at the time of annexation in the early-twentieth century, Korea's level of socio-economic development was stuck at the same stage as Japan had been near the end of its ancient period in the late-tenth century. Their contention was that Japanese colonial rule had the benefit of bringing a Korea that had never progressed beyond the ancient stage of socio-economic development into the modern world in one giant step.

The arguments of these apologists for Japanese colonialism had a veneer of believability in the way in which they employed modern Western geopolitical theory to contend that it was the peninsular location of Korea that made it susceptible to outside rule and the way in which they used modern Western positivist historical methodology to substantiate their conclusions. As a consequence, their arguments were frequently accepted as 'objective' and continued to exert influence long after Korea was liberated in 1945.

REFERENCES

O Ch'ŏnsŏk, *Han'guk sin kyoyuksa* (History of new education in Korea), Seoul: Hyŏndae kyoyukch'ongsŏ ch'ulp'ansa, 1964.

Kim Yongsŏp, 'Ilche kwanhakchadŭl ŭi han'guk sagwan' (Japanese imperialist historians' views of Korean history), *Han'guksa ŭi pansŏng*, Seoul: Sin'gu munhwasa, 1969.

An Kyehyŏn, 'Han'guk pulgyosa ha' (History of Korean Buddhism, part two), *Han'guk munhwasa taegye 6, chonggyo/ch'ŏrhaksa*, Seoul: Koryŏ taehakkyo minjok munhwa yŏn'guso, 1970.

Kim Yangsŏn, 'Han'guk kidokkyosa, 2,'(History of Christianity in Korea, part two), ibid.

Son Insu, *Han'guk kŭndae kyoyuksa* (History of modern education in Korea), Seoul: Yŏnse taehakkyo ch'ulp'anbu, 1971.

Pak Kyŏngsik, *Nihon teikokushugi no Chosen shihai* (Japanese imperialist rule of Korea), Tokyo: Aoki shoten, 1973.

Kang Wijo, *Nihon tochika no shukyo to seiji* (Religion and politics under Japanese rule), Tokyo: Seibunsha, 1976.

Yi Manyŏl, 'Ilbon kwanhakcha tŭl ŭi singmin sagwan' (Colonial Historical Views of Japan's government scholars), *Han'guk ŭi yŏksa insik ha*, Seoul: Ch'angjak kwapip'yŏngsa, 1976.

Chŏng Kwangho, 'Ilche ŭi chonggyo chŏngch'aek kwa singminji pulgyo' (Japan's religion policy and colonial buddhism), *Han'guk kŭndae pulgyo ŭi inyŏm kwa chŏn'gae*, Seoul: Han'gilsa, 1980.

Kang Tongjin, *Ilche ŭi han'guk ch'imnyak chŏngch'aeksa* (History of Japanese policies of imperialist aggression in Korea), Seoul: Han'gilsa, 1980.

Han Cheйi, *Nihon no chosen sihai to shukyo seishyaku* (Religious policy in Japan's rule over Korea), Tokyo: Miraisha, 1988.

SECTION TWO

The Development of the Anti-Japanese Cultural Movement

ANTI-COLONIAL HISTORIOGRAPHY

At the beginning of the twentieth century, when Japanese aggression in the Korean Peninsula was intensifying and the distortion of Korean history by Japanese government-controlled historians was taking shape, Korean scholars of the Patriotic Enlightenment Movement began the struggle to correct the distortions of Korean history perpetrated by the Japanese and to establish a systematic narrative of Korean history in which Koreans were the subjects driving their own historical development.

These scholars resisted colonialist depictions of Korean history by describing the achievements of national heroes who beat back foreign aggression. Hyŏn Ch'ae (1886–1925), a Korean scholar who authored an adaptation of Hayashi Taizuke's *Chosenshi*, used the *Tongguk saryak* (a fifteenth century history of Korea from Tan'gun down to the fall of the Koryŏ dynasty at the end of fourteenth century) to undercut or reject Japanese contentions regarding the Chinese Han dynasty's four commanderies in northern Korea and the Mimana government in southern Korea. Hyŏn also followed the lead of eighteenth century Practical Learning scholars to argue for the legitimacy of the Korean Three Han as the subjects of Korean history and to emphasize the historicity of Tan'gun, whom the Japanese had consciously disposed of as a myth from later times. Scholars such as Hyŏn, followed a simple anti-foreign line to stress that the Koreans were the subjects of their own national history and had no historical sense of popular sovereignty. Their historical understanding was still based on Confucian concepts of loyalty and filial piety so that they focused on the achievements of heroes and great men as the driving force of historical development. Furthermore, they continued to write their histories in the pre-modern annals format.

In the face of the intensification of Japanese historical abuse after annexation, some more advanced scholars developed a new trend of historical scholarship. This new trend is what is now referred to as nationalist historiography. Pak Ŭnsik, who had been active in the Patriotic Enlightenment Movement, engaged himself directly in the national liberation front movement after 1910 while writing such histories as the *Painful History of Korea* to narrate the process of Japanese aggression against Korea and the *Bloody History of the Korean Independence Movement* to tell the story of Korean resistance to Japanese aggression. Pak followed the line of Hyŏn and others in emphasizing the Koreans as the subjects of their own history in opposition to Japanese historical arguments, but he was able to transcend the limits of Confucian historical understandings. Pak believed that the rise and fall of states and nations was dependent on their national spirit (*kukhŏn*) and that it was that national spirit that was the driving force of history. He argued:

> The physical embodiment of a nation is the state and the history of a nation is its spirit. Korea's physical embodiment may have collapsed, but if its spirit still lives, there will be a restoration of the Korean state.

Pak thought that the writing and teaching of history centred on the subjective autonomy of the Korean people were essential to fostering a spirit of independence and maintaining the spiritual props of the national liberation movement. Even though his emphasis on national spirit meant that he had fallen into the idealist view of history, Pak's historical research and writing constituted one method for the national liberation movement.

Sin Ch'aeho was another historian who had been active in the Patriotic Enlightenment movement before throwing himself into the national liberation movement front. He focused primarily on ancient history, writing such books as *A Draft History of Korea* (*Chosŏnsa yŏn'gu ch'o*) and the *History of Korean Antiquity* (*Chosŏn sanggosa*). He argued that such ancient Korean states as Koguryŏ had displayed a strong sense of independence and national spirit, but that those attributes had been lost in medieval times as Koreans adopted an attitude of subservience towards China, leading to the decline of the Korean nation. He believed that the study of ancient history would enable Koreans to recover their original national spirit and attain the goals of the national liberation movement.

Sin's understanding of history, however, was not limited to the simple recovery of ancient glory. Even in the years of the Great Han Empire prior to annexation, Sin criticized the historical views of men like Hyŏn Ch'ae as those of 'men who, even as they live in the land of Korea at the beginning of the twentieth century, are unable to dream of a French revolution or an American war of independence and dream instead of the old three kingdoms of ancient China'. In his 1923 'Declaration of the Korean Revolution', Sin understood the national liberation movement as a revolution and argued that it was the *minjung* (popular masses) who formed the main revolutionary camp while contending that it was only through the direct revolution of the *minjung* that national liberation could be achieved. He also set forth a view of history as the struggle between the 'self' and the 'non-self'. It is not clear exactly what Sin meant by the *minjung* 'self', but it is clear that Sin believed that the leadership of the national liberation movement should not be limited to a small number of elites but expanded to include the workers and peasants whose levels of consciousness were rising rapidly at that time.

The 'nationalist historiography' established and developed on the overseas liberation movement front by such men as Pak Ŭnsik and Sin Ch'aeho spread into Korea where it was adopted by such men as Chŏng Inbo (1892–1950), An Chaehong and Mun Ilp'yŏng (1888–1939). These scholars edited and published the writings of such Practical Learning scholars as Yi Ik (1681–1763) and Chŏng Yagyong (1762–1836) in an effort to perpetuate Korea's national scholarly traditions while producing historical writing in opposition to colonialist historiography.

Chŏng Inbo, who had been trained as a scholar of Han Learning (*Hanxue*; Qing dynasty Confucian learning), argued in the article '5,000 Years of Korean Ôl' contained in his book *Studies on Korean History* (*Chosŏnsa yŏn'gu*) that the essence of history was to be found in the Ôl, or unique national spirit, of the Korean people. He contended that historical facts were reflections of Ôl and that the purpose of historical research was to establish the stream of Ôl. He had fallen deeply into the idealist view of history, but he did strive to write a systematic history of Korea based on his understanding of a unique national spirit as a way to combat the colonialist historiography and to establish and maintain nationalism under colonial rule.

An Chaehong, a journalist who had participated in the New Korea Society movement, stated that in the circumstances of severe colonial oppression inside Korea 'the highest duty is to preserve the national essence for later generations'. An Chaehong devoted himself to the study of history and wrote the *Mirror of Korean Antiquity* (*Chosŏn sangsosa kam*), in which he depicted Korean history from the time of Tan'gun Chosŏn to the Three Kingdoms period as a process of ancient historical development in refutation of the colonialist contention that ancient Korean society was formed out of the confluence of external cultural influences from the north and the south. He also set forth his 'new nationalism' theory in which he reaffirmed the autonomy of the Korean nation *vis-à-vis* other nations while contending that the class contradictions inside Korea should be resolved through democratic methods. An Chaehong emphasized that the study of history had to be linked closely to the broad range of problems in national development.

Another journalist who wrote history was Mun Ilp'yŏng, whose writings were collected in his three-volume anthology, *Collected Works of Hoam* (*Hoam chŏnjip*). He understood to some degree that the *minjung* were the driving force of historical development and showed strong interest in popularizing historical scholarship. Furthermore, he fought against colonialist distortions of Korean history by arguing that in the ancient period Korea was the cultural centre of north-east Asia and that its influence extended to Manchuria and Japan.

The 'nationalist historians' were not the only Korean historians to fight against colonialist historiography during the colonial period. There were also the so-called 'socio-economic historians' who based their studies on the materialist view of history. Mostly economic historians, they set out to fight against the colonialist claims that Korea's history was stagnant and backwards. They laboured to demonstrate that Korea, too, had followed the developmental path of world history and thus to expose the fallacies of the argument that 'Korea had no medieval stage'. The representative works of this group included Paek Namun's *Socio-economic History of Korea* (*Chosen shakaikeizai shi*) and *Socio-economic History of*

Feudal Korea (*Chosen hoken shakaikeizai shi*) and Yi Ch'ŏngwŏn's *Reader in Korean Social History* (*Chosen shakai shi tokuhon*). These histories relied on theories of the developmental stages of social formation while searching for the motive force of historical development exclusively in the popular masses. They thus made major contributions to the development of the study of history in Korea. On the other hand, however, they were criticized for too rigidly applying materialist theory and formulas to Korean history at the cost of recognizing other aspects of Korea's past.

The development of both 'nationalist' and 'socio-economic' history was thwarted, however, by Japanese suppression. The revival and further development of these two types of history were also delayed for some time after liberation because of the loss of some of the more important scholars and because of the division of Korea. To the extent that there was any continuation of colonial historiography in South Korea, it was in 'nationalist history', but there was strong tendency towards national chauvinism and towards providing support for military dictatorship.

THE DEVELOPMENT OF SCHOLARSHIP ON THE KOREAN LANGUAGE

The Korean phonetic script which we call *han'gŭl* was known as the 'proper sounds to instruct the people' at the time it was created in the fifteenth century, and later as the 'vulgar script' throughout all the entire Chosŏn dynasty, only becoming known as the Korean national script after the opening of the ports in 1876. As the use of the phonetic script became more widespread, scholars began to look into the issue of the standardization of orthography. Chi Sŏgyŏng (1855–1935) published his *New Revision of the National Script* (*Sinjŏng kungmun*) while other active research was done by a group led by Chu Sigyyŏng, who was at that time employed in the Great Han Empire's Education Ministry.

Study on the Korean language had just barely gotten off the ground when Korea was colonized. After annexation, the Japanese referred to their own language as the 'national language' even in Korea while relegating Korean to the sidelines as the 'language of Korea'. They also promoted their language in schools, offering more hours of instruction in Japanese than in Korean. After the outbreak of war with China, the Japanese eliminated all instruction in the Korean language and launched the so-called 'Movement for the Regular Use of the National Language' which required the use of Japanese for all public business. As a consequence, the study of the Korean language was regarded as part of the national liberation movement by both Koreans and Japanese, with the Japanese attempting to repress such research.

During the years of military rule immediately after annexation, the National Script Research Centre that had been established by the Great Han Empire was abolished and the publication of all newspapers and magazines except those put out by the Government-General itself was banned. Under such a situation, there was little opportunity to engage in study of the Korean language.

With the shift to cultural politics after the March First Movement, however, Korean language newspapers were published and the study of the Korean language gained new life. Men who had studied directly or indirectly under Chu Sigyŏng, such as Chang Chiyŏng (1887–1976) and Kim Yun'gyŏng, organized the Korean Language Research Society in 1921. The Society arranged research symposia and public lectures, worked toward the regularization and standardization of grammar and spelling, and carried out a campaign to teach basic literacy skills to the unlettered masses. The name was changed to the Korean Language Society in 1931, after which it prepared and published its 1933 *Standardized Spelling Rules for the Korean Script* (*Han'gŭl match'um pŏp t'ongil an*) while collaborating with the newspapers to sponsor frequent public lectures on the Korean language.

A group of scholars led by Kwŏn Tŏkkyu (1890–1950) and Ch'oe Hyŏnbae (1894–1970) began the publication of a journal devoted to the study of the Korean language under the name *Han'gul* in 1927. Although that journal soon suspended publication, it was subsequently revived by the Korean Language Society and published regularly until it was shut down by the Government-General in 1942 as it prepared to put out its ninety-third issue.

Although the phonetic script had been adopted as the national writing system and put into wide general usage during the years of the Great Han Empire, its orthography had yet to be standardized, giving rise to considerable inconvenience, not to mention a sense of national embarrassment. Hence, the Great Han Empire government established its National Script Research Centre to regularize and standardize orthography but that Centre was soon disestablished by the Japanese. Nonetheless, private associations of scholars continued the work that had been begun by the Centre. That work culminated in the above-mentioned 1933 publication of rules for standardizing spelling by the Korean Language Society, a project that took the twelve men, including Kwŏn Tŏkkyu, Ch'oe Hyŏnbae, Yi Kŭngno (1893–1978) and Yi Hŭisŭng (1896–1989), who served on the committee two years to come up with a draft and another year to make revisions in response to criticisms offered at two separate reading sessions. There had been some opposition to the Korean Language Society's standardization plan from another group of scholars led by Pak Sŭngbin (1880–1943) but the Korean Language Society's plan enjoyed the support of the media and literary figures. While in the process of establishing its standardization plan, the Korean Language Society joined up with the *East Asia Daily News* to hold a series of public lectures during 1931 throughout the country in order to propagate its plan among the people. The student-led *vnarod* movement's Korean language lecture programme continued for another three years until it was stopped by the Japanese who were alarmed at the positive reaction of the people to the programme.

The colonial period also saw the compilation of dictionaries as part of the movement to protect and propagate the Korean language. Korean-French, Korean-Russian and Korean-English dictionaries had been made by foreigners during the years after the opening of the ports, but nobody had been able to compile a comprehensive Korean dictionary. The Korean Language Society, feeling that the lack of such a dictionary was a national disgrace, did form a committee for that purpose in 1929, but the first dictionary of the Korean language wasn't published until 1939 when Mun Seyŏng's *Dictionary of the Korean Language* came out. The Korean Language Society had actively pursued various preparatory activities such as the 1936 'Collection of Select Standard Korean Language Terms' and the 1938 'Plan for Standardization of the Han'gŭlization of Foreign Words', but its plan for publishing a comprehensive dictionary was stymied when the Japanese fascists suppressed the Korean Language Society after Japan had provoked war with the United States.

The Japanese, who had already prohibited the use of the Korean language in all schools and public meetings, and had shut down such Korean language newspapers as the *East Asia Daily News* and the *Korea Daily News*, next set out to disband the Korean Language Society. They fabricated the Hamhŭng student incident of 1942 as a pretext to arrest the vast majority of the members of the Society and other people who participated in the Society's activities. The Japanese ended up trying eleven men who were given jail sentences ranging from two to six years. One of those eleven, Yi Yunjae (1888–1943), died in prison.

Even though Japanese oppression prevented the publication of the Korean Language Society's comprehensive dictionary of the Korean language, the Korean phonetic script, which, because it had been looked down upon as a 'vulgar script', had never been systematically studied or standardized throughout the Chosŏn dynasty, attained standardization of orthography and also experienced a growing movement for the compilation of a comprehensive dictionary. This was one of the biggest successes of the national cultural movement during the colonial period.

THE LITERATURE OF RESISTANCE

The expanding use of the national script and the intensification of foreign aggression after the opening of the ports led to widespread writing and singing of patriotic poems and songs. Most of the poems and songs of that time, however, still reflected the old Confucian values of loyalty, as seen in the following:

> Great Chosŏn of Asia,
> Independence is yours.
> Eya, eya, love your land.
> Eya, eya, die for your land
> Be loyal to your king
> And love your land
> Do your very utmost to
> Be loyal to your king.

> And love your land.
> Uphold your government.
> And support your king.

Other songs, such as the following, denounced the Japanese and those who collaborated with them:

> Ilchinhoe, Ilchinhoe.
> Even after 1905
> Your exploits are already high;
> Even after 1907,
> Your ambitions are satisfied;
> Now with annexation,
> Are you filling a bottomless valley?

Although poems and songs of this type could no longer be sung publicly inside Korea after annexation and thus had no direct connection with domestic literary circles, the tradition was carried on in the overseas national liberation movement front in songs of the liberation armies, as seen in the following song:

> Step forth, liberation army, step forth.
> The long-awaited liberation war is at hand.
> The swift swords we have sharpened
> while waiting these ten years
> are now ready for the testing.

Inside post-annexation Korea, there were anti-Japanese songs such as the one below:

> Wŏnsan is a good place to live,
> but nobody can live there with
> the meddling of the Japanese.
> Inch'on is a good place to live
> but nobody can live there with
> the meddling of the Japanese.
> Those who talk go to the courts,
> those who work join the party.

Around the time of the March First Movement, there was new literary activity inside the colony, resulting in the publication of such journals as *Ruins* (*P'yeho*) and *White Tide* (*Paekcho*). Under the conditions of colonial oppression, the literary activity represented by these journals was unable to express pent-up national frustrations as direct resistance to the Japanese and was instead oriented towards a kind of nationalism and romanticism that was somewhat divorced from the realities of the Korean people. Even those writers who were actively concerned about the national situation often had to seek expression indirectly through symbolism, decadence and aestheticism. There were a few writers who produced works expressing some concern with the bitter realities of colonial Korea, such as Hyŏn Segŏn (1900–43), author of the 1921 short story *Impoverished Wife* (*Pinch'ŏ*) and Yŏm Sangsŏp (1897–1963), who wrote the 1924 short story *Before the Hurrahs* (*Mansejŏn*).

On the other hand, there were some works that evidenced a clear line of resistance from such writers as Han Yongun and Sim Hun (1901–36). Han Yongun, a Buddhist leader and a poet who devoted himself to the national liberation movement, wrote the following celebration of death as love of his country in his 1926 work, *The Silence of the Beloved* (*Nim ŭi ch'immuk*):

> However, I must turn myself to finding a way in this world.
> One way is to surrender myself to the embrace of the beloved.
> The other is to surrender myself to the embrace of death.
> That is because the third choice is even worse than death.

For Han, the beloved of the first choice was the nation, or the national liberation movement, while the fate worse than death of third was Japan, or the acceptance of Japanese rule.

Sim Hun made clear the miserable reality of the nation in his 1926 poem *In the Midst of Lament*:

> Crying sounds arise from the Koreans crowding the road.
> In places made raucous by the hoofbeats of soldiers' horses,
> the angry mobs are pushed away and trampled asunder
> as they fall to the ground and issue their dying screams.
> The sounds of their fists beating angrily on the ground
> and sounds of their voices shouting angrily at the sky
> reach all the way to the nine directions of the heavens.

Again, Sim expressed his longing for the day of national liberation in his 1930 poem, *When the Day Comes*:

> I will use my sword to peel even my skin
> and make a great drum to strap to myself
> as I step forth to the front of your parade.

Sim's works heralded the rise of the so-called 'new trend' in literature that reacted against romanticism and naturalism to show particular concern for the realities faced by the nation, particularly the increasingly impoverished livelihood of the popular masses. Influenced by the socialist thinking that arose in the national liberation movement front in the second half of the 1920s and inspired by the significant growth in the consciousness of the peasants and workers, the new literary movement naturally developed into a literature of resistance to colonial rule.

The 'new trend' literature was significant in that it embodied an awareness of the plight of the nation and a hostility to Japanese colonial rule as seen in such novels as *Famine* and *The Slaughter* written by Ch'oe Hansong (1901–33) and such poems as *Will Spring Come to the Dispossessed*, written by Yi Sanghwa (1901–43). The perception of reality by the 'new trend' was, however, superficial and limited to then-and-there descriptions of such things as the growing gap between rich and poor in urban areas without being able to give concrete representations of reality.

The formation of the KAPF (Korean Proletariat Artists Federation) in 1925 and the publication of its *Literary Arts Movement Journal* (*Munye undong chi*) marked the beginnings of a genuine proletarian literary movement in Korea. The KAPF movement was a progressive movement in that it intensified the understanding of national reality and promoted literary depiction of reality in its arguments over the issue of how to make literature accessible to the masses. Yi Kiyŏng's full-length novel *Hometown* has been appraised as a novel that succeeded in the depiction of colonial reality. KAPF literature, however, was also criticized for its formalism and its inability to adapt Soviet theoretical arguments in ways that reflected Korean realities.

On the other hand, the citizen (*kungmin*) literature group rebelled against the KAPFs movement's one-sided emphasis on class and stressed 'nation over class'. The argument for 'nation over class' suffered, however, from an ahistorical and excessively abstract notion of nation, leading inevitably in the direction of restorationism. Under the circumstances of colonial rule, the true direction of nationalist literature lay not in the beautification of the nation's past, but rather in resistance to colonial rule.

The literary resistance to colonial rule suffered continuous oppression after 1930 when the Japanese expanded their wars of aggression to Manchuria, China and the United States. KAPF was disbanded after its members were subjected to two rounds of arrests in 1931 and 1934 while other authors oriented toward nationalism and resistance found themselves forced underground. On the other hand, the collaborationist literature movement flourished and many authors became pro-Japanese writers.

After onset of hostilities with China, the Japanese demanded Korean co-operation with their war effort and mobilized many Korean writers and intellectuals to form pro-Japanese organizations for such purposes as 'the moral transformation of society' and 'consolation of troops in the field'. The Japanese also prompted Koreans to create such organizations as the 1937 Korean Literary Arts Society headed by Ch'oe Namsŏn and Yi Kwangsu, the 1938 'All-Korea Thought League to Respond to the Urgent Situation and Repay the Nation' whose members included such former anti-Japanese activists as Pak Yŏnghŭi (1901–?) and Kim Kirin (1903–85) and the 1939 Association of Korean Writers headed by Yi Kwangsu, whose leading members included such men as Kim Tonghwan (1901–?), Chŏng Insŏp (1905–83) and Chu Yohan (1900–79).

These organizations supported the Japanese war effort through their writings, but also through such activities as giving public lectures and making visits to Japanese military units.

Pro-Japanese literature figures did not simply write and lecture, but also developed theories to rationalize their actions. Representative of those was the 'Japanese National Literature' (*kokumin bungaku*) theory, regarding which Ch'oe Chaesŏ (1908–64) said: 'Japanese National Literature is not just an extension of the so-called modern literature which is rooted in European traditions. Rather it is a literature based on a synthesis, through the Japanese spirit, of Eastern and Western cultures that expresses the ideals of the rapidly advancing Japanese nation. Thus it will come to lead the East.'

Even in the 'period of darkness' for literature from the late-1930s, the literature of resistance continued, albeit on a smaller scale. Yi Wŏllok (penname Yuksa; 1904–44) graduated from Beijing University and the officer training school of the Righteous Fighters' Corps. He threw himself into the national liberation movement and was jailed several times, published his poetry collection *Grapes* (*Ch'ongp'odo*) in 1940, after which he fled to China, where he was caught by the Japanese police and eventually died in jail. His poem *Kwangya* (*Wide Plain*) spoke of national liberation with a clear historical consciousness:

> Now as the snow is falling
> and the fragrance of pear blossoms is far away
> I will plant here the seeds of my poor song.
> A great man on a white horse
> will come again as in times of old
> I will open my throat and call him here to this wide plain.

Yun Tongju (1917–45), a poet from northern Jiandao, hoped to live 'without shame until I die', and 'lit a lamp to push back the dark, as I wait for the dawn of a new era'. Yun, unfortunately, never saw that dawn. He was arrested as a thought criminal and died in prison in 1945.

Writers of the colonial period often ignored the realities of the nation, pursuing 'pure literature' and indulging in decadence, and in some cases becoming little more than tools for colonial rule. Even many of the writers who were concerned about the national situation lacked the will to resist and fell into a reactionary celebration of old tradition. The true Korean national literature of the colonial period was unable to destroy Japanese imperial rule and could only become a literature of resistance.

REFERENCES

Im Chongguk, *Ch'inil munhak non* (On pro-Japanese literature), Seoul: P'yŏnghwa ch'ulp'ansa, 1966.
Pak Hyŏngch'ae, 'Ilche ha ŭi kugŏ undong yŏn'gu' (A Study on the national language movement under Japanese imperialism), in *Ilche ha ŭi munhwa undong*

sa (The Cultural Movement under Japanese imperialism), Seoul: Koryŏ tae-hakkyo Asea munje yŏn'guso, 1970.

Song Minho, *Ilche ha ŭi han'guk chŏhang munhak* (Korean Literature of Resistance under Japanese imperialism), ibid.

Yi Kibaek, *Minjok kwa yŏksa* (Nation and History), Seoul: Ilchogak, 1971.

Kim Yongjik & Yŏm Muung, *Ilche sidae ŭi hangil munhak* (Anti-Japanese literature of the period of Japanese Imperialism), Seoul: Sin'gu munhwa sa, 1974.

Kim T'aeyŏng, 'Kaehwa sasangga wa Aeguk kyemong sasangga ŭi sagwan' (Kaehwa and patriotic enlightenment thinkers' views of history) in *Han'guk ŭi yŏksa insik ha* (Perceptions of history in Korea, volume 2), Seoul: Ch'angjak kwa pip'yŏngsa, 1976.

Kim Yongsŏp, 'Uri nara ŭi kŭndae sahak ŭi sŏngnip' (The establishment of modern historiography in Korea), ibid.

An Pyŏngjik, 'Tanje Sin Chaeo ŭi minjokchuŭi' (The Nationalism of Sin Ch'aeho), ibid.

Kim Yunsik, *Han'guk kŭndae munye pip'yŏng yŏn'gu* (Studies in the modern literary criticism of Korean), Seoul: Ilchisa, 1976.

Im Yŏngt'aek & Ch'oe Wŏnsik, *Han'guk kŭndae munhaksa ron* (On the literary history of modern Korea), Seoul: Han'gilsa, 1982.

Kang Man-gil, 'Ilche sidae ŭi pan singmin sahak non' (On the anti-colonial histo-riography of the period of Japanese Imperialism) in *Han'guk minjok undongsa ron* (On the history of the Korean national movement), Seoul: Han'gilsa, 1985.

Yŏksa munje yŏnguso munhwasa yŏn'gu moim, *K'ap'u munhak undong yŏn'gu* (Studies in the KAPF literature movement), Seoul: Yŏksapip'yŏngsa, 1989.

PART 2

National Division and the Development of the Reunification Movement

5

The Formation and Intensification of the Division System

INTRODUCTION

The basic underlying cause for the division of post-liberation Korea lay in Japanese colonial rule, while the immediate reason was the occupation of northern Korea by the Soviet Union and of southern Korea by the United States. Nonetheless, it is important to note that arguments that place the primary responsibility for the division of Korea on the interference of foreign powers are rooted in a perception of history that ignores the historical agency of the Korean people themselves. A view of history that sees the Korean people as the subjects of their own history is not limited to the rectification of distortions of Korean history and the extolling of Korea's past glories; rather it seeks to strengthen itself by recognizing the degree to which the Koreans themselves must bear responsibility.

From this point of view, there are a number of causes for the division of Korean that can be attributed to the Korean people. First, at the time of liberation in 1945, the Korean national community lacked a clear and objective perception of the historical significance of the liberation of their nation. Second, Koreans did not have a good international political understanding of the geo-political importance of Korea to the great powers. Third, there was the failure to maintain the momentum of the liberation movement as it had developed in the final years of Japanese rule.

The national liberation movement continued, in the face of great sacrifice, throughout the colonial period. Nonetheless, it was not the first, nor the primary, agent of the liberation of Korea. Even though Korean military forces were active in concert with the Allied Forces in a number of places during the final years of the Second World War, unfortunately they were not able to advance into Korea to disarm or accept the surrender of Japanese forces. Furthermore, there was no Korean government-in-exile or any other political force that gained recognition from the allies.

During the nearly half-century of Japanese colonial rule that was almost without parallel in its harshness, Koreans inside the country managed to preserve their national identity while Koreans outside the Peninsula persisted in the national liberation movement. This meant that Koreans thought that the defeat of Japan was a victory for them, and were unable to recognize that the real position Korea occupied in the heartless world of international politics was that of a colony of a defeated country.

Even the defeated Japanese had at least a superficial cabinet, but in Korea there was only the Government-General and no Korean regime recognized by the occupying forces. The consequence was the imposition of military government. Rather than settling for a few years of joint US-USSR administered trusteeship, however, certain elements caught up in 'national passion' rushed to have an 'independent country,' even if it meant only half a country.

Throughout most of its pre-modern history, the Korean Peninsula had close links with the continent and was heavily influenced by political developments there. In the modern period, however, the maritime power of Japan, which enjoyed support from two other major maritime powers, Britain and the United States, won successive victories over the continental powers of Qing China and Russia, and eventually colonized Korea. In the years leading up the Russo-Japanese War, the continental power of Russia and the maritime power of Japan sought to avoid war through negotiations that included a plan for dividing Korea, but the negotiations failed and the Korea problem was resolved through war.

At the end of the Second World War, the communist Soviet Union, which was a continental power, and the capitalist United States, which was a maritime power, agreed to a divided occupation of Korea in order to attain some kind of balance of power. In the face of the greatest danger to national unity in Korea's long history as a unified state, Korea needed political leadership with the wisdom to use the Peninsula's strategic geo-political position to establish a unified nation-state as a buffer zone or a neutral area between continental and maritime power. Instead, certain political elements used the divided occupation of the country to push for the establishment of two separate states in Korea, and the majority of the popular masses followed them.

Ideological antagonism between left and right had existed in the colonial era national liberation movement and was, in fact, an element that impeded the development of a stronger national liberation front. But there were also continuous efforts to overcome differences in ideologies and lines in order to create a strong national liberation front, with the result that near the end of the war substantial agreement had been reached and a united national front was being formed. Once Japan had been defeated, however, the unified front forces were pushed away as elements willing to settle for a divided country linked up with the occupying forces.

Tragically, there were no other political forces strong enough to force a change in the situation, with the result that before too long two separate governments were established in Korea. This situation soon led to a war between the two governments that quickly developed into an international conflict. The three-year Korean War ended without any resolution except the strengthening of the division system. The division system, which featured mutually reinforcing dictatorial regimes on both sides of the demilitarized zone (DMZ), has had crippling effects on the cultural, social and economic development of the Korean people throughout the second half of the twentieth century.

In the early-1960s, the 19 April popular uprising in South Korea overthrew the dictatorial regime of Syngman Rhee (Yi Sŭngman). Thirteen months later, however, south Korea was put under military rule as a result of a coup led by Park Chung Hee (Pak Chŏnghŭi). Park's military dictatorship, which placed first priority on economic development, intensified the division system. In the early-1970s, Park declared the establishment of his *'yushin'* (restoration) system, a move that even further strengthened the division system. At the same time, however, movements for democratization and the peaceful and independent reunification of the country continued to develop in south Korea. These movements were the main underlying force behind the end of the Park regime in 1979. After a brief moment of hope, the 'new military' seized power, suppressed the Kwangju *minjung* resistance, and re-established military dictatorship.

The division of the Korean nation, arising from the establishment of separate regimes and hardened by the Korean War, developed into the division system within the context of the cold war between the Soviet Union and the United States. The division system saw both regimes promoting different political, economic, social and cultural changes in ways that enabled them to build their own power bases. The two regimes strengthened their power bases through confrontation and competition with each other. All thought and action that sought to overcome the division system and to recover national homogeneity were continuously suppressed as Korea fell deeper into the morass of national division.

The continuing confrontation and competition between the two regimes have consumed the power and resources of the nation on both sides of the DMZ and have become major roadblocks to the development of the national history of the whole nation during the second half of the twentieth century. Even as world history has developed to weaken ideology, give new life to democracy and produced a new sense of crisis in the unlimited competition of globalization, Korea remains the only divided nation on earth and the Korean people continue to consume their energies and resources in confrontation and competition with each other. Although the advance of the democratic movement and the unification movement in south Korea since the 1970s have, along with changes in world historical development, brought the demise of military dictatorship and a limited weakening of the division system, the overcoming of the division system is the greatest historical task the Korean nation faces today.

SECTION ONE
The Process of National Division

THE DEFEAT OF JAPAN

Japan, which had made Korea its colony after winning the Russo-Japanese War of 1904–45, continued to expand its wars of aggression through the Manchurian Incident of 1931 by which it made Manchuria a *de facto* colony and through its invasion of China in 1937. Although Japan expected an easy victory over China, it found itself bogged down on the continent, attacked Pearl Harbor and declared war on the United States and Great Britain in 1941. Thus Japan followed Germany and Italy into the Second World War.

Japan enjoyed success in the early years of the Second World War, occupying Singapore, the Philippines and Indonesia while pushing into Burma. Before long, however, Allied forces' counter-attacks put Japan on the defensive. The fall of Saipan to the United States on 7 July 1944 was a major setback to the Japanese. With Saipan as a base, the US was able to conduct major air campaigns against the home islands of Japan, to occupy Okinawa and thus to prepare for landing operations in Japan itself. Furthermore, the US succeeded in building an atomic bomb, which it used against the Japanese at Hiroshima on 6 August 1945 and Nagasaki on 9 August 1945, thus driving the Japanese to the verge of annihilation.

Earlier, after Italy, one of the Axis countries, had surrendered, the Allies met in Cairo on 12 November 1943 to discuss how they would order the world after the end of the war. At that time, they decided to 'guarantee the freedom and independence of Korea'. Once Germany had surrendered on 7 May 1945, the Allies met again at Potsdam where they once again affirmed the independence of Korea by deciding to 'limit Japanese sovereignty to Honshu, Hokkaido, Kyushu, Shikoku and other small islands to be determined by the Allied forces'.

Faced with certain defeat, in May 1945 Japan decided to use the Soviet Union as an intermediary in the hope of avoiding unconditional surrender. The Soviet Union, however, had already received guarantees from the other Allies for the return of Sakhalin, the ceding of the Kurile Islands and the maintenance of the *status quo* in Inner Mongolia at the Yalta Conference of 11 February 1945 and had committed itself to participating in the war against Japan within two to three months of the end of the war in Europe. Once the US used the atom bomb against Japan, the Soviets immediately moved against Japan on 9 August 1945, thus putting further pressure on Japan to surrender.

Japan, no longer able to avoid unconditional surrender after the US used atomic bombs and the Soviet decision to enter the war, had no choice but to accept the declarations of the Potsdam Conference. This brought to an end four years of war in the Pacific and liberation for Korea. After Japan notified the Government-General of Korea of its intention to surrender on 10 August 1945, the Government-General, concerned about the security and safe return to Japan of over 800,000 Japanese civilians and soldiers in Korea, entered into discussion about the transfer of power with such influential Koreans as Yŏ Unhyŏng and Song Chinu.

Song Chinu refused to respond and also refused to work with Yŏ Unhyŏng. This meant the transfer of power to Yŏ Unhyŏng's group. Yŏ, on the base of the already extant National Foundation Union, established the Committee for the Preparation for Korean Independence and set out to release persons who had been imprisoned as thought criminals and to establish public safety units. When the public safety units attempted to take over Japanese police offices on 16 August, however, the Government-General suddenly turned against transferring power. The commander of Japanese military forces in Korea proclaimed, 'the Japanese military will take resolute measures against anything that agitates the people or disturbs public order', and re-established Japanese control over police stations, newspapers and schools.

A few weeks later on 6 September 1945, US troops arrived in Seoul. On 9 September, the commander of the US troops accepted the surrender of Abe Sinko (1879–9953), the last Japanese Governor-General of Korea. This brought to an end the thirty-five years of Japanese colonial rule over Korea. The US troops now stationed in Korea, however, refused to recognize either the Shanghai Provisional Government or the People's Republic of Korea that had been proclaimed by the Committee for the Preparation for Korean Independence. The US troops implemented a system of military government to replace the Government-General. Whereas Yŏ Unhyŏng's organization had branches throughout all of Korea, the US Army Military Government in Korea was limited only to Korea south of the 38th parallel.

DEMARCATION AT THE 38TH PARALLEL

Although the divided occupation of Korea in 1945 along the 38th parallel was carried out by the occupying forces of the US and the USSR, the danger of the division of Korea was nothing new. The Korean Peninsula, because of its particular geopolitical position, had frequently been the focal point of collisions between great powers, and more than once those powers had sought to avoid conflict by dividing Korea. For that reason, some Koreans sought to avoid division and colonization by presenting plans for making Korea a buffer zone or a neutral state. Nonetheless, Korea found itself colonized and then divided in the twentieth century.

Following the failure of their attempt to emulate the Meiji Restoration in Korea (the 1884 *coup d'état*), such Enlightenment thinkers as Kim Okkyun (1851–94) and Yu Kilchun (1856–1914) presented proposals for the neutralization of the Korean Peninsula but met with no success. When Japan and Russia were facing off over control of Korea in 1896, the Japanese suggested that the two powers divide Korea at the 38th parallel but the Russians, feeling that they had gained the upper hand after

Kojong fled to the Russian legation in 1897, rejected the Japanese proposal. After Japan entered alliance with Great Britain in January 1902, the Russians, feeling threatened and anxious to secure their position in Manchuria, set forth a plan that would have recognized Japanese interests south of the 39th parallel and neutralized the rest of Korea north of that line. The Japanese refused, demanding instead the control of all of Korea and rights in Manchuria, rejected the plan. When war finally broke out between Japan and Russia in 1904, the Great Han Empire government proclaimed wartime neutrality. The Japanese, however, paid no heed to the Korean government's position and went on to establish a protectorate and then a colony in Korea.

At the very end of colonial rule, the Soviet Union, acting according to the decisions made at the Yalta Conference, joined in the war against Japan, and crossed the Tuman River into Korean territory and occupied Unggi on 11 August 1945. Soviet troops then landed at the northeastern port cities of Najin on 12 August and Ch'ŏngjin on 13 August. The Japanese Kanto army that occupied the northern reaches of Korea collapsed without offering any serious resistance and the Soviet forces swiftly swept southward. The US, whose forces were still engaged in mopping up operations in Okinawa, knew that it would take them some time to prepare for the occupation of Korea and was concerned that the Soviets would occupy the whole of the Peninsula. The US, in a move that echoed earlier plans to divide Korea, presented a proposal that its forces accept the surrender of Japanese troops south of the 38th parallel and Soviet forces accept the surrender north of that line. The Soviets, hoping for US aid and also hoping to participate in the occupation of Japan, agreed.

US policymakers, fearing that the Soviets would occupy the whole of Korea or at least push far south, were surprised at the Soviet acceptance of their plan. In reality, however, the sudden end of the war caught the Soviets unprepared to occupy the whole of Korea. In other words, Japan was still in a position to prevent the Soviets from gaining what they really wanted, which was the occupation of all of Korea and also parts of Japan proper such as Hokkaido. Thus Japan, even in defeat, still played a key role in the division of the Korean Peninsula.

Nonetheless, because the Allies had secretly agreed at the Yalta Conference to implement a long-term trusteeship in Korea, the 38th parallel represented nothing more than a temporary demarcation line for accepting the surrender of Japanese troops until such time as the Allies arranged for an interim government for the whole of Korea. Because of the opposition of some of the residents of Korea and because of the growing confrontation between the US and the USSR, plans for the establishment of one single interim government under Allied trusteeship were never realized. Instead, the 38th parallel became a true line of national division with the establishment of separate northern and southern governments.

The external factors behind the hardening of the 38th parallel as a line that divided the Korean nation included the geopolitical position of the

Korean Peninsula and Japanese colonial rule, the US proposal to prevent the total occupation of Korea by the Soviets and the Soviet acceptance of that proposal, the US decision to abandon the agreements of the Moscow Conference and instead to take the Korean problem to the United Nations, and the intensification of the Cold War between the US and the Soviet Union in the years following the end of the Second World War. The internal factors included nationalist sentiments that failed to recognize the realities of the international political position of Korea as the colony of a defeated power and refused to accept any delay in independence, those political forces inside Korea that sought to use those feelings to gain power even if only over part of the nation and the willingness of some of the ordinary Koreans to go along with those forces.

THE BREAKUP OF THE SOVIET-US JOINT COMMISSION

The immediate cause of the failure to establish a unified national government and the creation instead of two different governments in Korea was the breakdown of the Soviet-US Joint Commission established at the Moscow Conference to discuss the establishment of a unified provision government. The US forces accepting the surrender of Japanese troops south of the 38th parallel refused to recognize either the Korean People's Republic hastily proclaimed by Yŏ Unhyŏng's Committee for the Preparation for Korean Independence or the Provisional Government of the Republic of Korea, formerly in Shanghai but now in Zhongjing (Chungking). The US Pacific Command implemented its military government with the proclamation that: 'Complete authority over the Korean land and Korean people south of the 38th parallel resides for the time being in this command.'

The commander of US forces in Korea, General John R. Hodge (1894–?), initially attempted to administer Korea through the Japanese Governor-General, but immediately backed off in the face of strong resistance from the Koreans, dismissed the Governor-General and set up a military government. But he chose to use the institutions of the Government-General and the pro-Japanese Koreans who staffed them. On the other hand, north of the 38th parallel, the Soviets immediately detained the Japanese soldiers, police and bureaucrats, removed the pro-Japanese elements and organized people's committees in each province centred around Korean communists. The first people's committee was organized in South Hamgyŏng Province on 16 August 1945 and was immediately followed by people's committees in the remaining four provinces north of the 38th parallel: North Hamgyŏng, North P'yŏngan, South P'yŏngan and Hwanghae. On 9 February 1946, a North Korean Interim People's Committee was formed as a new ruling system was stabilized and strengthened earlier than in the south.

The Allied Powers, who had decided on a trusteeship in Korea at the Yalta Conference, held the Moscow Conference to discuss the post-war situation on 28 December 1945. The Conference was attended by the foreign ministers of the USSR, the US and Great Britain who made the following decisions about the Korean Peninsula. One, a unified interim government for all of Korea was to be established according to demo-cratic principles in order to prepare for an independent Korean state. Two, a USSR-US Joint Commission was to be established to support the creation of the interim government. Three, the trusteeship of Korea, which was to be jointly administered by the USSR, the US, Great Britain and the Republic of China, was to last no longer than five years.

The proposal for implementing a post-war trusteeship in Korea in order to separate Korea from Japanese rule and prepare Korea for inde-pendence was first raised by the US in 1942. This was reiterated in the declaration of the Cairo Conference that called for Korea to become independent 'in due course'. There was, however, no certain agreement about what 'in due course' meant. Whereas the US president Franklin D. Roosevelt (1882–1945) said that Korea needed a trusteeship of 'twenty to thirty years', the Soviet Union's Josef Stalin (1879–1953) declared that the trusteeship should be 'as short as possible'. No further agreement was attained by the time the Second World War ended and the Soviet Union moved into the northern reaches of the Korean Peninsula.

At the Moscow Conference, the US, which had elements of strong support in the United Nations, proposed that the UN administer trustee-ship in Korea, while the Soviet Union presented a 'guardianship plan'. As a compromise plan, the US proposed a trusteeship by three capitalist states and one socialist state. The Soviet Union, having received guaran-tees – never fulfilled – of participation in the occupation of Japan, went along. The result was the adoption of a plan for the establishment of the USSR-US Joint Commission, the creation of a unified interim govern-ment, and the drafting of a trustee agreement by the US, the USSR, Great Britain and the Republic of China.

The Moscow Conference decision, which opened the way for the establishment of a pro-American, pro-Soviet or a neutral government in Korea, was in fact an attempt by both the US and the USSR to gain time in order to create governments under their own influence in Korea. Even so, trusteeship was intended to be a means and a process for ensuring the independence of the former Japanese colony of Korea and not an end in itself. But once word of the agreement reached Korea, the big issue for Koreans became not the creation of interim unified government but rather the idea of trusteeship.

Initially both the left and the right in Korea stepped forth in oppos-ition to trusteeship, but the left, led by the Korean Communist Party, in a statement of total support for the decision of the Moscow Conference, soon shifted to a position of support for trusteeship. The Korean Independence Party, which was made up of old members of the Provisional Government, and the Korean Democratic Party, which was made up primarily of landlords, sought to overcome their weakness and consolidate their power through anti-trusteeship movements. In the midst of intensifying confrontation between right and left over the trusteeship issue, the USSR-US Joint Commission opened its first meeting on 20 March 1946.

The USSR-US Joint Commission's first task was to negotiate with political parties and social organizations to create an interim government to rule Korea during the period of trusteeship. For that reason, the Joint Commission decided on 18 April 1946 to negotiate only with those parties and organizations that accepted the decisions of the Moscow Conference. This presented no problem for the leftist forces that had already expressed a line of support for trusteeship, but the right-wing Korean Independence Party refused to participate in negotiations with the Joint Commission on the grounds that participation in such negotiations constituted a *de facto* acceptance of trusteeship. The Korean Democratic Party, however, eventually accepted the US military government's assurances that participation in the negotiations did not necessary mean giving up its opposition to trusteeship.

But the Soviet Union, however, took the position of refusing to allow right-wing groups or individuals to participate in negotiations unless they dropped their opposition to the Moscow Conference decisions. Regarding the list presented by the US of twenty political parties and social organizations to be invited to the negotiations, the USSR accepted only the three parties and organizations that belonged to the left-wing Democratic National Front and rejected the other seventeen on the grounds that they were parties or organizations opposed to the Moscow Conference decisions. The USSR also complained about the absence from the list of such organizations as the 600,000-member All-Nation Conference of Korean Labour Unions, the 300,000-member Korean Women's League, the 650,000 member All-Nation Youth Organization General League, and the 3,000,000 member All-Nation Farmers' Union General Federation. In response, the US noted the absence of right-wing organizations from the USSR's list and argued that the labour, women's, youth and peasant bodies cited by the Soviets were nothing more than destructive terrorist entities headed by radical Communists who exaggerated their membership. The US also proposed that discussions about the abolition of the 38th parallel and the economic integration of north and south should precede discussions about an interim unified government. The USSR responded that the disposition of the 38th parallel was an issue to be determined by the interim unified government and that the issue of the economy was not included in the Moscow Conference decisions. The consequence was the break up of the USSR-US Joint Commission meeting on 6 May 1946.

After the failure of the first Joint Commission meeting, a group of right-wing forces led by Syngman Rhee launched a movement to establish a separate government in south Korea. Once the US and the USSR began negotiations to open a second Joint Commission meeting, the right wing again refused to participate and carried out a large scale anti-trusteeship movement. The second Joint Commission meeting opened in the midst of the anti-trusteeship movement and appeared to be making some progress until the Soviets demanded that the 425 southern organizations registered as participants be reduced to 118. At the time there were 425 political parties and organizations in the south that had applied to participate and 36 in the north. The total number of members claimed by these organizations was over 70,000,000, a figure that was more double the entire population of Korea. The Soviets argued for the exclusion of the political parties and organizations involved in the anti-trusteeship movement and the many small organizations with fewer than 10,000 members. The US refused on the grounds that the anti-trusteeship forces had the right of 'freedom of expression'.

At the same time, the Chŏngp'an Company forgery incident of 15 May 1946 led to the suspension of publication of the Communist Party organ, the *Liberation Daily News* (*Haebang ilbo*), and orders were given to arrest Communist Party leaders. The left-wing forces led by the Communist Party abandoned their hitherto co-operative line of recognizing the US military government as a legal entity and on 26 July 1946 announced their 'new tactics', turning to a combative line. The left was experiencing internal strife over the issues of left-right collaboration and the combining of the three parties. Nonetheless, it was able to use worker discontent over severe high prices and food shortages to organize the September General Strike to put pressure on the US military government. This was followed by the *minjung* struggle that erupted on 1 October 1946 in Taegu and other parts of North Kyŏngsang Province. Over 300,000 persons participated in this huge outbreak of popular resistance that produced over 300 dead, over 3,600 missing, over 26,000 injured and over 15,000 arrested. The confrontation and friction deepened between the US military government and the left and between the left and right.

The US, in order to revive the deadlocked Joint Commission, demanded a meeting of all four allies – the US, the USSR, Great Britain and the Republic of China. The US also proposed that legislative organs be established in both north and south through regular elections, and that a unified interim body to be made up of the representatives of those legislative bodies negotiate the withdrawal of US and Soviet troops and the establishment of a completely independent state with the four powers. The USSR refused on the grounds that it was not appropriate to take the question of the creation of a temporary government to the four powers and that the formation of separate legislative organs in north and south would foster division. At that point, despite Soviet opposition, the US took the Korean question to the United Nations where its supporters formed an absolute majority. This marked the final dissolution of the Joint Commission on 21 October 1947.

THE ESTABLISHMENT OF SEPARATE STATES

Immediately after the break up of the first Joint Commission meeting, Syngman Rhee made his so-called Chŏngŭp declaration of 3 June 1946 in which he called for the establishment of a separate government in the south, saying: 'We must organize an interim government or committee in the south and appeal to world opinion to force the Soviets to withdraw from the north.' This was supported by the Korean Democratic Party and other right-wing forces. On 7 December 1946, Rhee went to the US to pursue his 'diplomacy' of asking the UN to discuss the Korea problem and asking the US for support for the establishment of a government in Korea.

At the United Nations General Assembly, the US Secretary of State attempted to make Korea independent by discussing ways to implement the decisions of the Moscow Conference with the Soviets. He concluded, however, that there had been no progress over the previous two years in the task of making Korea independent and stated: 'I hope that bringing the Korean question to the United Nations General Assembly will yield a means to make Korea independent without going through trusteeship.' This made clear the US position of abandoning the decisions of the Moscow Conference and turning the Korea problem over to the UN.

The Soviet representative opposed the US move on the grounds that it violated the agreement made in Moscow. The Soviet representative argued that the Korean problem had to be solved through an agreement among the USSR, the US and Great Britain and further declared that the best way to resolve the situation was for the Soviet and American armies to withdraw from Korea and let the Korean people themselves resolve their own future.

The US, however, presented a resolution to the UN calling for the establishment of a United Nations Temporary Commission on Korea to supervise free elections to be held throughout both north and south Korea before the end of March 1948 to establish a national assembly and a government. The resolution also called for the withdrawal of both US and Soviet forces from Korea. The UN approved a plan for the establishment of the United Nations Temporary Commission on Korea (UNTCOK), for Korea to become independent without going through trusteeship, and for a UN supervised general election in north and south. Thereafter, a UN commission composed of Australia, Canada, China, El Salvador, France, India, the Philippines and Syria went to Korea. The Soviets, however, prevented the commission from entering North Korea, thus stymieing the UN decision.

At this point, the anti-trusteeship right wing split into two major groups. Syngman Rhee and his followers in the Korean Democratic Party called for the establishment of a separate government in the south in a move to divide the nation. The Korean Independence Party, led by Kim Ku, opposed the establishment of a separate government, calling for the withdrawal of both the US and the Soviet armies and a general election to be decided by negotiations between major figures in the north and the south. It was, however, too late to prevent the establishment of a separate government.

After the UN commission was refused entry into the north, the United Nations, approved on 26 February 1948 the suggestion of Krishna Menon, the Indian representative who headed the commission, to carry out an election 'only in the area where it is possible.' Thus the election was implemented only in south Korea on 10 May 1948. Following the election, the newly-elected National Assembly established a constitution on 17 July 1948. The constitution provided for a president to be elected by the National Assembly and to be limited to two four-year terms. The National Assembly elected Syngman Rhee as president. Rhee took office on 15 August 1948 as the first president of the Republic of Korea.

In the process, the left wing led by the Korean Worker's Party of south Korea, as well as right-wing and moderate forces, opposed the formation of a separate southern government and formed the Association for the Promotion of Unified Independence on 21 July 1948. There were also many movements, including the 3 April Cheju Island resistance, against the establishment of a separate government that arose throughout the country.

On the other hand, north of the 38th parallel, the North Korean Provisional People's Committee, with Kim Il Sung as its chair, was established in February 1946 and carried out land reform on 5 March 1946. The North Korean Worker's Party was established separately on 28 September 1946, along with the formal North Korean People's Committee. After the Korean People's Army was founded and a constitution adopted on 29 April 1948, an election was held to select representatives to the Supreme People's Assembly on 25 August 1948, and the Democratic People's Republic of Korea was established on 9 September 1948.

Whereas the separate state in the south refused to negotiate with political forces in the north, the separate state in the north continued to express its desire to negotiate with southern political forces and proclaimed itself to be a unified government that had representatives from the south.

REFERENCES

Morita Hofu, *Chosen sosen no kiroku* (Records of the end of the war from Korea), Tokyo: Annando shoten, 1964.

Kuksap'yonch'an wiwŏnhoe, *Charyo taehan min'guk sa* (Historical materials on the Republic of Korea), Seoul: 1970.

Yi Hojae, *Han'guk oegyo chŏngch'aek ŭi isang kwa hyŏnsil* (Ideals and realities of Korea's foreign policy), Seoul: Pŏmmunsa, 1972.

Song Namhŏn, *Haebang 30nyŏn sa, 1 kwŏn* (History of 30 years of liberation, volume 1), Seoul: Han'guk saryo yŏn'guwŏn, 1976.

Cho Sŭngsun, *Han'guk pundansa* (History of the division of Korea), Seoul: Hyŏngyongsa, 1982.

Yi Wanbŏm, 'Han pando sint'ak chŏngch'i munje 1943–6' (The question of trusteeship for the Korean Peninsula, 1943–6) in *Haebang chŏnhusa ŭi insik* (Perceptions of history at the time of liberation), Seoul: Han'gilsa, 1987.

Han'guk yŏksa yŏn'guhoe hyŏndaesa yŏn'guban, *Han'guk hyŏndaesa 1* (Modern history of Korea, 1), Seoul: P'ulpit, 1991.

SECTION TWO
The Korean War

THE BACKGROUND TO THE WAR

The external causes of the Korean War can be seen as Japanese colonial rule and the divided occupation of the Korean Peninsula by the armies of the US and the USSR. Japanese expansionist aggression, which began with the colonization of Korea subsequently expanded to war with China, the US and the USSR, and the end of Japanese colonial rule brought the divided occupation of Korea. The divided occupation led to the establishment of separate governments in north and south Korea, which in turn led to the Korean War. Another partial reason was the success of the Communist revolution in China.

The internal cause can be found in the ideological confrontation within the nation. The split between left and right began in the process of the national liberation movement. Although continuous efforts were made in the unified front movement to overcome this ideological confrontation throughout the colonial period and in the movement to establish a unified national state during the post-liberation years, those efforts ultimately failed and a divided nation was created by division-oriented forces. Even if the two separate states expressed their desire for the peaceful reunification of the nation, in reality the north was pursuing revolutionary reunification and the south military reunification. The Korean War arose out of these external and internal factors dating back to the colonial period and the confrontation between the two separate states after liberation.

The Syngman Rhee government, which was established in collusion with the landlord elements that had enjoyed protection under colonial Government-General policies, gave shelter to pro-Japanese elements because it needed their support in the confrontation with left-wing forces, and thus became the target of attacks from the left wing. Furthermore, it alienated the right-wing forces that had participated in the national liberation movement. Thus it suffered from weak legitimacy. The nature of the Syngman Rhee regime is clearly revealed in its suppression of the Special Committee to Investigate Anti-National Activities that had been established for the purpose of punishing those Koreans who had collaborated with the Japanese during the colonial period.

From the time it took office, the Rhee regime was plagued with economic and political difficulties. In 1949, for example, the government's income was only 40% of its expenditures. In the first year since it took power, the amount of currency in circulation had doubled and inflation had more than doubled. Industrial output, on the other hand, was only 18.6% of that of 1944. In early-1950, as the time for new elections approached for the National Assembly, Syngman Rhee realized that his party's chances for victory were not good. He sought to postpone the elections but was prevented from doing so by US pressure. In the 30 May 1950 elections, Syngman Rhee's supporters won only 30 seats out of a total of 210 in the National Assembly, whereas 126 independents were elected. Many of those newly elected Assemblymen were moderates regarding north-south relations, a fact that cast a dark shadow on Rhee's chances for reelection in 1952.

In the meantime, there was continuing armed resistance to the Rhee regime. Elements of the South Korean Labour Party formed 'mountain units' that began to engage actively in guerilla warfare after the 3 April struggle on Cheju Island. The south Korean constabulary established by the US military government on 14 January 1946 had become the Army of the Republic of Korea with the founding of the republic in August 1948, but its ranks included substantial numbers of left-leaning soliders. Some of those leftist soldiers participated in the 3 April insurrection on Cheju Island, while others of the Sixth Regiment in North Kyŏngsang Province rose in rebellion on three occasions between 2 November 1948 and 30 January 1949.

The largest uprising by ROK soldiers, however, began in Yŏsu on 20 October 1948, just two months after the Rhee regime took office. Some 700 hundred soldiers stationed in Yŏsu arose in rebellion and fled to the area of Mount Chiri on the border between South Kyŏngsang and South Chŏlla provinces. They were joined by over 1,300 civilians, organized people's committees throughout large areas of the two provinces and began a guerilla war. Other areas of significant anti-Rhee guerilla activity included the Mount Odae and Mount T'aebaek regions of Kangwŏn Province, various locales in North Kyŏngsang Province and Cheju Island.

At the same time, US policy towards Korea can also be seen as setting the stage for war. Pursuant to the UN resolution calling for the withdrawal of foreign military forces from Korea, the US withdrew its troops from south Korea on 30 June 1949, leaving behind a roughly 500-member Korean Military Advisory Group. The US also set up a plan to provide south Korea with $10 million in military aid and concluded a mutual security pact with the south Korean government. However, once the Rhee regime's economic policy proved to be a failure and political chaos continued to erupt in south Korea, the US Secretary of State Dean Acheson (1893–1971) made a public statement that omitted Korea from the list of areas in Asia that the US would defend. On the other hand, on 19 June 1950 a representative of the US Department of State told the South Korean National Assembly that the 'US would gladly provide all necessary moral and material support if south Korea were to fight against the Communists'. These contradictory aspects of the US Department of State's attitude towards Korea revealed the uncertainty of US policy in the Peninsula. They are also considered by some scholars to have encouraged North Korea to launch its war against the South.

In contrast with the instability of the Rhee regime, Kim Il Sung's regime in the north was quickly able to attain stability. The Kim Il Sung regime, with its secure political system, achieved rapid improvement in north Korea's economy. Its 1949 industrial output was 20% higher than in 1944 while its agricultural production also increased by 40%. North Korea was able to claim that its gross national product more than doubled after liberation in 1945. The Kim Il Sung regime, bolstered by this kind of political and economic stability, declared that the democratic national fronts of north and south Korea must unite to 'make the whole people advance to the struggle to remove US forces and reunify the Fatherland', and proclaimed the organization of the Democratic Front for the Unification of the Fatherland on 25 June 1949. The northern regime also sent a message to the Secretary-General of the United Nations on 2 July 1949 in which it called for the 'peaceful reunification of Korea by the Korean people themselves', and a 'concurrent election in both north and south'.

The northern regime also sought to further the development of guerilla struggles in south Korea by organizing the guerilla forces into People's Guerilla Units at Mount Odae, Mount Chiri and Mount T'aebaek. The Mount Odae People's Guerilla Unit, also known as the Yi Hojae Unit, had five companies made up of about 300 students from the Kangdong Political School. The Mount Chiri Unit, with Kim Talsam as commander and Nam Tobu (alias Ha Chunsu) as vice-commander, had about 360 men. The Mount T'aebaek Unit, under the commander of Yi Hyŏnsang, had four regiments. The Rhee regime established combat headquarters in the Mount Chiri and South Chŏlla Province districts in March 1949 and engaged in a major campaign to eradicate the guerillas. The result was the almost total elimination of all the guerilla units except a few deep in the mountains that continued scattered activities thereafter.

The Kim Il Sung regime concluded economic and cultural agreements with the Soviet Union, along with another agreement that provided north Korea with military support for six infantry divisions and three mechanized divisions, along with 150 airplanes. The Kim regime also entered into a secret agreement with the People's Republic of China on 18 March 1949, to bring back to Korea the roughly 5,000 Korean soldiers who had been part of the Chinese People's Army. Those soldiers were incorporated in the Korean People's Army. The result was that the Kim regime was able to strengthen its military forces rapidly.

At the same time, the Rhee regime, in order to overcome its domestic political setbacks, began to call for military action against the north under the slogan 'Advance north for unification' (*pukchin t'ongil*). Nonetheless, south Korea was vastly inferior to north Korea militarily and suffered from increasing political and economic instability.

THE DEVELOPMENT OF THE WAR

After the 1948 establishment of separate states in north and south Korea, there were continuing clashes, large and small, between the military forces of the two states. Those clashes led to all out war on 25 June 1950.

The Korean War, which lasted three years and one month, can be generally broken down into four stages.

The first stage was the occupation of the entire country, except for the Pusan Perimeter in south-eastern Korea, by the People's Army. The People's Army occupied Seoul on 28 August, the fourth day of the war, and subsequently occupied Taejŏn on 20 July after fighting with the hastily dispatched US 24th Division. By early September, the People's Army had control of all of south Korea except for the area of Kyŏngsang Province behind the Pusan Perimeter, which stretched from Kyŏngju in the east to Taegu in the west and Masan in the south. But neither the People's Army's Second Corps, which was in North Kyŏngsang Province, nor its First Corps, which was in South Chŏlla Province, was able to break through the Pusan Perimeter, behind which the UN forces, composed mainly of Americans, began to regroup and prepare for a counter-attack.

The entry of UN forces during the first stage marked the transformation of the Korean War from a civil war to an international conflict. At that time, the USSR was boycotting the UN Security Council over the issue of the replacement of the Republic of China, now in Taiwan, with the People's Republic of China in Beijing. The Soviets were not there to exercise their veto power when the US proposal to have the Security Council declare the People's Army to be an aggressor and to dispatch UN forces to Korea was adopted. The consequence was not only the intervention by UN forces made up of sixteen nations but the transformation of a civil war into an international conflict.

The second stage was the counter-attack by the UN forces, both along the Pusan Perimeter and at the port of Inch'ŏn near Seoul, where they landed on 15 September 1950. They retook Seoul on 28 September. On 30 September, the UN forces crossed the 38th parallel and continued north to near the Korean-Chinese border, with one unit reaching as far as the banks of the Amnok (Yalu) River on 26 October 1950. The turning point of the second stage was the decision to have UN forces proceed north of the 38th parallel. As soon as Seoul was retaken, Syngman Rhee called for an attack across the parallel. The Democratic Party administration in Washington DC, facing midterm congressional elections, also needed a military victory in Korea. The US-dominated UN agreed to push north across the 38th parallel and established the United Nations Commission for the Unification of Korea (UNCURK). This UN decision was not made in the Security Council, where the USSR had made a reappearance, but at the General Session. Some elements in US political circles warned about Chinese intervention if UN forces passed the 38th parallel, but the commander of UN forces, General Douglas McArthur (1880–1964), discounted those warnings and send his forces north.

The third stage of the war began with the 25 October 1950 intervention by Chinese Communist forces. The UN forces were forced to retreat, giving up P'yŏngyang on 4 December and Hŭngnam on 24 December 1950, and even evacuating Seoul on 4 January 1951. The UN forces withdrew as far south as Osan before regrouping and retaking Seoul on 14 March 1951.

They again crossed the 38th parallel on 24 March and by 11 June occupied places north of the parallel in central Korea such as Ch'ŏrwon and Kŭmhwa. At that time, the Soviet Union, which had secretly sent its air forces to fight in Korea, presented a proposal at UN for a cease-fire. As a result, negotiations for a cease-fire began on 23 June 1951.

The largest issue of the third stage was the question of the expansion of the war. After the intervention of Chinese forces, McArthur argued for expanding the war by bombing Manchuria, using Nationalist Chinese forces from Taiwan in Korea, and opening up a new front by having Nationalist Chinese forces land in southern China. Great Britain and other countries, however, were strongly opposed to expanding the war. The US government, concerned about the possibility of Soviet intervention leading to another world war, was also opposed to McArthur's proposals. Eventually, McArthur was dismissed from his post as commander-in-chief of the United Nations forces on 11 April 1951. The US policy toward Korea thus shifted from the line of unifying Korea under American influence to a line of ending the war through negotiations.

The fourth stage of the war was the process of conducting talks and concluding an agreement for a cease-fire. The US's ready acceptance of the Soviet proposal for a cease-fire led to the opening of talks at Kaesŏng on 10 July 1951. The talks focused on establishing a line of demarcation for a demilitarized zone, the formation of an organization to oversee the implementation of the cease-fire and the exchange of prisoners of war.

The Syngman Rhee regime, which was strongly against the US suggestion of a cease-fire, set forth a number of conditions for accepting a cessation of hostilities, including the withdrawal of Chinese Communist forces, the disarmament of north Korea and the implementation of a general election under UN supervision. There was no chance for the acceptance of these conditions. In the midst of continuing combat, the US pushed on with the cease-fire talks.

One of the issues was the question of where to establish the cease-fire line. The Communist forces argued for the 38th parallel, whereas the UN forces, who had pushed somewhat north of the parallel, held out for establishing the line at the current point of contact between the two sides. Eventually, the Communist side gave in and agreement was reached on 31 October 1951. The two sides also agreed to establish a committee of neutral countries to oversee the implementation of the cease-fire. The committee was made up of Switzerland and Sweden, suggested by the UN forces, and Poland and Czechoslovakia, suggested by the Communist forces.

The biggest difficulty for the cease-fire talks was the exchange of prisoners of war. The UN side presented a list of 132,474 People's Army and Chinese Communist prisoners, while the Communist side presented a list of 11,559 Republic of Korea and United Nations prisoners. Among those prisoners on the Communist side, including men who had been mobilized as volunteers by the People's Army during its occupation of southern Korea, there were many who did not want to be sent back south. This led the UN to argue for interviews of each prisoner, with the prisoners to be allowed to choose north Korea, south Korea, Communist China or Thailand. The Communist side countered that all prisoners had to return to their original countries. It looked like yet another impasse, but the Communist side backed off and the talks continued. The result of the UN side's interviews of its prisoners was that 83,000 men wanted to be returned. The Communist side declared that it could not trust the UN's interviews. This led to a halt in the talks and intensification of combat. The US Air Force bombed the Sup'ung Dam on the Amnok (Yalu) River, which had to that time been spared, and fierce fighting in the Kŭmhwa area produced large numbers of UN and south Korean casualties.

The stalled talks were renewed at the suggestion of the Communist side following the change of administrations in the US in January 1953 and the death of Josef Stalin in the Soviet Union on 5 March of that year. Initial agreement was reached on 26 April 1953 on the exchange of injured and ill prisoners. But progress in the cease-fire talks produced even greater opposition from the Syngman Rhee regime. The US attempted to persuade Rhee by promising to raise twenty combat divisions in the south Korea army, to provide 100 million dollars in economic aid and to maintain US forces on alert status in or around south Korea. Rhee not only refused to respond to the US enticements, but as soon as the agreement to exchange prisoners was signed he shocked the world by the unilateral release of 25,000 'anti-Communist' prisoners of war. Although Rhee's action almost brought the breakdown of the talks, the US continued actively to pursue a cease-fire and won the agreement of the Communists with the result that a cease-fire agreement was signed on 27 July 1953. Before the signing of the agreement, the US mollified Rhee with the signing of a mutual defence pact between the US and the Republic of Korea and with promises of long-term economic aid and the strengthening of the South Korea military.

The cease-fire agreement called for the opening of political talks to determine the future of the Korean Peninsula within three months. In a joint statement issued on 7 August 1953, the US and south Korea promised that 'if peaceful reunification of the historic Korea Peninsula under a democratic and independent state cannot be achieved within 90 days' the two countries would withdraw together from the political talks. Political talks were opened in Geneva on 26 April 1954, but broke up without achieving any success.

In the meantime, remnants of the People's Army who were unable to retreat north after the Inch'ŏn landing, together with Korean Worker's Party elements who had been reorganized and strengthened during the period of north Korean occupation and surviving members of the pre-Korean war guerilla units, had begun to organize new guerilla units in each of the southern provinces. These Communist guerilla units, centred on the 'southern army' commanded by Yi Hyŏnsang, opened up guerilla activities in such places as Mount Chiri in order to open up a second front in anticipation of another southern push by the People's Army. These units, however, were almost completely annihilated by the south Korean military by the time of the signing of the cease-fire agreement.

THE SIGNIFICANCE OF THE WAR

The Korean War, which arose out of the two sides' efforts to impose unification by revolution and unification by military force, failed to achieve the goal of reunification. The one thing it did produce was national fratricide. During the war, however, each side enjoyed a short-term occupation of the other side, during which each implemented its own limited occupation policy. An examination of the occupation policies pursued by the two sides can give us some insight into what kinds of historical and practical goals they hoped to achieve.

Seen from the side of the Kim Il Sung regime, the Korean War was a continuation of the people's democratic revolution that had been pursued during the years of Japanese colonial rule. The unified front policy adopted at the Seventh Comintern of 1935 allowed for flexibility in its application in various national societies. It was a people's democratic revolution strategy that allowed for the total expulsion of imperialism from colonized nations and nations that were satellites of imperialist powers, for their complete independence and for the liquidation of feudal remnants. Regimes pursuing this revolutionary strategy were ultimately committed to the dictatorship of the proletariat, but they were less concerned at this stage with a socialist revolution than with liquidating imperialist and feudal forces. Thus the role of these regimes was less that of a proletariat dictatorship than that of a people's democratic dictatorship that sought to represent the interests of a broad spectrum of the people.

After liberation in August 1945, the Kim Il Sung regime, following the people's democratic revolutionary line and the programme of the Fatherland Restoration Association developed during the anti-Japanese struggle, set up the north Korean branch of the Korean Communist Party in October 1945, followed by the establishment of a people's regime in the North Korean Provisional People's Committee in February 1946. It then proceeded to carry out land reform, nationalize major industries, implement democratic labour laws, and establish equality between men and women.

The Korean War broke out while the Kim regime, having reorganized the Provisional People's Committee as the North Korean People's Committee, was moving from the stage of the people's democratic revolution to the second stage, the socialist revolution. The Kim Il Sung regime, which occupied nearly 90% of south Korea in the early months of the war, pursued an occupation policy that was an extension of the people's democratic revolution. In preparation for pursuing a people's democratic revolution in the south, the Kim regime first restored the organizations and people's committees of the Korean Workers' Party, which it had earlier created on 1 July 1947 as a union of northern and southern Korean Workers' Party branches. This restoration of the Korean Worker's Party in the south was done using members of the Southern Branch of the Korean Workers' Party who were freed from jail after the People's Army occupied the south, surviving members of Communist guerilla units and underground Party members.

In late August and early September of 1950, the Kim regime used such elements to establish metropolitan and provincial parties in Seoul (chairman Kim Ûngbin), Kyŏnggi (Pak Kwanghŭi), North Ch'ungch'ŏng (Yi Sŏnggyŏng), South Ch'ungch'ŏng (Pak Uhŏn), North Chŏlla (Pang Chunp'yo), South Chŏlla (Pak Yŏngbal), North Kyŏngsang (Pak Chonggŭn) and South Kyŏngsang (Nam Kyŏngu). In addition to such party organs, the Kim regime also set up such social organizations as the Democratic Youth League, Woman's League, Vocational League, Peasant's League and the General League of Cultural Organizations.

At the same time, the people's committees that had been organized immediately before and after liberation but had subsequently been oppressed by the US military government re-emerged as collectives of revolutionary forces based on labour-peasant leagues at each administrative level to form a unified front political organ. This organ pursued a programme of liquidating pro-Japanese and anti-national elements, the seizure and redistribution of land without compensation, the establishment of equality between men and women, and the confiscation of property that had been owned by the Japanese imperialists.

The class composition of county, township and village people's committees was 8.1% industrial workers, 85.5% peasants and 3.7% office workers. By comparison, the elections conducted in the north before the war resulted in industrial workers and peasants accounting for 50.9% of provincial, city and township committee members and 66.2% of county committee members.

The socio-economic occupation policy pursued by the Kim Il Sung regime in the south featured land reform, the implementation of labour laws, the collection of agricultural taxes in kind, and the purge of pro-Japanese and pro-American forces. The principles for land reform called first for 'the permanent eradication of feudal landownership relations and the tenant system and the ownership of land only by those who actually cultivated it', and second for 'the seizure and redistribution of land without compensation'. The second principle, in particular, was significantly different from the land reform plan of the Rhee regime.

At the beginning of the war, on 4 July 1950, the Kim regime promulgated its 'Provisions for Implementing the Programme of Land Reform in the Southern Half of the Republic'. These provisions were carried out in all of Seoul, the parts of Hwanghae and Kangwŏn province south of the 38th parallel, and Kyŏnggi, South Ch'ungch'ŏng , and North Chŏlla provinces and in part in the areas of South Kyŏngsang, North Kyŏngsang, and South Chŏlla provinces that were under the control of the People's Army. Land reform was completed in 1,198 of the 1,526 townships in south Korea. About 38% of the land seized was nationalized, while 66% of the total peasant households in the occupied area received redistribution of land without compensation. The debts owed by peasants who had already bought land from landlords were cancelled. As the UN forces recovered territory in south Korea, they nullified the land reform of the Kim regime and restored lands to the original landlords. Nonetheless, the Kim regime's land reform greatly weakened the position of south Korean landlords and made it impossible for the Rhee regime to pursue its programme of land reform.

On the other hand, the Kim regime decided on 6 July 1950 to raise volunteer soldiers in the areas of south Korea under its occupation. The volunteers, who were eighteen years or older, came largely from the poor peasants. Also all the former members of the southern branch of the Korean Workers' Party who had joined the People's Guidance League were forced to join the army. As the fortunes of war turned against them, the North Koreans intensified their recruitment of volunteers, and nearly 400,000 young south Koreans were mobilized to fight in the war. Furthermore, the north Korean forces pursued a policy of purging anti-national forces in the area under their occupation. A large number of right-wing persons were disposed of through people's courts and many others of various backgrounds were kidnapped and taken to the north by the retreating north Koreans.

After the Inch'ŏn landing brought the war to its second stage, the US Joint Chiefs of Staff, who had authorized McArthur to cross the 38th parallel, made a statement regarding measures to be taken after the People's Army no longer offered resistance. The statement said that UN had not granted the right of the Republic of Korea to rule over the territory north of the 38th parallel, so any recognition of the automatic extension of the Republic of Korea's authority must wait for action from the UN. The Syngman Rhee regime, on the other hand, contended that 'once combat has ceased, the authority of the Republic of Korea to exercise its legal rights over the territory of north Korea must be realized as quickly as possible', and called for a UN supervised election to be carried out in the northern half of the country. The US, however, took the position that the Republic of Korea was a legal government only in the southern half of Korea and rejected Rhee's claim of authority over the north. The British representative to the UN argued that the election to be carried out in Korea after the cessation of hostilities should not be limited just to the north, but should also include south Korea.

The UN general meeting on Korea passed a resolution on temporary administrative measures in the territory north of the 38th parallel by the UN forces that in effect recognized McArthur's headquarters' rule over the area of north Korea under UN occupation and also decided to form the United Nations Commission on the Unification and Rehabilitation of Korea (UNCURK). This was done without any prior consultation with the Rhee regime. The UN also formed an interim committee and authorized the use of south Koreans as officials, guards and police in north Korea until the time that UNCURK could arrive in Korea. The McArthur headquarters placed a temporary freeze on issues relating to land ownership, banking and currency, and allowed the use of north Korean currency.

On 10 October 1950, the Syngman Rhee regime declared its own imposition of military law over the entire area north of the 38th parallel, followed by the establishment of military rule civil affairs office on 16 October. The Rhee regime announced the creation of a police force to be made up of 3,000 soldiers to control nine cities in north Korea and also sent right-wing youth, mostly members of the North-western Youth Association, to the north in an effort to establish its control there. This resulted in conflict with the UN forces. In P'yŏngyang, for example, the UN forces established a military government under the US I Corps headed by a US Army colonel and set up a P'yŏngyang civil affairs office that appointed Kim Sŏngju (1919–54), a former member of the Northwestern Youth Association, as acting governor of South Py'ŏngan Province. This meant the rejection by the US forces of Syngman Rhee's appointee, a man named Kim Pyŏngyŏn. Kim Sŏngju was appointed by the UN forces as acting governor of South P'yŏngan Province so that once the war was over a new government could be established in north Korea that would be able to enter negotiations, on an equal basis, with the Syngman Rhee regime to create a coalition government over all of Korea. The Rhee regime, however, later executed Kim Sŏngju on the grounds that he suppressed the governor dispatched by Rhee and other men commissioned to handle domestic affairs.

Through the Korean War, which broke out less than two years after the establishment of separate governments, each side attempted to create a unified nation state centred on its own regime. The intervention in the war by the US-led UN forces and the Chinese Communists and the subsequent signing of a cease-fire meant that neither regime could attain its goal of unification. A difference between north and south was that whereas the Kim regime had been able to implement its own policy of occupation in the south, the Rhee regime, which had already yielded operational command of its forces to the UN, experienced difficulties in establishing its right to pursue both an occupation policy and a reunification policy.

The Korean War, which lasted for three years and one month, produced about 1,500,000 dead and 3,600,000 injured on both sides and devastated almost the entire Korean Peninsula, ended with nothing changed except moving the border between the two regimes from the 38th parallel to the cease-fire line. Furthermore, this war solidified the internal division of the nation and led to the rise of dictatorial political systems in both north and south. The war also intensified the cold war between the West and the East.

This was a war that demonstrated that at least in the 1950s – and later, as well – that the geopolitical significance of the Korean Peninsula and the ideological division of the nation made it impossible for either regime to attain reunification through the use of military force. At the same time, the war also resulted in the economic, political and military revival of Japan, a turn of events that was of great historical significance for both East Asia and the world as a whole.

When the People's Army had occupied almost all the Korean Peninsula in the first stage of the war, the US mobilized the UN to intervene. Following the success of the Communist revolution in China, the US felt the urgent need to keep Japan under its influence. If the entire Korean Peninsula were to fall under Communist rule, Korea would became 'a dagger pointed at the heart of Japan', and the US felt unable to guarantee the security of Japan. The US wanted to keep south Korea under its influence so that south Korea could act as an outpost or a buffer for the defene of Japan.

When nearly the entire Peninsula came under UN occupation during the second stage of the war, Communist China intervened. This was because the control of all of Korea by maritime capitalist powers would present a threat to China's revolution and China's security. The same was true for the security of the Soviet Union.

The Korean War became the occasion for the US to push for the rearming of Japan in the so-called Self-Defence Forces. During the war, the US concluded its own peace treaty with Japan, thus bringing Japan into the 'camp of freedom'. The US also spent over 1.3 billion dollars in special military procurements in Japan, thus enabling the resurrection of the Japanese economy. It was the Korean War that made it possible for Japan to grow into a great economic power and subsequently to begin to try to remake itself as a great military power, thus threatening the East Asian countries that had experienced Japanese aggression during the Second World War.

REFERENCES

Kaneguchi Funi, *Chosen senso* (The Korean War), Chuo koronsha, 1966.

Chŏnsa p'yŏnch'an wiwŏnhoe, *Han'guk chŏnjaengsa* (History of the Korean War), 1967.

Cumings, Bruce, *Han'guk chŏnjaeng ŭi kiwŏn* (The origins of the Korean War), Ch'ŏngsa, 1986.

Hyŏndaesa yŏn'guhoe p'yŏn, *Haebanghu mujang t'ujaeng yŏn'gu* (Studies in the armed struggles after liberation), 1988.

Ch'oe Changjip, (ed.), *Han'guk chŏnjaeng yŏn'gu* (Studies in the Korean War), T'aeam, 1990.

Han'guk chŏngch'i yŏn'guhoe chŏngch'isa punkwa, *Han'guk chŏnjaeng ŭi ihae* (Understanding the Korean War), Yŏksa pip'yŏngsa, 1990.

Han'guk yŏksa yŏn'guhoe hyŏndaesa yŏn'guban, *Han'guk hyŏndaesa* (Contemporary history of Korea), vol. 2, P'ulpit, 1991.

SECTION THREE

The Process of Strengthening the Division System

THE SYNGMAN RHEE REGIME

At the time of its establishment, the Syngman Rhee regime was unable to get support from left-wing forces or from right-wing forces of the national liberation front movement such as the Korean Independence Party. Its support came from only the landlord-based Korean Democratic Party and pro-Japanese forces. Before long, however, it lost even the support of the Korean Democratic Party.

The Syngman Rhee regime, which was fated to come to an end after only one term, gained new strength from the outbreak of the Korean War and was able to perpetuate itself. The Rhee regime based itself ideologically on a thorough anti-Communism and a superficial anti-Japanese stance, while it used the police, the military and youth groups, along with its Liberal Party, which was in effect simply a private organization, to enforce its rule and to engage in repeated acts of tyranny.

The Rhee regime was implicated in such problems of wartime misgovernance as the Kŏch'ang incident of 11 February 1951 in which 500 civilians were massacred on suspicion of being Communist guerillas or the Citizens' Army incident of March 1951 in which the officers of the Second National Defence Corps appropriated more than 2.3 billion *wŏn* and over 50,000 *sŏm* of rice, driving nearly 1,000,000 soldiers to the verge of death from starvation and disease. As his term in office drew to a close in 1952, Syngman Rhee realized that there was no chance that he would be re-elected by the National Assembly, where he had little support.

The result was the political upheaval of May 1952 when Rhee set out to amend the constitution to permit direct election of the president. He declared military law in and around the wartime capital of Pusan, organized such groups of thugs as the 'White Bones Corps' and had them demand the dismissal of the National Assembly, and had over 50 opposition party members of the National Assembly arrested by the military police on suspicion of having received funds from the Communist Party. Finally, on 4 July 1952, Rhee culminated his campaign of terror by holding a stand-up vote in the National Assembly amidst an intimidating police presence on a constitutional amendment to allow direct election of the president. This amendment to the constitution allowed him to be elected for a second term.

The second act of political violence Rhee committed in order to stay in power for life was the so-called 'rounding up' amendment of 1954. Although the amendment of 1952 allowed Rhee to be re-elected to a second term, he still faced the constitutional limitation of two terms as president. In order to amend the constitution once again, he needed a two-thirds majority in the National Assembly, but the elections of 1954 produced only 114 Liberal Party members, far short of the 136 needed to amend the constitution. Rhee and the Liberal Party then sought to enlist independent assemblymen in their cause but the result of the 28 November 1954 votes was 135 in favour, one vote short of the total needed to pass the amendment. Even though the National Assembly had announced the failure of the amendment, overnight Rhee and his henchmen decided that 135 rounded-up to two-thirds and declared on the morning of 29 November that the amendment had passed. This allowed Rhee to run for a third term and to be re-elected on 15 May 1956.

From this time on, the Rhee dictatorship grew stronger as his followers supported him with 'excessive loyalty'. Chang Myŏn (1899–1966), the opposition party figure elected as vice-president, was attacked on 28 September 1956, while Cho Pongam (1898–1959), head of the Progressive Party who is said to have actually beaten Rhee in the 1956 election, was executed on suspicion of being at spy on 29 July 1959. Rhee also used the police to stifle political opposition to the passage of a new national security law on 24 December 1958 while organizing gangs of thugs such as the Anti-Communist Youth League (22 January 1959) which he used to shut down the opposition paper, the *Kyŏnghyang sinmun*, on 29 April 1959.

The final act of political violence perpetrated by Rhee, the one that brought his downfall, was the fourth presidential and vice-presidential election of 13 March 1960. In the election of 1956, Rhee's Liberal Party candidate for vice-president, Yi Kibung (1896–1960), had lost to the opposition leader Chang Myŏn. Rhee, who was getting on in years and was worried about who would take over after his death, employed all imaginable means to ensure the Yi Kibung would be elected in 1960. In order that the Liberal Party could claim 85% of the votes, the Minister of the Interior, Ch'oe In'gyu (1919–61), seized 40% of the ballots and secretly ordered his subordinates to ensure that the Liberal Party get another 40% of the votes through a system of three-member and nine-member team voting in which the team head supervised the voting of the other members. Ch'oe also gave orders to be prepared to change ballots and ballot boxes if necessary in order to reach the 85% goal. The results of this rigged election gave Syngman Rhee, who was running alone after the death of his challenger Cho Pyŏngok, 92% of the vote, and gave Yi Kibung a victory over Chang Myŏn of the Democratic Party with 72% of the vote.

Demonstrations protesting voting irregularities arose in Masan on the day of the election and spread throughout the country, culminating in the 19 April 1960 struggle by college students in Seoul. Vice-president elect Yi Kibung announced on 24 April that he would not take office as vice-president, after which he and his family committed suicide. On the other hand, Syngman Rhee attempted to retain his hold on power by announcing that there were reasons to believe that the Communist Party was behind the demonstrations in Masan while also shifting all responsibility for the elections to the Liberal Party and resigning from his post as head of the party. Rhee, however, was eventually forced to step down on 26 April in the face of protests by college professors and the fresh eruption of popular demonstrations demanding his resignation.

The Syngman Rhee regime, which lacked legitimacy and strong support from the beginning, used anti-Communism to gain US backing at each critical juncture. Examples of this include the National Assembly *p'ŭrakch'i* incident of 1949, the International Communist Party incident of 1952, and the secret meeting incident in Dehli, India in 1954. Nonetheless, the Rhee regime was brought down after twelve years by the opposition of the people in what has come to be known as the April Revolution.

THE CHANG MYŎN REGIME

After Syngman Rhee stepped down following the 19 April struggle, the reins of power passed on to Hŏ Chŏng (1896–1988), who had been appointed by Rhee as Minister of Foreign Affairs, the top-ranking post in the cabinet. The Hŏ government set forth the 'five measures of the interim government'. The first measure was to strengthen anti-Communism. The second was to limit punishment for election irregularities to persons who held positions of responsibility and to persons who committed acts of brutality. The third was to carry out revolutionary political reform by non-revolutionary methods. The fourth was to declare that stating that the US role in the April Revolution amounted to intervention in Korea's domestic affairs would be considered an act benefiting south Korea's enemies. This fifth was work for the regularization of Korean-Japanese relations and to permit Japanese news reporters to enter Korea. These five measures give a clear indication of the nature of the Hŏ government.

The Hŏ government, which was to rule until general elections could be held, did implement some policies that upheld the spirit of the 19 April struggle, such as arresting officials of the Rhee government and the Liberal Party who were known to have been behind the rigged election and establishing a time frame for those who had amassed wealth through corruption to surrender themselves. On the other hand, however, the Hŏ government arranged for Syngman Rhee to flee to exile in Hawaii and thus to avoid responsibility for his twelve years of misgovernment and for the deaths and injuries of the 19 April struggle.

After Rhee stepped down, the National Assembly, the majority of whose members belonged to the Liberal Party, established a committee to deal with the emergency situation. This committee passed three proposals on 26 April. The first declared the 15 March presidential and vice-presidential elections invalid and called for new elections. The second called for a constitutional amendment to establish a parliamentary system. The third called for new National Assembly elections as soon as the constitutional amendment was passed. Although general popular opinion called for the immediate disbanding of the National Assembly, this committee chose to defer disbanding until after amending the constitution.

Subsequently, the National Assembly agreed to the arrests of National Assemblymen implicated in election irregularities and passed the National Security Law. It also set out to expand the basic rights of the people which had been severely restricted during the Rhee era by revising laws related to the registration of newspapers and political parties and the freedom of assembly. On 15 June 1960, it adopted a constitutional revision establishing a bicameral parliamentary system. It also established basic committees to draft legislation for direct elections of city mayors, and county and township chiefs and for ensuring police neutrality.

In response to the public's wishes, the National Assembly also formed a committee to investigate massacres of civilians, such as that at Kŏch'ang, perpetrated by the Rhee regime. The committee conducted its investigations for about one month and found that over 8,500 civilians had been massacred by soldiers and police during the Korean War in such locales as Kŏch'ang, Kŏje, Hamyang, Masan and Taegu. The investigators called for an expanded investigation by all three branches (legislative, judicial and administrative) of government and the passage of special measures to handle incidents of civilian massacres.

With the adoption of the new constitution, the National Assembly was automatically dissolved. An election was held on 29 July to elect a new National Assembly made up of two new bodies, the House of Representatives and the House of Councilors. There were a number of unfortunate incidents in places such as Ch'angnyŏng where efforts were made to prevent the election of Liberal Party candidates, but the final outcome of the election was a huge victory for the Democratic Party.

Reformist political forces, which had suffered badly due to the execution of Cho Pongam and the suppression of the Progressive Party, once again emerged on the political surface. They were unable, however, to form a unified body and split into several groups, such as the Socialist Masses Party. Although they fielded candidates in 123 electoral districts, they succeeded in having only five of their number elected.

The Democratic Party, which was established in response to Syngman Rhee's dictatorship, was a conservative organization made up of such forces as members of the old Korean Democratic Party, independents who had belonged to the Liberal Party but subsequently broken away, men from the Young Korean Academy (Hŭngsadan), Catholics and men who had been officials under the Japanese. From the time of its founding, the Democratic Party had been split into an old faction, made up of landlords from the Korean Democratic Party and a new faction, made up of Catholics and colonial era officials. There had been continuous rivalry between these two factions, rivalry that intensified after the fall of the Rhee regime gave them hope of attaining power.

After the 29 July elections, the struggle for power between the two factions of the victorious Democratic Party grew even more intense.

The National Assembly elected Yun Posŏn (1897–1990) of the old faction to the largely ceremonial office of President and chose Chang Myŏn of the new faction to be Premier on 23 August. This meant victory for the new faction in the struggle for power. The Chang regime formed its first cabinet made up almost entirely of the new faction, but was forced by the old faction to form a second cabinet on 12 September that included five members of the old faction. Nonetheless, the old faction soon withdrew from the Democratic Party on 22 September to establish its own party, the New Democratic Party with Kim Toyŏn (1894–1967) as chairman. Those remaining in the Democratic Party then split into a young group, known as the New Wind Society, and an older group that made up the mainstream of the party. The Chang regime formed another cabinet on 30 January 1961 in an unsuccessful effort to dispel the dissatisfaction of the New Wind Society and to resolve the tensions between the two groups. It wasn't until it formed its fourth cabinet on 3 May 1961 that the Chang regime was able to attain some degree of stability, only to meet with a military *coup* eleven days later.

The students, the *minjung* and the media, having overthrown the Rhee regime in the 19 April struggle, stepped forth to demand immediate political, social and economic reforms. But the conservative Chang regime, which was embroiled in ceaseless factional struggles, was not able or even inclined to meet those demands. Furthermore, the Chang regime failed to win the will of the people. The consequence was continuing political instability.

One significant issue was the punishment of those implicated in the 15 March election irregularities and of those responsible for the shootings on 19 April. The judicial branch found eight of the men arrested to be innocent and dismissed charges against three others. With the exception of Seoul police chief Yu Ch'ungnyŏl, who was held responsible for the shootings and sentenced to death, the remaining defendants were all given light sentences. Unhappy with the government's half-hearted efforts to bring the culprits to justice, students who had been wounded on 19 April occupied the House of Representatives on 8 October 1960. The House of Representatives, shaken by the students' protest, then passed a retroactive law to 'dispose of anti-democratic persons' and promulgated such measures to deal with election irregularities and to delineate citizens' rights but the Chang regime fell before it was able to implement these measures.

Another important problem was dealing with those who had accumulated wealth illegally. This issue, however, was complicated by the way in which the US had fostered the growth of monopoly capital and the power of the state. The US needed to create a capitalist system based on monopoly capital in Korea in order to strengthen the anti-Communist system, while domestic monopoly capital desperately needed to maintain its power. The Chang regime, unable to resist the demands of the US and Korean monopoly capital, had no choice but to restrict the application of the law passed by the House of Representatives to deal with illegally accumulated wealth to those who had provided or received 30,000,000 *hwan* used to corrupt the 15 March elections.

The Chang regime, which had come to power as a result of 19 April explosion of the dissatisfactions accumulated among the citizens under the Rhee dictatorship, experienced continuing internal political strife before finally beginning to attain some stability in early 1961. Nonetheless, it was unable to provide an appropriate plan for national reunification which was demanded by progressive political elements and students. Instead the Chang regime sought to control them by passing such measures as a law restricting large-scale demonstrations and another anti-Communist law, but these measures only provoked stronger demonstrations. The Chang regime came to an end after only eight months with the 16 May 1961 military *coup d'etat*.

THE PARK CHUNG HEE REGIME (1): FROM MILITARY RULE TO 'CIVILIAN GOVERNMENT'

The command of the Republic of Korea armed forces, which began as the national defence force under the US military government, was made up primarily of men who had served in the Japanese army and the Manchukuo army before liberation in 1945, along with a small number of men who had served in the Korean Restoration Army of the Shanghai Provisional Government. Not only was the south Korean military created by the US, but it also surrendered its operational control to the US during the Korean War and most of its high-ranking officers were subsequently trained by the US. The predictable result was that the south Korean military became a pro-American group on which the US could always rely for support in implementing its policies in Korea.

When Syngman Rhee declared martial law and ordered the mobilization of the military at the time of the political upheaval of May 1950, the military refused to comply on the grounds that it was under the operational control of the US. At that time, one group of officers, whose numbers included Park Chung Hee (Pak Chŏnghŭi, 1917–79), planned a *coup* to oust Rhee with the support of the US forces in Korea. Later, when Syngman Rhee attempted to obstruct the cease fire negotiations, one of the options considered by the US was a military *coup* to overthrow Rhee. Support for Rhee in US political circles dropped sharply during the final years of his rule because of his corruption and tyranny while reports came out expressing concern over the growth of progressive forces among students and young people. There was yet another plan among certain elements of the military, including Park Chung Hee, for a *coup* against Rhee, but that was put on hold after the April Revolution and Rhee's abdication. Nonetheless, a military *coup* led by Park took place only eight months after the establishment of the Chang regime.

The Park-led military group carried out their *coup* on 16 May 1961. They declared martial law and assumed legislative, executive and judicial powers. They also made six public promises. Those pledges included pursuing a state policy of anti-Communism, observing the UN charter, strengthening ties with the US and other allies, eradicating old evils and revitalizing the national spirit, developing the capacity to overcome Communism and attain reunification, and turning political power over to civilian politicians of good conscience. They established a Military Revolutionary Committee, with Chang Toyŏng, who had been head of the Joint Chiefs of Staff of the Chang regime, as chair and Park Chung Hee as vice-chair. On 19 May, they renamed the committee the Supreme Council for National Reconstruction.

The military junta, which forced the mass resignation of the Chang cabinet and got President Yun Posŏn to authorize the imposition of martial law, solidified its position by promulgating a series of measures to establish a central intelligence agency, to relieve peasants and fishermen of high-interest loans, to promote a citizen's movement for national reconstruction, to organize a revolutionary judiciary and to reaffirm anti-Communist policies. Almost immediately, however, strife arose within the military ranks as Chang Toyŏng and his supporters were arrested in an 'anti-revolutionary incident', opening the way for Park Chung Hee to assume the chairmanship of the Supreme Council for National Reconstruction. This marked the actual beginning of the Park regime.

One of the features of the military regime's power structure can be found in the 10 June 1961 establishment of the Korean Central Intelligence Agency (KCIA). The KCIA, put together by a man named Kim Jong Pil (Kim Chongp'il) who had been one of the main planners of the *coup*, was established to 'organize and oversee domestic intelligence and criminal investigations related to national security and the intelligence collection and investigation activities of all agencies of the government including the military'. The KCIA, which operated in secrecy and had massive manpower and financial support, formed the nucleus of the military regime. It was the real organ for planning and implementing domestic political, anti-Communist and north Korea policies.

On the other hand, the commander of US forces in Korea and the US embassy issued a statement that the US 'supported the lawful government of Korea' as if the US stood behind Chang Myŏn, but the US government soon invited Park Chung Hee to Washington DC in November 1961. As a means to gain solid support from the US, the Park regime displayed a willingness to improve relations with Japan. At the same time, it announced an economic development plan and promulgated its 16 March 1962 'law to purify political activities', by which it prohibited 4,374 'old politicians' from engaging in political activity.

The Park military junta established a presidential constitution through a national referendum on 17 December 1962 and announced plans for a presidential election in April, a National Assembly election in May and the return of government to civilian hands in August 1963, while indicating that Park Chung Hee would run for president. Shortly thereafter, the junta issued its 18 February statement which proclaimed that the military would not participate in the civilian government.

Pak Pyŏnggwŏn, the Minister of Defence, issued a statement supporting the 18 February statement, declaring the political neutrality of the military, and stating that Park Chung Hee would not be a candidate for the presidency. The next day, however, following a motorized demonstration by military commanders demanding a continuation of military rule and a demonstration by soldiers of the Capital Defence Command, Park Chung Hee announced that a national referendum on the question of extending military rule for four more years would be held. Once opposition politicians and the US came out strongly against such a move, Park made a statement putting the referendum on hold.

In the meantime, the military forces behind the *coup* had already formed the Democratic Republican Party and designated Park Chung Hee as its candidate for president even before the formal authorization of the resumption of political activities. Park promoted himself to four-star general, resigned from the military, and ran for president in the 17 December 1963 election, in which he defeated Yun Posŏn by some 150,000 votes.

In the process of 'returning political power to civilian authorities', the military junta forbade political activities by all other political forces through its 'law to purify political activities' while secretly preparing for its own Democratic Republican Party to assume power as a 'civilian government'. In order to raise political funds, it also perpetrated the 'four great suspicious incidents'. Those were the 'stock disturbance' in which it created bogus companies whose stocks were sold on the stock market, the 'Walker Hill incident' in which luxurious resort facilities were built on the pretext of providing recreational facilities for US forces in Korea, the '*pachinko* incident' and the 'Saenara automobile incident', in which *pachinko* machines and automobiles were imported duty-free from Japan and sold at great profits.

The Park regime, which had to overcome repeated difficulties in 'returning political power to civilian authorities', also concluded a 31 October 1964 agreement with the US to dispatch Korean troops to Vietnam, by which it first sent non-combatant units, but eventually also sent combat divisions. The Park regime also faced another major crisis over the issue of regularizing relations with Japan. The Park regime, which had decided soon after the *coup* to enter into talks with Japan and had agreed on the issue of reparations from Japan through the Kim Jong Pil – Ohira memorandum, now sought to hold those talks with the Japanese. However, over 200 representatives from the opposition party and religious and cultural organizations organized a 'pan-national committee opposed to the humiliating diplomacy with Japan' and college students carried out strong demonstrations against the talks. On 3 June 1964, the Park regime quelled popular protests by announcing the imposition of emergency martial law in the Seoul area, but when it presented the agreement with Japan for ratification in the National Assembly, 61 opposition lawmakers presented their resignations. This led to further demonstrations by college students and Seoul was put under garrison rule.

Having gotten past this crisis, Park Chung Hee ran again for president and was re-elected by a large margin over Yun Posŏn of the opposition party on 3 May 1967. After the National Assembly elections of 8 June, student demonstrations denouncing election fraud arose throughout the country and 31 universities and 136 high schools were temporarily closed on 19 June 1967. Park ran into another crisis in 1969. Although the military regime's constitution of 1962 called for limiting the president to two four-year terms, Park, like Syngman Rhee before him, decided to force through an amendment allowing him to run for a third term. Park, who had revealed his intention to amend the constitution in a press conference at the beginning of 1969, pushed aside the opposition party and suppressed student demonstrations to pass a constitutional amendment at a session held in the National Assembly annex building and attended only by Assemblymen from the Democratic Republican Party on 14 September 1969. This was then confirmed by a national referendum.

The New Democratic Party selected Kim Dae Jung (Kim Taejung) as its candidate and the two parties entered into a full-fledged presidential campaign. Opposition figures formed a 'Citizens' Association for the Protection of Democracy' on 19 April 1970 to carry out a campaign against Park's re-election while Kim Dae Jung took the offensive by claiming that Park was planning to become president for life and predicting that this would be the last open presidential election. After a hard fight, Park was re-elected as president on 27 April 1971. Demonstrations against Park continued after the election, with the result that martial law was again declared in the Seoul area on 15 October 1971. Armed soldiers occupied ten university campuses in Seoul and 156 students were expelled from universities for their roles in protest demonstrations.

Although the Park regime was able to maintain itself through this constitutional amendment, its system of military rule faced serious challenges in the early-1970s internationally, domestically and in its relations with north Korea. The regime needed to find a way to overcome those challenges and stay in power after Park's third term came to an end. Thus immediately after the election, the Park regime began to plan its '*yusin*' (restoration) system.

THE PARK CHUNG HEE REGIME (2): THE RISE OF THE 'YUSIN' SYSTEM

Major changes arose in US world strategy and its strategy in Korea in the early-1970s. The US, concerned about growing domestic anti-war sentiment and struggling with the economic costs of its massive involvement in Vietnam, began in August 1970 to discuss a reduction of its forces in Korea. The US president Richard Nixon, in search of a relaxation of tensions with the Communist block, announced his 'Nixon Doctrine' on 25 July 1969, opened his 'ping-pong diplomacy' with Communist China on 7 April 1971, and visited Beijing on 17 February 1972. The Nixon Doctrine was expressed in his Korea policy as a withdrawal of US forces from south Korea, as north-south talks as a precondition for continuing US military aid and as a 'two-Korea policy'.

In response to these changes, the Supreme People's Assembly of north Korea passed resolutions on 12 April 1971 strengthening the Kim Il Sung system, arming the whole people and fortifying the whole nation. It also set forth an 'Eight Point National Reunification Proposal' that called for the withdrawal of US forces, the reduction of north and south Korean military forces to under 100,000 each, the abrogation of south Korea's treaties with the US and Japan and the establishment of national autonomy, the creation of a unified central government through elections in both north and south, the guarantee of free political activity in both north and south, the implementation of a confederal system as an interim measure, economic, cultural and social exchanges, and the opening of political talks between north and south. The Park regime also responded to the changes in the international situation by proposing a 'movement to reunify divided families' through the south Korean Red Cross on 12 August 1971, a move to which the north responded positively. A standing liaison office was established at P'anmunjŏm, a direct telephone line was set up between Seoul and P'yŏngyang, and a number of preliminary Red Cross meetings were held. Eventually, after secret meetings were held between high-ranking officials of north and south, the 4 July Joint Statement of 1972 was issued simultaneously in both Seoul and P'yŏngyang.

At the same time, the Park regime was suffering domestically from severe inflation, worsening deficits in international trade, and a continuing recession. This situation produced a number of incidents in which workers burnt themselves to death in protest, most notably the 13 November 1971 self-immolation of Chŏn T'aeil, a garment worker in Seoul's P'yŏnghwa Market, and in the struggles to survive of the urban poor as seen in the August 1971 uprising of the residents of Kwangju in Kyŏnggi Province. The deteriorating domestic situation not only produced a surprisingly high 43.6% of the popular vote for Kim Dae Jung in the April 1971 presidential election, but also a doubling of New Democratic Party seats in the National Assembly, from 44 to 89 seats, in the 25 May 1971 National Assembly elections. These election results brought a feeling of insecurity to the Park regime.

The domestic situation made it all but impossible for the regime to attempt to extend its rule through a fourth term constitutional amendment and the changes in the international situation meant that the ideology of security based on Cold War logic was losing its validity as an excuse for continuing military rule in south Korea. Furthermore, improvement in north-south relations made it difficult for the Park regime to prolong its policy of 'development first, unification second' while the grounds for maintaining the National Security Law and the intelligence agencies that had formed the backbone of the Park regime were also evaporating. Together, these various factors produced a sense of crisis in the Park military regime.

While opening preliminary Red Cross talks with north Korea, the Park Chung Hee regime gave top priority to ensuring the security of the state and declared a 'state of national emergency' on 6 December 1971. That declaration indicated there would be no acceptance of any sort of social unrest that threatened the state and called for the establishment of a new value system centred on national security. The regime pushed aside the desperate struggle of the opposition party and passed in an irregular session of the National Assembly its 'Law for Special Measures to Defend the State' on 27 December 1971. This law retroactively legalized the 6 December declaration of 'a state of national emergency' and gave the president a broad range of emergency powers including the authority to freeze prices and wages, to mobilize the country's human and natural resources, to restrict public gatherings and demonstrations, publications and collective bargaining, and to reallocate the budget.

While continuing to negotiate with north Korea in the first full session of the Red Cross talks on 29 August and the first joint session of the chairs of the North-South Co-ordinating Committee on 12 October 1972, the Park regime took further measures to strengthen its hold over south Korea. On 17 October, in what he called the 'October Restoration' (*yushin*), Park suddenly dissolved the National Assembly, declared the imposition of martial law over the entire country, shut down all of the nation's college campuses, and implemented a system of censorship over newspapers, radio and television. He then prepared his Yushin Constitution which he had ratified through a national referendum. The Yushin Constitution provided for indirect election of the president through an electoral college known as the National Council for Reunification. On 23 December, Park, who was the only candidate, was chosen as president by the electoral college. The Yushin Constitution stated that 'the citizens exercise their sovereignty through their representative or through national referenda', a provision that allowed Park to legalize his major policies through national plebiscites. The constitution also institutionalized restrictions on the rights of labour and permitted the president to take emergency measures. It also greatly restricted basic human rights by abolishing arraignment hearings and allowing convictions based solely on confessions.

The legislative branch was deprived of its power to audit the administration and it was allowed to meet only 150 days during the year. Furthermore, one-third of the members of the National Assembly were nominated by the president. The consequence was a great reduction in the powers of the legislative branch which was now easily manipulated by the president. The judicial branch also lost its independence. The president had the authority to appoint all judges and the Supreme Court's authority to make judgments on the constitutionality of laws and actions was transferred to a constitutional committee.

Not only did the president take for himself almost all the three powers of government, but he was to be elected indirectly through the National Council for Reunification. His term of office was set at six years, with no limitations on the number of terms he could serve. In effect, the Yushin Constitution made Park Chung Hee president for life. There is no need to emphasize that this strengthening of presidential authority was intended to bolster Park's dictatorship.

Talks between north and south continued with little progress during the time when Park was establishing his Yushin system, but the talks were suspended by the north on 28 August 1973 after Kim Dae Jung, who had been carrying out a movement against the Yushin system, was kidnapped from Japan. Resistance against the system also continued inside south Korea in a million-person petition movement led by Chang Chunha to revise the Yushin Constitution. This led the Park regime to impose nine emergency measures that prohibited any rejection, opposition, or criticism of the constitution, any calls for its revision or abolition, and any initiatives, proposals, or requests to change the constitution.

Despite the imposition of these emergency measures, resistance continued, as seen in the April 1974 National League of Democratic Youth and Students incident or the order closing Korea University. Under this pressure, the Park regime conducted yet another national referendum on the Yushin Constitution on 12 February 1975. That referendum, in which 79.8% of eligible voters participated, resulted in a vote of 73.1% in favor of the constitution. Nonetheless, there was no let up in the democratic movement led by intellectuals and opposition party politicians, as seen in the 15 March 1973 declaration signed by 165 literary figures of the 'Association of Writers for Democratic Practices', or the 1 March 1976 'March First Declaration to Save the Nation'. In the midst of this opposition, Park's six-year term came to an end. He was re-elected for another six-year term by the National Council for Reunification on 21 December 1978.

Park's re-election notwithstanding, his nearly twenty-year military dictatorship had reached its limits. It was rocked by a number of incidents, including the 11 August 1979 YH Industrial Company incident, the first explosion of the accumulated dissatisfactions of the workers; the expulsion of Kim Young Sam (Kim Yŏngsam), head of the New Democratic Party, from the National Assembly; and the 16 October eruption of popular protests in Pusan and Masan. Eventually, Kim Chaegyu (1926–80), the head of the Korean Central Intelligence Agency, who had been locked in a power struggle with Ch'a Chich'ŏl (1934–79), the head of Park's bodyguards, shot Ch'a and Park to death at a drinking party in a KCIA safehouse on 26 October 1979, bringing to an end Park Chung Hee's eighteen years of dictatorial rule.

In the final years of Park's rule, such incidents as the YH incident, the Pusan and Masan uprisings, and the expulsion of Kim Young Sam, brought together the various forces opposed to the Yushin system, including working class people, youth, students, intellectuals, religious leaders and opposition politicians in a joint front to struggle for democratization. Furthermore, the unreasonable expansion by the Park regime of heavy chemical industries deepened the economic recession, causing corporate bankruptcies, increasingly unemployment and dangerously high inflation. In addition, the Park regime was experiencing severe conflict with the US Carter administration over such issues as 'human rights diplomacy', the withdrawal of US troops from Korea, Park's pursuit of an independent military line, his export of weapons and his attempt to develop nuclear weapons. The 26 October assassination of Park was the product of all these various factors.

THE CHUN DOO HWAN REGIME

A State Council meeting called after Park Chung Hee's assassination put the entire country except Cheju Island under emergency martial law and chose Prime Minister Choi Kyu Hah (Ch'oe Kyuha) to be acting president. Choi was subsequently elected as president by the National Council for Reunification on 6 December 1979, but Choi was unable to exercise effective power and found it difficult to control the military.

A 'new military' group was forming around Major General Chun Doo Hwan (Chŏn Tuhwan), who was head of the Army Security Command at the time of Park's assassination and thus took charge of the investigation, and division commander Major General Roh Tae Woo (No T'aeu). The new military, which was made up of officers who belonged to a private organization known as the 'Hanahoe' and of other military commanders who were deeply loyal to Park Chung Hee, manufactured an excuse that General Chŏng Sŭnghwa, Army Chief of Staff and head of the Martial Law Command, was implicated in the assassination of Park, mobilized troops loyal to themselves and attacked Chŏng's office where they arrested him on the night of 12 December 1979.

The new military moved quickly to solidify its position, sentencing Kim Chaegyu to death on 20 December, and having Chun Doo Hwan appointed as acting director of the KCIA on 14 April 1980. After some discussion about replacing the Yushin system with a dual system of governance, the new military extended martial law to Cheju Island on 17 May with its Martial Law Decree Number Ten. This decree prohibited political activities, required censorship for print and broadcast media, shut down all colleges and universities, and prohibited the use of arguments or terminology like that used by north Korea. The new military also arrested potential presidential candidates Kim Dae Jung and Kim Jong Pil and put Kim Young Sam under house arrest, while also arresting many other opposition figures, dismissing Prime Minister Sin Hyŏnhwak and his cabinet and forming its own new cabinet.

On 18 May, student demonstrations opposing the extension of martial law arose in the southwestern city of Kwangju. The military forces sent in to suppress the demonstrations over-reacted with bloody results. The outraged citizens of Kwangju then joined in the demonstrations, seized weapons, formed a 'citizen's army' and forced the military out of the city. After a stand off of several days, on 27 May the new military sent its forces in again to eradicate the citizens army and bring an end to the Kwangju *minjung* resistance.

The new military, which was actively expanding its control through martial law and the suppression of the Kwangju *minjung* resistance, set up a 'State Protection Emergency Measures Committee' with Chun Doo Hwan as chair on 31 May. Through this committee the new military seized control of all three branches of government. It brought Kim Dae Jung and 23 others to trial in a military court in the 'plotting treason incident' and prohibited political activities by 210 of the 231 National Assembly members, by 254 high ranking officers of political parties and by 347 high-ranking former officials. Furthermore, in July of that year, the new military carried out a 'purge' in which it forced the dismissal of over 8,500 persons, including 232 high-ranking civil servants, 4,760 mid- and low-ranking civil servants, 86 college professors, 611 school teachers, 431 employees of banks, insurance, and investment companies, 1,819 employees of state-run investment firms, and 711 journalists and reporters.

The committee also revoked the licences of 172 periodical publications on 31 July, and the licences of 617 publishers on 19 August as part of its policy of social purification. A few months later, on 14 November, it pushed through a consolidation of newspaper and broadcast companies, merged the wire services into one company and forced capital-based newspapers to recall their reporters stationed out in the provinces. Military forces stormed Buddhist monasteries throughout the country and illegally arrested 153 monks. The new military also proclaimed that it was going to conduct a sweep of thugs and persons who committed crimes injurious to public morality, and arrested over 57,000 persons. Over 3,000 of those arrested were jailed, while over 40,000 were sent to the notorious 'triple purification' (*samch'ŏng*) education camps.

The US did express its displeasure at the 12 December *coup*, but the US media pointed out the deficiencies as presidential candidates of the so-called three Kims (Kim Dae Jung, Kim Young Sam, Kim Jong Pil). Furthermore, the commander of US forces in Korea made a statement in support of Chun Doo Hwan's seizure of power in which he likened the Korean people to lemmings who will obey any leader and declared that democracy was not appropriate for the Korean people. In a 9 August press conference with US reporters, Chun Doo Hwan asserted that Korea needed the leadership and control of the military and strongly hinted at the reappearance of a military regime led by himself.

Choi Kyu Hah resigned as president on 16 August and a meeting of major military commanders adopted a resolution calling for the elevation of Chun Doo Hwan to head of state on 23 August. The following day, following Park Chung Hee's precedent, Chun had himself promoted to full general and then resigned his military commission. On 27 August, Chun was elected as president with 2524 votes out of the 2525 cast by the National Council for Reunification. The new Reagan administration in the US signalled its support for Chun by making him the first foreign leader to be invited to the Reagan White House on 3 February 1981. The Reagan administration also promised that it would not enter into bilateral talks with north Korea and would not withdraw any more troops from south Korea.

The Chun Doo Hwan regime, which had come to power under the Yushin Constitution, set out to make a new constitution which it then ratified through a national referendum on 22 October 1980. The regime also sought to create the appearance of party politics by creating the Democratic Justice Party with Chun Doo Hwan as chair and a 'loyal opposition' party in the Democratic Korea Party headed by Yu Ch'isong. The new constitution stipulated that the National Council for Reunification would be replaced by an electoral college. On 25 February 1981, Chun went through the formality of having himself re-elected by the electoral college.

Students and intellectuals continued the anti-dictatorial democratization movement even under the Chun regime's policy of suppression. Large numbers of students had to endure repeated suspension and restoration. Even in the midst of the Chun regime's harsh suppression, 264 students from Korea, Yonsei and Sungkyunkwan universities succeeded in occupying the Democratic Justice Party's headquarters on 14 November 1984. All 264 were, of course, arrested. After enduring such experiences as the 29 June 1985 police raids at nine universities to arrest 66 students involved with the Struggle Committee for Liberation of the Masses, Attainment of Democracy and Unification of the Nation (Sammin t'ujaeng wiwŏnhoe), the 14 January 1987 torture death of Pak Chongch'ŏl (1965–87), and the 9 June 1987 killing of Yi Hanyŏl (1967–87) by a riot police tear gas grenade, over 4,000 students from 95 colleges and universities met on 19 August 1987 at South Ch'ungch'ŏng University where they organized the National Association of University Student Councils (Chŏndaehyŏp) to resist the oppressive regime and lead the student movement.

Intellectuals also stepped forth in opposition to the Chun regime. On 1 August 1985, 401 writers made a public declaration calling for freedom of creation and expression. Thirty-nine opposition organizations launched a movement that forced the regime to back down when it attempted to promulgate a campus security law in order to suppress student demonstrations. On 28 March 1986, the faculty at Korea University made public a statement calling for democratization, which was then followed by similar statements from the faculties at colleges and universities throughout the country. Furthermore, 546 elementary- and middle-school teachers also made public a declaration calling for the democratization of education on 10 May 1986.

The Chun regime years also witnessed the rise of an active anti-American movement. Based on the fact that the US supported the establishment of the Chun regime and on the widespread perception that the army units used to suppress the Kwangju resistance could not have been mobilized without the permission of the US, an anti-American movement, unthinkable in earlier years, now developed openly. The 18 March 1982 arson incident led by Mun Pusik at the American Cultural Center in Pusan was followed by an explosion at the American Cultural Center in Taegu on 22 September 1983. Students also occupied the American Cultural Center in Pusan on 21 May 1985 and twenty-five students were arrested for the occupation of the American Cultural Center in Seoul on 23 May 1985.

Coming into 1984, the Chun regime three times lifted restrictions on political activities. Those men now freed from restrictions formed the New Korean Democratic Party, with Yi Minu as chair, on 18 January 1985. The New Korean Democratic Party won 67 seats in the National Assembly elections and gained further strength when 29 Assemblymen switched over from the Democratic Korea Party. The emergence of the New Korean Democratic Party as the main opposition party marked a major change in the political situation. The movement for constitutional revision gained strength when Kim Dae Jung, who had been sentenced to death in the 'plotting treason incident', but then was released and allowed to go to the United States, returned and joined forces with Kim Young Sam, who had been engaged in a hunger strike to demand democratization. The New Korean Democratic Party and the Association for the Promotion of Democratization carried out a 10 million person petition movement in February 1986. The democratization movement reached new highs in August 1986 when the New Korean Democratic Party decided on a proposed constitutional amendment to allow for direct election of the president and also opened, in concert with 34 opposition organizations, a 'pan-national convention to expose sexual torture and fabrications of pro-Communism'. The Chun Doo Hwan regime responded with conventional tactics of heightening tensions by charging on 30 October that north Korea's Kŭmgang Mountain dam is being built to turn Seoul into a sea of water and launching a 'citizens' movement' to build a 'peace dam'.

The Chun regime also continued to insist on indirection election of the president by announcing its 13 April 1987 'measure to protect the constitution'. The opposition reacted by founding the 'headquarters of the citizens' movement to seize democracy' and organizing peaceful parades on 26 June 1987, in which over a million persons participated, throughout the nation demanding the revision of the constitution to allow for the direct election of the president. This June 1987 democratization movement was different from the past movements in that ordinary citizens stepped forth alongside the opposition politicians. The government and the Democratic Justice Party, aware that it would be difficult to maintain the system of indirect election, now had Roh Tae Woo, who had already been designated as its presidential candidate, make his 29 June announcement accepting the direct election system.

The opposition forces sought to have Kim Dae Jung and Kim Young Sam form a unified slate, but the two Kims eventually split. Four principle candidates for the presidency emerged: Roh Tae Woo of the Democratic

Justice Party; Kim Young Sam, who had dissolved the New Korean Democratic Party and formed a new Unification Democratic Party; Kim Jong Pil, who presented himself as the successor to Park Chung Hee and organized the New Democratic Republican Party; and Kim Dae Jung, who founded his one People's Party for Peace and Democracy. The 16 December 1987 vote resulted in the election of Roh Tae Woo.

The Chun Doo Hwan regime, which perpetuated the system the military rule established by Park Chung Hee, began by proclaiming its intention to 'realize a welfare society' and attempted to create an atmosphere of reconciliation by attracting the Olympics to Seoul, allowing middle- and high-school students to discard their uniforms and grow their hair, abolishing the night-time curfew that had been in effect since the Korean War, establishing a Ministry of Physical Education and launching a professional baseball league. Nonetheless, the Chun regime, which was the beneficiary of the Yushin system and came to power by crushing the Kwangju *minjung* resistance, faced real limits in its ability to gain a broad base of support among the people.

Furthermore, as a dictatorial regime that did not come to power through democratic means and thus lacked legitimacy, the Chun government found it difficult to prevent corruption by those who had power. There were frequent incidences of corruption among relatives of the regime's power holders. In the Chang Yŏngja and Yi Ch'ŏrhŭi incident of May 1982, Chun Doo Hwan's relatives were involved in a financial fraud of over 700 billion *wŏn*. Nonetheless, their role in the scandal was hidden and the case wound up with the arrest of a bank president and sixteen other men. Another such case was the Myungsung (Myŏngsŏng) Group scandal of August 1983, which was concluded with the arrest of sixteen men, including bank personnel and the Minister of Transportation, again without dispelling suspicions of involvement by relatives of powerful members of the regime. In addition, an audit of the operations of the New Village Movement's Central Headquarters, headed by Chun Doo Hwan's brother Chun Kyung Hwan (Chŏn Kyŏnghwan), revealed serious irregularities, but Chun Kyung Hwan was not arrested until after the end of the Chun Doo Hwan regime.

An indication of the extent to which the Chun regime lacked popular support can be found in the fact that Chun Doo Hwan hid himself away in a Buddhist monastery for two years after he stepped down. Nonetheless, the Chun regime did have its own bases of support. The most important of those bases was, of course, the military, particularly the Army Security Command. The Army Security Command played a crucial role in establishing and maintaining the Chun regime by 'purging' officials and consolidating the media. Another important base was the National Security Planning Agency. When Chun first took power, he renamed the Korean Central Intelligence Agency the National Security Planning Agency and appeared to have greatly weakened its powers. The agency, however, recovered its old powers while handling the Kim Dae Jung 'plotting treason incident' and subsequently became

a central force for the political, economic, social and cultural maintenance of the Chun regime through such stratagems as the 'meeting for
measures by related organs'. In addition, the riot police were greatly
strengthened under Chun Doo Hwan and played the major role in suppressing anti-regime demonstrations as the regime evolved into a police
state. The Democratic Justice Party, which was formed around a nucleus
of men from the Army Security Command, was unable to gain popular
support and persisted only as window dressing for the Chun regime.

While the bases of popular political support for the Chun Doo Hwan
regime continued to shrink during its seven years of power, the political
capacities of the *minjung* forces continued to grow. The *minjung*'s capacities forced the Chun regime to withdraw its '13 April measure to protect
the constitution', to issue its 29 June statement allowing direct election
of the president and, eventually, achieved the first 'peaceful' transfer of
power in the history of the Republic of Korea.

THE ROH TAE WOO REGIME

The Roh Tae Woo regime, which assumed power on 25 February 1988
after winning 36.6% of the valid ballots in the direct election of the
president that it was forced to allow by the June democratization
movement of 1987, was unable to win even half of the seats in the
thirteenth National Assembly elections held on April 26, 1988. The
thirteenth National Assembly, in which the opposition outnumbered
the ruling party, passed revisions to the National Assembly Law to allow
for the establishment of legislative hearings and, in accordance with the
demands of the citizens, opened hearings to uncover the misdeeds of
the Chun regime.

Roh Tae Woo himself had been a member of the new military that had
been formed after the assassination of Park Chung Hee on 26 October
1979 and had been a central member of the Chun Doo Hwan regime that
was established through the 12 December 1979 *coup* and the suppression
of the Kwangju *minjung* resistance. Even though it had been put in office
by a direct election of the president, the Roh regime came to power as
the offspring of the Chun regime. Nonetheless, the Roh regime found
itself in the difficult position of having to conduct some sort of 'liquidation of the Fifth Republic' (the Chun regime) in order to attain some
degree of stability.

Even before Roh took power, the government established a 'committee to further democratic consensus' on 20 January 1988 in order to deal
with the Kwangju incident that had been taboo during the Chun years
and promised to listen broadly to the 'views of citizens of all social groups
and social strata'. The result was a determination by the government that
'investigation or punishment' was inappropriate and that the Kwangju
incident should be defined simply as an 'attempt to realize democratization'. Accordingly, the government sought to dispose of the incident by
providing compensation and erecting monuments and a memorial hall

for those who were killed or injured. These gestures, however, fell short of satisfying the demands of the people or of the opposition politicians. The result was the opening of a 'hearing on the Kwangju incident' in the National Assembly where many witnesses provided testimony. Nonetheless, the hearing concluded without achieving any clarification of what had really happened and of who was responsible for ordering shots to be fired.

Once the wrongdoings of the Chun regime were exposed through National Assembly hearings, the public and the opposition parties began to demand the direct testimony of former presidents Choi Kyu Hah and Chun Doo Hwan. The Roh regime, however, actively avoided requiring their appearance at the hearings on the grounds that it amounted to 'political retribution'. Unable to resist the demands of the citizens, however, Chun Doo Hwan appeared before the public on 23 November 1988 and said 'I now realize that I must willingly accept whatever punishment is deemed necessary and await the judgment of the citizens.' He also promised to donate to the state and to society all of his property, including his residence and 13 billion *wŏn* in political funds that he had prepared for his retirement. He then went into seclusion at Paektam Monastery in Kangwŏn Province.

Attention was diverted away from the issue of resolving the wrongdoings of the Chun regime in early 1989 by the incident in which reverend Mun Ikhwan (1918–94) and the novelist Hwang Sŏgyŏng made an unauthorized visit to north Korea. Nonetheless, the opposition parties' continuing determination to struggle against the Roh regime and the students' continuing demonstrations demanding 'punishment of Chun Doo Hwan and overthrow of the Roh regime' eventually forced Chun to give testimony before the National Assembly on 31 December 1989. Chun strongly asserted that the decision to open fire at Kwangju was made by the commander in the field. This was greeted by strong rejection from opposition party legislators and his testimony was suspended.

A year earlier, on 13 December 1988, the Roh regime had established a 'special office for the investigation of the Chun regime's wrongdoings'. The special office arrested 47 men, including such major figures of the regime as Chang Sedong and such relatives of Chun as his brother Chun Kyung Hwan and indicted 29 other persons. It was then disbanded.

The Roh regime, struggling with the issue of resolving the wrongdoings of the Chun regime under the situation where the ruling party was a minority in the National Assembly, made a secret agreement to amend the constitution to provide for a parliamentary system and created a new political party, the Democratic Liberal Party, by merging the Democratic Justice Party with Kim Jong Pil's New Democratic Republic Party and Kim Young Sam's Unification Democratic Party on 1 January 1990. The new party now controlled 216 seats in the National Assembly, far more than the 198 votes needed to amend the constitution. This in effect reversed the results of the general election and created a huge new ruling party, a move that shocked the citizens.

After the creation of the new party, however, Kim Young Sam came out in opposition to amending the constitution. The secret agreement for combining the three parties was leaked. The agreement called for three things: the formation of a parliamentary democracy in which both the National Assembly and the cabinet are responsible to the people; amending the constitution within one year; and beginning the process of amendment within the current year.

Kim Young Sam's opposition to the constitutional amendment plunged the new Democratic Liberal Party into crisis. The Roh regime, however, was determined to maintain the kind of huge ruling party majority that had been a feature of Park Chung Hee's Yushin system and Chun Doo Hwan's government. Against strong opposition from the opposition party, it pushed through, at times by irregular means, a broad range of legislative measures. Those measures included a 'revision of laws related to broadcasting', a 'revision of military organization laws', a 'revision of the Kwangju compensation law', a 'police law', a 'special law to enhance the position of teachers', a 'revision of the National Security Law', a 'measure to purchase grain', a 'special law to develop Cheju Island', a 'law to foster organizations for the "live right movement" ' and a 'basic law for youth'.

Although the Roh regime was thus able to keep the huge new ruling party together, it soon faced a new crisis in the Susǒ incident of February 1991, in which the Hanbo Group had bribed Blue House secretaries, the chairman of the National Assembly's Construction Committee, and a number of National Assemblymen and in return had obtained residential land in the Susǒ district of Seoul. This incident provoked a great protest from the public who regarded it as the greatest wrongdoing of the Roh regime. The Roh regime was able to overcome this crisis by reinstituting local assembly elections, which had been suspended after the 16 May 1961 military *coup*, and succeeding in having a large majority (over 70%) of members friendly to the ruling party elected on 27 March 1991.

Despite the Roh regime's successes in manipulating the system, student demonstrations continued, leading to the death of Myǒngji University student Kang Kyǒngdae (1971–91) on 26 April. This led to further demonstrations demanding democratization and the dissolution of the Democratic Liberal Party, along with a number of incidents of students burning themselves to death, once again plunging the Roh regime into crisis. The Roh regime got through the crisis by implementing local elections, this time an election for wide area local assemblies in which Democratic Liberal Party candidates won 65% of the seats.

In July 1992, the Roh regime faced another crisis when a group of swindlers that included the Military History Materials Section Head of the Joint Chiefs of Staff headquarters, bilked an insurance company of 6.6 billion *wǒn* by promising to sell lands owned by the army. This was the greatest instance of fraud under the Roh regime. Although there were questions about who may have really been behind this act of malfeasance, but it was disposed of as a simple case of fraud.

After undergoing a number of difficulties, including its failed attempt to implement a competitive election to select its presidential candidate, the Democratic Liberal Party nominated Kim Young Sam, the Speaker of the National Assembly, to be its candidate for the upcoming presidential election. The Roh regime declared its neutrality in the election and formed a 'neutral cabinet' on 7 October 1992. Kim Young Sam was chosen to be president in the 18 December election. This marked the rise of the first civilian government since the 1961 military coup thirty-two years earlier.

The years of the Roh regime were a time of radical changes in the international situation with the collapse of the socialist block. The regime, gaining momentum from the 1988 Seoul Olympics and its 7 July 1988 statement laying out its policy toward reunification, began to purse an ambitious 'Nordpolitik' (northern policy). The regime began to open relations with socialist countries when it announced the establishment of standing representatives between south Korea and Hungary on 13 September 1988, followed by the exchange of ambassadors on 1 February 1989. It next opened relations with Poland on 1 November and Yugoslavia on 28 December. It also agreed to exchange consuls with the Soviet Union on 8 December 1989 and eventually entered into full-scale diplomatic relations with the Soviet Union on 30 September 1990 – a full eighty-six years after the treaty of amity and commerce between the old Taehan Empire and the Russian Empire was abrogated in 1904.

Although there were certain strategic reasons for the opening of diplomatic relations with all the socialist countries, such was particularly true in the case of the Soviet Union. The USSR, which was mired in economic difficulties, was looking for economic co-operation from south Korea while south Korea was seeking to isolate north Korea by establishing relations with the Soviet Union which was northern regime's ally and friend. Before diplomatic relations were established, there was a Moscow meeting between the two governments to discuss economic co-operation, and one of the conditions for accelerating the establishment of full diplomatic relations was an economic co-operation package worth two to three billion dollars.

Change was also taking place gradually in south Korea's relations with China, which was P'yŏngyang's sole remaining ally. The Chinese began with such statements as 'We hope for peace and security in the Korean Peninsula and we are engaging in civilian trade with south Korea,' and 'Relations between south Korea and China are limited to non-governmental trade relations,' appearing to adhere to a line of distinction between politics and economics. At the time of the Beijing Asian Games in October 1990, however, south Korea participated in a nine million dollar advertising project and provided Beijing with over 400 automobiles. This led to discussions about the establishment of trade representative offices that eventually resulted in the establishment of full diplomatic relations in August 1992.

Even as it was wrapping up its Nordpolitik by establishing diplomatic relations with the countries of eastern Europe, the Soviet Union and

China, the Roh regime also attained the simultaneous admission of south and north Korea to the United Nations on 17 October 1990. The Roh regime claimed that its Nordpolitik towards north Korea was designed to encourage the Kim Il Sung regime to open up and was part of its larger reunification policy. In reality, however, it was a policy intended to isolate Kim Il Sung. With regard to admission to the UN, the Roh regime rejected the Kim Il Sung regime's position that there should be only one seat for both Koreas and instead launched a campaign for the admission of south Korea alone. The compromise result was the simultaneous admission of both states.

Whether the Roh regime's Nordpolitik and UN policy will lead to the peaceful reunification of the nation, to unification by absorption as happened in Germany, or to a permanent 'two Korea' policy is unclear at the time of this writing. That depends on the north Korea policy and the national reunification policies of the civilian government that has finally re-emerged after over thirty years of military rule.

REFERENCES

Chungang ilbosa, *Kwangbok 30 nyŏn chungyo charyo chip* (Collection of major materials for the first thirty years after liberation), 1975.

Tonga ilbosa, *Kaehang 100 nyŏn yŏnp'yo wa charyo chip* (Timetables and materials for the 100 years since the opening of the ports), 1976.

Chin Tŏkyu et al., *1950 nyŏndae ŭi insik* (Perceptions of the 1950s), Han'gilsa, 1981.

Han Sŭngju (Sung-ju Han), *Che2 konghwaguk kwa han'guk ŭi minjujuŭi* (The Second Republic and democracy in Korea), Chongno sŏjŏk, 1983.

Han'gyŏre sahoe yŏn'guso chŏngch'i punkwa, *Yŏnp'yo, inmul, charyo ro pon nambukhan 45 nyŏnsa* (The 45-year history of north and south Korea seen through timetables, persons, and materials), Wŏlgan tari, 1989.

Han'guk yŏksa yŏn'guhoe hyŏndaesa yŏn'guban, *Han'guk hyŏndaesa* 3, 4 (Contemporary history of Korea), P'ulpit, 1991.

6

The Development of the Movement for Democracy and Reunification

The colonial period saw continuous efforts to create a unified front in the national liberation movement. The Shanghai Interim Government, at the time of its founding, represented a left/right united front, while the united national party and the New Korea Society movements of the late-1920s and early-1930s were also attempts to form a united front. Following the demise of the New Korea Society in the early-1930s, ceaseless efforts were made in the overseas national liberation front to establish a unified nation-state. A united front movement centred on the Interim Government arose on the overseas front right before liberation in 1945, while secret organizations such as the National Foundation League that were formed inside Korea attempted to link up with the overseas united front movement. Those organizations eventually provided the foundation for the Committee for the Preparation for Korean Independence.

If the goal and task of the national liberation movement during the colonial period had been to get out from under Japanese colonial rule and to establish a democratic state in lieu of the old Taehan Empire, then under the conditions after liberation when the factors of division, including the establishment of the 38th parallel, the goal was to create a unified national state. Indeed, the post-liberation movement for democracy and the establishment of a unified national state constituted a continuation of the main thrust of the colonial period national unification front movement.

This movement manifested itself in the activities of the Committee for the Preparation for Korean Independence at the time of Japan's defeat in the Second World War. With the exception of some landlords, both the left and the right participated equally in the Committee, whose programme and policies were the same as those of the national unified front of the liberation movement. This enabled the Committee to gain broad support from the *minjung*. Once, however, leftist forces gained strength in the Committee's organizations, the right wing broke away in opposition. Furthermore, the Korean People's Republic government which the Committee hastily declared in anticipation of the arrival of US forces failed to gain recognition from the Americans who instead implemented their military government in Korea. This meant that the Committee was unable to fulfil its role in initiating the creation of a unified nation-state.

After the demise of the Committee for the Preparation for Korean Independence, and divisions deepened between left and right over the trusteeship issue, the movement for the establishment of a unified nation state re-emerged in the activities of the left-right alliance committee. Those activities were pursued by moderate leftists and moderate rightists in a coalition that excluded the far right and the far left. Although this movement clearly laid out the conditions for co-operation between the two sides and attempted to resolve their differences, it also ended in failure as a result of the left wing's suspicions that it was intended to further the divisions among leftist forces and the right wing's efforts to create a separate government in south Korea, efforts that coincided with the US policy towards Korea.

After the Syngman Rhee forces intensified their efforts to create a separate government in south Korea, the movement to establish a unified nation-state brought in the previously excluded left- and right-wing elements to participate in the 1948 north-south negotiations. This effort, however, came too late to prevent the establishment of separate northern and southern regimes. Within less than two years, the Korean War, an attempt to attain unification by military force, broke out. The Korean War was a conflict that demonstrated clearly the extent to which the geopolitical significance of the Korean Peninsula was related to the issue of national unification.

The Peninsula was the meeting point of the continental Communist powers and the maritime capitalist powers. The Kim Il Sung regime, supported by the continental forces of the Soviet Union and China, attempted to reunify Korea by force, but the maritime forces, led by the United States, could not allow that to happen. When the maritime forces under the flag of the United Nations, reached as far north as the Amnok River, the continental forces were not willing to accept that situation. The result was a three-year long war that brought massive casualties and in the end left the Korean Peninsula still divided.

After the April Revolution of 1960, the talk of reunification by force in South Korea briefly subsided. In its place arose discussion of peaceful reunification and of the neutralization of Korea, but such discussion was made illegal after the 16 May 1961 military coup. For a short time after the 4 July 1972 north-south joint statement, it appeared as though the door to peaceful reunification might be opening, but that too came to nothing. Still, the 4 July statement left a number of important lessons for the problem of national reunification.

First, it demonstrated that national reunification must be discussed and realized by the Korean people themselves. The 4 July statement set forth the principle that reunification must be achieved autonomously without the intervention of outside powers. Nonetheless, to the extent that the negotiations between north and south came about as a result of the thaw in relations between the US and the Soviet Union and the US and China and at the urging of those powers, the negotiations ultimately did not represent the true national agency of the Korean people and had no real chance to succeed.

Second, the joint statement showed that reunification could be attained not in the interests of any political power group but only when pursued in the true interests of the nation as a whole. Even though the statement called for a great national unity transcending the ideological and institutional differences in the two systems, to the extent that the reunification issue was a means for the ruling groups of each of the two regimes to strengthen themselves, then there could be no real progress toward reunification.

Third, the joint statement showed that reunification was impossible if the political and social forces involved were not willing to make sacrifices. Even though the two sides declared themselves to be in favour of peaceful reunification, because they were not prepared to compromise, yield and make sacrifices, the declaration represented nothing more than an attempt to buy time in order to gain diplomatic, economic or military advantage. In the final analysis, both sides were still committed to reunification by force, a policy that meant the conquest of one part of the nation by another.

Even though the 4 July statement did not lead to national reunification, it had the unintended consequence in south Korea of stimulating the development of an autonomous peaceful reunification movement among the people throughout the 1970s and 1980s. The labour movement, student movement, intellectual movement and opposition movement of those years that erupted in such events as the 18 May Kwangju resistance of 1980 and the June *minjung* resistance of 1987 were democratization movements that were ultimately linked to the movement for autonomous and peaceful national reunification.

The two regimes of the divided nation were forced to change their reunification policies in response to demands from the *minjung* and the changing world situation. In the case of the Kim Il Sung regime, it reformulated its 1960s' call for a north-south alliance as its Koryŏ Confederal Republic proposal in the 1970s. In the case of south Korea, the Chun Doo Hwan regime had a 'plan for peaceful national reunification through national conciliation', while the Roh Tae Woo regime put forth a 'plan for the reunification of the Korean national community'. Even though the two sides were struggling to gain advantage over each other, the gap between their proposals began to narrow. That led to the holding of talks between the two sides' prime ministers, limited economic exchange, and the signing of a 'basic agreement between north and south' that called for a *détente* and co-operation and that foreswore military aggression. On the other hand, however, such issues as the conducting of Operation

Team Spirit exercises between US and south Korean military forces and nuclear inspections in north Korea showed that there were still serious obstacles to be overcome. Seen from a historical perspective, the experiences of divided nations in the twentieth century show that the interests of the nation as a whole must take precedence over political or diplomatic manoeuvring for power. Attaining reunification remains the guiding principle and the single greatest task of the Korean nation in the second half of the twentieth century. Only the conscience, the wisdom and the courage of the nation, rather than any sort of political or diplomatic ploys, can enable us to move forward and resolve this problem.

SECTION ONE

The Committee for the Preparation of Korean Independence and the Korean People's Republic

THE ACTIVITIES OF THE COMMITTEE FOR THE PREPARATION OF KOREAN INDEPENDENCE

Yŏ Unhyŏng, who had entered into negotiations with the Government-General of Korea, received firm promises of the freeing of political and economic prisoners, of rations for three months, and of noninterference in the Koreans' political activities and the formation of youth, student, worker, and peasant organizations. He then launched the Committee for the Preparation for Korean Independence (CPKI), based on the National Foundation League, on 15 August 1945. The activities of the CPKI, with Yŏ as chair and An Chaehong as vice-chair, commenced on 16 August when Yŏ made a public statement about his negotiations with the Government-General. On the same day, An Chaehong made a radio broadcast called 'a report to the Korean people at home and abroad' that discussed the issues of the formation of a constabulary and a regular military, issues of obtaining foodstuffs, currency and prices, and issues relating to the freeing of political prisoners, and the treatment of pro-Japanese collaborators and of Japanese living in Korea. This was a clear statement of the assumption of power from the Japanese.

On 17 August, the CPKI established as its central organs a Department of General Affairs (headed by Ch'oe Kŭnu), a Department of Finance (Yi Kyugap), a Department of Organization (Chŏng Paek), a Department of Information (Cho Tongu) and a Department of Police and Military Affairs (Kwŏn T'aesŏk). The heads of these departments were evenly distributed between left and right. It formed a National Foundation Constabulary made of 2,000 youth and students to handle public security and its also set up a Committee on Foodstuff Measures in an effort to ensure the supply of foodstuffs after the end of the war.

At the time of its launching, the CPKI placed its top priorities on ensuring public security, unifying national capacities for the work of establishing a state, and taking measures for foodstuffs, transportation, communications and finances. During the days before the 38th parallel emerged as a demarcation line, 145 local people's committees were formed in major cities and counties throughout the country, from Hoeryŏng and Kyŏngsŏng in the north to Cheju Island in the south. Most of those local committees were branches of the CPKI. Following the growth of its provincial organization, the CPKI central expanded and restructured its central organs to include departments of Foodstuffs, Culture, Public Security, Transportation, Construction, Planning, Public Welfare, Inspections and Secretariat. Again the CPKI selected men evenly from both left and right, including Kim Chunyŏn, Yi Yongsŏl (1894–?), Kim Yaksu (1992–?), Yi Tonghwa, Yi Kangguk, and Ch'oe Yongdal.

The CPKI put forth a programme with three major provisions that further clarified its goals. One was the establishment of a completely independent state. Another was the establishment of a democratic government that would fulfil the nation's basic political and social needs. The third was the maintenance, by Koreans themselves, of public safety and the ensuring of the livelihood of the masses during the temporary transition period.

Some right-wing forces, such as Song Chinu, did not participate in the CPKI. Nonetheless, participants in the CPKI included such right-wing and moderate elements as Yŏ Unhyŏng, An Chaehong, Kim Pyŏngno, Yi In (1896–1979) and Hŏ Hŏn, along with such left-wing elements as Pak Hŏnyŏng and his supporters and Chŏng Paek of the Changan (Seoul) faction Communist Party. Simply put, the CPKI got its start as an organization made up of both left and right. As its organization and its influence grew, however, conflicts of interest emerged that led to internal divisions. Strife between left and right surfaced over the issue of holding a congress of national leaders as each side sought to expand its representation in the congress, leading eventually to the resignation of vice-chair An Chaehong on 31 August. After An's resignation, Hŏ Hŏn became vice-chair and carried out a reorganization on 4 September that resulted in an increase in the power of the left wing. Two days later, the CPKI announced the formation of the 'Korean People's Republic' and dissolved itself.

The failure to gain the participation of the Song Chinu group at the time of its founding meant that the CPKI was not able to launch itself as an organization that represented all the nation's domestic political forces. There is also room to question the extent to which close communications existed between the CPKI's central organs and its local branches. Nonetheless, as a kind of 'upper stratum united front' entity participated in by moderate leftists such as Yŏ Unhyŏng, rightists such as An Chaehong, and leftists such as Yi Kangguk and Ch'oe Yongdal, the

CPKI received support from the entire citizenry to handle domestic politics and public security during the political void following the surrender of Japan. Once the Communist Party-centred leftists gained control, however, the CPKI no longer constituted a left-right collaborative organization and dissolved itself with the founding of the Korean People's Republic. The political line pursued by Yŏ Unhyŏng has been evaluated as either moderate left or as a centre national line that was neither left nor right. Yŏ subsequently organized the Korean People's Party on 11 November 1945 and participated in the leadership of the Democratic National Front until he resigned in opposition to the merger of the three left-wing parties. After that, he joined with Kim Kyusik to lead the movement for a left/right alliance.

THE DECLARATION OF THE KOREAN PEOPLE'S REPUBLIC

On 6 September the CPKI, now under the dominance of the left wing, declared the foundation of the Korean People's Republic. It announced the holding of a Congress of National People's Representatives, the forming of a Central People's Committee made up of 55 members such as Syngman Rhee and Yŏ Unhyŏng and 20 candidate members such as Ch'oe Ch'angik, and the creation of a twelve-person advisory council that included such men as O Sech'ang (1864–1953). It also released the names of major officials of the central government, along with a political programme and a list of 27 political guidelines.

The list of major officials had Syngman Rhee as president, Yŏ Unhyŏng as vice-president and Hŏ Hŏn as prime minister, and included men from the Shanghai Provisional Government such as Kim Ku and Kim Kyusik, from the Yenan Independence League such as Mujŏng, domestic leftists such as Yi Sŭngyŏp, men from the CPKI such as Yi Man'gyu, and domestic rightists such as Kim Sŏngsu (1891–1955). Most of the men named to ministerial posts, however, were either still overseas or were domestic figures who were named to office without their concurrence. That meant that once the government assumed power, actual authority would be exercised by vice-ministers, men who were mostly left-wing members of the CPKI.

The programme of the Korean People's Republic had four provisions. First was the establishment of a completely autonomous state. Second was the purge of all Japanese and feudal elements and the establishment of a truly democratic government that would realize the entire nation's political, social and economic demands Third was the rapid enhancement of the livelihoods of all the masses, including workers and peasants. Fourth was the making of alliances with all the democratic countries of the world and the attainment of world peace. This was similar to the programme of the CPKI, except for the addition of the provision for purging all Japanese and feudal elements. This issue appeared prominently in the list of 27 political guidelines that called for 'the nationalization of all land owned by the Japanese and national traitors and the distribution of that land to the peasants without compensation', and the 'nationalization of all facilities owned by the Japanese and national traitors, including mines, factories, railways, ports, ships, communications organs and financial organs'. Other key guidelines included the establishment of a rationing system to ensure fairness and equality in the provision of daily necessities and the implementation of a compulsory education system whose costs were to be borne by the government.

The call for such socialist economic systems as the nationalization of land and factories brought forth strong opposition from some right-wing elements. Nonetheless, the fact that most of the country's land and major production facilities had come under the control of the Japanese or of pro-Japanese Koreans during the colonial meant most people on both the left and the right considered nationalization an appropriate measure. The rightist Interim Government had issued, in anticipation of Japan's defeat, a 1941 programme for national foundation that called for the 'nationalization of major production facilities, of land, fisheries, mines, forests, irrigation works, land, sea and air transportation, banking, communications, transportation, major agricultural, industrial and commercial enterprises, and major co-operative production facilities administered by cities and industrial zones'.

Nonetheless, the proclamation of the Korean People's Republic was done hastily, leading to questions about how representative it was. Yŏ Unhyŏng explained the sudden formation of the Republic:

> This is unavoidable as an emergency measure at a time when our efforts to establish a state are in danger. We need to have a body that represents the will of the nation in order to negotiate with the Allied forces that will soon occupy the country and that means that we have to convene a Congress of National Representatives in order to establish such a body. Our work now must be directed towards foreigners.

It would appear that he foresaw direct rule by the Allied forces unless Korea had some form of government before the Allies arrived.

Japan, even though it was a defeated nation, had its own cabinet and thus was not subjected to direct rule by Douglas McArthur. Even north of the 38th parallel, the people's committees of each province were exercising administrative authority. The declaration of the Korean People's Republic, coming after the Allied forces refused to recognize the rightist Shanghai Interim Government, represented a move by leftist-led domestic political forces to create a unified front government that could gain recognition from the Allies. It also was an attempt to counter the formation of the right-wing Korean Democratic Party led by Song Chinu, who was hurrying his efforts in hopes of establishing control over the Interim Government once it returned to Korea.

Nonetheless, the Korean People's Republic was seen by many as having lost the upper–stratum unified–front aspect of the CPKI and as having turned to a leftist line by excluding such national bourgeoisie as An Chaehong and by emphasizing the establishment of a mass unified front. It has also been contrasted by some with the 10 October 1945 Congress of Responsible Activists of the Korean Communist Party in northern Korea that abandoned the effort to attain political power through a people's republic and set forth instead basic guidelines for forming a broad national front embracing persons of all groups and all strata as a base for a reform movement that would lead to the establishment of a state.

REFERENCES

Yi Man'gyu, *Yŏ Unhyŏng sŏnsaeng t'ujaengsa* (History of the struggles of Yŏ Unhyŏng), Seoul: Minŭmsa, 1946.

Yŏ Unhong, *Mongyang Yŏ Unhyŏng* (Biography of Yŏ Unhyŏng), Seoul: Ch'ŏnghagak, 1967.

Song Namhŏn, *Haebang samsimnyŏnsa* (History of thirty years of liberation), Vol. 1, Seoul: Han'guksa yŏn'guso, 1976.

Song Kŏnho, '8.15hu ŭi han'guk minjokchuŭi' (Korean nationalism after liberation), *Han'guk minjokchuŭiron*, Seoul: Ch'angjak kwa pip'yŏngsa, 1982.

Han'gilsa, ed., *Haebang chŏnhusa ŭi insik* (Perceptions of history before and after liberation), vol. 3, Seoul: Han'gilsa, 1987.

Han'guk yŏksa yŏn'guhoe hyŏndaesa yŏn'guban, *Han'guk hyŏndaesa* (Contemporary Korean history), vol. 1, Seoul: P'ulpit, 1992.

SECTION TWO

The Left-Right Coalition Movement and the North-South Meeting

PEOPLE'S REPUBLIC – INTERIM GOVERNMENT NEGOTIATIONS AND THE FOUR-PARTY COMMUNIQUÉ

After the leftists gained a dominant position in the CPKI and declared the establishment of the Korean People's Republic, they sought to bring in rightist forces by making Syngman Rhee president and including right-wing elements in their people's committee. After Rhee arrived in Korea, the Korean People's Republic published a welcome statement that offered 'loyal thanks and whole-hearted welcome to the great leader'. Rhee's broadcast response was to say: 'I have good feelings toward the Communist Party and approve of its ideology. There are many points in Communism that we can use to establish economic measures.' This marked the beginning of serious negotiations between Rhee and the People's Republic.

Talks among Rhee, Yŏ Unhyŏng and Pak Hŏnyŏng on 23 October 1945 resulted in a resolution for the left and right to form a Central

Association for the Realization of Independence. When representatives met to form the Association, however, and adopted a 'Statement to Be Sent to the Four Great Allies' that called for opposition to division, opposition to trusteeship and opposition to occupation of Korea, Pak Hŏnyŏng announced that the Communist Party would break away from the Association unless the statement included the 'principle of national unification based on the exclusion of pro-Japanese elements'.

This led to a stand off between the right, which called for 'unification first, exclusion of pro-Japanese elements second', and the left, which wanted 'exclusion of pro-Japanese elements first, unification second'. On 6 November the leftist National Youth Representative's Assembly issued a resolution stating: 'If Syngman Rhee refuses the presidency of the People's Republic, we will not only refuse to support him but will consider him ultimately responsible for the division of the national reunification front.' The next day Rhee responded by stating that while he was grateful to the Korean People's Republic for designating him president, he was a man of the Provisional Government and could not be involved in anything without the collaboration of the Provisional Government. On 5 December, the Korean Communist Party declared its separation from the Association, marking an end to negotiations between Rhee and the People's Republic.

In the meantime, members of the Interim Government returned to Korea as private individuals, as demanded by the Allies, with the first group arriving on 23 November and the second on 2 December. The Interim Government had proclaimed that: 'Until such time as a transitional government is formed inside Korea, the Interim Government will be responsible for maintaining domestic order and handling all external affairs.' In effect, therefore, whether the US military government recognized it or not, there were two governments, the Interim Government and the People's Republic, claiming authority in Korea. The People's Republic invited Kim Ku and Kim Kyusik to join its Central People's Committee, but the two Kims refused.

The Korean Communist Party presented a principle for unification that called for a fifty-fifty split among left and right, with collaborationists, national traitors and chauvinist extremists to be excluded. This was rejected by the Interim Government, which demanded recognition of its legitimacy along with acceptance of its offices and officers and offered to add two or three new offices to accommodate left-wing participation.

Once the plan for trusteeship was announced, a meeting was held at the suggestion of the People's Republic on 31 December attended by such representatives of the Interim Government as Ch'oe Tonghŏn, Sŏng Chusik and Chang Kŏnsang and such representatives of the People's Republic as Hong Namp'yo (1890–?), Hong Chŭngsik (1895–?) and Yi Kangguk. On the next day, 1 January 1946, the People's Republic presented a plan for a committee made up of representatives from both sides to engage in concrete discussions about the establishment of a unified government and called for an agreement to be reached before the

US-Soviet Joint Commission convened. The Interim Government rejected this proposal on procedural grounds. Not only did the Interim Government refuse to accept the People's Republic as an equal partner in negotiations, but there was a huge gap between the two sides on the trusteeship issue, with the left generally supporting the decision of the Moscow Conference and the Interim Government seeking to establish its leadership over the anti-trusteeship movement.

When negotiations between the two 'governments' began to flounder, the People's Party led by Yŏ Unhyŏng launched discussions for unification among major right- and left-wing political parties. At the suggestion of Yi Yŏsŏng of the People's Party, a meeting was held between Wŏn Sehun and Kim Pyŏngno of the Korean Democratic Party, An Chaehong, Paek Honggyun, and Yi Sŭngbok (1895–1978) of the National Party, Yi Chuha and Hong Namp'yo of the Korean Communist Party, and Yi Yŏsŏng and Kim Seyong of the People's Party. The result was the 'Four Party Communique' of 7 January 1946 that declared: 'With regard to the decisions of the Moscow Conference, we totally support the intention and the spirit of ensuring the independence of Korea and of assisting the development of democracy. The issue of 'trusteeship' must be resolved based on the spirit of autonomy and independence by the soon-to-be-established Korean government.' The Korean Democratic Party, however, opposed the communiqué on the grounds that it lacked a clear expression of opposition to trusteeship and calls were made for the censure of Kim Pyŏngno and Wŏn Sehun. The National Party also came out in opposition on similar grounds. At that point, the New Korean National Party opened a 'five party meeting' in support of unification efforts on 9 January. This five party meeting adjourned after a stand off between the right-wing New Korean National Party, the National Party and the Korean Democratic Party on one side, and the left-wing People's Party and the Korean Communist Party on the other side over the issue of whether the five party meeting should be considered a preliminary session of an emergency political conference, as demanded by the right, or an extension of the four party talks as demanded by the left.

The People's Party subsequently sought to revive the five party talks with a compromise proposal that called for 'supporting the Moscow Conference's decision to aid the establishment of an independent government in Korea and opposing trusteeship', but was unable to bring the five parties back together. The People's Party tried again with a proposal of four principles for unification that called for the exclusion of collaborators and national traitors, for the establishment of the independent state decided at the Moscow Conference, for both the People's Republic and the Interim Government to abandon their claims to sole legitimacy, and for proportional representation according to the actual numbers and sizes of organization. That attempt also came to nothing. Yŏ Unhyŏng tried once more to overcome the division between left and right over the trusteeship issue and to unify the People's Republic and the Interim Government with yet another compromise proposal to support the decisions of the Moscow Conference while calling for autonomous resolution of trusteeship. That final proposal also failed, but Yŏ's efforts towards an alliance between left and right continued.

THE ACTIVITIES OF THE LEFT-RIGHT ALLIANCE COMMITTEE

The opposition between left and right over the trusteeship issue intensified after the failure of the attempt to unify the People's Republic and the Interim Government and collapse of the 'four party communiqué'. On 23 January 1946, such Korean National Revolutionary Party and Korean National Liberation Movement Activist League progressives as Kim Wŏnbong, Kim Sŏngsuk, Sŏng Chusik and Chang Kŏnsang, who had joined with the Interim Government's united front line during the final stages of the Second World War, left the Interim Government in opposition to its turn to the right.

On 2 February, the Interim Government held an emergency national conference at which it reaffirmed its legitimacy as the successor to the national liberation movement of the colonial period and pushed on with its movement in opposition to trusteeship. Syngman Rhee's Central Association for the Realization of Independence joined with the Committee for the All-out Mobilization of the Citizens against Trusteeship to form the Korean Citizen's Association for the Realization of Independence. This organization then established a Democratic Council of Representatives of the Citizens of Korea in order to prepare for the US-Soviet Joint Commission. This represented the unification of the right-wing forces.

On the other hand, on 15 February, the progressive forces that did not participate in the Democratic Council also prepared for the Joint Commission by forming their own Democratic National Front, based on the four principles set forth by the People's Party at the five party conference. A wide variety of political parties and social organizations participated in the Democratic National Front, including the Korean Communist Party, the People's Party, the New Korean National Party, the National Revolutionary Party, the National Council of Labour Unions, the Nationwide General League of Peasant Unions, the Youth League and the General League of Women. Yŏ Unhyŏng, Pak Hŏnyŏng, Hŏ Hŏn, Kim Wŏnbong and Paek Namun were co-chairs. At the beginning, the Democratic National Front strove to make itself a broad, popular-based united-front organization and included such persons as Kim Sŏngsuk, Sŏng Chusik and Chang Kŏnsang who had left the Interim Government along with such domestic moderates as Yi Kŭngno and O Chiyŏng (?–1950) of the Religion of the Heavenly Way. Before long, however, it became simply a narrow left-wing united front led by the Communist Party.

The divisions between the right-wing Democratic Council and the left-wing Democratic National Front in early 1948 was such that the two organizations held separate commemorations of the March First Movement.

The antagonisms between left and right and between the left and the US military government were deepened even further following the 6 May breakup of the first US-Soviet Joint Commission and the 15 May outbreak of the Chosŏn Chŏngp'an Company counterfeiting scandal, which the left contended was a plot fabricated to besmirch the Korean Communist Party.

During this time, north of the 38th parallel all farmlands owned by Japanese and all farmlands greater than five chŏngbo, including tenant farms, were seized and redistributed without compensation on 5 March and a twenty-point programme emphasizing the struggle against reactionary elements was announced on 23 March. In the south, foreign wire services were beginning to report right-wing talk about establishing a separate government south of the parallel, reports that were given credence by Syngman Rhee's 3 June Chŏngŭp announcement regarding the need to establish a separate government.

It was under such circumstances that Yŏ Unhyŏng and Kim Kyusik began to make contacts for the creation of a left-right alliance. On 14 June, a four-person meeting among Yŏ, Kim, Wŏn Sehun of the rightist Korean Democratic Party and Hŏ Hŏn of the Democratic National Front took place. This was followed by the formation of a Left-Right Alliance Committee made up of Kim Kyusik, Wŏn Sehun, An Chaehong, Ch'oe Tongho and Kim Pongjun (1888–?) from the right and Yŏ Unhyŏng, Sŏng Chusik, Chŏng Nosik and Yi Kangguk from the left. This committee held its first meeting in Tŏksu Palace on 25 July 1946. The left put forth a programme that called for support of the decisions of the Moscow Conference, the establishment of an interim government through the reopening of the US-Soviet Joint Commission, land reform without compensation, nationalization of major industries, the elimination of pro-Japanese collaborators and national traitors, and the transfer of political power in the south to the People's Committee. The right set forth its own 'eight principles for a left-right alliance'. Those principles included resolving the trusteeship issue after establishing an interim government, creating a society that provided institutional and legal equality in all such areas as politics, economy and education through a meeting of national representatives after the establishment of an interim government, and punishing pro-Japanese collaborators and national traitors through a special court to be convened after the establishment of an interim government.

The major differences between the programmes set forth by the left and the right revolved around the issues of trusteeship, such economic issues as the disposition of land and major industries, and the handling of the issue of the pro-Japanese collaborators. These were in fact the big impediments to the realization of a left-right alliance and the talks broke off after the initial meeting did little beyond confirming the differences between left and right.

The left-right alliance movement receded into the background while the Communist Party, the People's Party and the New Korean Democratic

Party announced the merger of the three parties on 5 September, the political office of the US military government ordered the arrest of Communist Party leaders, and *minjung* resistance movements arose in Taegu and other areas of North Kyŏngsang Province. Despite the intensification of the left-right split, there were continuous efforts to reconcile the two sides. On 7 October, the Left-Right Alliance Committee announced its 'seven principles of left-right alliance' as a compromise between the five principles of the left and the eight principles of the right. This announcement called for resolution of the trusteeship issue after establishing a 'democratic left-right alliance interim government according to the decisions of the Moscow Conference'. It called for the nationalization of major industries but provided some guarantee of the interests of the landlords by stipulating that land reform would be carried out through 'purchase at reduced prices', with land being redistributed free to the peasants. It also called for punishing pro-Japanese collaborators and national traitors through a legislative body.

The right-wing Korean Independence Party of Kim Ku approved these seven principles. Syngman Rhee said: 'I am not satisfied because there are conditions that go against democratic policies. We should wait until after the establishment of an interim government to discuss the issues of trusteeship and land and deal with them according to the wishes of the people.' The Korean Democratic Party turned away from the left-right alliance movement altogether, arguing that land reform should be done through purchase from landlords and sale to peasants. This led to the resignation of some 270 of the more progressive members of the Korean Democratic Party, including such men as Wŏn Sehun, Kim Pyŏngno and Kim Yaksu.

On the other hand, Pak Hŏnyŏng of the left said: 'The issues of reaction or progress, independence or subjugation at this critical time do not allow for the existence of a moderate line.' Pak went on to explain his opposition on the grounds that the seven principles did not fully support the decisions of the Moscow Conference, that compensation for the sale of land sacrificed the people's economy to the interests of the landlords, that there was no provision for transferring power to the people's committees and that the decisions of a legislative organ were subject to veto by the US military government.

Although the left-right alliance movement was stymied by its inability to gain agreement from central figures of the left and the right over the issues of trusteeship, land reform and punishment of pro-Japanese collaborators, it was gaining broad public support. The committee itself expanded its membership to include persons from religious circles, youth groups, women's groups and academic circles along with persons from various political parties and social organizations. In addition, on 3 July 1947 over 100 persons from various circles, including Kim Kyusik, Yŏ Unhyŏng, Hong Myŏnghŭi, An Chaehong, Wŏn Sehun, O Hayŏng (1870–1959), Ch'oe Tongho, Kim Pongjun, Yun Kisŏp (1881–?) and Yi Kŭngno, formed a Council for Measures to Deal with the Situation that strongly supported the left-right alliance movement. There was also wide support for the left-right alliance movement from a broad range of political parties and other political groups. These included the National Autonomy Alliance headed by Kim Kyusik with the support of An Chaehong and Hong Myŏnghǔi; the National Alliance also chaired by Kim Kyusik with the participation of Kim Yaksu and Yi Sunt'ak (1897–?); the New Progress Party, created by the merger of the New Korean National Party, the New Korean Democratic Party, the Korean Revolutionary Party, the Alliance of Korean-Americans, and the Pure Friends' Party, the Social Democratic Party headed by Yŏ Unhong (1891–1973), the Religion of the Heavenly Way National Protection Party led by Sin Suk, the Working Masses Party of Kang Sun (1898-?), the Korean Republican Party with Kim Yaksu as secretary, and Korean Masses Party chaired by Yi Tusan, the New Korean Citzens' Party led by Pak Yonghǔi (1884–1954), and the Democratic Unification Party headed by Hong Myŏnghǔi.

At its beginning, the left-right alliance movement received policy and financial support from the US military government. The US, still hoping for some sort of resolution of the Korea problem through the decisions of the Moscow Conference, was not yet able to support actively such 'far right' elements as Kim Ku and Syngman Rhee who were strongly pushing the anti-trusteeship movement. Not only did the anti-trusteeship movement go against the Moscow accords, but if the US openly supported Syngman Rhee's plan for the establishment of a separate government, it would have run the risk of forcing the moderate forces to join with the left in a strong movement against a separate government. The US thought that if it supported the establishment of a government by moderate forces it would be able to prevent the communization of the Korean Peninsula. In order to strengthen the position of the moderate forces and broaden support for the US military government, the US created, in the face of leftist opposition, a South Korean Interim Legislature headed by Kim Kyusik on 12 December 1946 and a South Korean Interim Government headed by An Chaehong on 5 February 1947. The Interim Legislature was composed of forty-five representatives chosen by the people and forty-five appointed by the US. The Syngman Rhee group and the Korean Democratic Party won a majority of the popularly elected seats amidst controversies over electoral fraud, while the appointed seats were filled with men from the Left-Right Alliance Committee and other moderates.

Syngman Rhee made a trip back to the US in early 1947 where he lobbied strongly for the establishment of a separate government in south Korea. Shortly after the US State Department's hints of a plan to establish a separate government led to the final breakup of the US-Soviet Joint Commission on 19 July 1947, Yŏ Unhyŏng, the left-wing leader of the left-right alliance movement was assassinated on 19 July. The US then abandoned the decisions of the Moscow Conference and took the Korea problem to the United Nations, where it had an absolute majority. This meant the final failure of the left-right alliance movement and the finalization of the plan to establish a separate government in the south.

There are scholars who contend that the left-right alliance movement began as part of a US plan to divide the leftist elements of the democratic national movement. Nonetheless, considering the central roles played by such men as Kim Kyusik and Yŏ Unhyŏng, who had led the unified front movement in the colonial period through such entities as the Korean National Revolutionary Party and the National Foundation League, the left-right alliance movement can be said to have been a post-liberation continuation of the movement to establish a unified nation-state that had broad support from among moderate political forces.

Although there may have been problems in the overall reporting of numbers, what we have indicates that the moderate political parties had memberships close to those claimed by left- and right-wing parties. Furthermore, a public opinion survey taken by the US military government showed that whereas only 17% of the population supported capitalism and only 13% supported communism, 70% supported socialism. This tells us that there was a broad base of support for the left-right alliance movement during the 'liberation space' (the period between liberation in 1945 and the establishment of separate regimes in 1948). Nonetheless, the division of Korea along the 38th parallel by foreign powers and the way in which domestic forces used that division to curry favour with the occupiers spelled frustration for the left-right alliance as a movement to create a unified nation-state.

THE NORTH-SOUTH MEETING

Once the US changed its Korea policy from one of supporting a plan for the creation of a unified government led by centrist forces to one of supporting a separate government led by Syngman Rhee and the Korean Democratic Party and the Korea problem had gone over to the US-dominated United Nations, there arose a strong movement in opposition to the creation of a separate government. After the assassination of Yŏ Unhyŏng, Kim Kyusik joined forces with such moderate elements as the *Minjung* League, the New Progressive Party and the Social Democratic Party, excluded elements from the far left and far right and formed a 'National Independence League' on 20 December 1947 that proclaimed a line of national autonomy.

Kim Ku, who had allied himself with Syngman Rhee and the Korean Democratic Party against trusteeship, rejected Rhee's and the Korean Democratic Party's turn toward the establishment of a separate government in south Korea and joined forces with Kim Kyusik to send a letter to Kim Il Sung and Kim Tubong in the north proposing a meeting of key figures from both north and south. Kim Ku also presented a plan to the United Nations delegation to Korea for a joint meeting of northern and southern leaders on 6 February 1948, published his 'Tearful Report to My 30 Million Compatriots' on 10 February, and again suggested north-south negotiations on 8 March.

Kim Il Sung and Kim Tubong sent a response to Kim Kyusik's and Kim Ku's letter on 25 March, proposing a north-south meeting to discuss an exchange of views on the Korean political situation, measures to oppose the UN resolution for conducting an election intended to create a separate government in the south, and an investigation of ways to establish a unified and democratic government in Korea. They also sent a letter proposing a 'joint meeting of representatives of all the political parties and social organizations in Korea' on 30 March.

Problems arose, however, over trips to the north for those who had been invited, including Kim Kyusik, Kim Ku, Cho Soang and Hong Myŏnghŭi. The US military government opposed allowing these men to go north right before the elections in the south. Organizations such as right-wing youth and student groups, Christian groups and groups made up of persons who had fled the north all stepped forth against allowing those men to travel to the north. On the other hand, there were also many entities, including moderate political parties and legal organizations, that supported the meeting as seen in the 4 April joint statement signed by 104 men in support of the north-south meeting.

Before they went north, Kim Ku and Kim Kyusik published 'five principles for negotiations' that called for the rejection of dictatorial politics and the construction of a democratic state, for the rejection of monopoly capitalism and the recognition of private ownership of property, for the establishment of a unified central government through a nationwide general election, and for opposition to providing military bases to foreign powers. By the time they arrived in P'yŏngyang, the All Korea Meeting of Political Party and Social Organizations Representatives of 19–26 April had already begun. This meeting resulted in the adoption of a message to be sent to all Koreans demanding the immediate withdrawal of both US and Soviet forces and opposing the creation of separate governments. This was followed by a 27–30 April Conference of the Leaders of Political Parties and Social Organizations in north and south Korea attended by eleven delegates from the south, including Kim Kuk, Kim Kyusik, Pak Hŏnyŏng and Paek Namun, and Kim Il Sung, Kim Tubong, Ch'oe Yonggŏn and Chu Yŏngha from the north. This conference agreed on four points: the immediate withdrawal of foreign military forces; the prevention of civil war after the withdrawal; the formation of an 'All-Korea Political Assembly' to implement a general election and establish a government; and opposition to the establishment of a separate government in the south. A four person meeting was also held by Kim Ku, Kim Kyusik, Kim Il Sung and Kim Tubong that reached agreements on such issues as the north continuing to send electric power to the south, the opening of the Yŏnbaek irrigation co-operative that straddled the 38th parallel, and allowing Cho Mansik (1882–1950) to go south.

In order to negotiate the withdrawal of US and Soviet troops, which was the necessary precondition for the other points agreed upon in the Conference of Leaders, Kim Tubong was sent to the Soviet military and Yŏ Unhong to the US military to convey the decisions of the conference and ask for the withdrawal of forces. The Soviet commander said that 'the Soviet forces are prepared to withdraw immediately if the US forces withdraw at the same time'. The US commander Hodge, however, replied that: 'The UN resolution specifies that the troops of both countries are to withdraw as quickly as possible after the implementation of a general election throughout all of Korea and the establishment of a Korean national government,' adhering to the plan of withdrawing troops only after the establishment of a government. As a consequence, the agreements of the Conference of Leaders came to nothing.

Upon their return to Seoul, Kim Ku and Kim Kyusik made a joint statement that laid out the course of the north-south negotiations in P'yŏngyang and the points of agreement and rejected the 10 May elections for the establishment of a separate government in south Korea. The north, which was laying its own plans for elections to establish a separate government, subsequently proposed a second north-south conference to be held in Haeju which they urged the two Kims to attend. The two Kims, however, refused to participate on the grounds that the northern plan to establish a separate state, even if done in response to the southern plan, was a move to divide the nation.

The north went ahead without the two Kims to held a 29 June Second Conference of the Leaders of Political Parties and Social Organizations in north and south Korea at which it denounced the south's Korean National Assembly as an illegal organization and decided to establish the central government of the 'Democratic People's Republic of Korea'. The two Kims then issued a statement on 19 July that foretold the coming of the Korean War. The statement said:

> The north has unilaterally decided on a constitution, declared the founding of a people's republic, and even adopted its own national flag. Differences in timing, location and methods notwithstanding, the north and the south are each intending to establish a state in half of the country. From this point on, north and south will compete over our divided land and lead us into national fratricide.

After the two Kims rejected the Second Conference of Leaders, 'representatives' of cities and counties throughout south Korea gathered in Haeju on 21 August to hold a South Korean Congress of People's Representatives. There they selected 360 delegates drawn from all the political parties and social organizations that had attended the first Conference of the Leaders of Political Parties and Social Organizations in north and south Korea. The South Korean Worker's Party accounted for the 132 delegates, the Korean People's Republic Party for 68, the New Progress Party for 31, the Social Democratic Party for 43, the Democratic Korean Independence Party for 35, the Working Masses Party for 62, the National Association of Labour Unions for 66 and the Democratic Independence Party for 53. The two Kims' attempts at north-south negotiations ended with the first 'Conference of Leaders'. The Second

Conference of Leaders and the Haeju South Korean Congress were held for the purpose of supporting the establishment of the Democratic People's Republic of Korea in the north.

Even after elections in the south, the two Kims brought together forces opposed to the establishment of a separate government, such as the Korean Independence Party and the National Autonomy League, on 21 July 1947 to form the Association for the Promotion of Unification and Independence. The Association's goals included 'bringing together all unification and independence activists' and 'resolving the national problem autonomously'. As they pushed on with their movement for national unification, they demanded that the UN dissolve the two separate governments in north and south and establish a unified government through a general election held in both north and south. Ultimately, however, Kim Ku was assassinated on 26 June 1949 and the Korean War broke out on 25 June 1950.

Once the danger of national division became apparent as the result of the machinations of certain domestic political groups and foreign powers, the political forces that had led the united front movement of the national liberation front during the colonial period stepped forth again to push for a coalition between the People's Republic and the Interim Government, for an alliance between left and right, and for north-south meetings in order to establish a unified nation-state in Korea. The 1948 north-south meeting is particularly noteworthy as an autonomous and peaceful movement for the establishment of a unified nation-state that had broad participation from all those forces that had been part of the national liberation movement and all those forces oriented towards a unified nation-state. The only exceptions were the Syngman Rhee group and the Korean Democratic Party.

REFERENCES

Song Namhŏn, *Haebang samsimnyŏnsa* (History of thirty years of liberation), Vol. 1, Seoul: Han'guksa yŏn'guso, 1976.

Yi Tonghwa, '8.15 rŭl chŏnhuhan Yŏ Unhyŏng ŭi chŏngch'i hwaltong' (Yŏ Unhyŏng's political activities before and after liberation), *Haebang chŏnhusa ŭi insik*, Seoul: Han'gilsa, 1979.

Song Kŏnho, '8.15hu ŭi han'guk minjokchuŭi' (Korean nationalism after liberation), *Han'guk minjokchuŭiron*, Seoul: Ch'angjak kwa pip'yŏngsa, 1982.

Kim Chŏngwŏn, 'Haebang ihu han'guk ŭi chŏngch'i kwajŏng' (Political process in Korea after liberation), *Han'guk hyŏndaesa ŭi chae chomyŏng*, Seoul: Tol pegae, 1982.

Kang Man-gil, 'Chwau hapchak undong ŭi kyŏngwi wa kŭ sŏngkyŏk' (Course and nature of the left-right alliance movement), *Han'gu kminjokchuŭi ron*, Seoul: Ch'angjak kwa pip'yŏngsa, 1983.

Kang Man-gil, 'Kim Ku wa Kim Kyusik ŭi nambuk hyŏpsang' (The north-south negotiations of Kim Ku and Kim Kyusik), *Hyŏndaesa rŭl ŏttŏhkae pol kŏsin'ga?*, Seoul: Tonga ilbosa, 1987.

Yi Wanbŏm, 'Haebang chikhu minjok t'ongil undong e kwanhan yŏn'gu' (A study on the national unification movement right after liberation), *Wŏnu nonjip* 15–1, 1987.

Seoul taehakkyo inmun taehak han'guk hyŏndaesa yŏn'guhoe, *Haebang chŏngguk kwa minjok t'ongil chŏnsŏn* (The political situation of liberation and the national unification front), Seoul: Segye, 1987.

Sŏ Chungsŏk, *Han'guk hyŏndae minjok undongsa yŏn'gu* (Studies in the modern Korean national movement), Seoul: Yŏksa pipyŏngsa, 1991.

Han'guk yŏksa yŏn'guhoe hyŏndaesa yŏn'guban, *Han'guk hyŏndaesa* (Contemporary Korean history), vol. 1, Seoul: P'ulpit, 1992.

SECTION THREE

The 19 April Movement for Democracy and Unification

THE 19 APRIL DEMOCRATIZATION MOVEMENT

The Syngman Rhee regime, which came into being in south Korea following the failure of the Committee for the Preparation of Korean Independence, the left-right alliance movement and the north-south negotiations to achieve the creation of a unified nation state, established its dictatorial system under the slogans of anti-Japanism and anti-Communism. The Rhee regime proclaimed a superficial anti-Japanism in order to establish itself as the successor to the national liberation movement of the colonial period, but in fact it had very weak grounds for making such a claim.

If the national liberation movement of the colonial period can be divided methodologically into independence through war and independence through diplomacy, Syngman Rhee's group falls into the latter category. If it can be divided into arguments for absolute independence and relative independence, the Korean Democratic Party, one of the forces that established the Rhee regime, falls into the latter. The first government to be founded in Korea after liberation was one that excluded the national forces that had called for a war of independence and absolute independence.

Even though the Rhee regime paid lip service to anti-Japanism, in reality it was a government very much based on the pro-Japanese collaborators of the colonial period. The US military government in Korea retained almost all the Koreans who had been officials of the Japanese Government-General and Syngman Rhee, in turn, retained the vast majority of the officials of the US military government. The consequence was that most of the Korean officials of the Government-General, including the police, continued to hold office under Rhee. The way in which the Special Committee to Investigate Anti-National

Activities was illegally disbanded stands as testimony to this aspect of the Rhee regime.

The issues of punishing pro-Japanese collaborators and of carrying out land reform were the constant focus of contention during the activities of the Committee for the Preparation of Korean Independence and the left-right alliance movement. The Rhee regime attempted to establish its nationalist credentials by setting forth anti-Japanese policies and promulgating the 22 September 1948 Law to Punish Anti-National Activities. However, once the law's application reached the Rhee regime's top police officials, Rhee suddenly had the police surround the Special Committee to Investigate Anti-National Activities and forced the Committee to disband on 6 June 1949. This meant the effective end of any serious efforts to punish the pro-Japanese collaborators.

From that time on, the Rhee regime's anti-Japanism was nothing more than a diplomatic strategy aimed at Japan while pro-Japanese collaborators remained safely ensconced in important political, cultural and educational positions. The Rhee regime's failure to punish the pro-Japanese collaborators meant the loss of its nationalist legitimacy. All that was left to justify the regime was a policy of anti-Communism that was supposed to bring the establishment of a liberal democratic system in Korea. The US, in order to maintain its triangular US-Japan-south Korea security system in North-east Asia, urged the Rhee regime to reopen diplomatic relations with Japan, but negotiations stalled over issues of compensation and economic aid. This led to friction between the Rhee regime and the United States.

The 19 April movement, which was a *minjung* movement in resistance to the Rhee regime that had lost its legitimacy and had developed into a dictatorship, began as a movement to recover popular sovereignty. Whenever the Rhee regime engaged in acts of tyranny, the opposition politicians carried out limited anti-dictatorship movements such as the founding of the Association to Defend the Constitution, the 18 September 1955 establishing of the Democratic Party, the launching of the Association to Struggle for the Protection of Popular Sovereignty and the forming of the Citizens' General League to Protect Civil Rights. The opposition, however, was never able to overthrow the Rhee regime.

The Liberal Party's manipulation of elections reached a climax in the 15 March 1960 election to choose the president and vice-president, particularly in the effort to ensure the election of the Party's vice-presidential candidate, Yi Kibung. On the day of the election, a *minjung* demonstration broke out in Masan in protest of voting irregularities. The demonstrators attacked the police station, resulting in over eighty dead and injured. Student demonstrations protesting the corrupt election spread to Seoul, Pusan and other cities, while a second *minjung* demonstration arose in Masan on the occasion of the transfer of the body of a dead student demonstrator, Kim Chuyŏl (1943–60).

The Syngman Rhee regime followed its usual practice of claiming that Communist elements were behind the unrest in Masan. However, students at Korea University in Seoul demonstrated on 18 April, sparking the uprising by more than 20,000 students and ordinary citizens on 19 April who denounced the corrupt election and set fire to the government's newspaper, the Seoul Sinmun, the Anti-Communist Hall and the police station. In the process, the police opened fired and killed 186 persons. The dead included 66 common labourers, 36 high school students, 22 college students, 19 elementary and middle school students, 10 office workers, and 5 others.

Shaken by the turn of events, Syngman Rhee attempted to contain the situation and retain power by declaring martial law, reshuffling his cabinet, forcing the resignation of Yi Ki-bung and stepping down himself from his position as head of the Liberal Party. Nonetheless, the 26 April demonstration by college professors was followed by additional *minjung* demonstrations, leading Rhee finally to resign as president on 27 April after twelve years in power. After Rhee's resignation, Foreign Minister Hŏ Chŏng assumed power. Hŏ's transitional government presided over a revision of the constitution to provide for a parliamentary system and general elections that resulted in the 23 August formation of a Democratic Party cabinet with Chang Myŏn as Prime Minister.

The direct cause of the explosion of the 19 April movement was the shameless manipulation of voting by the Liberal Party in the fourth presidential election. More than that, however, it was a democracy movement seeking to recover popular sovereignty. The movement for popular sovereignty in Korea can be traced back to the years of the Great Han Empire, but that came to an end during the colonial period. Such a movement was also not tolerated under trusteeship. The result was a strong pent-up demand for popular sovereignty during the 'liberation space' that was once again denied during the process of the formation of the Rhee regime and the Korean War. During the second half of the 1950s, there again arose strong demands for democracy, led largely by students and youthful intellectuals. The workers' and peasants' movements, which had been suppressed by the dictatorship and the strengthening of the anti-Communist system, became active once again as cuts in US economic aid led to industrial stagnation and increasing unemployment. An additional factor enabling the overthrow of the dictatorial regime was the weakening of US support for the Rhee regime.

THE 19 APRIL NATIONAL REUNIFICATION MOVEMENT

From the time of its founding, the Syngman Rhee regime rejected the north's proposals for talks and argued that unification should be attained by the dissolution of the Kim Il Sung regime and free elections carried out in the north under UN supervision, a plan that changed to one of reunification by force before the outbreak of the Korean War. After the war, the Rhee regime rejected the 'plan for a general election in both north and south under UN supervision' recommended by the participants in the Geneva Conference and contended instead that 'an election should be held under UN supervision in the north while an election in the south should be carried out according to the provisions of the constitution of the Republic of Korea'. After the Geneva Conference broke up, however, the Rhee regime reverted to its earlier plan of 'an election under UN supervision only in the north'. When Cho Pongam's Progressive Party proposed its 'plan for peaceful reunification through a general election in both north and south', the Rhee regime declared the Progressive Party illegal on the grounds that the proposal went against state policy and executed Cho Pongam as a spy.

After the 19 April movement brought down the Rhee regime, new changes began to appear in discussions about reunification. The prime reason was that it was now possible for progressive political forces to become active again. After the progressives forces split into the Social Masses Party and the General Alliance for Reform and failed miserably in the 29 July general elections, they split once again into the Social Masses Party made up of old Progressive Party elements, the Social Party and the Reform Party composed of former Labouring Masses Party members, and the Unification Social Party made up of former Democratic Reform Party forces. Nonetheless, all these different groups took roughly the same position regarding reunification. That position can be boiled down to three things: autonomous national reunification without any intervention from the UN or the great powers; peaceful reunification through negotiations between north and south; and making the Korean Peninsula neutral.

After their disastrous defeat in the 29 July elections, the progressive forces began to seek unity. The result was the 30 August 1960 establishment of the Central Association for Autonomous National Reunification headed by Kim Ch'angsuk (1879–1962) of the Association for the Confucian Way. The Central Association's membership was not limited to progressive political parties. Its participants included the Association for the Confucian Way, the Religion of the Heavenly Way, some teachers' unions and the Association of College Professors. The Central Association put forth proposals for a practical citizen's movement for reunification that included calls for immediate talks between north and south, the formation of a Supreme Committee for the Establishment of a Unified Nation State, the rejection of foreign powers, and the opening of talks between northern and southern representatives to discuss reunification.

The Central Association's concrete plan for reunification provided for three stages. The first stage was to include the exchange of civilian organizations, the opening of mail services, and economic and cultural exchanges. The second stage was to have the two governments engage in joint economic planning targeted towards reunification and to implement various projects in preparation for unification. The third stage featured the establishment of democratic election procedures, the guaranteeing of various freedoms and free elections. The Central Association pushed its reunification movement while also carrying out movements against the Chang regime's 8 February 1961 economic agreement with the US and against the anti-Communist Law and various laws restricting large-scale demonstrations.

In contrast to the clear and progressive reunification plans of the progressives, the Chang regime's reunification policy was makeshift. The Chang regime was aware it could not simply continue the Rhee regime's reunification policy of overthrowing the north, but it was unable to prepare a reunification plan that answered the wishes of the general public. After agonizing over the issue for some time, the regime presented a plan to the UN General Assembly for 'peaceful, free and democratic reunification through a general election held under UN supervision in both north and south'. This plan, however, came under fire from some conservative groups for 'treating north and south Korea as equals and therefore denying the legitimacy of the Republic of Korea'. It was also derided in the media:

> The plan for general elections in north and south under UN supervision presented by the Democratic Party government to the United Nations is something that will be batted back and forth interminably and represents nothing but an attempt to seize the initiative in the propaganda of the Cold War between the US and the Soviet Union.

Once the huge gap between the reunification plans of the progressives and the Chang regime became apparent, the reunification discussions among the youth and college students who had led the 19 April movement picked up speed and took a radical turn. The national reunification movement became most active in the first half of 1961. The students' association of Korea University called for the opening of mail services, the exchange of persons, and the conclusion of a technology agreement between north and south. The National Reunification League of Seoul National University proposed talks between the students of north and south, including academic debates, an atheletic meet and exchange of university newspaper reporters. Furthermore, fifty representatives of seventeen universities gathered on 5 May 1961 to form the 'National League of College Students for National Reunification' and issued a call for talks between students from the north and the south at P'anmunjŏm within five days.

In the face of the students' radical reunification movement, the Chang regime persisted in its call for a general election under UN supervision, its rejection of the Korean Peninsula being made neutral, and its determination that it was still too early to have exchanges between north and south. Nonetheless, some progressive members of the old faction of the Democratic Party that had broken away to form the New Democratic Party went so far as to propose the exchange of observation teams and the exchange of letters. In addition, the progressive elements of the Central Association for Autonomous National Reunification welcomed the proposal for north-south students' talks and broadened its base of support by holding a 13 May 1961 mass rally for the promotion of reunification. Three days later, however, the 16 May military coup made all reunification movements illegal.

Although the 19 April movement started as a democratic movement in opposition to Syngman Rhee's dictatorship, after Rhee was ousted and the Chang regime took power, it rapidly developed into a movement for national reunification. Just as the anti-Japanese movement and the democracy movement were pursued together during the colonial period, so were the reunification movement and the democracy movement pursued together after liberation in 1945. The reunification movement of this time was an extension of the colonial period national united front movement and of the post-liberation movement to establish a unified nation-state as seen in the activities of the Committee for the Preparation of Korean Independence, the left-right alliance movement and the north-south talks of 1948.

REFERENCES

Kang Man-gil, et al., *Sawŏl hyŏngmyŏng non* (On the April revolution), Seoul: Han'gilsa, 1983.

Han Wansang, et al., *4.19 hyŏngmyŏng non* (On the 19 April revolution), Seoul: Irwŏl sŏgak, 1983.

Kim Hakchun, 'Che2 konghwaguk sidae ŭi t'ongil nonŭi' (Debates on reunification in the time of the Second Republic), *Minjok t'ongillon ŭi chŏn'gae*, Seoul: Hyŏngsŏngsa, 1983.

Han Sŭngju (Sung-ju Han), *Che2 konghwaguk kwa han'guk ŭi minjujuŭi* (The Second Republic and democracy in Korea), Seoul: Chongno sŏjŏk, 1983.

Sŏng Yubo, '4wŏl hyŏngmyŏng kwa t'ongil nonŭi' (The April Revolution and debates on reunification), *Han'guk minjokchuŭi ron II*, Seoul: Ch'angjak kwa pip'yŏngsa, 1983.

No Chungsŏn, *Minjok kwa t'ongil (1) charyop'yŏn* (The nation and reunification (1) materials), Seoul: Sagyejŏl, 1985.

Kim Kwangsik, '4.19 sigi hyŏkseryŏk ŭi chŏngch'i hwaltong kwa kŭ han'gye' (Political activities and limits of the progressive forces at the time of 19 April), *Yŏksa pip'yŏng*, summer 1988.

Yu Chaeil, '4wŏl hyŏngmyŏng chikhu minjat'ong ŭi t'ongil undong' (The reunification movement of the Central Association for Autonomous National Reunification right after the April Revolution), *Sahoe wa sasang*, May 1989.

Han'guk yŏksa yŏn'guhoe hyŏndaesaban, *Han'guk hyŏndaesa (2)* (Contemporary Korean History, volume 2), Seoul: P'ulpit, 1991.

SECTION FOUR
The 4 July North-South Joint Statement

THE NORTH-SOUTH RED CROSS TALKS

The national reunification movement that had advanced so rapidly after 19 April was completely outlawed with the 16 May military *coup d'état*. The military government, which had declared 'anti-Communism to be the basic state policy' at the very beginning of its 'revolutionary promises', declared in its eighteenth decree issued on 19 May 1961, that 'persons organizing anti-state associations, joining such associations, or urging others to join such associations shall be severely punished.' Subsequently, the military government dissolved all political parties and social organizations on 22 May, announced its law to establish a Central Intelligence Agency on 10 June, and a new anti-Communist law on 4 September. It also arrested the students and progressive forces such as the 'Central Association' who had led the reunification movement after 19 April and turned them over to military courts, thereby totally suppressing talk of reunification.

On the other hand, the Kim Il Sung regime, which had pursued a policy of reunification that established north Korea as a 'democratic base' for revolution in the south, now recognized the presence of 'revolutionary capacities' in the south and changed to a policy of 'regional revolution in the south'. At the same time, the Kim regime also presented on 8 August 1960 its 'plan for the confederal unification of north and south' which had as its basic principles 'leaving in place the political systems of north and south for the time being and preserving the activities of the governments of the Democratic People's Republic of Korea and the Republic of Korea', forming a 'Supreme National Committee' made up of representatives of both governments, and the 'unified co-ordination of the economic and cultural development of north and south Korea'. In effect, the Kim Il Sung regime was pursuing a two-faced policy.

The Park Chung Hee regime, in the first presidential election after 'transferring power to civilian authority' in 1963 presented as the unification plan of its Democratic Republican Party a 'plan for general elections in both north and south based on free democratic principles under UN supervision' while emphasizing total preparation for victory over Communism in all sectors, including politics, economy, education and culture. Subsequently the Park regime continued to suppress progressive forces through the 1964 'Incident of the People's Revolutionary Party' that had called for the 'withdrawal of US forces and peaceful reunification through the exchange of letters, culture and economy between north and south' and the 1968 'Incident of the Reunification Revolutionary Party' which had set forth a programme of the 'autonomous peaceful reunification of the Fatherland'.

In the late-1960s and early-1970s, the world situation changed rapidly with the defeat of the US in Vietnam. The 1969 US 'Nixon Doctrine' demanded that the US allies bear a greater share of their defence while shifting to a policy of peaceful coexistence with such Communist states as the USSR and China. At the UN, the number of new states from Africa and Asia increased, giving the Third World greater influence. As a result, the UN principle that outlawed north Korea was abandoned and a plan was passed to invite both north and south Korea to join the UN simultaneously. These changes in the world situation led the US to follow a 'two Korea policy' and a 'policy of building a Korea-US-Japan triangular security system'.

These changes in great power postures toward the Korean Peninsula amounted to a policy of making the division of Korea permanent. Korean reaction against such a policy may have provided momentum toward a pan-national resolution of the reunification issue. In the south, the Park regime was struggling with both the change in the world situation and with domestic opposition such as the spread of college student demonstrations against compulsory military training and the 19 April 1971 formation of the 'National Association for the Defence of Democracy' by a broad range of democratic forces and needed some sort of breakthrough. In the north, the Kim regime was also motivated by the thaw between the US and the USSR and China and stated on 6 August 1971 that it was willing to negotiate with all south Korean political parties including the Democratic Republican Party of Park Chung Hee. Thus the stage was set for the resumption of peaceful contact between north and south for the first time in over twenty years.

Peaceful contact began when the south Korean Red Cross proposed a meeting to discuss reuniting divided families on 12 August 1971 and the north Korean Red Cross responded positively two days later, on 14 August. Things then moved rapidly, with delegates from the two Red Cross societies meeting at P'anmunjŏm to exchange credentials on 21 August. The first preliminary talks were opened at P'anmunjŏm one month later, on 20 September. The 4 July North-South Joint Statement was issued while the preliminary talks were still underway and appears to have hastened the process. Agreements were reached on such issues as holding alternate meetings in Seoul and P'yŏngyang, on procedures for crossing the DMZ at P'anmunjŏm, on the agenda for the talks, on the guarantee of transportation and communication, on rules for the conduct of the meetings, on providing shelter, food and other conveniences for delegation members, on the size of delegations, and on meeting dates. The first meeting was held in P'yŏngyang on 8 August 1972.

The first meeting showed substantial progress as the two sides agreed to discuss such issues as determining if members of divided families were still alive, ascertaining addresses and informing each other; allowing members of divided families to visit and exchange letters freely; allowing the reunion of divided families according to their free wishes; and dealing with other humanitarian problems. The second meeting, held in Seoul on 12 September, saw agreement on three items and the future looked bright. The first item said:

> Reflecting the will and the desire of the whole nation, both sides will apply democratic and free principles to the resolution of all problems that have been put on the agenda, and will realize the comradely love and spirit of the 4 July Joint Statement as well as the spirit of humanitarianism of the Red Cross.

The second stated:

> Based on the mutual trust that we have gained through the first two meetings, both sides agree to engaged in discussions on the agenda items beginning with the third meeting.

The third item stipulated:

> The third meeting will be held in P'yŏngyang on 24 October 1972 and the fourth in Seoul on 22 November 1972.

The Red Cross talks, however, were influenced by the difficulties the political talks were encountering over the establishment of a North-South Co-ordinating Committee, and did not continue past the sixth meeting held in Seoul on 9 May 1973. In the end, the Red Cross talks served only to open the way for political talks.

THE NORTH-SOUTH JOINT STATEMENT

Once contact had been established through the Red Cross talks, the two regimes entered into secret contacts to arrange for political talks. Eventually, the South Korean Central Intelligence Agency Director Yi Hurak and the North Korean Organizational Guidance Director Kim Yŏngju (Kim Il Sung's brother) issued a simultaneous joint statement in Seoul and P'yŏngyang on 4 July 1972. This '4 July North-South Joint Statement' was the first joint statement by the two sides since the division of the nation. It was important as an agreement between the rulers of the two sides, but it was even more important historically because it represented the first agreement between north and south on the principles for reunification.

The two sides reached agreement on the following three principles:

> First, reunification must be achieved autonomously with no reliance on or interference from outside forces. Second, reunification must be achieved peacefully without resort to military force by either side. Third, national unity as a single people must take precedence over differences in ideology or institutions.

In short, north and south agreed on peaceful reunification by the Korean people themselves and rejected the intervention of any outside force, including the United Nations.

The Joint Statement also provided for lessening tensions and cultivating an atmosphere of trust by halting all acts of armed provocation and by halting all vilification and criticism, to engage in exchanges in all areas in order to promote national solidarity and mutual understanding, active co-operation for the success of the Red Cross talks, to establish a direct phone line between Seoul and P'yŏngyang to prevent unintended military clashes and quickly and accurately dispose of any problems that might arise between the two sides, and to establish a North-South Co-ordinating Committee for the resolution of the reunification problem based on agreed principles.

The first meeting of the chairmen of North-South Coordinating Committee was held in the 'Freedom House' at P'anmunjŏm on 12 October 1972. Immediately afterwards, however, both sides strengthened their one-man dictatorships as Park Chung Hee declared martial law, dissolved the National Assembly and proclaimed his *'yushin'* on 17 October, while ten days later Kim Il Sung announced the promulgation of the 'socialist constitution'. Rather than striving for a grand national unity as one people that transcended ideological and institutional differences, the two sides were strengthening their respective systems which were totally different from each other.

The second meeting of the chairmen of the Co-ordinating Committee was held shortly thereafter on 2 November in Pyongyang. A statement was issued that said:

> We have carried out negotiations in an atmosphere of brotherly love based on the deeply-held desire to improve north-south relations and to achieve the independent and peaceful reunification of Korea. As a result, we have deepened our mutual understanding and have made progress in resolving a series of problems.

The meeting agreed that the two sides would work together in all areas to carry out joint projects, would create and operate a North-South Co-ordinating Committee, would halt all radio broadcasts and DMZ loudspeaker broadcasts against each other, and would refrain from scattering propaganda leaflets in each other's territory.

The agreement reached between the chairmen for the creation and operation of the North-South Co-ordinating Committee specified that the Committee would have five functions, functions that truly could have enabled the Committee to fulfil its role as an agency to prepare for autonomous national reunification.

> First, based on the agreed principles for reunification of the Fatherland, the Committee will negotiate the problem of how to attain independent and peaceful reunification and will ensure the implementation of

its decisions. Second, the Committee will negotiate the problem of how to realize broad exchanges among political parties, social organizations, and individuals of north and south and will ensure the implementation of its decisions. Third, the Committee will negotiate the problem of how to carry out joint projects based on political, economic and cultural exchanges and will ensure the implementation of its decisions. Fourth, the Committee will negotiate the problem of how to reduce tensions between north and south, prevent military clashes, and ease military confrontation and will ensure the implementation of its decisions. Fifth, the Committee will negotiate the problem of how to co-ordinate diplomatic activities and enhance our pride as a unitary nation and will ensure the implementation of its decisions.

After Park Chung Hee was re-elected as president according to the Yushin constitution, the North-South Co-ordinating Committee held meetings alternately in Seoul and P'yŏngyang on three occasions, the last being the 12 June 1973 meeting in Seoul. After that meeting, the Park regime issued its 23 June 'Peaceful Reunification Diplomatic Policy' statement that called for peaceful reunification, for north and south to refrain from interfering with or attacking each other, for the simultaneous admission of both Koreas to the UN and other international bodies, and for opening up to states with different ideologies. On the same day, the Kim regime published its 'Five Great Principles for the Reunification of the Fatherland', calling for resolution of the military issue as the first priority, for joint projects in such areas as politics, military, diplomacy, economy and culture, for the calling of a great national assembly for reunification, for a confederation between north and south, and for admission to the United Nations as one country.

Park's 23 June statement's provision for simultaneous admission to international bodies drew fire from the south Korean opposition party as 'a statement designed to make division permanent and an anti-national act'. The subsequent kidnapping of Kim Dae Jung from Japan became a reason for the north to declare the suspension of talks on 28 August. The Co-ordinating Committee was no longer able to pursue its goals and the Korean Peninsula was once again plunged into a tense stand off.

The north-south talks, which progressed rapidly due to the Red Cross talks and the 4 July North-South Joint Statement, arose within the context of the *détente* policies of the US and the Soviet Union and the improvement in relations between the US and China. Although the *détente* policies of the great powers appear on the surface to have led to the relaxation of tensions in the Korean Peninsula, the easing of tensions between the great powers also appears to have produced policies to perpetuate the division of the Peninsula as the 'two Koreas'. That means that genuine dialogue between north and south, even as it took advantage of the relaxation of tensions between the great powers, should have come about as autonomous national opposition to policies intended to make the division of Korea permanent. Even though the 4 July Joint Statement proclaimed the principle of autonomous reunification, that was not done in opposition to the great powers' 'two Koreas' policy but rather as a means for the Park and Kim regimes to strengthen their rule through the 'Yusin' and the 'socialist constitution'.

Even though the 4 July Joint Statement proclaimed the principle of peaceful reunification, neither side pursued reunification through reconciliation, compromise, yielding and coexisting; rather each sought to strengthen its system of defence and system of political rule in order to overcome the other. This was the unavoidable result of discussions on national reunification led by the ruling forces of the two sides. That was the reason why the day after the 4 July Joint Statement was announced, the National Association for the Defence of Democracy, an entity that embraced almost all of the opposition in south Korea, said that it supported the opening of exchanges for the relaxation of tensions between north and south but that the participation of the *minjung* as the real constituents of the nation should be guaranteed, that the perpetuation of national division through discussions on reunification that served the interests of the regime should be guarded against, and that the National Security Law, the anti-Communist law and other related laws should be abolished and the declaration of an emergency situation should be withdrawn.

REFERENCES

Chungang ilbo, *Kwangbok 30nyŏn charyo chip* (Collected materials on the 30 years since liberation), Seoul, Chungang ilbosa, 1975.

Kim Hakchun, *Panoese ŭi t'ongil iron* (Anti-foreign reunification theory), Seoul: Hyŏngsŏngsa, 1979.

Yang Homin, Yi Sangsŏl and Kim Hakchun, *Minjok t'ongillon ŭi chŏn'gae* (Development of the debate on national reunification), Seoul: Hyŏngsŏngsa, 1983.

Song Kŏnho, '70nyŏndae ŭi t'ongillon' (Debate on reunification in the 1970s), *Han'guk minjokchuŭiron*, vol. 2. Seoul: Ch'angjak kwa pip'yŏngsa, 1983.

Han'guk yŏksa yŏn'guhoe hyŏndaesa yŏn'guban, *Han'guk hyŏndaesa 3* (Contemporary Korean history), Seoul: P'ulpit, 1991.

SECTION FIVE

The Kwangju *Minjung* Resistance and the 10 June Democratization Movement

THE KWANGJU *MINJUNG* RESISTANCE

The 12 December 1979 incident, coming less than six weeks after the assassination of Park Chung Hee, brought the 'new military' centred on Chun Doo Hwan to the centre of power. This provoked a movement among people of all walks of life against the reappearance of military rule and in favour of democracy. On 24 April 1980, 361 college professors in Seoul signed a petition calling for the 'democratization of academia'. Rumours that the military would soon take action were circulating as student demonstrations spread throughout the country. Two events occurred on 16 May. One was the gathering of roughly 100,000 college students in front of Seoul Station to demand the revocation of martial law; the other was the publication of the 'declaration of 134 intellectuals for democratization' in opposition to the reimposition of military rule.

On the same day, the leaders of the student movement decided to halt student demonstrations in order to deprive the military of an excuse to seize power. Nonetheless, on the next day the new military expanded martial law to the entire country in preparation for the seizure of total power. Student demonstrations against the expansion of martial law continued in the city of Kwangju in South Chŏlla Province, demonstrations that led to the takeover of the city of Kwangju by an armed 'citizens' army' that held out for four days before being defeated in battle by government soldiers. This was the Kwangju *minjung* resistance.

The Kwangju *minujung* resistance began on 18 May with a clash in front of South Chŏlla National University between the military and students demonstrating against the expansion of martial law and the order shutting down their university. The students, prevented from entering their school by the military, began to hold demonstrations in various locations throughout the city of Kwangju. The excessive brutality of the soldiers attempting to quell the students provoked further demonstrations, leading in turn to even more brutal actions by the soldiers. Incensed by the soldiers' behaviour, ordinary citizens joined in the struggle against the military. The alliance between the students and the citizens developed into the Kwangju *minjung* resistance as the people of Kwangju took the offensive against the military.

The 20 May demonstration against the military by over 200 taxi drivers inspired large numbers of ordinary labourers, poor people, office workers and store clerks to arm themselves with metal pipes and pieces of lumber. At the same time, the civilian government led by Prime Minister Sin Hyŏnhwak stepped down and discord within the military in the Kwangju area between the locally-based forces and the incoming martial law forces led to the creation of two different 'chains of command'. Once negotiations between the citizens' representatives and the governor of South Chŏlla Province on 21 May failed the participants in the resistance began to arm themselves in earnest.

Among the roughly 100,000 persons gathered in the city centre, there were persons who had armed themselves with carbines seized from various armouries. The demonstrators also seized armoured cars from neighbouring automotive plants, while miners from the nearby Hwasun mine provided large amounts of explosives and detonators. Over 800 carbines and M-1s were seized from police offices in Naju, Yŏngsanp'o and

Hwasun and brought into the city. The result was the formation of a true 'armed citizenry' in Kwangju.

The 'armed citizenry', made up mostly of labourers, construction workers, shoeshine boys, rag-pickers, bar, restaurant and hotel employees, vagrants, and day workers, attacked the temporary headquarters of the military in the South Chŏlla Province offices with machine guns and carbines and forced the military into a 'tactical retreat'. On 21 May, the entire city of Kwangju except for the jails were under the control of the citizens' army. The retreating military sealed off the city of Kwangju in order to prevent the spread of the insurrection.

Within in the surrounded city of Kwangju, a Citizens' Committee to Resolve the Situation was formed on 22 May. Its members included government officials, Christian pastors, Catholic priests and businessmen. The committee entered into negotiations with the military after resolving to oppose the intervention of the military prior to the reestablishment of order, to demand the freeing of all persons who had been detained, to demand the military's recognition of its brutality, to prohibit future retaliation, to demand treatment and compensation for those who were injured or killed, and to disarm after its demands were fulfilled.

The conditions set forth by the committee, however, failed to gain the support of the *minjung* because even as they provided for disarming, they did not include the original demands of the resistance: the repeal of martial law, the freeing of Kim Dae Jung and the withdrawal of the military from politics. The conditions also were rejected by the military. Nonetheless, the committee was able to get the citizens to turn in roughly half the weapons they had acquired.

On 23 May, as a citizen's rally to defend democracy was being held and a Students' Committee to Resolve the Situation was being formed, a new Citizens' Committee to Resolve the Situation was formed under the leadership of Catholic archbishop Yun Konghŭi. This new committee included ten members of the old committee and twenty student representatives. A group of the committee members gave 200 of the 1,200 weapons that they had collected to the military in return for the release of 33 prisoners. By the evening of that day, over 2,500 carbines, M-1s and pistols – fully half of the citizens' army's weapons – had been turned in.

By the sixth day of the resistance on 24 May, there arose differences among the resisting *minjung* over the questions of whether to negotiate, to surrender, or to continue to fight by expanding the resistance to other areas. The efforts of the Citizens' Committee to Resolve the Situation to collect weapons and turn them over to the military ran into resistance from the *minjung* groups determined to resist. The Students' Committee to Resolve the Situation also split between those who wanted to surrender and those who wanted to resist, but the resisters gained control. On 25 May, amidst continuing citizens' rallies, a new executive group was formed out of the resisters, leaders of the youth movement and persons from the lower classes with Kim Chongbae as chair.

The new executive group formed an organizational structure under the leadership of the Citizens' Army Struggle Committee Chair. It included a vice-chair for internal affairs and a vice-chair for external affairs, directors of planning, civil affairs, the situation room, supply, public relations and investigations, along with military directors of mobile attack and guard units. The citizens' army's only hope is said to have been buying time in hopes that US pressure and the resistance of their fellow countrymen would force the new military to abandon its plans to seize power. Of the total 5,400 weapons held by the citizens' army, 4,000 had been turned in by this day, 25 May.

On the other hand, the new military launched its pacification operation with roughly 4,000 soldiers, including a combat division and special forces, at 3:00 a.m. on 27 May. The exact numbers of the citizens' army cannot be determined, but they are said to have included eight mobile attack squads at the South Chŏlla Provincial Office, roughly 100 members of patrol units, 50 guards, 80 unarmed members and one armed company at the Kwangju Park. The pacification operation lasted about four hours and produced many dead and wounded. This marked the end of the ten-day Kwangju *minjung* resistance. The martial law headquarters announced that 148 of the resisters had died, of which 118, or 71%, had been killed by gunfire and that fifteen of its soldiers had also died.

The Kwangju *minjung* resistance represented the continuation of a long tradition of popular resistance, from the 1894 peasants' war and the Chŏlla righteous army wars of the late-nineteenth and early-twentieth centuries, to the Kwangju Student Movement of the colonial period and the various armed resistance movements of the immediate post-liberation period. It also represented the explosion of popular resentment against the policies of the Park Chung Hee era, including the excessive investment in heavy industries that brought the economic stagnation of the late-1970s, the fostering of regional antagonism between Kyŏngsang and Chŏlla provinces, and the relative neglect of the Chŏlla region in the Park regime's economic development plans. Other elements behind the Kwangju *minjung* resistance included the 'YH incident', and the 'Pusan and Masan resistances' of the Yushin period, the hopes of the 'Seoul Spring' after the assassination of Park Chung Hee, opposition to the plans of the new military to seize power and to the arrest of Kim Dae Jung, and, most immediately, the excessive suppression of student demonstrations by the new military that was anxious to demonstrate its power.

A public opinion survey taken in Kwangju eight years after the resistance revealed that 55% of the respondents identified the cause as 'the sophisticated machinations of the new military group to take power', 25.7% said the cause was 'the cruel suppression of demonstrations by the military', 11.5% blamed it on the 'instigation of particular politicians', and only 2.4% saw the source to have been 'regional antagonism'.

There are a number of historically noteworthy things about this movement against military rule. First, it began in one city, developed into an armed insurrection, and showed signs of spreading to other areas. Second, it was the turning point that brought the Chun Doo Hwan regime to power. Third, the question of the US officials' authorization of Chun's redeployment of forces to Kwangju from the DMZ produced an anti-US movement much stronger than had ever been seen before in south Korea.

THE 10 JUNE DEMOCRATIZATION MOVEMENT AND THE NATIONAL REUNIFICATION MOVEMENT

The democratization movement and the national reunification movement fell into a temporary slump after the military's suppression of the Kwangju *minjung* resistance. Nonetheless, the democratization movement, the national reunification movement, the workers' movement and the peasants' movement which had experienced rapid growth during the 1970s, were ultimately able to overcome the Chun regime's 13 April measure to 'protect the constitution' and realize the direct election of the president. At the same time, the democratization movement and the national reunification movement followed the path of the world-wide changes occurring in the late-1980s.

The national reunification movement and the democratization movement that had been temporarily immobilized by the tyranny of the Chun regime came back to life with the formation of the Alliance of Youth for Democratization in September 1983, the Dismissed Professors' Association in December 1983, the Korean Workers' Welfare Association in March 1984, the Democratization Movement Association in April 1984 and the Democratic Media Movement Alliance in December 1984. Out in the provinces, such youth and religious organizations were formed as the October 1984 North Chŏlla Province Democratization Movement Association, the November 1984 South Chŏlla Province Democratic Youth Movement Association and the November 1984 Inch'ŏn Area Social Movement Association. Furthermore, there came into being such national democratic alliances as the 29 June 1984 *Minjung* Democratic Association and the 16 October Democratic Reunification Citizens' Association. The various isolated national democracy groups that had existed before the Kwangju *minjung* resistance were now oriented towards forming a united front, but they split into two major groups. One was the *Minjung* Democracy Movement Association centred on the Alliance of Youth for Democratization and the other was the Democratic Reunification Citizens' Association led by Protestant Christian elements.

Eventually, however, these two groups merged in March 1985 into the Democratic Reunification *Minjung* Alliance that set forth its tasks to be 'democratization and national reunification', and its principles to be 'an organization of opposition political groups and an orientation towards the *minjung* line'. This alliance was able to fulfil its role by stepping to the front of the June 1987 democratization movement as the unifying body of the democratic movement and the reunification movement.

1985 also saw the formation of the Association of the Family Movement for the Realization of Democracy, an organization that demanded the freeing of prisoners of conscience, the abolition of the National Security Law and a halt to the use of torture. Other groups that were active during this period included the National Association of College Professors formed in 1987 for promoting the democratization of academia and society and for facilitating the contributions of intellectuals to the *minjung* national movement, and the Attorneys' Group for a Democratic Society established in 1988 to provide legal assistance in human rights cases.

The torture and death at the hands of the police of Seoul National University student Pak Chongch'ŏl on 14 January 1987 led to a rapid escalation of the anti-government and democratization movements. After the Chun regime announced its '13 April measure to protect the constitution', the Unification Democratic Party and the Alliance for Democracy and Unification joined forces on 27 May to establish the Headquarters of the National Movement to Attain a Democratic Constitution with the 'ultimate goal of establishing a democratic government through the attainment of a democratic constitution'.

On 10 June, the Democratic Justice Party selected Roh Tae Woo as its candidate for president, one day after the death of Yonsei University student Yi Hanyŏl, who was killed by a tear gas grenade on 9 June. At that point, the '10 June citizens' assemblies' were held by students and ordinary citizens in eighteen cities throughout the country. These demonstrations called for the withdrawal of the '13 April measure to protect the constitution', the overthrow of military dictatorship, the attainment of a democratic constitution and the cessation of US interference in Korea's internal affairs. These demonstrations began peacefully amidst the sounds of citizens clapping their hands and passing automobiles honking in support, but they were broken up by strong police suppression. One city hall, 15 police boxes and two local offices of the Democratic Justice Party were damaged as over 3,800 demonstrators were taken into custody.

A group of protestors then locked themselves in the Myŏngdong Cathedral while demonstrations broke out again in such cities as Seoul, Pusan, Taegu, Inch'ŏn, Taejŏn, Chinju, Chŏnan and Suwŏn. Continuing demonstrations in 127 locations in ten cities resulted in damage to 16 police boxes, three Democratic Justice Party offices, and two KBS regional offices. The Headquarters of the National Movement held the '18 June assemblies to ban tear gas' in 247 locations in 14 cities throughout the country. Over 200,000 persons, according to police estimates, participated in these demonstrations, demanding the repeal of the '13 April measure to protect the constitution', the overthrow of dictatorship, the attainment of democracy and the 'withdrawal of the US forces that are supporting military dictatorship'. Over 80 combat police were disarmed by demonstrators in Seoul. In the midst of continuing violent demonstrations causing, according to police calculations, the destruction of

21 police boxes and nine police vehicles and injury to 621 policemen, rumours circulated about the declaration of martial law and deployment of the army. On 20 June, Roh Tae Woo declared that he 'had no particular attachment to the position of candidate for president', and a meeting was held between Chun Doo Hwan and Kim Young Sam, head of the Unification Democratic Party, but broke up without achieving any agreement.

The Headquarters of the National Movement led huge demonstrations attended by over one million persons in 370 cities, towns and counties throughout the country on 26 June. Two police stations, 29 police boxes and four Democratic Justice Party local offices were damaged or burned and scores of police vehicles were damaged while 3,467 demonstrators were arrested. At this point, the Chun regime, with Roh Tae Woo as its spokesman, made its '29 June declaration' based on negotiations with the opposition. The declaration promised the amendment of the constitution to allow direct election of the president, the implementation of fair and open elections, a pardon and restoration of civil rights for Kim Dae Jung, the freeing of persons arrested in relation to the situation, correction of human rights abuses and institutional reform, the freedom of the media, the formation of local legislatures, and academic freedom and educational autonomy.

On the other hand, the US government had reacted to Chun's '13 April measure to protect the constitution' by urging the government and the opposition to compromise for democratization, and continued to urge the regime to compromise with the opposition after the 10 June 'citizens' assemblies' demonstrations. After the 18 June demonstrations against the use of tear gas, the US continued to press for discussions on amending the Korean constitution, announced its opposition to martial law and made clear its opposition to the deployment of the South Korean army to control the demonstrations. The Human Rights Committee of the US House of Representatives adopted a 'Resolution to Promote the Democratization of Korea' and the US Senate passed a 'Resolution for the Democratization of Korea'. The US also indicated that it strongly welcomed the '29 June statement'.

The June democratization movement was, as an anti-military dictatorship democratization movement, an extension of the Pusan and Masan *minjung* resistance of the 1970s and the Kwangju *minjung* resistance of 1980. Whereas the Pusan, Masan and Kwangju resistances had been short-term affairs limited to specific locales, the June movement took place throughout the entire country, had as many as 4–5 million participants and involved street demonstrations and other struggles for three weeks. The June movement was not limited to a small number of large cities but erupted at the same time in 20–30 cities throughout the country and also showed signs of spreading to rural villages. This nationwide, large-scale, and continuous movement was successful in preventing the Chun regime from perpetuating itself and in stopping the indirect election of the president.

The June democratization movement did not develop into an armed struggle as had been the case in Kwangju. The Headquarters for the National Movement had declared its programme for action to be non-violent struggle. Nonetheless, the movement was, for a large-scale nation-wide movement, a fierce and aggressive movement as seen in such things as the disarming of large numbers of combat police. There was no way from the Chun regime to put down the movement without mobilizing the army. In the end, the movement succeeded in its goals of 'repealing the measure to protect the constitution' and 'attaining direct election of the president'.

The 10 June democratization movement, whose participants were students, office workers, factory workers, small urban merchants and self-employed persons, and peasants, was a *minjung*-led movement that displayed autonomy and democracy. It was one of the *minjung* movements that erupted to play important historical roles at every critical juncture in Korea's modern history. It was also closely tied to the labour movement that developed in Korea from July through September of 1987.

After attaining the direct election of the president, the national democratic movement developed into a movement for the joint north-south hosting of the 24th Olympiad in 1988. The National Association of University Student Councils and eight other organizations called for 15 August talks between students from north and south while forces from the social movement formed an Association of Democratic Organizations for the Peaceful Reunification of the Fatherland as the national unification movement spread throughout the national democratization movement forces. After the Roh Tae Woo regime announced its '7 July declaration', over 90 opposition figures formed a National Conference for Independent and Democratic Reunification on 8 August 1988.

Following the 9 September formation of a Nation-wide Conference to Promote National Democratic Associations, the All-Korea National Democratic Movement Alliance was launched on 21 January 1989 as a coalition of associations from eight sectors, including labourers and peasants, and twelve regional associations. It was set up as a 'general association of patriotic national democratic movement forces centred on the working *minjung* and with the student movement as its fighting force and was open to conscientious educators, writers, religious figures, attorneys, reporters, medical professionals and scientists, as well as small businessmen and overseas Koreans'. Its Fatherland Reunification Committee made a proposal to north Korea for a 'pan-national congress'. Earlier, on 9 December 1988, the north had proposed the convening of a 'pan-national congress' to be participated in by social organizations from north and south and by overseas Koreans, and the North Korean Student Committee had invited the south's National Association of University Student Councils to attend the World Youth Festival to be held in P'yŏngyang.

The Roh regime set forth its 'one-window policy' on negotiations with the north and refused to allow national democratic movement forces to go North Korea. Nonetheless, Mun Ikhwan, an adviser to the All-Korea National Democratic Alliance went to P'yŏngyang, along with Yu Wŏnhyo, at the north's invitation on 25 March 1989. While there, they presented a joint statement on 2 April on nine points of agreement related to peaceful reunification. The National Association of University Councils also sent Im Sugyŏng, a student at the Hankook University of Foreign Studies, through Europe to attend the World Youth Festival on 30 June. The Catholic Priests for the Realization of Justice also sent Father Mun Kyuhyŏn to accompany Im Sugyŏng on her trip back to the south. The national democratic movement was at a fever pitch.

Furthermore, in August 1988, the Headquarters for Holding a Pan-National Congress and a World Congress for the Peace and Reunification of the Korean Peninsula was formed and announced the holding of a pan-national congress for the purposes of uniting the whole nation in peaceful reunification, of evaluating and providing alternatives to existing reunification proposals, and of joining the world-wide trend of casting off the Cold War regime and pursuing peace. The north responded by indicating that its Committee for the Peaceful Reunification of the Fatherland would attend. The All-Korea National Democratic Movement then replied with a 'proposal for the holding of preliminary talks for the Pan-National Congress' in January 1989. The activation of the Pan-National Congress represented the 'civilian-led reunification discussions' as counterpart to the Roh regime's 'one-window policy'.

The Roh regime prevented the holding of preliminary talks. Thus the only way left in 1989 was to hold separate Pan-National Congresses in the south, the north, and overseas, and the 1990 Congress was also only a half-congress. However, the Berlin 'three party talks' of November 1990 resulted in the formation of the 'Pan-National Alliance for the Reunification of the Fatherland, followed by the formation of an overseas headquarters led by Yun Isang and a South Korean headquarters led by Mun Ikhwan in January 1991.

Whereas earlier national democratic movement efforts had been limited to calls for autonomous exchanges and for the repeal of impediments to reunification such as the National Security Law, the Pan-National Congress Movement took the initiative towards reunification by calling for peace, for the realization of reductions in arms and declarations of non-invasion, and preparing concrete plans for reunification. This pan-national civilian reunification movement was one of the factors behind the changes in the reunification policies of the southern and northern governments that produced the conclusion of the basic agreement between north and south.

SECTION SIX

The Conclusion of the North-South Agreement

THE NATIONAL RECONCILIATION AND THE CONFEDERATION REUNIFICATION PLANS

During the 'Seoul Spring' after the 26 October 1979 assassination of Park Chung Hee, the north proposed a joint north-south team for the Moscow Olympics on 20 December. The south rejected the north's proposal, but came up with its own proposal for an exchange of friendly competitions between north and south on 11 January 1980. In response, the north suggested talks between prime ministers on 14 January. The south accepted this and preliminary talks got underway at P'anmunjŏm, where it was agreed to reopen the phone line between P'yŏngyang and Seoul and to continue preliminary discussions. Ten subsequent preliminary meetings were held before the northern representatives called a halt to the talks because of disagreement over agenda items on 24 September.

After the talks were suspended, the north announced its proposal for the creation of an internationally neutral 'Koryŏ Confederal Republic' on 10 October. Specifically, the proposal called for 'north and south to recognize each other's ideologies and systems and on that foundation the north and south would as equal partners form a confederal national unification government under which north and south would have equal authority and responsibility and would each implement its own system of local autonomy'. This plan claimed that 'in a confederal-style unified state, there would be a supreme national confederal assembly made up of equal numbers of representatives from north and south and an appropriate number of representatives from overseas Koreans. The supreme national confederal assembly would then constitute a standing confederal committee to guide the governments of north and south and to oversee all projects of the confederal state as a whole.' The north also set up a number of conditions for the forming of a supreme national confederal assembly. Those included the repeal of the south's anti-Communist law and National Security Law, the legalization of all social organizations and political parties, the replacement of the armistice agreement with a peace treaty, and the withdrawal of all US troops from the south.

The north's proposal also contained 'ten great guidelines for political affairs'. Those included the maintenance of autonomy in the conduct of state affairs; the implementation of democracy and the realization of grand national unity in all sectors; economic co-operation and exchange for the development of a self-reliant economy; exchanges and co-operation in such fields as science, literature and education; the linking and free use of transportation and communications facilities between north and south; promoting the livelihood and welfare of all the people; the organization of a military alliance between north and south to protect against foreign invasions; the protection of the rights and interests of overseas Koreans; unified co-ordination of foreign affairs; and policies to maintain good relations with all the countries of the world and to promote peace.

Only five days later, the south denounced the north's plan as false. On 12 January, the south suggested an exchange of visits between the highest officials of each side. On 22 January, the south proposed its own 'national reconciliation reunification plan' that called for the 'formation of an association made up of representatives from north and south, tentatively called the national reunification association, to draft a reunification constitution for a unified democratic republic that would pursue the ideals of national democracy, freedom and welfare'. It also called for 'the reunification constitution to be ratified through a democratic free national referendum in both north and south, with general elections to be held as provided by the constitution to form a unified national assembly and a unified government'.

This 'reunification plan' proposed seven interim practical steps:

> First, both sides will maintain relations based on the principles of reciprocity and equality. Second, both sides will resolve conflicts through peaceful means. Third, both sides will refrain from interference in each other's internal affairs. Fourth, both sides will ease the armed confrontation by adhering to the armistice agreement. Fifth, both sides will engage in exchanges and co-operation. Sixth, both sides will recognize the other's international treaties and agreements. Seventh, permanent liaisons will be established in both Seoul and P'yŏngyang.

Somewhat later, on 1 February, the south presented a list of 'twenty model projects', including the opening of the highway between Seoul and P'yŏngyang, the opening of the area between Mount Sŏrak in the south and the Diamond Mountains in the north as a free tourism zone, and the opening of the ports of Inch'ŏn and Namp'o for free trade.

The north rejected the south's proposal for an exchange of visits between the highest officials and the 'national reconciliation reunification plan' on 20 February. Instead it offered a proposal for a North-South Politicians' Alliance to be made up of fifty delegates from each side. The south, on the other hand, persisted in its demand for talks between the highest officials. Thus, even in the early-1980s, both sides recycled for propaganda purposes reunification plans and proposals for meetings that had no realistic chance of success. Nonetheless, the north's 'confederal plan' of the 1980s, with its call for a 'confederal system as a total unified form', represented a substantial change from its 1970s call for 'a north-south confederal system as an interim measure', while the south's proposals introduced concrete steps and methods toward reunification so that even though its proposals were one-sided at least it was beginning to set up reunification as a goal and policy and to think concretely about how to attain national reconciliation as a step in that direction.

After the Aungsan Incident of 9 October 1983, in which seventeen high-ranking south Korean officials were killed by a bomb while visiting Burma, the north proposed on 10 January 1984 'three-party talks among the north, the south and the US' while calling for a 'declaration of non-aggression' between north and south'. The south responded with a demand for 'direct dialogue between north and south'. The north then again proposed a joint north-south team for the Olympics. The south responded but nothing came of the three meetings held to discuss the issue.

On 8 September 1984, the north proposed to provide the south with rice, medicines and cement to aid the victims of flooding. The south accepted the north Korean offer on 14 September. Both sides continued to propose various talks, including economic meetings, national assembly meetings, Red Cross talks, high-level political and military talks, and foreign minister talks. A few sports and economics meets were held, but were suspended over such issues as joint US-south Korean Operation Team Spirit exercises and achieved no real results.

THE AGREEMENT FOR RECONCILIATION, NON-AGGRESSION, EXCHANGE AND CO-OPERATION

As Roh Tae Woo was preparing to take office at the beginning of 1988, the north put forth a 1 January proposal calling for the adoption of a declaration of non-aggression, the suspension of Team Spirit exercises, joint north-south hosting of the 1988 Olympics, and a joint meeting of north and south Korean political authorities and political party and social organization leaders. President-elect Roh set forth his ideas for the conclusion of a tentative basic agreement between north and south, for the holding of regular meetings among the cabinet ministers of both sides and the formation of a north-south co-operative community.

After the breakup of the National Association of Student Councils' attempt to hold north-south student talks on 10 June, enthusiasm for reunification continued to rise as seen in such things as the proposal for the 15 August student talks. In response, the Roh regime announced its '7 July declaration'. The declaration proclaimed a 'promise to achieve a social, cultural, economic and political community based on the principles of autonomy, peace, democracy and welfare in which all the members of the nation can participate and which will led us into a new era of national survival and prosperity'.

The declaration contained six proposals. The first called for the active promotion of exchange between Koreans north and south and the free travel to north and south by overseas Koreans. The second called for the active promotion of the exchange of letters and visits by members of divided families. The third declared that trade between north and south should be seen as domestic trade. The fourth called for the balanced development of the national economy and promised not to oppose the exchange of non-military goods and materials with the north as a friendly country. The fifth called for co-operation for the good of the nation as a whole in foreign affairs. The sixth promised to help the north improve its relations with capitalist states and to seek improvement in the south's relations with socialist states. Even as the '7 July declaration' excluded overseas Koreans from prosecution under the National Security Law for visiting North Korea, it also sought to bring the rising fervour for reunification in the national democratic movement within the regime's 'one-window policy'.

As preliminary meetings for the north-south national assembly meeting and the Red Cross meetings continued after the '7 July declaration', the north proposed on 16 November 1988 a high-level north-south political and military meeting to discuss relaxation of political and military tensions. The south came back on 28 December with a proposal for talks between high-ranking authorities of north and south which the north accepted on 16 January 1989. As preliminary talks were underway, the south published what can be seen as the essence of the Roh regime's reunification policy in the Korean National Community Reunification Plan of 11 September 1989. The plan specified autonomy, peace and democracy as the principles and provided for establishing a north-south council and cabinet level talks through a north-south summit conference; for general elections to be held according to a reunification constitution to be drafted by the north-south council; and for realizing unification through a bicameral legislature to be chosen by the election. The plan also called for the reunified state's policies to pursue a democratic republic system, to promote the welfare and lasting security of all members of the nation, and to pursue friendly relations with foreign nations. It also demanded that north Korea respect the human rights of its people and abandon its line of reunification through Communism.

The reunification 'process' envisioned in the Korean National Community Reunification Plan was a 'north-south alliance' different from the confederal republic of the north's proposal and the 'state alliance' of the south's opposition party. According to Roh's plan:

North and south will each remain as a sovereign state with its own foreign relations and military forces, but that does not mean that the Korean Peninsula will be divided. Although this may appear at first glance to be contradictory, it is born of the policy needs that require both the recognition of the existence of two different systems and the need to maintain the tradition of our nation that has had thousands of years of history as a unified people.

This policy that 'may appear at first glance to be contradictory' in its call for two sovereign states with their own foreign policies and military forces was in fact not a policy of 'one state and two systems' but rather a policy of 'two states and two systems'.

On the other hand, after a series of eight preliminary meetings between 8 February 1989 and 26 July 1990, the first north-south meeting of high-ranking authorities was held in Seoul from 4 September to 7 September 1990. The south presented a proposal for a basic agreement between north and south, while the north presented a proposal for resolving the political and military stand off between the two sides. At the 16–19 October second meeting in P'yŏngyang, the south presented a draft agreement for north-south reconciliation and co-operation, while the north presented a draft of a non-aggression agreement. At the 11–14 December third meeting in Seoul, the south presented a draft of a basic agreement for improvement of relations and a draft of a declaration of non-aggression, while the north presented a draft of statements on non-aggression and on reconciliation and co-operation.

As the high-level talks were alternating back and forth between Seoul and P'yŏngyang, 'north-south reunification soccer matches' were held in P'yŏngyang on 11 October and Seoul on 21 October 1990. Joint north-south teams were formed for the Forty-first World Table Tennis Tournament on 25 March and the Sixth World Youth Soccer Tournament on 6 May 1991, occasions where the joint teams enjoyed considerable success. North and south subsequently joined the United Nations simultaneously on 17 September 1991.

At the fourth high-level talks held 22–25 October in P'yŏngyang, the south presented a single draft basic agreement for improving north-south relations that called for a declaration of non-aggression, the opening of communications and transportation, and for economic exchange and co-operation, while the north presented a statement for the denuclearization of the Korean Peninsula. Finally, a basic agreement to be known as the 'Agreement for Reconciliation, Non-aggression, Exchange and Cooperation' was adopted at the fifth round of talks in Seoul from 10 December to 13 December. The agreement consisted of twenty-five articles.

The articles related to reconciliation provided for recognition and respect for each other's systems, for non-interference in each other's domestic affairs, for prohibition of acts of destruction or acts intended to overthrow the other side, adhering to the armistice agreement until the cease-fire situation could be converted to a peace treaty, the cessation of competition in the international arena, the establishment and operation of a north-south liaison office at P'anmunjŏm, and the formation of a north-south political subcommittee.

The articles related to non-aggression called for the prohibition of the use of military force or aggression, for the peaceful resolution of disputes, the transformation of the military line of demarcation into a line of non-aggression, for the formation and operation of a joint north-south military committee, for the establishment and operation of a direct telephone line between the two sides' military commands, and the formation of a north-south military subcommittee.

The articles related to exchange and co-operation stipulated the joint development of resources, exchange of products and materials, joint investments, exchange and co-operation in such areas as science, technology, education, culture, arts and sports, freedom of travel and contact for members of the nation, freedom of communication, travel, meeting and visiting for members of divided families and their reunion according to their own free will, the linking of railroads and highways and the opening of sea routes, the linking of mail and communications systems and the guarantee of privacy, and the formation and operation of a committee for economic exchange and co-operation. This opened the way for linking and regularizing all the sectors that had been cut off by national division and particularly by the Korean War.

The basic agreement was a continuation of the 4 July 1972 joint statement, but it represented a much more concrete, substantial and progressive charter for independent and peaceful reunification. It also constituted a great success for the national democratic movement that had persisted at the cost of great sacrifice ever since the division of the nation. Such hopes not withstanding, such issues as the Team Spirit exercises and the nuclear problem continued to hinder the efforts of north and south to attain reunification and no progress was made in the implementation of the articles of the basic agreement. In the case of the south, the question of implementing the basic agreement was left to the new 'civil government' that took power after thirty years of military rule.

REFERENCES

Kukt'o t'ongirwŏn, *Han minjok kongdongch'e t'ongil an ŭi iron chŏk kich'o wa chŏngch'aek panghyang* (The theoretical basis and policy direction of the Korean national community reunification plan), Seoul, 1990.

Tonga ilbo sa, *Tonga yŏn'gam* (The Tonga Yearbook), 1989–92.

Cho Hŭiyŏn (ed.), *Han'guk sahoe undongsa* (History of Korean social movements), Seoul: Chuksan, 1990.

Han'gyŏre sahoe yŏn'guso chŏngch'i punkwa, *Yŏnp'yo.inmul.charyo ro pon nampukhan 45nyŏnsa* (Forty-five years of north-south history seen through chronology, persons, and materials), Seoul: Wŏlgan tari, 1989.

Han'guk yŏksa yŏn'guhoe hyŏndaesa yŏn'guban, *Han'guk hyŏndaesa* (Contemporary Korean history), 4, Seoul: P'ulpit, 1991.

7

The Economy: Decolonization and Development

Just as it was on the verge of forming a modern society, Korea became a colony of Japan and thus was unable to accumulate its own national capital and to introduce modern technology on its own terms. Furthermore, during the thirty-five years of colonial rule, most of Korea's resources were appropriated by the Japanese. The consequence was that the most pressing economic problem facing Korea at the time of Japan's defeat and its liberation on 15 August 1945 was transforming the economic legacy of the colonial period in a democratic direction and establishing a self-reliant economy.

As the prospects for national liberation began to brighten in the late-1930s, both the left wing and the right wing of the national liberation front agreed that the post-liberation economic system should include the nationalization of major industries and land as national resources. After liberation, however, the establishment of the US military government and the establishment of separate states made it impossible to realize the economy policy that had been established in the national liberation movement front. In the case of south Korea, land reform was carried out in an unthorough manner that left many peasants without their own land. Furthermore, not only was the ownership of industries by Koreans recognized, but even Japanese-owned industries were transferred to persons with connections. Simply put, the national liberation front's economic plans were completely stymied.

No genuine national capital could be formed during the colonial period. What Korean-owned industries that had come into being simply limped along in their role as supporters of the economy of their Japanese colonial motherland. Their inability to function fully was made even worse by the division of the country after liberation. The Syngman Rhee regime's economy, crippled by the lack of capital and technological backwardness of these industries, could only survive through the assistance of the United States. That assistance, furthermore, was designed to establish a south Korean economy dependent on the US and to erect an anti-Communist system.

The economic system of the Rhee regime, which developed around the 'three white' industries of flour, cotton and sugar using excess US agricultural products, inhibited the productive motivation of the peasants and made south Korea a permanent importer of foodstuffs. Furthermore, the industrial sector continued to develop along the pattern inherited from the colonial period of the reproduction of consumer goods. The industrial sector was dominated by a few entrepreneurs with connections to the regime and the economic-aid system as the post-liberation economic system shifted from one dependent on the Japanese economy in the colonial period to one dependent on US aid. The Rhee regime's economic system fostered dependence, monopoly and consumption, and hindered the formation of a self-reliant national economic base. As a result, demands for a more democratic and self-reliant economy grew louder in the late-1950s even as reductions in aid because of the US's deteriorating balance of trade led to the *chaebŏl* (conglomerates; J. *zaibatsu*) cutting back on operations and a general slow down in the economy until the Rhee regime itself was dissolved by the 19 April movement.

The Chang Myŏn regime attempted a small amount of economic democratization but it soon fell. The Park Chung Hee regime's economic plans replaced the old foreign-aid economic system with a new foreign-capital economic system. The time when the Park regime established itself was a time when US foreign aid was drying up and the advanced capitalist countries were seeking to export their capital to underdeveloped capitalist countries to support the development, to a limited degree, of light industries. The Park regime actively sought out foreign capital and took advantage of south Korea's cheap labour to achieve a high rate of growth in light industries and rapid expansion of exports. It also established free export zones to attract direct foreign investment. Nonetheless, the old problems inherited from the colonial period of consumer oriented production, large enterprise monopolies, a high degree of dependence on an external economy and the sacrifice of the agrarian sector remained uncorrected.

In the 1970s, the advanced capitalist powers began to focus on monopolizing advanced high technologies and began to transfer some heavy industries and capital to later developing capitalist countries. The Park regime actively developed such heavy industries as steel and automobiles. However, by the late-1970s the Park regime's excessive investments in heavy industries and its failure to open foreign markers brought a severe economic downturn. That downturn was one of the major factors behind the fall of the Park regime.

Simply put, the economic system from the 1980s on has been one of an open economy due to pressure from the advanced capitalist countries. The Chun Doo Hwan regime, which came to power through the

12 December coup and the 17 May expansion of martial law, sought to overcome the economic slump of the late-1970s and early-1980s by disposing of poorly performing enterprises, reorganizing the overall economic structure to open up as demanded by the US and other advanced capitalist powers, and seeking continued growth in the heavy economic sector. The Chun regime was able to overcome the economic slowdown and strengthen the monopolistic economic system due to the 'three lows' (low interest rates, low oil prices, low dollar) of the mid-1980s but the result was greater dependence on foreign economies. The 'three lows' did not last forever, but the international pressure for the opening of the Korean economy persisted, bringing back a negative balance of trade under the Roh Tae Woo regime.

The open economy system of the 1980s brought major changes to medium and small businesses. Although medium and small businesses had continuously been bankrupted or absorbed by monopoly businesses in the past, the further strengthening of the export-based monopoly capital system in the 1980s meant that, on the one hand, the monopoly enterprises were incorporated into the international division of labour systems while, on the other, medium and small enterprises were transformed into subcontractors dependent on monopoly enterprises. This brought a transformation in the position held by medium and small businesses in the overall national economy.

The open economy system of the 1980s also brought changes in the financial system. The low interest and policy loans of financial organs that had been based on government ownership were reversed as a result of privatization of ownership and self-regulating management. This was the result, in part, of domestic economic changes but it was also the consequence of the demands of multi-national corporations for the opening of south Korea's financial markets. While the privatization of bank ownership and the expansion of the secondary financial sphere resulted in the ever greater domination of finance by domestic monopoly capital, on the other hand the opening of the financial markets also brought increasing multinational corporate control of south Korea's finances.

The sector that suffered most from the open economy system of the 1980s, particularly the consequences of the 'Uruguay Round', was the agrarian sector. The agrarian sector, which had earlier been sacrificed to chemical industry-centred heavy industrial development, was totally unprepared for the new open economy system and was incapable of competing internationally. After the government's comprehensive agricultural management policy failed, it set forth a new 'integrated farming and fishing village development plan', declared the establishment of a new trust fund for the management of farmlands and asserted that it was promoting rural industrialization, but there are serious doubts as to whether it can succeed in the face of demands for opening up all agricultural products, including rice.

SECTION ONE
Economic Decolonization

THE US MILITARY GOVERNMENT'S DISPOSAL OF LAND UNDER
ITS CONTROL

There were signs of the partial collapse of the large landownership system during the years after the opening of the ports in 1876, and the 1894 peasant soldiers demanded peasant ownership of land. However, the landlord system was strengthened under Japanese colonial rule to the extent that fully 63% of Korea's arable land was rented out to tenants at the time of Japan's defeat in 1945. That was the reason why even the right-wing Shanghai Interim Government of the national liberation front called for the nationalization of farmland after liberation, with the peasants to manage their own lands, and why the Interim Government planned to prohibit the inheritance and sale of land and to plan the management of lands according to the peasant's traditional practice of *'ture'* (co-operative planting and harvesting). Such plans to the contrary, after liberation there were major problems in realizing the liquidation of the landlord system and the realization of peasant ownership in Korea south of the 38th parallel.

The problems began with the 25 September 1945 promulgation of the second regulation of the military government that announced that it would take over and manage all publicly-owned and Japanese-owned lands and invalidated the decisions of the local people's committees to seize the land held by Japanese individuals and the Japanese Oriental Development Company. Furthermore, in its 5 October ninth regulation, the US military government announced its 'determination of land rents' that set rents at a maximum of one-third of harvests, prohibited landlords from dissolving contracts before they expired and made new contracts with rents that exceeded one-third illegal. Subsequently in February 1946, the US military government made the property owned by the Oriental Development Company and Japanese corporations its own property and established the Sinhan Public Corporation to manage those properties.

The US military government did bring limited change to the landlord system by taking control of all Japanese-owned lands and by reducing rents, which had been higher than 50% during the colonial period, to 30% of harvests. The US military government itself had no further plans for land reform. The reality, however, was that in the situation of 1945, when only 13.8% of peasants cultivated their own land, 34.6% were mixed self-cultivators/tenants and 48.9% were pure tenants, economic democracy could not be realized without land reform. For that reason, all political parties in Korea, both left and right, set forth programmes and policies for land reform in one way or another. The early 1946 land reform without compensation to landlords or payment by peasants carried out north of the 38th parallel led to strong demands among the south Korean peasants for land reform. The National League of Peasant Unions formed in December 1945 demanded the seizure and redistribution to the peasants of lands owned by the Japanese and by national traitors and prepared its own draft land reform law which it presented to the US military authorities on 21 February 1947.

In response, the US military government announced the formation of the interim south Korean legislature and said that the land reform issue would be decided there. Although the US military government authorities came to realize the importance of land reform after experiencing the *minjung* resistances of Taegu and the North Kyŏngsang Province area in 1947, the interim legislature, which was dominated by the Korean Democratic Party and Syngman Rhee supporters, delayed even the appearance of the land reform issue on the legislature's agenda until 23 December 1947 when 'legislation for land reform' finally came up. Even then, however, a boycott by the right-wing legislators who were manoeuvring to have the Korea question turned over to the United Nations and were planning to establish a separate government prevented a committee from being formed and the land reform question from being discussed. Although the US military government did propose that the interim legislature deal with land reform, in reality the issue was postponed until after the formation of a separate government and the US military government's efforts went no further than planning the disposition of the former Japanese-owned lands that were under the management of the Sinhan Public Corporation.

Once it became impossible for land reform to be considered by the interim legislature, the US military government announced its 179th regulation on 10 March 1948 that dissolved the Sinhan Public Corporation and established a Central Land Administration Office on 22 March to dispose of the lands that had been administered by Sinhan. The new office established three conditions that applied to the disposition of lands of 2 *chŏngbo* (1 *chŏngbo* = 2.45 acres = 1 hectare) or less. First, the first right of purchase was given to the tenants farming the land with second priority going to peasants and workers who had come south from north Korea, to peasants disposed by natural disasters and peasants returning from overseas. Second, the price of the land was set at 300% of the annual yield of the land's primary crop, with payment to be made in kind at the rate of 20% of harvests over fifteen years. Third, sale, leasing and pawning of the land was restricted for a fixed period of time.

As seen in Table 1, the lands managed by the Sinhan Public Corporation totaled over 324,000 *chŏngbo*, including over 270,000 *chŏngbo* of agricultural land plus orchards, mulberry fields, residential land and forests.

The land disposed of by the US military government, however, was limited to only fields and paddies, 85% of which were sold by the time the Syngman Rhee regime took power. The vast bulk of those fields and paddies were sold to the tenants who had been farming them. One of the goals of the US military government's rapid disposition of the lands that

Table 1: Lands managed by the Sinhan Public Corporation (in *chŏngbo*)

Type of land	Area	Percent of total
Paddies	205,988	75.5
Dry Fields	62,631	23.0
Orchards	3,618	1.3
Mulberry Fields	670	0.2
Total Cultivated Lands:	272,907	100.0
Residential Land	3,342	
Land for Other Agrarian Uses	10,518	
Forested Land	37,697	
Grand Total:	324,464	

Source: Nongnim sinhansa, ed., *Nongŏp kyŏngje yŏn'gam*, 1949.

had been owned by the Japanese was to blunt the left wing's political offensive in the forthcoming 19 May 1948 elections.

LAND REFORM UNDER THE SYNGMAN RHEE REGIME

The plans for total land reform and the nationalization of land that had been a major policy of the national liberation movement front forces of both left and right during the colonial period were not realized under the three-year long US military government whose land reform was limited to the disposal of lands that had been owned by the Japanese. That meant that the problem of fundamental land reform was left for the Syngman Rhee regime.

The 86th article of the constitution under which the Rhee regime was formed specified that 'agricultural lands will be distributed to the peasants with the method of distribution, limits to the size of owned lands, and the nature and limitations of ownership to be determined by law'. Accordingly, on 5 February 1949 the regime presented to the National Assembly a plan that had three features. First, the government was to purchase lands cultivated by tenants and self-cultivated lands exceeding three *chŏngbo* and to redistribute those lands with compensation to tenants, agricultural labourers, descendents of deceased national liberation fighters and persons returning from overseas in that order. Second, the plan established the purchase price of land at two times the annual harvest, with the government to compensate the landlords over a ten-year period beginning three years after the transfer of land. Third, peasants receiving these lands were to repay the purchase price of the land in equal instalments over a ten-year period.

The National Assembly prepared its own separate land reform plan. It was generally similar to the regime's plan except it called for the purchase price of land to be three times the annual harvest, a measure that was unfavourable to the peasants. The provision calling for repayment of the purchase price over ten years was also unfavourable to the peasants in comparison to the US military government's fifteen-year repayment plan. It was a reform plan that reflected the interests of the landlords who made up a large portion of the National Assembly's membership.

After considerable conflict over the differences between the regime plan and the National Assembly plan, a compromise plan calling for compensation to landlords of 150% of annual harvests, for peasants to pay 125% of annual harvests, and for the payment period to be reduced to five years was presented to the administration on 28 April 1949. The reduction of the peasants' purchase price from the rate of twice the annual harvest set by the regime and three times the annual harvest put forth in the National Assembly's original plan was the result of public opinion that the reform should be done on terms favourable to the peasants.

The establishment of a rate of compensation to landlords greater than the peasants' purchase price created a financial burden for the government. The government then declared that it was impossible to implement the reform and demanded that compensation and purchase price be equalized. The National Assembly refused the government's demand and the law was promulgated without change on 21 June 1949, but the government did not implement the reform on the grounds that it was too heavy a burden. Criticism from the people forced the National Assembly to pass a revised law that equalized compensation to landlords and payments from peasants on 10 March 1950, but the revised law did not lessen the compensation to landlords, but rather raised the peasants' payments to 150% of harvests, while leaving the repayment period at five years. This meant that the peasants had to pay an amount equal to 30% of annual harvests each year.

Although a land reform programme was finally passed after many ups and downs, it ended up being handled in the same extremely half-hearted manner as the other main issue of decolonization, the punishment of pro-Japanese collaborationists. This became a major factor behind the weakening of the legitimacy of the Syngman Rhee regime, the first government after liberation.

The land reform plan of the Rhee regime was favourable to the landlords. The post-liberation period discussions of land reform in south Korean political circles centred on three propositions: seizure and redistribution of land without compensation or payment; seizure with compensation and redistribution without payment; and seizure with compensation and redistribution with payment. Whether it was the uncompensated seizure of Japanese-owned lands and their redistribution with payment to the peasants of the US military government or the compensated seizure of lands from landlords and their redistribution with payments to the peasants of the Rhee regime, both were unfavourable to the peasants and beneficial to the landlords.

Not only did the south Korean land reform take five years to be implemented, but it also failed to include a large portion of the lands in

Table 2: Land in tenancy in 1945 and land redistributed by reform (in *chŏngbo*)

	Amount of land in tenancy	Amount of land redistributed	Percent redistributed
Paddies	895,313	395,794	44%
Dry Fields	552,046	155,174	28%
Totals:	1,447,359	550,968	38%

Source: Sakurai Hiroshi, *Kankoku nochi kaikaku no saikento*, p . 120.

tenancy at the time of liberation. That was because much land was sold privately before the reform. As seen in Table 2, the total amount of land in tenancy at the end of 1945 was over 1,447,000 *chŏngbo*, but the amount of land distributed under the land reform was only 550,000 *chŏngbo*. Only 38% of lands in tenancy at the end of the colonial period were redistributed through the land reform. Most of the rest was sold privately.

The original intent of the land reform was to enable peasants to own their own land and to create a complete self-cultivating agricultural system. Although the Rhee regime's land reform did bring about the creation of a self-cultivating system in legal terms, in reality it was an incomplete reform that left self-cultivating peasants in an insecure situation.

As the land reform was being implemented, the Korean War broke out. This led to a decline in agricultural productivity while at the same time the government, suffering from severe budgetary difficulties, instituted a temporary land tax. Total payments and taxes on redistributed lands came to 39% of harvests, a heavy burden for the peasants. Furthermore, severe inflation, as high as 100% per year, continued throughout the war. Whereas some sectors benefited from the inflation, it only made matters worse for the peasants who had to remit their land payments and land taxes in kind.

The peasants were still mired in poverty after the land reform, causing them great difficulty in making the payments on their land. In March 1953, when the peasants were to have finished paying off their debt, the total amount of grain remitted was only 56.8% and by 1962 it reached 98%. Furthermore, there were increasing numbers of peasants who had no choice but to sell their lands even before they had finished paying for them. As of the end of 1954, there had been 13,000 such sales involving 3,146 *chŏngbo* of paddies and dry fields. As mentioned earlier, the Interim Government had announced a programme to nationalize lands, redistribute them to the peasants, and prohibit inheritance and sale. The Rhee regime, however, simply prohibited the sale or giving away of lands until they had been paid for. The result was the reappearance of landlords renting out lands to tenants, which meant that the land reform failed to create a permanent self-cultivating agricultural system.

The land reform also had the goal of encouraging landlords to invest the funds they received in payment for their land in tenure as industrial capital, but that goal, too, was not achieved. The government calculated that the total amount of money received by ex-landlords by 1954 was 132,700,000,000 *hwan*. The government's hope was to use that, along with the proceeds from the sale of properties that had once belonged to the Japanese, to promote industrial development. However, the land sale bonds that the government issued to landlords were held as savings in the Korean Industrial Bank while the Bank provided the landlords with 300,000 *hwan* per month to cover their living expenses and refused to recognize the bonds as a form of payment for anything other than taxes or the purchase of property formerly owned by Japanese. Loans against the bonds were also restricted only to operational funds for enterprises formerly owned by Japanese.

Restrictions on the bonds were subsequently relaxed somewhat, but the owners of the bonds, hard pressed by inflation, sold their bonds at 20–30% discounts. The consequence was that little progress was made in converting agricultural capital into industrial capital. Except for a few large landlords who purchased discounted bonds and benefited from the disposition of properties formerly owned by the Japanese, the vast majority of smaller landlords did not make the transition to industrial capitalists. The result was the demise of what had once been a comparatively broad landlord class.

The plans for land reform set forth by both the left and right sectors of the national liberation movement front called for the nationalization of all the property held by persons who engaged in anti-national activities, but the Rhee regime did not include any such provisions in its land reform. Furthermore, the Rhee regime's plan excluded redistribution of orchards and forest lands whose ownership by both ordinary landlords and anti-national landlords was recognized. Those lands were inherited by the landlords' descendents. Once such example is the inheritance of large amounts of land by the descendents of Yi Wanyong, who had acquired that land through his anti-national actions at the time of the annexation of Korea by Japan in 1910.

One view of the historical nature of the Rhee regime's land reform holds that it was a landlord-centred reform that brought the dissolution of semi-feudal land ownership through compromise. Another view is that it was a bourgeois reform that dismantled feudal land ownership and established peasant land ownership. The one thing that is clear is that it was not the kind of land reform that had been envisioned by either the right or the left elements of the national liberation movement front. It failed to transform the landlords, especially the medium and small landlords, into industrial bourgeoisie and because it prohibited the sale of lands for only a limited period of time, it also failed to created a complete system of peasant land ownership.

DISPOSITION OF JAPANESE-OWNED BUSINESSES BY THE US MILITARY AND THE RHEE REGIME

The national liberation movement front of the colonial period established a policy for the nationalization of all the factories and other properties owned by Japanese government agencies, Japanese corporations and Japanese individuals. As mentioned earlier, the Interim Government had called for the nationalization of all Japanese-owned production facilities, transportation operations, banks and communications along with all such large-scale facilities owned by Koreans.

After liberation, the US military government took a hands-off approach to enterprises owned by Koreans and issued on 25 September 1945 its second order providing for 'freezing or limiting the transfer of all properties owned by Japan', thus freezing all properties owned by the Japanese government or public entities. On 23 December, the US military government issued its 33rd order on 'the reversion and management of Japanese-owned property in Korea', thereby taking over control of property privately that had previously been owned by Japanese individuals.

During the period between Japan's surrender on 15 August and the arrival of the US forces in mid-September, much of the property owned by the Japanese government, Japanese companies and Japanese individuals was managed autonomously by Korean workers. By the time the 33rd order had been issued in mid-December, nine out of ten Japanese property owners had returned to Japan. Most of their properties had either been sold to Korean individuals who paid for them with the Bank of Chosen notes that were still in circulation, were being managed by persons designated by the departing Japanese or were being managed by self-directed committees of Korean workers.

Rather than being intended to bring all Japanese-owned properties under US military government control, the 33rd order was intended to revert to US military control the properties that had been sold to Koreans, that were managed by Koreans on behalf of Japanese owners and especially the properties that were being managed autonomously by Korean workers. This brought to an effective end the workers' autonomous management movement in enemy enterprises. Businesses that reverted to US military government control accounted for 21.6% of all businesses in Korea at that time, while the employees of the reverted businesses accounted for 48.3% of all employees. This shows that the reverted businesses included a relatively high proportion of large-scale enterprises. The US military government appointed officials to manage these businesses. The officials who were so appointed held positions similar to those in government-owned enterprises and were mostly persons who had been employers of or investors in the businesses during the colonial period, persons who had had business relations with the businesses, or persons who had been invited by the post-15-August workers' autonomous management organizations.

The US military government began to dispose of reverted businesses from March 1947. But the military government's disposal was limited to 513 businesses, 839 parcels of real estate and 916 other items. The 513 businesses represented no more than 10–20% of the total number of reverted businesses and were limited to small-scale enterprises. Those to whom the military government sold the businesses were mostly managers or leaseholders. The disposition of most large-scale enterprises such as mines and banks was put off until after the Rhee regime took power. The Rhee regime followed the military government's lead in selling enterprises to managers and leaseholders. Thus it can be said that the general direction of the disposition of reverted properties was set by the US military government.

The redistribution of reverted agricultural land was done through sale, but first priority was given to the peasants who had suffered under the Japanese landlords on the principle of creating a system of peasant land ownership. By contrast, the US military government rejected the workers' autonomous management organizations that had been formed in some reverted businesses and instead sold those businesses to Koreans who had been closely tied to the Japanese owners and to whom the Japanese had entrusted management as they left Korea. In effect, the military government opened the way for these Japanese-linked elements to become the leaders of the capitalist economy in south Korea.

Shortly after the establishment of the Rhee regime, an 'Agreement Regarding Finances and Property' was concluded between south Korea and the US on 11 September 1958. The agreement's fifth article stipulated that 'the Republic of Korea will recognize and respect the US military government's dispositions of publicly- and privately-owned Japanese property in Korea that had reverted to its control according to the 33rd order'. This meant that the Rhee regime was prepared to follow the US lead in the disposition of reverted property.

The Rhee regime disposed of approximately 330,000 pieces of formerly Japanese-owned property in an effort to attain financial stability. It excluded three categories: first, major natural resources, forests and historically-significant lands, buildings, and cultural treasures of a public nature or in need of preservation; second, resources needed for the use of the government and public organizations; and third, enterprises essential to national defence and the livelihood of the people and major mines, steel mills and machine factories of a public nature that it designated to be operated by the state or by state-owned corporations. All other reverted properties were sold to individuals or corporations. Properties sold to civilians were divided into four categories: businesses and real estate, moveable property, stocks, and other property. Priority was given to persons with links to the property, to employees and to persons, and their descendents, who had rendered great services to the country. After that, properties were sold to designated individuals or to the general public. The price of real estate was to be paid in instalments over a fifteen-year period.

The subsequent outbreak of the Korean War resulted in the destruction of 67% of reverted enterprises, a change that greatly diluted the effectiveness of the disposition of reverted property as a means to provide finances for the government. Nonetheless, 43% of the cases of sale of reverted property occurred during the war years as the government sought to increase the production of war materials, to control inflation by expanding the supply of goods and to ease its wartime deficits through the conversion of reverted enterprises to civilian management. Nonetheless, inflation severely eroded the value of the payments the government received while the decline in productivity due to the paralysis of production facilities led to a serious problem of late payments.

In the end, the disposition of reverted properties had little effect on the government's budget. Income derived from the sale of reverted properties from 1949 to 1955 accounted for an annual average of only 1.5% percent of the governments' tax revenues during those years. Some monies received from the disposition of reverted property after 1957 were used for such things as funds for housing, medium and small businesses, and agriculture. Nonetheless, during the six years from 1949 to 1955, the government – in order to supplement its income by a mere 1.5% – sold off properties that had been stolen from the people during the forty years of Japanese rule and sold them mostly to persons who had been connected with the Japanese.

Generally speaking, roughly 40% of the payments the government received from its disposition of reverted property during the years up to 1958 came in the form of land bonds. That did not, mean, however, that old landlords had bought up that much of the property; during and after the war, many landlords had sold their bonds at discounts to merchants and industrial capitalists. When reverted enterprises were sold, priority was given, as it had been under the US military government, to some stockholders, leaseholders and managers. These enterprises then pushed aside the new medium and small industries that were just getting started and used their special privileges as beneficiaries of aid from the US to develop into monopoly enterprises.

In short, the bulk of the Japanese businesses that had been targeted for nationalization during the national liberation movement of the colonial period were converted into privately-held businesses by the US military government and the Rhee regime who had stymied the workers' efforts at autonomous management after liberation. It is particularly significant that the way in which the US decided to appoint managers of reverted businesses resulted in most of the businesses being sold to persons who had been closely connected to the original Japanese owners. Furthermore, the Rhee regime's priority policy and its practice of sale to designated individuals perpetuated the trend that started under the US military government. The outcome was that persons who had had close links with the Japanese during the colonial period emerged as the leading forces of the post-liberation south Korean capitalist economy. Thus the disposal of reverted businesses, which was second only to land reform in the economic decolonization of Korea, resulted in the sale of important assets at bargain prices to pro-Japanese elements. Furthermore, the sale was accompanied by all sorts of special privileges, meaning that the disposal of reverted businesses was even more anti-historical than the land reform. That was because the US military government and the Syngman Rhee regime placed their first priority on fostering the growth of a class to lead the capitalist economy as a way to establish their anti-Communist system.

REFERENCES

Han'guk sanŏp ŭnhaeng, *Han'guk sanŏp kyŏngje simnyŏnsa* (Ten year history of industrial economy in Korea), Seoul, 1955.

Sakurai Hiroshi, *Kankoku nochi kaikaku no saikento* (Re-examination of Korean land reform), Ajia keizai kenkyujo, 1976.

Yi Chonghun, *Han'guk kyŏngjeron* (The Korean economy), Seoul: Pŏmmunsa, 1979.

Yu Inho, 'Haebanghu nongji kaehyŏk ŭi chŏn'gae kwajŏng kwa sŏngkyŏk' (Process and nature of land reform after liberation), *Haebang chŏnhusa ŭi insik*, Seoul: Han'gilsa, 1979.

Kim Pyŏngt'ae, 'Nongji kaehyŏk ŭi p'yŏngka wa pansŏng' (Evaluation of and reflections on land reform), *Han'guk kyŏngje ŭi chŏn'gae kwajŏng*, Seoul: Tol pegae, 1981.

Yi Taegŭn, 'Mi kunjŏng ha kwisok chaesan ch'ŏri e taehan p'yŏngka' (Evaluation of the disposition of reverted property under the US military government), *Han'guk sahoe yŏn'gu*, 1, 1983.

Hwang Hansik, 'Mi kunjŏng ha nongŏp kwa t'oji kaehyŏk chŏngch'aek' (Agriculture and land reform policy under the US military government), *Haebang chŏnhusa ŭi insik*, 2, Seoul: Han'gilsa, 1985.

Chang Sanghwan, 'Nongji kaehyŏk kwajŏng e kwanhan silchŭng chŏk yŏn'gu' (A positivist study on the process of land reform), *Haebang chŏnhusa ŭi insik*, 2, Seoul: Han'gilsa, 1985.

Han'guk nongch'on kyŏngje yŏn'guwŏn, *Nongji kaehyŏksa yŏn'gu* (Studies in the history of land reform), Seoul: 1989.

SECTION TWO
The Development of the Aid Economy

US ECONOMIC AID

With the intensification of Japanese aggression on the continent in the 1930s, partial colonial industrialization of the Korean Peninsula came about as Japan sought to make Korea a base for its military operations. Such industrialization, however, entailed economic dependence on Japan and severe regional imbalance, and allowed virtually no opportunity for the accumulation of capital by Koreans. Once Japan was defeated and industries in Korea were cut off from their colonial motherland, the economic structure of the Korean Peninsula was almost totally unable to function independently. To make matters even worse, the economy of south Korea was further crippled by the division of the country which left most heavy industry in the north.

Furthermore, the Syngman Rhee regime was unable to obtain the support of left-wing forces or even of such right-wing forces of the national liberation front as the Korean Independence Party, leaving it with very weak legitimacy. Before long, the Rhee regime also parted forces with the rightist Korean Democratic Party and its base of support was rapidly diminishing. Even under such unfavourable economic and political conditions, the US was determined to maintain a capitalist system in south Korea in order to prevent the Korean Peninsula becoming communist. Thus the US applied its foreign-aid policy, which it had developed to stop the expansion of the socialist block after the end of the Second World War, to south Korea.

The economic aid given to south Korea under the US military government was part of the GARIOA (Government and Relief in Occupied Areas) policy applied to such major recipients of US aid as Germany, Japan and Austria. The aid given to south Korea during the three years of US military government rule totaled $410 million. It came primarily in the form of consumer goods such as foodstuffs (41.6%), agricultural goods (17%) and clothing (10%). Once the Rhee regime was established, the US implemented a more long-term aid policy in order to maintain economic stability in south Korea. This was the Economic Co-operation Administration (ECA) aid provided for in the 'US-Korea economic aid agreement'. ECA aid changed into SEC aid after the outbreak of the Korean War and continued until 1953. On the other hand, south Korea also received, in the name of the United Nations, emergency relief during the war and United Nations Korea Reconstruction Agency aid to help in rebuilding after the war. US aid to south Korea intensified with the signing of the cease-fire in 1953. US aid from that time on came through Foreign Operations Agency (FOA) and the International Co-Operation Agency (ICA), the Agency for International Development (AID) and Public Law 480. After the US international balance of payments deteriorated in 1957, such free aid gradually diminished and was replaced by loans.

The total amount of US aid during the years from 1945 to 1961, the year before Park Chung Hee's first-five year plan, was roughly $3.1 billion. Of that, approximately 41% came in the form of raw materials and semi-finished products to be used in the manufacturing sector and in social indirect investment in airports, harbours, etc. 25% came as such agricultural products as wheat and corn, while 9% came as capital goods and 5% as technological support. The aid provided by the US during the seventeen years helped to overcome the chaos of the immediate post-liberation years and the severe shortage of foodstuffs and the decline of manufacturing during the Korean War to maintain the Rhee regime and to establish some degree of stability in the south Korean capitalist economy. Nonetheless, the US played a negative role in regard to the tasks faced by the south

Korean economy after liberation: economic decolonization and the establishment of a self-reliant economy; and the formation of a autonomous forces to lead democratic and productive economic development. Consumption-oriented economic aid centred on foodstuffs and raw cotton hindered the development of a self-reliant economic structure.

Although the introduction of US agricultural surplus as food aid did help to resolve the food crisis at the time of war, it retarded the development of Korean agriculture and opened the way for south Korea to become a permanent importer of foodstuffs. Aid in the form of raw cotton resulted in the creation of textile *chaebŏl* that were reliant on special privileges and brought a reduction in the production of cotton in Korea. The consumption-oriented US economic aid caused problems in south Korea's industrial development policy that impeded development while at the same time rapidly raising south Koreans' levels of consumption and creating a consumption structure highly reliant on the outside world. At the same time, such aid was also a means for the US to overcome its post-war economic problems. Even though it was free aid, it helped to strengthen US capitalism's position in the world market and in the long-term expansion of US markets. Furthermore, US foreign aid also was a means to promote the export of American capital.

Generally speaking, economic aid allowed the donor nation to overcome the economic problems resulting from post-war excess production and to promote the export of its products and capital while it also allowed the donor to strengthen its political and military power in the receiving nation. Such aid was the most important factor in strengthening US influence in international relations after the Second World War. But the aid also hindered the formation of an autonomous economic structure and national capital in the receiving nations and made their economic systems dependent on outside assistance. It also made possible the existence of dictatorial regimes and the formation of monopoly capital linked to those regimes, thus fulfilling the role of establishing non-democratic political and economic systems.

Furthermore, in the case of south Korea, it contributed to the building of an 'anti-Communist base on the front line against the Soviet Union and China'. Also, the 'Far East Economic Aid Act' of February 1950 specified that aid would be suspended if 'south Korea established a coalition government that included even one member of the Communist Party, one person under the control of the north Korean regime, or one person who espoused those ideals', thereby embracing the goal which hindered peaceful reunification in Korea.

US AGRICULTURAL SURPLUS AND AGRICULTURE IN KOREA

Throughout the colonial period, Korea fulfilled the role of supplier of foodstuffs to Japan and during the war years from the 1930s on, it experienced forced appropriation of foodstuffs through the 'rice collection' system as well as extreme suppression of consumption through the rationing system. Even under such harsh conditions, Korean agriculture was able to provide a minimal level of self-sufficiency. After liberation, however, such factors as the return of large numbers of Koreans from overseas and shortages of fertilizer caused a worsening of the food situation.

This was made even worse by the damage of the Korean War. In 1949, the year before the war, domestic rice supplies totaled about 2.4 million *sŏm* (one *sŏm* = 5.12 US bushels), but that declined to about 2 million *sŏm* in 1951. Production shortages and severe inflation meant that rice prices continued to climb. The average annual price per *sŏm* rose rapidly from 191 *wŏn* in 1949 to 906 in 1950, 2,570 in 1951 and 9,300 *wŏn* in 1952.

In the case of aid provided under the provisions of Public Law 498, which was the mainstay of US agricultural surplus foreign aid, about $203 worth of US agricultural products were brought into Korea. These surplus agricultural products were then sold for Korean currency. The US used about 10–20% of those proceeds for its own needs and the rest went to the south Korean government as national defence funds. Wheat accounted for 41%, while raw cotton, barley and rice together accounted for 50%. US surplus agriculture economic aid did help to ease foodstuff shortages in post-war south Korea. It was also a means for the US to prevent an agricultural depression coming from surplus production. Most of the funds received from the sale of US agricultural aid went to south Korea's defence budget and thus supported the US policy of blocking the spread of communism and keeping south Korea under its influence. However, it also had huge influence on south Korea's agricultural economy and the livelihoods of south Korea's peasants. First, the agricultural surplus brought in from the US was not intended simply to make up the shortage in Korea's domestic food supply. It was also brought in to help resolve the Rhee regime's budgetary problems.

As seen in Table 3, during the years from the initial introduction of US agricultural surplus aid according to Public Law 408 in 1956 until it ended in 1969, the actual amount brought in exceeded government estimates of food shortages almost every year. The actual average amounts brought in during those thirteen years exceeded the government estimates of shortages by no less than 223%.

The reasons why actual imports more than doubled estimated shortfalls were the government's need to raise large military funds through sales as well as the desire to control severe inflation in grain prices and in overall prices. However, even after the national economy recovered in the years after the war and south Korea reached 97% self-sufficiency in food supplies, excessive amounts of US agricultural products continued to be imported, driving down domestic grain prices.

The introduction of US agricultural surpluses had the effect on south Korea's agricultural economy of maintaining low grain prices, reducing peasant incomes and diminishing the peasants' will to produce thus making south Korea a continuing importer of foodstuffs. Agriculture income formed 74.3% of rural household incomes, and 78.5% of agricultural income came from the sale of grains. But the policy of maintaining

Table 3: Introduction of US surplus agricultural products
(unit: 1,000 *sŏm*)

Year	Gvt. estimates of need	Domestic production	Gvt. estimates of Shortfall	Actual imports	Imports as % of estimated shortfall
1956	26,643	24,785	1,858	3,092	166%
1957	28,444	21,126	7,318	6,318	86
1958	29,256	25,270	3,986	6,465	162
1960	31,822	26,885	330	3,512	1064
1961	31,143	25,500	3,042	3,979	131
1962	33,232	30,325	2,157	3,677	170
1963	33,683	31,567	10,814	9,235	85
1964	38,436	28,398	3,963	6,391	161
1965	43,843	35,346	1,438	4,910	341
1966	56,652	44,570	4,110	4,205	102
1967	65,693	61,772	3,921	8,102	207
1968	69,680	60,918	8,762	11,171	127
1969	75,167	59,268	15,899	17,118	108

Source: Nongnimbu, *Nongnim t'onggye wŏlbo*, 1971–72.
* Estimates of shortfall from 1960 on exclude amounts carried over from and amounts not yet received in the previous year.

low grain prices through the import of surplus agricultural aid, meant that the prices peasants got for their grain were artificially low. In the period from October 1958 to September 1959, the peasants were able to get on average 22,744 *hwan* per sŏm. That was 2,374 *hwan* less than the cost of production. Whereas urban household incomes in 1959 averaged 95,073 *hwan*, rural household incomes averaged only 45,311 *hwan*. As a consequence rural household debt rose rapidly, from 3,997 *wŏn* per household in 1957 to 11,294 *wŏn* per household in 1962.

The import of US surplus agricultural products also had the effect of introducing severe distortions in the south Korean economy. The so-called 'three white' industries that led the recovery of the economy after the war were all based on cheap surplus agricultural products brought in as economic aid. This resulted in the disruption of production of crops other than rice. Changes in diet following the introduction of US wheat brought the rapid development of flour milling, but domestic production of wheat, which had once been as important as barley, decreased due to the introduction of cheap foreign wheat. As late as 1955, 70% of south Korean consumption of wheat was met by domestic production, but by 1958 it had fallen to only 25%. Thus even in the face of changes in dietary habits away from rice, the peasants concentrated excessively on rice production.

A similar situation obtained in the case of cotton. Before liberation, the Government-General of Korea, in order to provide war material, had demanded the cultivation of cotton in south Korea by implementing such policies as 'cotton in the south and wool in the north' and the 'plan to increase cotton production'. As a result, even after the appropriation of much of the cotton crop for military uses, cotton production in Korea came close to meeting domestic demand. From the late-1950s onwards, however, even with great increases in textile production, the amount of land devoted to cotton cultivation decreased sharply. Whereas the amount of land used to grow cotton reached a peak of 257,682 *chŏngbo* in 1942, by 1962, it had dwindled to 16,443 *chŏngbo*. The division of the country was one factor behind this drop in cotton cultivation, but the formerly large proportion of land in cotton in the south shrank to only 6% of all land under cultivation. This was because, as in the case of wheat, raw cotton accounted for a large proportion of surplus agricultural aid.

The case of the third 'white industry,' sugar, was different because Korea had not produced raw materials for making sugar. Nonetheless, both the flour milling and textile industries turned away from domestically produced raw materials in favour of cheap surplus agricultural products from overseas. These light industries led the way in the development of Korean capitalism after the Korean War and eventually grew into monopoly *chaebŏl*.

THE AID ECONOMY AND INDUSTRY

South Korea's industry under the aid economy system of the Rhee regime showed two characteristics. One was the development of industries producing consumer goods; the other was the growth of some of those industries into monopoly enterprises. These characteristics arose out of the foreign dependency fostered by the aid economy.

Except for the final years of colonial rule when the colony was being turned into a base for the production of war materials, Korean industry had developed mostly in the areas of food processing and textiles. After liberation, the south Korean economy suffered from both the distortions of the colonial regime and the distortions introduced by US economic aid. This resulted in the strengthening of the pre-existing trend toward light industries producing consumer goods, centred on the 'three white' industries.

The comparison of the production of consumer good and industrial goods in Table 4 below shows clearly the extent to which south Korea's industry was distorted under the aid economy system.

In south Korea in 1953, the consumer goods sector accounted for 74.4% of all manufacturing production, while the productive goods sectors accounted for only 18.3%. This distorted industrial structure had not improved at all by the time of the end of the aid economy system in 1961. On the contrary, the output of consumer goods increased to 77.3% of the total while the output of productive goods increased by barely 1%. This severe structural imbalance in favour of consumer goods arose out of the foreign dependence of industries under the aid economy system,

Table 4: Comparative output of productive goods and consumer goods

	South Korea		Japan
	1953	1961	1959
Productive Goods	18.3%	19.4%	57.7%
Chemicals	7.6%	8.2%	11.1%
Machines	–	–	34.3%
Steel, Nonferrous metals	10.7%	11.2%	12.3%
Consumer Goods	74.4%	77.3%	30.1%
Foodstuffs	27.0%	28.6%	12.8%
Textiles	17.9%	17.4%	8.8%
Ceramics	3.7%	4.2%	4.9%
Miscellaneous Goods	25.8%	27.1%	3.6%
Other Production	7.3%	3.4%	12.2%

Source: Kim Taehwan, '1950nyŏndae han'guk kyŏngje ŭi yŏn'gu', *1950nyŏndae ŭi insik.* Seoul: Han'gilsa, 1981, p. 211.

as shown clearly in their reliance on foreign raw materials. For example, of the total of 1.75 billion *wŏn* of raw materials used by Korean industries during the twelve-month period beginning in September 1962, 11.2 billion *wŏn* was accounted for by imports. Korean industry depended on imports for no less than 63.7% of its raw materials. Furthermore, textile production, which constituted over 30% of total domestic manufactures, relied on imports for 79% of its raw materials, most of which were US agricultural surpluses provided as aid according to the provisions of Public Law 480. In addition, such other major industries as chemicals and pulp each relied on imports for 64.7% of their raw materials.

The second characteristic of the south Korean industrial structure under the aid economy system was the growth of monopoly enterprises, a feature that arose out of the way in which reverted businesses were disposed of after liberation. As discussed earlier, the US military government refused to recognize the workers' autonomous management of Japanese-owned properties and appointed officials who had ties with the Japanese to manage them. Because the Rhee regime disposed of those properties through a system of preference and the practice of sale to designated persons, most major formerly Japanese-owned enterprises fell under the ownership of particular persons who were closely tied to political power.

In the circumstances where the old national economy was destroyed and the distribution structure dismembered by the Korean War, large numbers of medium and small industries engaged in locally limited divisions of labour came into being. These small industries developed using raw materials produced in their immediate locales and producing goods for the domestic market. Once, however, the aid economy system took hold, these small industries were excluded from the privileges of foreign aid, financing and foreign exchange. Instead, the production of consumer goods was dominated by large reverted enterprises that had been sold to particular persons who enjoyed access to US aid and other privileges bestowed on them by the Rhee regime.

The growth of the textile industry in the 1950s was based on the disposition of reverted enterprises, on access to raw cotton provided by the US as aid, and on special loans arranged by the Rhee regime. Access to raw cotton and special financing was not made available on a democratic and fair basis to all enterprises but only to a few that had connections with the government, leading to the concentration of production in a small number of enterprises. Even though the textile industry grew significantly, it was not able to stimulate production in related domestic industries such as raw materials or machines. Rather it acquired its raw materials and machinery from overseas markets controlled by foreign capital. In the case of the developed countries, the textile industries led the way to the formation and development of self-reliant national economies in the eighteenth and nineteenth centuries, but in the case of Syngman Rhee's south Korea, the textile industry developed in a way that relied heavily on access to foreign raw materials and foreign machinery and contributed very little to the development of a self-reliant national economy.

This privileged development of the consumer goods industries naturally led to the domination of industry by a small number of large monopolistic enterprises. As can be seen in Table 5, an extremely small number of large enterprises with 200 or more employees dominated the market to an extremely high degree in most sectors.

In the flour-milling sector, two large enterprises out of a total of 58 controlled 10% of the market, while in the sugar refining sector, two out of a total of 44 controlled 91.2% and in the soap sector, one out of

Table 5: Degrees of productive concentration in major industrial sectors

Industrial sector	Numbers of enterprises		Total sales (million *wŏn*)	
	Total	Large (%)	Total	Large (%)
Flour Milling	58	2 (3.4)	2,337	233 (9.9)
Sugar Refining	44	2 (4.5)	3,480	3,173 (91.2)
Spinning and Weaving	174	39 (19.0)	11,089	9,834 (88.7)
Plywood	8	5 (62.5)	14,497	7,067 (48.7)
Tires and Tubes	10	2 (20.0)	1,105	1,023 (92.6)
Soap	98	1 (1.0)	528	255 (49.2)
Cement	5	1 (40.0)	1,337	129 (9.6)
Rubber Footwear	48	9 (18.8)	1,845	1,437 (77.9)

Source: Kim Taehwan, '1950nyŏndae han'guk kyŏngje ŭi yŏn'gu', *1950nyŏndae ŭi insik*. Seoul: Han'gilsa, 1981, p. 211.

*Large enterprises are those with 200 or more employees.

98 controlled 49.2%. In the rubber-footwear sector, nine large enterprises out of a total of 48 controlled 78% of the market.

Under the aid economy system of the Syngman Rhee regime, large enterprises came to monopolize the production of consumer goods while developing as monopolistic and dependent *chaebŏl* enterprises. These were formed with special privileges in the process of the disposition of reverted properties formerly owned by the Japanese and enjoying the benefits of access to raw materials in the form of foreign aid and special financing from the government. As a result, the medium and small businesses that should have become the base of a self-reliant national economy were unable to grow.

The 1950s development of foreign dependent consumer goods industries by monopoly enterprises based on US foreign aid meant the relative lack of growth of a self-reliant national industrial base. The narrowing of control of the domestic market by such a dual economic structure brought the overdevelopment of productive facilities in a small number of sectors by a small number of monopoly enterprises. Furthermore, the late-1950s reduction in US aid resulted in the closure of a large proportion of large-scale factories. The contradictions that had been developing under the aid economy system had reached their limit. The 19 April movement was an eruption not only of political discontent, but also of unhappiness over the rise of foreign dependent monopoly enterprises centred on the production of consumer goods, over political corruption in the economy, and over the weakness of the agricultural, labour and small business sectors. That was why the Chang Myŏn regime set up the goal of establishing a democratic and self-reliant economy and why it attempted to implement policies punishing those who had become wealthy through corruption and fostering the growth of medium and small businesses.

REFERENCES

Han'guk sanŏp ŭnhaeng, *Han'guk sanŏp kyŏngje simnyŏnsa* (Ten year history of industrial economy in Korea), Seoul: 1955.

Pak Hyŏnch'ae, *Minjok kyŏngjeron* (The national economy), Seoul: Han'gilsa, 1978.

Yi Chonghun, *Han'guk kyŏngjeron* (The Korean economy), Seoul: Pŏmmunsa, 1979.

Pak Hyŏnch'ae, 'Mi ingyŏ nongsanmul wŏnjo ŭi kyŏngje chŏk kwigyŏl' (The consequences of US surplus agricultural product aid), *1950nyŏndae ŭi insik*, Seoul: Han'gilsa, 1981.

Kim Taehwan, '1950nyŏndae han'guk kyŏngje ŭi yŏn'gu' (A study in the Korean economy of the 1950s) *1950nyŏndae ŭi insik*, Seoul: Han'gilsa, 1981, p 211.

Pak Ch'anil, 'Miguk ŭi kyŏngje wŏnjo ŭi sŏngkyŏk kwa kŭ kyŏngje chŏk kwigyŏl' (The nature and economic consequences of US economic aid), *Han'guk kyŏngje ŭi chŏn'gae kwajŏng*, Seoul: Tol pegae, 1981.

SECTION THREE

The Development of the Foreign Capital Economy System

THE INTRODUCTION AND NATURE OF FOREIGN CAPITAL

After the April Revolution of 1960, the Democratic Party set forth a platform of such things as recovering ill-gotten wealth, elimination of special privileges and monopolies, fair distribution of national income, relief for the unemployed, revival of rural villages, fostering of medium and small businesses, and free access by all to financing. While planning a large-scale 4 billion *wŏn* 'national construction project', the Chang regime adopted 'comprehensive measures to foster medium and small industries' and set up an economic development plant intended to provide the foundation for the creation of a self-reliant economy. The plans of the Chang regime, however, were delayed due to intense political strife until they were finally nullified by the 16 May 1961 military coup that led to the formation of the Park Chung Hee regime's foreign-capital economy system.

During the final years of the Syngman Rhee regime, US capital that had once been provided without compensation had begun to change into a programme of loans. But the real transformation of the aid economy system to the foreign-capital economy system began with the implementation of Park's first five-year economic development plan in 1962. The shift to the foreign-capital economy system intensified after the 1965 signing of the agreement normalizing relations between South Korean and Japan.

The Park regime's economic development plan depended heavily on the introduction of foreign capital. Thus the regime implemented a full range of policies to bring in foreign loans for its expenditures as well as for commercial ventures, to bring in foreign investments and to pay for the import of foreign technology. The regime, however, found few foreign investors willing to make commercial loans or direct foreign investments in south Korea. Thus the regime depended largely on loans to the government until 1965, when the conclusion of the agreement to normalize relations with Japan brought a rapid increase in foreign commercial loans and direct foreign investment. Foreign loans increased rapidly from $99 million in 1964 to $177 million in 1965 and $261 million in 1966.

The signing of the normalization agreement with Japan was a major turning point in the development of the foreign-capital economy system. The agreement brought the active introduction of Japanese capital, including commercial loans and opened the way for a new penetration of Korea by Japanese capitalism twenty years after the defeat of Japan and the liberation of Korea in 1945. It also provided the occasion for south Korea to lessen its almost total dependence on the US and to bring in loans not only from Japan but also from such other developed capitalist nations as West Germany, Great Britain and France. The agreement also marked the beginning of the large-scale introduction of foreign commercial loans. Such loans increased to $623 million in 1969 and resulted in the 1970 appearance of large numbers of enterprises that defaulted on their foreign commercial loans. The government adopted measures forcing the disposition of such enterprises and implemented its 1972 '3 August measure freezing private debts' designed to force improvements in the financial structure of enterprises. On the other hand, it shifted to a policy of giving priority to foreign direct investment and establishing free export zones in such places as Masan and Iri to host foreign enterprises.

Once direct foreign investment declined due to the 'oil shock' of 1973 and Vietnam becoming Communist in 1975, the regime obtained greater amounts of governmental loans from such international agencies as the International Monetary Fund (IMF). The government also shifted its commercial loans from the previous form of commodity loans to cash loans and raised considerable funds from the issue of bonds on international financial markets. As a general rule, the introduction of foreign capital to underdeveloped countries started out as free aid, moved to public loans, then to commercial loans, followed by direct investment and then the establishment of free trade zones. South Korea was no exception to the general pattern.

Foreign loans brought into south Korea by these various changing means amounted to $23.7 billion in 1979. These included public loans of $8.87 billion, commercial loans of $10.8 billion and foreign investments of $1.7 billion. The US was the largest overall lender at 23.9% of the total, while Great Britain at 22.4%, Japan at 12.7% and the IMF accounted for much of the total commercial loans. Japan and the US accounted for most foreign direct investment – the US provided 20.7% while Japan provided the lion's share at 54.7%. Most of the public loans were used for social indirect investment, purchase of grains and manufacturing, and most of the commercial loans went to manufacturing, social indirect investment and maritime industries, while most of the foreign direct investment was concentrated in manufacturing and hotels. The terms and conditions for over half the public loans in June 1976 were for payments to begin after five years and to be spread over 20 years or more at interest rates of 5% or less. In the case of commercial loans, terms and conditions were tougher, with over 53% requiring payment to begin in fewer that three years, with repayment to be completed within 10 or fewer years, and at interest rates ranging between 4% and 8%.

Foreign direct investment began in the form of joint investments in the refinery industry and spread to the fertilizer and chemical fibre industries. In the case of the refinery company, the power to make management decisions was vested in a board of directors made up of equal numbers of foreign and local members but when the board was split evenly on decisions, the final authority was given to the foreign side. Although such issues as changes in capitalization, changes in rules and regulations, and acquisitions and dissolutions were to be decided jointly by both sides, such basic issues as finances, employment, purchasing and sales were handled almost completely by the foreign side. Such favourable conditions for foreigners were guaranteed until such time as they had recovered 150% of their investment.

The capital directly invested by foreigners enjoyed a guarantee of a minimum fixed annual return. Typically, the foreigners received an annual priority return of 20% on their investment. That meant the full recovery of invested capital in five years, but in many cases the foreigners received guarantees of annual 20% returns for fifteen years and also maintained their superior position in operations for the same time.

Direct foreign investments were often made in monopoly daily necessities. The materials were supplied from companies owned by the foreign investors, allowing them additional profits beyond those they earned from their investments. There were also many instances in which government agencies, both Korean and foreign, were required to purchase the goods produced by the joint investment ventures, thus guaranteeing profits even greater than those earned from the commercial loans. As seen in Table 6, Caltex, which invested in the Honam Refinery Company, was able to obtain remittances that exceeded its original investment in only four years.

Despite these many problems in the foreign-capital economy system, south Korea was able to enjoy an average annual growth rate in exports of 40.7%, was able to save an average of 20% of foreign investments and was able to attain an overall annual average growth rate in the economy of 8.9% during the years from 1962 to 1980. Between 1966 and 1970, south Korea had the highest overall growth rate of 56 developing countries, the highest rate of increase in exports and the second highest rate in the growth of manufacturing, and received international recognition as a model case of development. The dark side, however, included an

Table 6: Remittance on foreign investment by two major refineries

Year	Yugong (Gulf)	Honam (Caltext)	Totals
1964–1971	$2,156,000	–	$2,156,000
1972	4,502,000	1,015,000	5,517,000
1973	4,502,000	4,144,000	8,646,000
1974	4,500,000	3,056,000	7,556,000
1975	5,300,000	7,498,000	12,798,000
Totals:	20,960,000	15,713,000	36,673,000
Original Investment:	30,000,000	12,147,000	42,147,000
Rate of Recovery:	69.9%	129.4%	87.0%

Source: Yi Taegŭn, 'Oeja toip', *Han'guk kyŏngujeron.* Yup'ung ch'ulp'ansa, 1977.

increasing dependence on foreign capital, technology, management and markets, and the accumulation of heavy foreign debts. Furthermore, imbalances between different regions and different social classes worsened. The dual social and economic structures intensified as the *chaebŏl* continued to expand their monopoly operations.

THE FOREIGN-CAPITAL ECONOMY AND INDUSTRIALIZATION

Industry under the aid economy system of the Syngman Rhee regime was characterized by the production of consumer goods, by a high degree of dependence on foreign sources of capital and materials, and the monopoly of major sectors by a small number of *chaebŏl*. Despite its external appearance of rapid development, the foreign-capital economy of the Park Chung Hee regime was not able to overcome these problems.

To begin with, the consumer-goods-centred structure of industry changed little even during the period of high growth rates. As shown in Table 7, the value added proportion of light industries, which can be seen as consumer goods industries, fell from 74.9% in 1962 to 44.6% in 1979, while that of heavy industries grew markedly from 25.1% to 55.3% during the same period. The growth in the proportion of heavy industries during the period up to 1976 was led by manufacturing, and oil and coal products. Although these sectors do belong to heavy industry, they are heavily oriented toward the production of consumer goods. By contrast, such sectors that make productive goods, such as the machine industry and basic chemicals industry, lagged behind and Korea continued to rely heavily of foreign productive goods.

Table 7: Trends in industrial structure (as % of value added)

	1962	1966	1970	1973	1976	1979
Light Industries	*74.9*	*71.1*	*54.3*	*51.2*	*48.8*	*44.6*
Foodstuffs and Tobacco	21.3	18.7	25.7	18.2	18.4	16.5
Textiles, Clothing and Leather	26.1	27.1	17.1	21.8	22.3	19.6
Lumber and Furniture	6.0	3.2	3.5	4.6	2.5	2.4
Paper, Printing and Publishing	7.2	7.5	5.1	4.4	3.6	4.3
Other Manufacturing	14.3	14.6	2.9	2.2	2.0	1.8
Heavy Industries	*25.1*	*28.9*	*45.7*	*48.9*	*50.2*	*55.3*
Chemicals, Oil, Coal, Rubber and Plastics	7.0	9.3	22.0	20.0	20.5	17.4
Non-metal Mining	3.5	4.3	5.9	5.1	4.7	5.8
Primary Metals	3.4	3.8	4.0	7.6	5.3	7.9
Metal Products, Machines and Equipment	11.2	11.7	13.8	16.2	19.7	24.2

Source: Kyŏngje kihoegwŏn, *Kwanggongŏp t'onggye chosa pogosŏ*, 1981.

We can subdivide the heavy industries into those that made primary productive goods, such as iron, steel, basic industrial chemicals and manufacturing machinery; those that made intermediate productive goods, such as chemical materials, intermediate metal goods, industrial machines and industrial electric machines; and those that made other final productive goods such as transportation equipment, we then find that the proportion of value added of the primary productive goods sector declined from 9.7% in 1963 to 6.0% in 1974. The intermediate productive goods sector increased from 25.4% to 27.6% and the final productive goods sector from 64.9% to 66.4%. The development of heavy industries was highly concentrated in the final productive-goods sector.

Next, heavy foreign reliance, which had been a basic weakness of the Korean economy throughout the colonial period and the aid economy years, grew even worse during the years of rapid growth under the foreign capital economy system. First, the proportion of self-capitalization by manufacturing industries gradually declined throughout the 1960s and early-1970s to 22.8% in 1975. This was considerable lower than that of mining at 41.2%, electricity at 33.0% and construction at 34.4% in the same year. Among manufacturing industry as a whole, the self-capitalization of heavy industry stood at 26.1% while that of light industry was at 19.7%. That of industries producing for domestic consumption was at 24.2%, but that of industries producing for export was only 21.0%. That of medium and small businesses was 36.1%, but that of large enterprises was comparatively low at 22.1%. The debts of the manufacturing industries in 1975 were structured as follows: bank loans and various private loans accounted respectively for 35% and 28% of floating liabilities while foreign loans accounted for nearly 48% of all fixed liabilities, a proportion that greatly exceeded the 28% of bank loans. A major structural feature of manufacturing-industry finance was heavy reliance on outside capital, much of which came from foreign loans.

South Korean industries were also heavily reliant on foreign sources for their materials. Reliance on Japanese sources of material for the export industries was particularly heavy and Korean manufacturers were 100% dependent on foreign sources for crude oil, raw cotton, raw wool, raw rubber, fats and raw sugar. In addition, over 80% of domestic demand for wheat, pulp and scrap iron had to be met through imports. One reason for the reliance of south Korean industries on foreign sources of materials is that some of those raw materials are not found in Korea, but another reason is that the development of agriculture and mining was delayed and not linked to the growth of manufacturing. The result was that Korean industries, which were already dependent on foreign capital and foreign technology, also grew increasingly dependent on foreign sources of raw materials.

Another factor behind the heavy foreign reliance of Korean industry was the limit of domestic demand. Part of the reason was the neglect of the agrarian economy in favour of rapid industrial development, which left the peasants with diminished purchasing power, but a more important reason was the structure of industrial manufacturing costs. The proportions of manufacturing costs made up by materials, labour and general management in 1974 were 81.6%, 8.4% and 10.0% respectively. The extremely low labour costs meant low purchasing power and were a direct factor behind limited domestic demand.

A third feature of south Korean industry under the foreign-capital economy system was the continuation of the pattern of regional imbalance and monopoly concentration that had characterized the Korean economy during the colonial period and the aid-economy-system years. There was a small number of locales that accounted for the overwhelming majority of added value: Seoul at 30.1%, Kyŏnggi Province at 15.5%, Pusan at 14.4% and South Kyŏngsang Province at 13.5%. A few seaside industrial parks were added, but most industry remained concentrated in the Seoul-Inch'ŏn area. There were no prospects for a regional dispersion of industry that would have promoted the agricultural economy through the use of domestically-produced materials.

The gap in the dual structure economy between major urban industrial centres and seaside industrial parks that were based on high technology and large-scale capital brought in from foreign countries and the conventional medium and small industries located in small cites and rural areas continued to grow, as did the gap between export industries that enjoyed tax exemptions, special financing, government support and access to raw materials and industries that produced for domestic consumption. The widening of the gaps in the dual structure economy eventually led to the destruction of medium and small industries by the large-scale enterprises that were built with foreign loans and the even greater concentration of production in a small number of *chaebŏl*. As seen in Table 8, the degrees to which the top three companies in various sectors controlled the market were extremely high. This was not the consequence of consumer goods manufacturers becoming dependent on productive goods sector monopoly capital, but rather the opposite as monopolies based on foreign-made productive goods developed first in the consumer goods industries and the productive goods sector then becoming dependent on the consumer goods sector.

The monopolistic concentration of manufacturing is also revealed in structures of scale. Table 9 below shows that while very small manufacturers with between five and nine employees accounted for 37.5% of all manufacturers in Korea, they accounted for less than 1.5% of total production. On the other hand, very large manufacturers with over 500 employees accounted for only 2% of all manufacturers but 55% of total production. These very large manufacturers were mostly those with foreign financing.

The foreign-capital economy system of the Park Chung Hee regime saw rapid development of the industrial sector based on the introduction of foreign capital and growth in exports. But it was unable to resolve the problems of making the transition from a consumer goods-centred structure to a productive goods-centred structure, of reducing

Table 8: Market shares of major industrial products (top 3 companies)

Product	Market share	Product	Market share
Powdered Milk	92.3%	Acrylic Thread	72.1%
Packaged Noodles	100.0%	Knitted Wool	68.2%
Refined Sugar	90.1%	Kraft Paper	92.1%
Soju Liquor	68.0%	Tires	68.3%
Beer	100.0%	Mortar	100.0%
Lemon-Lime Drinks	100.0%	Carbide	92.0%
Cola Drinks	65.8%	Toothpaste	100.0%
Polyester Fabric	92.0%	Cement	64.0%
Viscose Thread	100.0%	Steel Reinforcing	74.2%
Wire Rope	93.4%	Cultivators	100.0%
Bearings	100.0%	Television Receivers	86.6%
Refrigerators	86.7%	Passenger Automobiles	100.0%
Bicycles	67.4%		

Source: Tonga ilbo, 27 March, 1976.

Table 9: Structures of scale in manufacturing (1979)

% of:	# of Firms	# of Employees	Production	Added value
Very small (5–9 persons)	37.5	3.6	1.5	1.9
Small (10–49 persons)	42.0	14.1	7.6	8.8
Medium (50–199 persons)	14.8	21.8	15.1	17.4
Large (200–499 persons)	3.8	17.1	18.4	16.9
Very Large (500+ persons)	2.0	43.4	56.3	55.0
Total Numbers:	31,804	21,160,000	26 trillion wŏn	9.2 trillion wŏn

Source: Kyŏngje kihoegwŏn, *Kwanggongŏp t'onggye chosa pogosŏ*, 1981.

the dependence of industry on foreign capital, foreign technology, foreign raw materials and foreign markets, of addressing regional imbalances in development, of reducing the gaps in the dual structure economy, and of preventing the destruction of medium and small businesses by large-scale enterprise monopoly.

THE FOREIGN-CAPITAL ECONOMY AND GROWTH OF EXPORTS

The Park Chung Hee regime, which had established an economic development policy that was dependent on foreign resources, foreign capital and foreign technology, set forth its programme of 'exports first' in order

Table 10: Trends in exports and imports (unit: $1 million)

	Exports (Customs clearance)		Imports (Customs clearance)	
	Value	% Increase	Value	% Increase
1960	32.8	65.7	343.5	13.1
1961	40.9	24.7	316.1	−8.0
1962	54.8	34.0	421.8	33.4
1963	86.8	58.4	560.3	32.8
1964	119.1	37.2	404.4	−27.8
1965	175.1	47.0	463.4	14.6
1966	250.3	42.9	716.4	54.6
1967	320.2	27.9	996.2	39.1
1968	455.4	42.2	1,462.9	46.8
1969	622.5	36.7	1,823.6	24.7
1970	835.2	34.2	1,984.0	8.8
1971	1,067.6	27.8	2,394.3	20.7
1972	1,624.1	52.1	2,522.0	5.3
1973	3,225.0	98.6	4,240.3	68.1
1974	4,460.4	38.3	6,851.8	61.6
1975	5,081.0	13.9	7.274.4	6.2
1976	7,715.1	51.8	8,773.6	20.6
1977	10,046.5	30.2	10,810.5	23.2
1978	12,710.6	26.5	14,971.9	38.5
1979	15,055,5	18.4	20,338.6	35.8

Source: Han'guk ŭnhaeng, *Kyŏngje t'onggye yŏnbo*, 1982.

to earn the foreign exchange needed to pay for those resources, capital and technology. This led to rapid growth in exports from the 1960s. As seen in Table 10, earnings from exports in 1960 were less than $33 million, passed $100 million in 1964 and reached $250,000 in 1966. This means that exports grew an annual 44% during the years of the first five-year plan.

As Table 11 shows, however, 67.2% of exports in 1974 and an even higher 74.9% of exports in 1975 were made up of such light industrial products as processed foods and materials, textiles, plywood and footwear. By contrast, such heavy industrial products as steel goods and electric/electronic goods decreased from 32.8% in 1974 to 25.1% in 1975.

Heavy industrial export totals did increase somewhat after South Korea began exporting ships in 1978 but processed foods, materials and other light industrial products still accounted for 61.3% of total exports when the Park regime came to an end in 1979. This shows that the sharp increase in exports during the Park regime came about primarily through labour-intensive light industries based on low wages.

On the other hand, most of the major exports were made with materials imported from outside, meaning that the actual earnings of foreign exchange through their sale were limited. Although earnings of foreign

Table 11: Exports by major products (unit: $1 million)

Product	1974 Value	1974 % of increase	1975 Value	1975 % of increase
Foodstuffs and Direct Consumer Goods	347.3	7.8	669.9	13.2
Materials and Fuels	236.1	5.3	218.8	4.3
Other Light Industrial Products	2,414.1	54.1	2,916.0	57.4
Textile Products	1,526.0	34.2	1,840.2	36.2
Plywood and Wood Products	199.4	4.5	227.6	4.5
Footwear	179.5	4.0	191.2	3.8
Others	509.2	11.4	657.0	12.9
Heavy Industrial Products	1,463.0	32.8	1,276.3	25.1
Chemical Engineering Products	91.8	2.1	74.8	1.5
Steel Products	450.3	10.1	231.5	4.6
Transportation Equipment	121.1	2.7	183.7	3.6
Electric/Electronic Products	474.2	10.6	441.6	8.7
Others	325.6	7.3	344.7	6.8
Totals:	4,460.4	100.0	5,081.0	100.0

Source: Yu Tonggil, 'Kukche suji, muyŏk, oehwan', *Han'guk kyŏngjeron*, 1977.

exchange from industrial products rose from 34% in 1963 to 61.7% in 1973, the overall ratio of foreign exchange earnings from exports fell from 82.2% to 65%. The reason for the decline in the proportion of foreign exchange earnings from exports can be attributed to the way in which exports were centred around light industrial products whose production relied not on domestic materials but on materials that were purchased from abroad. That is why even though south Korea saw rapid increases in its absolute export totals, it continued to suffer from a negative balance of international payments.

Another problem arising from the rapid growth in exports was the growing dependence of the national economy as a whole on foreign trade. Foreign trade had accounted for 21.1% of the economy in 1961, but it increased to 73.9% by 1975. That meant that south Korea was subject to immediate and heavy influence from import restrictions growing out of such problems in the international economy as international inflation, oil shocks and international recessions. Yet one more weakness in the foreign-capital economy system was its excessive dependence on two countries: the US and Japan. In 1967, those two countries accounted for 69.4 % of Korea's foreign trade – by 1972 that had increased to 71.8%. This trend moderated somewhat later, but the close economic and politics relations south Korea had with those countries made it difficult for Korea to diversify its foreign trade.

THE FOREIGN-CAPITAL ECONOMY AND AGRICULTURE

The principle of 'exports first', rapid industrialization and the high rate of economic growth of the 1960s and 1970s brought major changes to the agricultural sector as well. First, the proportion of the gross national product accounted for by agricultural production decreased sharply and the proportion of the total population living in agricultural villages also dropped markedly.

As depicted in Table 12, farming and fishing made up 43.3% of the gross national product in 1962, but their share fell to on 19.2% in 1979 in contrast to the continuing increase in other sectors. Mining and industry accounted for only 11.1% in 1962, but grew to 33.8% by 1979. The proportion made up by farming and fishing fell most dramatically in the late-1960s and early-1970s and in 1974 the value of manufacturing production surpassed that of agriculture.

Also, as seen in Table 13, the proportion of total households contributed by farm families declined from 53.6% in 1961 to 27% in 1980, while the proportion to total population accounted for by peasants dropped from 56.1% to 28.4%. The percentage of persons engaged in agriculture also fell from 63.1% in 1963 to 45.9% in 1975, while during the same period the percentage employed in mining and industry grew from 8.7% to 19.2%.

Another major change in the agricultural sector during this time was the restructuring of the stratum structure of the rural population. The poor peasants largely fled the villages, while the proportion of middle peasants increased substantially. The number of poor peasant households with landholdings of less than one-half *chŏngbo* shrank from roughly 1,000,000 in 1960 to 690,000 in 1975, accounting for only 30.2% of all rural households. By contrast, the numbers of households with more than one-half *chŏngbo* increased across the board. The largest increase was seen in middle peasants who owned between one and two *chŏngbo*, followed by small peasants who had between one-half and one *chŏngbo*. The reasons why poor peasants left the farms were the growing gap between farm and non-farm incomes and the expansion of employment opportunities in the non-agricultural sectors of the economy.

Table 12: Proportions of GNP by production sectors

Year	Farming, Fishing, Forestry	Mining and industry	Social indirect investment
1962	43.3%	11.1%	45.6%
1965	42.9%	13.1%	44.0%
1970	30.4%	19.5%	50.1%
1975	24.9%	28.0%	47.1%
1979	19.2%	33.8%	47.0%

Source: Han'guk ŭnhaeng, *Kyŏngje t'onggye yŏnbo*, 1982.

Table 13: Proportion of farm households and population

Year	Farm households	% of total	Farm population	% of total
1961	2,327,000	53.6%	14,509,000	56.1%
1966	2,540,000	48.9%	15,781,000	53.6%
1970	2,483,000	42.4%	14,422,000	45.9%
1975	2,379,000	35.2%	13,244,000	38.2%
1980	2,156,000	27.0%	10,830,000	28.4%

Source: Han'guk ŭnhaeng, *Kyŏngje t'onggye yŏnbo*, 1982.

Other important changes in agriculture during the Park regime years included an increase in the number of farm families with outside employment and changes in the age and gender structure of the farming population. As late as 1964, only 10% of farm families had outside employment, but by 1968 that figure had increased to 15% and again to 18% by 1979. The primary cause was the creation of industrial parks in a few locations near farming villages. There was significant change in the age and gender structure of the farming population. In 1963, persons in their twenties accounted for 27% of the farming population, but by 1974 that figure had declined to 17%. During the same period, the proportion of elderly persons aged 50 or more increased from 19% to 26%. In 1963, men made up 62% persons engaged in agriculture, but that proportion dropped to 58.5% in 1974, while the proportion accounted for by women grew from 38% to 41.5%. The absolute increase in the numbers of people engaged in farming reflected the greater numbers of women working in the fields.

Despite the rapid industrialization and urbanization of the Park Chung Hee years, there was little change in the agricultural land situation. Total land under cultivation in 1960 was 2,042,000 *chŏngbo*. There was some increase to 2,233,400 *chŏngbo* by 1968, but after that there was a decrease to 2,224,000 *chŏngbo*. That was because of the expanding use of farmland for factories, residential projects and roads, and because there was little incentive to develop new fields. Even in the face of the decrease of arable land, the expansion of employment in non-agricultural sectors and the relative decrease in the proportion of the population engaged in agriculture, many peasants remained stuck in poverty. The average landholdings of farm families did not exceed one *chŏngbo*. The proportion of farm households owning one *chŏngbo* or less of land declined somewhat from 73.5% in 1956 to 66.4% in 1975; the proportion of households with between one and two *chŏngbo* increased from 20.4% to 27.1%; and the proportion of households with more than two *chŏngbo* barely changed, going from 6.1% to 6.5%.

According to government agricultural surveys, tenancy rates grew from 26.4% in 1960 to 33.5% in 1970, while the scale of lands in tenancy expanded from 12% of all farmland in 1960 to 17.2% in 1970. Tenant rents were usually around 50% of harvests, the same high rate that tenants had paid under the feudal landlord-tenant relations of the pre-modern period.

Whether one views the reappearance of tenancy as a revival of feudal landlord-tenant relations or as modern farmland rental relations, there is no question that it represented a departure from the goal of a peasant land ownership system. Nonetheless, the Park Chung Hee regime decided to overcome the chronic rural problem of poverty by encouraging the development of corporate agriculture by legalizing the new tenancy system as a system of management by consignment or a system of farmland rental and by doing away with upper limits on farmland ownership.

Such an agricultural policy, which sought to foster the development of capitalist agriculture by attracting urban capital and by mechanizing farm operations, did have the goal of increasing agricultural production but it also meant abandoning the hopes of the peasants for a democratic agricultural sector based on a peasant land ownership system and was seen as an essential attempt to transform the peasants into wage labourers. While this policy did bring about an increase in the land utilization and land productivity of self-managing peasants and also opened up possibilities for increased employment and better living conditions and for the development of organic agriculture, it has also been evaluation as an agricultural policy that ignored the possibilities of the employment of agricultural professionals and of agricultural mechanization through the shared use of machines.

REFERENCES

Pyŏn Hyŏngyun & Kim Yunhwan p'yŏnjŏ, *Han'guk kyŏngjeron* (The Korean economy), Yup'ung ch'ulp'ansa, 1977.

An Pyŏngjik oe, *Han'guk kyŏngje ŭi chŏn'gae kwajŏng* (Developmental process of the Korean economy), Seoul: Tol pegae, 1981.

Pak Hyŏnch'ae, *Han'guk nongŏp ŭi kusang* (A Plan for Korean Agriculture), Seoul: Han'gilsa, 1981.

Cho Yongbŏm, *Han'guk kyŏngje ŭi iron* (Theory on the Korean economy), Chŏnŭmsa, 1981.

SECTION FOUR

The Development of the Open Economy System

THE STRENGTHENING OF THE MONOPOLY CAPITAL SYSTEM

It was under the Yushin system in the late-1970s that the south Korean economy began to develop as a genuine monopoly capital system centred on heavy industry. However, excessive investment in heavy industry brought the severe economic downturn of the late-1970s and early-1980s. The Chun Doo Hwan regime sought to overcome the recession by preparing such measures as the July 1986 'Factory Development Law' and the December 1986 'Tax Reduction Regulation Law'. The Chun regime also implemented a 'policy to rationalize industry' and decided to dispose of poorly-performing enterprises.

The Chun regime divided the industries to be rationalized into those in need of investment regulation such as heavy construction machinery and automobiles and those suffering from structural stagnation such as textiles and non-organic chemical fertilizers. With regard to the former, it proscribed the creation of new companies and prescribed product specialization; with regard to the latter, it provided 210 billion *wŏn* of aid for supplementary investments and changeovers to new product lines. This approach strengthened the base of monopoly capital.

The disposition of poorly-performing enterprises took place on five occasions beginning in 1986 and involved a total of 78 enterprises. Of those, 57 were taken over by third parties, while 21 were disposed by such means as merging them with other corporations, putting them under court control, regularizing their corporate affiliates or shutting them down. In the process, the government provided 282.4 billion *wŏn* in loans and 214.4 billion *wŏn* in tax reductions. In order to cover the losses incurred by commercial banks, the Bank of Korea provided special loans of 1,722.2 billion *wŏn*. Takeovers by third parties were done in most cases by already established *chaebŏl* as a small number of monopoly *chaebŏl* received special benefits totaling the staggering amount of 782.4 billion *wŏn*.

The 1980s were the time when a new international division of labour took shape in Asia. US-based transnational capital was strengthening its entry into Asia, Japan was focusing on developing the high value added advanced technology sector, newly industrializing countries (NICs) such as Korea were taking over the intermediate sector and the ASEAN (Association of Southeast Asian Nations) countries of south-east Asia were specializing in the labour-intensive simple manufacturing sector. The industrial restructuring of the Chun regime was an internal consolidation undertaken in order to adjust to the reorganization of the international division of labour.

The *chaebŏl*, having gained investment security through the strong measures of the government, were now in a good position to take advantage of the three-year long 'three lows' (low interest, low oil prices, low dollar) boom to attain average annual growth rates of 12% in the heavy industries on which they were concentrating: automobiles, electronics goods, machinery and steel. Annual growth rates in exports also climbed back to the high levels of the 1970s. Booming exports and restrictions on imports produced a favourable trend in current accounts that led to a record high positive balance of $4.6 billion in 1986 and the following three years all saw increases in the positive balance. The 'three lows' boom did enable the south Korean economy to overcome the recession of the late-1970s and early-1980s, but the boom itself came about

Table 14: Major indices of economic development in the 1980s

Year	GNP (trillion *wǒn*)	Per capita GNP ($)	Industrial production	Labour productivity
1980	52.3	1,592	100.0	100.0
1981	55.4	1,734	112.7	116.8
1982	59.3	1,824	118.4	125.3
1983	66.8	2,002	137.0	141.9
1984	73.0	2,158	157.6	155.6
1985	78.1	2,194	164.5	166.4
1986	88.2	2,505	198.5	193.2
1987	99.6	3,110	236.2	219.3
1988	112.0	4,127	268.3	250.9
1989	119.5	4,968	276.0	279.5

Source: Han'guk sahoe yǒn'guso, *Han'guk kyǒngjeron,* p. 160.

primarily because of external factors and when those external factors changed near the end of the 1980s, the boom petered out. The 1989 increase in the gross national product dropped to 6.7%, the growth rate of the mining and manufacturing centres fell to 3.5% and the current balance of accounts slipped back into the red.

The extra funds monopoly capital gained from the 'three lows' boom were not available to deal with the end of the boom because they had been mostly used for speculative accumulation. The real estate holdings of the thirty largest *chaebǒl* increased from 394.0 square kilometres at the end of 1986 to 469.2 square kilometres in early 1989. Nonetheless, industrial production grew significantly through the 1980s as a whole. If we use 1980 as a base index of 100, 1989 reached an index of 276. This provided the basis for growth in the gross national product from 52 trillion to 120 trillion *wǒn,* and in per capita GNP from $1,592 to $4,968.

The 1980s also saw the structure of production moving to an advanced level, with the proportion of the agricultural, fishing and forestry sectors declining from 15% in 1981 to 10.2% in 1989, with manufacturing increasing from 29.9% to 31.3% and service industries from 51.2% to 61.3% during the same period. The proportion of exports accounted for by heavy industrial products increased from 47.3% in 1981 to 57.9% in 1989.

Heavy industry, which led economic growth in the 1980s through the fabrication of durable and non-durable goods, reduced the proportion of its total supply of production capability provided by imports from 25.3% in 1970 to 22.4% in 1987. The heavy industry sector also experienced high growth rates in exports. This was an indication of the degree to which a domestic production base had been established. Nonetheless, the increase in exports and the production of productive means were concentrated in low-cost, low-technology and low-value-added goods and imports of high-cost, high-technology and high-value-added goods actually increased.

Even as heavy industrial production increased, the import of productive goods continued to increase. That was because the South Korean output of productive goods, rather than being tied in with a domestic division of labour, was exported due to demand from the international division of labour in which Korean heavy industry filled the role of international subcontractors. On the other hand, even as investment by *chaebŏl* in technological research and development was increasing, the continuing weakness in technology meant that imports of technology by rapidly-growing industries grew substantially. Payments for technology increased from the level of $100 million in 1980 to $1 billion by 1989.

Despite the development of heavy industry, there was no real change in the basic structure of 'importing machinery and parts from Japan and exporting finished products to the US'. As a result, the Korean economy became, if anything, even more dependent on trade with the US and Japan, as seen in Table 15 below. Whereas in 1989 south Korea attained a positive balance of $9.4 billion dollars in trade with the US, south Korea's negative balance with Japan continued to grow, reaching nearly $40 billion in 1989.

South Korea's monopoly capital, facing a crisis in its foreign debt at the beginning of the 1980s, opened its doors to direct foreign investment, which required no repayment of principle or interest and which promised the transfer of high technology. The intensification of friction over trade imbalances and increasing outside pressure to open up in the mid-1980s brought the acceleration of the opening of the Korean economy. As a result, foreign direct investment increased from something over $10 billion in 1987 to $65.7 billion in authorized investments in 1989. As of 1986, direct foreign investment companies accounted for 13.0% of total value-added production and 29.3% of exports. In other words, foreign direct investment enterprises accounted for one fourth of south Korea's exports and imports. Of the $4.2 billion positive balance of trade recorded in 1986, direct foreign investment enterprises accounted for $2.6 billion

Throughout the continuing restructuring of the production sector in the 1980s, the domination of the economy by monopoly *chaebŏl* intensified. Sales by the top 30 *chaebŏl* continued to account for over 40% of

Table 15: Trade with the US and Japan (unit: $1 million)

	With the US			With Japan		
	Exports	Imports	Balance of trade	Exports	Imports	Balance of trade
1970	47.3	29.5	−165.9	28.1	40.8	−575.0
1980	26.3	21.9	552.0	17.4	26.3	−2,818.4
1989	33.1	25.9	937.9	21.6	28.4	−3,991.8

Source: Han'guk sahoe yŏn'guso, *Han'guk kyŏngjeron*, p. 189.

total sales, and the proportion of the gross national product constituted by the value added by the top 50 *chaebŏl* increased from 15.8% in 1980 to 20.8% in 1984. In the final analysis, the 1980s restructuring of the production sector strengthened the domestic monopoly capital system while externally adjusting to the international division of labour through the merging of capital and collaboration in technology.

CHANGES IN THE NATURE OF MEDIUM AND SMALL BUSINESSES

Until the mid-1970s, monopoly capital control over medium and small businesses was largely limited to driving them out of business or absorbing them. Once, however, the development of heavy industry got under way in earnest in the late-1970s, the structure of medium and small businesses also began to develop. Their share of total production rose from 38.4% in 1974 to 47.4% in 1985. Furthermore, as heavy industry's share of exports increased, so did that of medium and small businesses, evidence of the advancing development of their internal structure.

Whereas medium and small businesses had earlier been limited to finished products for direct consumption, they were now producing semi-finished products and parts for monopoly enterprises. Under the expansion of the social division of labour, medium and small businesses came to form part of the production base as suppliers to big enterprises.

In the process of establishing its domination over the economy, monopoly capital had oppressed and killed off small-scale businesses, but now that its control over the economy was secure, monopoly capital turned to a mode of coexistence with medium and small businesses in which they became dependent entities that helped strengthen monopoly capital's domination and accumulation of profits.

Furthermore, the government enacted its 'Law to Support the Creation of Medium and Small Businesses' in May 1986 in order to create and foster the development of various kinds of medium and small enterprises. Investment in facilities by medium and small businesses increased over 3 times during the years from 1981 to 1988. The proportion of such investments made up by purchases of machinery also increased from 46.0% to 56.0%. One result was an overall increase in sales from 1981 to 1987 of 530%, larger than the 330% increase recorded by heavy industry for the same period. Another result was a decrease in the import of parts used in such major assembly industries as electronics, automobiles and ships from 40.5% in 1978 to 29.3% in 1985.

Along with the restructuring of medium and small enterprises on a high level came the establishment of vertical relations in their ties with large enterprises. For example, whereas only 17.4% of medium and small businesses were suppliers for large enterprises in 1975, by 1988 that proportion had increased to 55.5%. In the machinery sector, in particular, in 1988 fully 80% of medium and small businesses were suppliers to large enterprises. These suppliers in most cases were essentially little more than affiliated subcontractors of large enterprises. Over 80% of suppliers

Table 16: Trends in medium and small business sales by type of sale

	Exports	Domestic sales	
		Sales to manufacturers	Market sales
1970	9.1%	20.9%	70.0%
1980	23.8%	28.1%	52.9%
1986	29.7%	33.2%	42.0%
1987	32.3%	42.0%	33.9%
1988	28.8%	40.8%	33.5%

Source: Han'guk sahoe yŏn'guso, *Han'guk kyŏngjeron,* p. 189.

were dependent on subcontracts with large enterprises for 80% or more of their business.

One the other hand, there were also medium and small businesses who were dependent on assembly production and exports. As early as 1980, medium and small enterprises accounted for 32.1% of exports, a share that expanded to 37.9% in 1988. Even as sales of medium and small suppliers to big enterprises increased, so did the exports of other medium and small businesses. As seen in Table 16, 23.8% of medium and small business total sales in 1980 came in the form of exports, a proportion that increased to 32.2% in 1987. Medium and small businesses were exporting roughly one-third of their products.

In the process of expanding their exports, medium and small businesses came to have a high degree of foreign dependence, either as subcontractors for large enterprises or through direct contact. This was true in the areas of capital acquisition, labour and markets. Their degree of reliance on the US and Japan was particularly high. The proportion of foreign materials they used continued to increase, as did foreign joint investments and the introduction of foreign technology. As Table 17 shows, in 1983 there were 53 instances of joint investment with foreign capital, a number that increased to 267 by 1987. Instances of the introduction of foreign technology also increased from 95 in 1982 to 325 in 1987.

Beginning in the 1980s, medium and small businesses underwent a process of differentiation that resulted in their division into several types: exporters; subcontractors for big enterprises; producers for domestic markets; affiliates of large enterprises; and companies formed by exclusive foreign investment. Each type had distinct characteristics according to its nature and position. Nonetheless, they all were faced with the problems of structural weakness and backwardness.

Companies with assets of less than 100 million *wŏn* formed 46.8% of the total in 1986, while companies with fewer than 100 employees accounted for 93.2% of the total in 1987. Most (73.0%) of the medium and small companies were not public corporations but privately held firms. They also suffered from low productivity due to the backwardness of their facilities and technology. The value-added productivity of

Table 17: Trends in medium and small business foreign joint investment

	1983	1984	1985	1986	1987	1983–87 Total
Total Foreign Investment (A)	75	104	127	203	363	872
Foreign Joint Investment with Medium and Small Businesses (B)	53	72	81	135	267	608
Foreign Joint Investment with Large Enterprises	17	20	23	29	44	133
Exclusive Foreign Investment	5	12	23	39	52	131
B as percentage of A	70.6%	69.3%	63.8%	66.5%	73.6%	69.7%

Source: Han'guk sahoe yŏn'guso, *Han'guk kyŏngjeron*, p. 230.

medium and small industries was only 68.8% of the total average and only 49.0% of the large enterprise average in 1987. During the 1980s, medium and small businesses were highly dependent on subcontracts with domestic and foreign monopoly capital large enterprises. Their position in the overall structure meant that they had relatively less access to funding from the government and assistance from abroad. They only received 5.4% of governmental financial aid to businesses in 1987, a proportion much lower that in Japan where medium and small businesses received 18.1% of government financial aid in 1985. Furthermore, unlike the financing privileges enjoyed by large enterprises, medium and small businesses had to provide security for bank loans. The result was continuing financial difficulties for medium and small businesses.

Despite the overall growth in medium and small business sales and the upward restructuring of the sector, the proportion of medium and small enterprises that had to cut back on production or even suspend or stop production altogether was relatively high. In 1987, 700 businesses suspended or stopped production and in 1988, that number grew to 1,037. Rates of the suspension or stopping of production were particularly high in the foodstuffs industry at 29.2%, the printing and paper industry at 22.6% and 21.4% in the chemical and plastics industries. These rates were much higher than the overall manufacturing rate of 13.7%.

In summary, although there was some degree of upward restructuring of medium and small businesses in the 1980s, the transformation of many such enterprises into subcontractors for domestic and foreign large enterprises meant that they were being subordinated to monopoly capital. Their degree of subordination was intensified by their reliance on monopoly capital to acquire materials and markets. That meant the gradual weakening of conditions that might have allowed the development of an economic system based on non-monopoly capital. Instead south Korea saw the development of a strong monopoly capital economy that was closely tied to foreign-monopoly capital.

CHANGES IN THE FINANCIAL STRUCTURE

The Syngman Rhee regime's public sale of reverted bank stock led to civilian operation of banks, but it also led to the banks being transformed into private depositories for the *chaebŏl*. After the 16 May 1961 military coup, the government recalled the stocks of major investors and in effect nullified the civilian operation of banks. The major roles fulfilled by government-managed bank capital were to provide low-interest rates and policy loans to finance specific government initiatives.

Banks provided loans to enterprises at rates much lower than available through private financing, and interest rates on policy loans were only half of regular rates. Policy loans were concentrated in the export and heavy-industry sectors. These were sectors dominated by monopoly-capital enterprises and policy loans helped to accelerate the accumulation of capital by those enterprises.

Under these circumstances, the banks were unable to attract sufficient savings to fund their loans. The government made up the difference with special financing from the Bank of Korea. That was a major factor behind the expansion of the money supply and the rise of inflation. During the years from 1963 to 1985, over 10% of the funds given out by banks as loans were obtained as special financing from the central bank. Excessive investment by enterprises that enjoyed monopoly access to low interest loans resulted in the failure of large numbers of companies. Funds provided to cover those losses totaled 1.256 trillion *wŏn* in 1985.

A 'plan to allow for the self-regulating management of ordinary banks' was announced in December 1980 as part of a drive to return banks to civilian operation. The government sold 50% of the stock it held in such banks as the Hanil, the Cheil, the Sin'tak and the Chohŭng. It also limited the percentage of total issued stock that could be held by any one individual or corporation to 8% in an effort to prevent the ownership of banks by monopoly capital. The *chaebŏl*, however, used such methods as disguised purchase of stock by affiliated companies to control from 20 to 27% of the stock of major banks. Table 18 shows percentage holdings of civilians in major banks.

The government also sought to promote the self-regulating management of civilian-owned banks. The 'temporary bank measures law' that had given the authority to approve or reject the appointments of officials at financial institutions to the Director of the government's Bank Supervision Board was repealed and over 600 different government regulations regarding the operation of financial institutions were abolished in January 1981 and December 1984. Also, in 1982 the government amended the banking law to eliminate the section that gave the Director

Table 18: Civilian ownership of banks (as of 4 August 1983)

Bank	Date privatized	Major stockholders	% of stock held
Sangŏp	7/31/73	Trade Association	21.6
		Samsung affiliates	13.8
		Sanhak cooperative foundation	6.7
Hanil	7/1/81	Taerim affiliates	12.1
		Hyundai affiliates	2.2
		LG affiliates	6.9
Cheil	9/10/82	Daewoo affiliates	18.0
		Hanjin Affiliates	10.9
		Hyundai affiliates	10.3
		LG affiliates	10.2
		Taehan education insurance	9.0
		Samsung affiliates	8.0
Seoul sint'ak	9/10/82	Tongguk steel affiliates	10.1
		Tonga construction affiliates	10.1
		Sŏju industries affiliates	6.7
		Sindonga affiliates	6.3
		Hyundai affiliates	6.9
Chohŭng	3/8/83	T'aegwang industries affiliates	11.4
		Samsung affiliates	9.8
		Sindonga affiliates	7.8
		Ssangyong affiliates	5.9

Source: Han'guk sahoe yŏn'guso, *Han'guk kyŏngjeron*, p. 324.

of the Bank Supervision Board the authority to issue instructions regarding bank operations. Even so, in November 1990, the banks presented a 'plan for strengthening bank competitiveness in preparation of the opening of the financial markets' in November 1990 that called for guarantees of self-regulated management such as autonomy in appointing their highest officers, the introduction of the chairman system and permission to allow banks to increase their capitalization and to merge.

One of the changes that occurred in the world capitalist system in the 1980s was the rise of transnational capital and the demands to open up the financial and service sectors of the newly industrializing countries. South Korea was no exception. Capital liberalization began with the government's 1981 announcement of a 'long-term plan to internationalize capital markets for capital liberalization'. The push for the liberalization of capital transactions through bonds, loans, insurance and real estate came as an extension of government's active effort to attract direct foreign investment during the economic downturn of the late-1970s and

Table 19: Major *Chaebŏl* dependence on foreign bank branches,
July 1987

Chaebŏl	Total loan amounts*	% from Foreign bank branches
Samsung	20,799	25.47
Hyundai	24,451	16.77
Daewoo	29,270	8.04
LG	14,272	32.31
Sunkyung	7,612	22.74

Source: Han'guk sahoe yŏn'guso, *Han'guk kyŏngjeron*, p. 320.
*Loan amount unit: 100 million *wŏn*

early-1980s and in tandem with the expanded opening of commodities markets during the mid-1980s years of a positive balance of trade.

As a result, there was an increase in dependence on foreign sources of monetary capital. The mode of limiting the introduction of foreign capital to state-brokered loans that prevailed until the 1970s gave way in the 1980s to allowing loans from foreign banks and allowing foreigners to invest in stocks and bonds. This led to the active penetration of south Korea by transnational banks and the total capital of foreign bank offices in Korea increased from 14.5 billion *wŏn* in 1970 to 7.901 trillion *wŏn* in 1989. As seen in Table 19, there was an increase in *chaebŏl* borrowing from foreign banks.

From the 1980s onwards, the subordination of the Korean economy to the international division of labour was intensified through the opening of financial markets while at the same time monopoly *chaebŏl* domination of domestic finances gradually increased. The *chaebŏl* exercised virtually total control over the short-term loan companies, the general finance companies and the securities companies that made up the secondary financial market, and also gained substantial control over the banks that were returned to civilian management in the early-1980s, thus paving the way for their domination of the full range of financial institutions.

In short, the full-scale penetration of Korea by foreign monopoly capital as the country shifted over to the open economy system in the 1980s led to the intensification of competition among domestic *chaebŏl* that intensified the trend towards ever larger, ever more monopolistic enterprises. This, in turn, led, despite the government's announced intentions of returning banks to civilian control and promoting their autonomy, to the strengthening of the direct control of financial institutions by monopoly capital.

THE OPEN ECONOMY SYSTEM AND AGRICULTURE

When south Korea enjoyed a temporary positive balance in current accounts and exports that reached the $10 billion level in the late-1970s, its trading partners reacted by strengthening import restrictions. This forced the government to implement a policy of the opening Korea to certain limited types of imports. On three occasions in 1978 and 1979, the government removed restrictions on the import of some 160 items, including a limited number of agricultural products that were not produced in Korea or whose limited supply resulted in severe price fluctuations. The government also began a staged abolition of the export recommendation system.

With the return and expansion of trade deficits at the end of the 1970s and the beginning of the 1980s, the lifting of restrictions on imports was delayed. In the case of rice, however, the reduction in the amount of land planted in the 'unification rice' strain that had previously been forced on the peasants by the government resulted in the import of 500,000 tons of rice in 1979, 1,119,000 tons in 1980, 1,830,000 tons in 1981 and 500,000 tons in 1982.

Beginning in 1985, the US implemented a new trade policy intended to reduce its negative balance of international trade by emphasizing the export of agricultural products. This policy included provisions for retaliatory trade measures. In order to speed up the process of concluding trade talks and to make it easier to apply retaliatory trade sanctions, the US delegated those powers, which had previously belonged to the president, to its chief trade representative. It also made the application of retaliatory trade sanctions mandatory and expanded its definition of unfair trade practices.

The US demanded of south Korea that it abolish its import quota system for fodder and raw grains and that it lift restrictions in three stages against the import of such high-value agricultural products as beef and oranges and such large quantity purchase items as wheat and corn by January 1991. The consequence was a great expansion of the opening of Korea to agricultural products. Furthermore, the lifting of restrictions against American cigarettes in September 1986 resulted in a decrease in the number of farm households cultivating tobacco plants from 91,389 in 1987 to 77,485 in 1998, while the amount of land used for tobacco cultivation shrank from 35,226.9 to 31,821.4 hectares.

On 4 August 1989, the government announced that it would lift import restrictions on 243 agricultural products over the next three years. Sixty-two of the 119 items demanded by the US were included therein. As shown in Table 20, the proportion of agricultural products on which restrictions were lifted increased from 71.9% in January 1989 to 84.9% in 1990.

With the full-scale development of heavy industry-led capitalism after the mid-1970s, the government's policy of guaranteeing relatively high rice prices began to receive criticism. Changes in dietary habits led to a reduction in rice consumption while the high rice price policy resulted in large amounts of rice being warehoused. In addition, the dual rice price policy by which the government sold rice on the market a lower price than it bought it from the producers caused an increasingly large drain

Table 20: Liberalization of Agricultural/Foresty/Martime imports by Year

Type of product	Dec. 1988	1989	1990	1991
Agricultural	75.1%	79.3%	82.8%	86.2%
Forestry	94.6%	94.9%	95.3%	97.3%
Maritime	40.2%	57.9%	57.9%	69.2%
TotalAnnual Averages:	71.9%	76.1%	80.3%	84.9%

Source: Han'guk sahoe yŏn'guso, *Han'guk kyŏngjeron*, p. 394.

on the budget. The government defrayed the shortfall not with ordinary tax revenue but with special loans from the Bank of Korea, which brought an expansion in the money supply and an increase in inflation.

At the time of the 10 June democratization movement there was a temporary increase in the price the government paid for rice. There was also a 1998 revision of the grain management law to require the agreement of the National Assembly to change the purchase price and to require that the opinions of a grain distribution committee composed of persons from all walks of life be reflected in any such decisions. But the government's grain purchase price policy and its grain production policy were not co-ordinated and grain purchase prices were determined by considerations of maintaining stable prices and by the political situation at any given time rather than by the interests of the peasants. In 1988 about 42 million *sŏm* of rice were produced of which 16%, or roughly 6.7 million *sŏm*, were purchased by the government, while in 1989 approximately 41 million *sŏm* of rice were produced of which 28.7%, or about 1.17 million *sŏm* were bought by the government.

In order to make up the difference in the decrease of farm household income following the freezing of grain purchase prices in 1984, the government pushed a policy of encouraging farmers to cultivate locally specialized crops and supplementary crops in addition to rice. For that purpose, the government created nearly 2,000 special zones to which it provided 245.3 billion *wŏn* in aid. Stimulated by the government's policy, the peasants actively engaged themselves in the production of commercial agricultural crops other than rice. The result, however, was overproduction and severe declines and/or fluctuations in prices. One representative example was the 'cattle price disturbance'. The government, which had experienced an earlier disturbance over cattle prices in the late-1970s due to a shortfall in supply, decided to encourage the raising of cattle as part of its policy of diversifying agricultural production. The number of cattle raised in Korea had remained at the level of about 1.53 million between 1973 and 1983, but the increasing import of live cattle and of breeding from 1983 resulted in an increase in the number of cattle to 2.65 million by June 1985. The consequence was a sharp drop in the price of cattle and in the incomes of peasants who were

Table 21: Trends in peasant debt (Household averages in 1,000 *wŏn*)

Year	Total (A) (% increase)	Institutional loans Total (B)	Nonghyŏp	Other	Private loans	B/A	B/C
1980	339	173	165	8	166	51	104
1981	437 (28.9)	227	216	11	210	52	108
1982	830 (89.9)	554	524	30	276	67	201
1983	1,285 (54.8)	864	823	41	421	67	205
1984	1,784 (38.8)	1,226	1,147	79	558	69	220
1985	2,024 (13.5)	1,440	1,337	103	584	71	247
1986	2,192 (8.3)	1,550	1,436	114	642	71	242
1987	2,390 (9.8)	1,876	1,718	158	514	75	365
1988	3,131 (31.0)	2,652	2,511	141	479	85	554
1989	3,899 (19.7)	3,272	3,069	203	627	84	552

Source: Seoul Sahoe kwahak yŏn'guso, *Han'guk esŏ ŭi chabonjuŭi paltalsa*, p. 310.

raising cattle. The amount of cattle breeding funds that was not repaid during the two years of 1983 and 1984 totaled 250.2 billion *wŏn* in 3.05 million farm households, for an average of 820,000 *wŏn* per household. This represented no less than 6% of the total farm household debt of 4,180 billion *wŏn*.

On the other hand, the discontinuance of the policy of increasing grain production, the relative retreat of the high rice price policy, and the lifting of restrictions against agricultural imports of the 1980s resulted in the rapid increase of farm family debt, forcing the government to take such steps as the 'measures to reduce the debts of farming and fishing households' and the 'comprehensive measures to revitalize the farming and fishing economies' of 1987. Such steps notwithstanding, the underlying financial weakness of farm families and of the structure of rural financing meant that the expansion of commercial farming and advances in agricultural mechanization resulted in further increases in farm household debt. As shown in Table 21, the average farm family debt of 339,000 *wŏn* in 1980 increased to 3,899,000 in 1989 and reliance on private financing gradually grew higher.

The deterioration of the rural economy brought an increase in the number of persons who left the villages and a corresponding decrease in agricultural labour power. In 1970, the rural population of 14,422,000 constituted 45.1% of the country's total population of 31,435,000. In1980, the rural population had declined to 10,830,000 or 28.4% of the total 38,124,000 persons and by 1987, it had fallen to 7,770,000 or just 18% of the total south Korean population of 42,400,000. There was also a continuous decline in the number of farm households which had peaked at of 2,580,000 households in 1967. Between 1967 and 1975, the average decrease in the number of farm households was 26,000 or an average of 1% per year. Between 1975 and 1988, the annual average climbed to 42,000 households, or 2% per year. The loss of farming population was concentrated in young men, bringing an intensification of the trend towards increasing numbers of elderly persons and women in the agricultural labour force.

There were also major changes in farm household management. The proportion of farm households owning less than 0.3 *chŏngbo* of land declined from 15.7% in 1970 to 13.4% in 1980 and 12.7% in 1986. Also, the decrease in agricultural labour power stimulated the mechanization of agriculture. This was limited to cultivators until the mid-1970s when the use of power transplanting and harvesting machines began to spread widely, bringing the total mechanization of rice cultivation. Advances in the mechanization of agriculture also enabled those households that owned more than one *chŏngbo* of land to begin expanding their holdings. At the same time, however, the amount of land needed to maintain a household at a minimal middle peasant level increased sharply from 0.5–1.0 *chŏngbo* in 1976 to 1.5–2.0 *chŏngbo* in 1983.

The rapid decline in the farming population from the late-1970s brought a greater expansion of landlord-tenant relationships than had been seen in previous periods. The proportion of land in tenure increased from 16.5% in 1977 to 34.8% in 1998 and the proportion of tenant farmers increased sharply from 27.8% in 1975 to 64.7% in 1985. The total value of rents paid by tenant farmers in 1985 was over 50 billion *wŏn*. Of that total, 32.15 billion *wŏn* went to absentee landlords who were not directly engaged in agricultural management. The average annual rent paid by tenant farmers was 419,000 *wŏn*, an amount that represented 11.3% of total farm income.

The government's policy of the diversification of agriculture, implemented to deal with the crisis in agriculture brought about by the declining profitability of farming that occurred in the process of the development of heavy industry-centred monopoly capital, the spread of landlord-tenant relations, the increase in farm household debt, the rapid increase in the population leaving the farms and the decline in foodstuff self-sufficiency, failed due to the lifting of restrictions against agricultural imports. The government then turned to a rural industrialization policy as seen in its April 1989 'comprehensive measures for the development of farming and fishing villages'. This policy sought to expand existing sources of farming and fishing income, develop new sources, and improve rural living conditions by establishing zones for agricultural industrialization.

The Farming and Fishing Village Promotion Corporation established by these measures acquired an agricultural land management fund of 2 trillion *wŏn* which it used to support the purchase of farm lands as part of a plan to foster the development of specialized commercial agriculture. It also established 53 special zones for agricultural industrialization near Seoul in North Ch'ungch'ŏng Province, and 53 others in areas of North and South Kyŏngsang provinces near Pusan, in order to promote rural industrialization. Even though agricultural land management fund aid was used to reduce tenancy and to expand the holdings of middle peasants, impoverished peasants who gave up on farming found it difficult to find opportunities to earn wages in most rural areas.

The greatest difficulty facing the agricultural sector under the open economy system was the Uruguay Round, the eighth session of the General Agreement on Tariffs and Trade. Under the leadership of the United States, the Uruguay Round demanded the repeal of import duties on all agricultural products designated as non-tariff items and the repeal of all domestic subsidies for agricultural products as well as subsidies to promote exports. In other words, it demanded the total liberalization of trade in such agricultural products as rice and the repeal of agricultural subsidies. It remains to be seen to what extent the south Korean government will be able to resist these demands and to what it extent it will be able to improve the structure of agriculture in order to make it internationally competitive. Other issues to be resolved include the implementation of a system of price guarantees for agricultural products, the improvement of distribution systems in order to stabilize the cost of agricultural products, and the effective implementation of measures to co-ordinate the production and shipping of agricultural goods.

REFERENCES

Han'guk sahoe yŏn'guso, *Han'guk kyŏngjeron* (The Korean economy), Paeksan sŏdang, 1991.

Seoul sahoe kwahak yŏn'guso, *Han'guk esŏ ŭi chabonjuŭi paltal* (The development of capitalism in Korea), Saegil, 1971.

Han'guk yŏksa yŏn'guhoe, *Han'guk hyŏndaesa* (Contemporary history of Korea), 4, Seoul: P'ulpit, 1991.

Pak Hyŏnch'ae yŏkkŭm, *Ch'ŏngnyŏn ŭl wihan han'guk hyŏndaesa* (A contemporary history of Korea for young people), Sonamu, 1992.

8

Society and Culture in the Division Period

INTRODUCTION

The post-liberation division system in south Korea, which began under the US military government, was strengthened in the political, economic, social and cultural spheres under the successive Syngman Rhee, Park Chung Hee, Chun Doo Hwan and Roh Tae Woo regimes. Educational policy played an important role in that process. The US military government replaced the colonial educational system that had been implemented in Korea for nearly a half century with an American style educational system. The Syngman Rhee regime added in anti-Communist education. On top of that, Park Chung Hee grafted his autonomy (*chuch'e sŏng*) education designed to legitimize his military dictatorship.

The Syngman Rhee regime, having hardened its resolve to unify Korea through an 'advance to the north' following the establishment of separate regimes and the Korean War, pursued an educational policy that emphasized anti-Communism and military training. The Park Chung Hee regime continued to intensify its anti-Communist education even after the '4 July joint statement' and strengthened its autonomy education, or 'education with nationality', as a means to emphasize its legitimacy.

Even though the Park regime proclaimed a policy of peaceful reunification instead of the Rhee regime's policy of reunification by conquering the north, there was no difference between the education policies of the Park regime and the Rhee regime. If anything, the Park regime intensified anti-Communist education and the teaching that north Korea was the enemy. The reactionary and chauvinist nature of Park's autonomy education worked against the overcoming of the division system and the attainment of national reunification. During the years of the Chun Doo Hwan and Roh Tae Woo regimes, even though world history was moving away from ideology and towards pacificism and even though a peaceful reunification policy was beginning to take root, the Chun and Roh regimes' educational policies remained within the old framework of confrontation and the Cold War system.

One concrete example can be found in the teaching of history. Even after such proclamations of peaceful reunification as the Park regime's 4 July joint statement, the Chun regime's national reconciliation democratic reunification plan, and the Roh regime's 7 July statement and its national community reunification plan, students were not taught the historical significance of the right-left united front movement of the colonial period, the right-left alliance movement and the 1948 north-south talks of post-liberation period, or the civilian reunification movement of the 1970s and 1980s.

The labour problem is another area that clearly shows the limitations of the division system. Even though Korea was a late developing former colony, the labour movement had been an important part of the national liberation movement during the colonial period and the workers of Korea had a heightened consciousness of politics, society and history. This meant that there was strong potential for the activation of the labour movement in the post-liberation period as working conditions worsened in the process of establishing a capitalist system that perpetuated many of the evils of the colonial period. Under the conditions of national division and confrontation between capitalist and socialist states, however, labour movement organizations were unable to establish their autonomy but rather became part of the state-centred power structure. Even as the collusion between labour movement organizations and the state intensified, there arose continuous disputes and strikes among organized labour and an active movement among unorganized workers. Nonetheless, because of the limitations of the division system, the labour movement of Rhee, Park and Chun years remained for the most part fragmented and limited.

Even under such conditions, the labour movement became quite active during periods of democratization. This was seen in the period after 19 April 1960 and again in the months from July to September after the 10 June democratization movement of 1989, when there was an increase in the formation of 'democratic labour unions' and the establishment of regional labour union associations led to the formation of the Confederation of Korean Trade Unions. Once again, however, the government and employers strengthened their oppression of the labour movement with the carrying out of a 'no work, no pay' policy and the implementation of an aggregate wage system. The end of military rule and the rise of a civilian government in the 1990s have yet to bring resolution of these problems.

On the other hand, the national cultural movement also experienced difficulties in finding its direction. First, the division of nation also produced the division of its cultural capacities and vast differences in understanding of what the national culture was. The establishment of separate regimes and the Korean War thoroughly divided the cultural world into two different groups each of which did its share in strengthening the division system. With the lengthening and deepening of the division system, however, cultural circles in south Korea split into two groups. One group affirmed the division system and sought its place therein. The other sought to express in its works the national and human pain brought by division and eventually developed into a new national cultural movement that sought to advance the cause of national reunification.

This new trend was largely limited to the literary sector, but from the 1980s onwards academic and fine arts groups also sought to overcome national division and there was a growing perception of these efforts as constituting a new national cultural movement. The result in the literary sector of the 1980s was the reorganization of the 1970s Association of Writers for Free Practice into the National Literature Writers Association. Stronger elements of class and party were introduced into national literature theory, giving rise to such more intense discussions and the appearance of a national liberation literary theory, labour liberation literary theory and labour liberation artistic theory. This period also saw the appearance of poets and novelists of working-class backgrounds who produced excellent works depicting the realities of labour in south Korea. This was a particularly distinctive period in the history of Korean literary thought.

Another distinctive feature of the 1980s was large amount of artistic activity based on progressive and *minjung* lines in a wide range of sectors, including art, music, motion pictures, drama, architecture, dance, and photography. These various sectors came together for the first time since the Korean War to form the General Alliance of Korean National Artists.

SECTION ONE

Education and the Academic Movement under the Division System

THE EDUCATIONAL POLICY OF THE US MILITARY GOVERNMENT

The various political parties of the national liberation movement front of the colonial period all adopted free compulsory education as part of their post-liberation educational policies. The Korean Independence Party adopted the Three Equalities Theory's principle that 'the state will assume the burden of all the costs of the people's education of all kinds' for its educational policy while the Korean National Revolution Party declared in its programme that 'compulsory education and vocational education will be financed by the state'. The Korean Independence League stated that 'the state will bear the burden of financing a national compulsory educational system'. These ideas were adopted as part of the Shanghai Interim Government's programme for establishing a state: 'The state will bear all the expenses for each kind of education for the people, will establish independence, democracy and solidarity as its central educational principles, and will edit new textbooks.'

Looking back, education up through the Chosŏn period was largely limited to the *yangban* class, but educational opportunities for commoners expanded and the number of schools increased rapidly after the opening of the ports in 1876. In the colonial period, however, education for Koreans was largely limited to producing workers with minimal skills in line with the Japanese policy of keeping Koreans ignorant. That was the reason why both left and right in the national liberation movement front sought to overthrow the Japanese educational system and adopted compulsory educational systems both to ensure equal opportunities but also to enhance the educational level of the people. In the case of south Korea after liberation, however, the educational policy of the national liberation front was not fully realized under the US military government.

The US forces that occupied Korea south of the 38th parallel first took over the Japanese Government-General's Bureau of Education, reorganized as the Ministry of Education, established a seven (later ten) person education committee on 16 September 1945. It then ordered the opening of elementary schools on 19 September and secondary schools on 24 September. In November 1945, the US military government established an educational council, chaired by An Chaehong and made up of ten subcommittees. The educational ideal selected at that time was to 'foster well-rounded and patriotic citizens of a democratic state based on the Korean national foundation principle of "widely benefiting humanity" '. At the time, there were those who criticized the use of the mythical 'widely benefiting humanity' as something that could not be proven scientifically and that was similar to the founding myth of Japan.

The educational council abolished the various rudimentary and temporary schools set up by the Japanese in rural areas and revised the school system to provide for six years of elementary school education, six years of middle school education, and four years of college education. It also divided middle school into lower and higher middle schools of 3 years each, thus following the US 6-3-3-4 system. Near its end, the US military government in December 1948, promulgated a law for the establishment of educational district assemblies in a move intended to promote local educational autonomy. Efforts were also made to cast off the colonial educational methods of repression, uniformity, and instructor and textbook-centred instruction and replace them with more democratic methods but achieved only limited success because of difficulties in finding qualified teachers and appropriate educational materials.

Although the US military government did not implement the national liberation movement front's policy of free compulsory education for all persons, nonetheless it did preside over a great increase in the number of students and schools. At the time of liberation in August 1945, there was a total of 2,834 elementary schools with 1,366,024 students; when the Syngman Rhee regime was formed in three years later, there were 3,443 elementary schools with 2,426,115 students. During the same period, the number of middle schools increased from 165 to 564 and the number of middle school students increased from 133,857 to 756,700. Higher education saw an increase in the number of colleges and universities from 19 to 31 and in the number of students from 7,819 to 24,000. In the case of secondary higher education in particular, the growth in the number of students greatly exceeded the expansion of educational facilities. This was a reflection of the pent-up demand for higher education in the colonial period, but it also brought a decline in the quality of education.

The great increase in the numbers of students within the context of rapid social change created many problems on the campuses. First, even if all the persons who had been teachers under the Japanese were mobilized, the number would have fallen far short of what was needed. Furthermore, those teachers who had been responsible for education under the Japanese should have been retrained, but they were not. Instead, they were sent directly out to the schools. Making matters even worse was the way in which the deepening left-right ideological split plunged the schools into chaos. Boycotts of classes arose in schools at all levels throughout the country.

A typical example was the movement in opposition to the plan to establish a national university. The US military government, citing financial reasons and the need to make the best use of existing human and material resources, announced on 19 June 1946 that it had 'decided to abolish the various government higher education facilities in and around Seoul and to create a great new university under new ideals and a new vision that can represent the whole country's education'. As soon as the US military government's Ministry of Education announced this plan, an alliance of technical school and college professors stepped forth in opposition. They were concerned that the way in which the board set up to establish the national university was made up completely of Ministry of Education officials would led to the loss of autonomy and dictatorial official control of higher education and also concerned that it would weaken schools in the technological sector, such as engineering, natural sciences and mining. The professors' alliance argued for expanding Kyŏngsŏng College (the old Keijo Imperial University) as a comprehensive university while preserving the individuality of its constituent colleges. Student opposition, led mostly by left-wing elements, took the form of boycotts of classes by students at the various schools that were to be incorporated into the new national university, to be known as Seoul National University.

As soon as the Ministry of Education declared the adjournment of classes at Kyŏngsŏng College and suspended the students who had participated in the boycotts, professors opposed to the national university plan left their schools and boycotts of classes spread to over 400 schools throughout the country. On 22 August 1946, Seoul National University was established as planned and boycotts gradually died away. The movement in opposition to the national university was the greatest academic problem faced by the US military government. It arose because of opposition to the one-sided way in which the Ministry of Education authorities handled thing, but also because the total abolition of already existing schools was widely perceived to be a method for getting rid of left-wing faculties.

THE EDUCATIONAL POLICY OF THE SYNGMAN RHEE REGIME

The 16th article of the constitution under which Syngman Rhee took office stipulated, 'all citizens have equal rights to education and the state shall provide, at a minimum, free compulsory elementary school education'. This made only elementary school education free and compulsory. The educational budget of the first year of the government in 1948 amounted to 8.9% of the total budget, and 69.4% of that was set aside for compulsory educational expenses. The 1949 budget for education increased to 11.4% of the total budget, and 71.6% of that was used for compulsory education. Even so, the amount provided by the budget covered less than 30% of costs and the remaining 70% had to be made up by parents through such things as school support association fees and teacher-parent association fees. It wasn't until 1962, fourteen years after the government was established, that the school support associations and teacher-parent associations were abolished.

Although a new education law was passed on 31 December 1949, its educational principles perpetuated the 'widely benefiting humanity' of the US military government, to which it added Rhee's 'one people-ism' (*ilminjŭi*) as an 'ideal of democratic national education' and also organized the Student National Protection Corps through which it implemented military training for students at the middle school and higher levels. Although the Rhee regime paid lip service to the ideal of democratic education, concerns were raised that its 'one people-ism' was strongly fascist, that its Student National Protection Corp was reminiscent of the Hitler Youth of Nazi Germany, that it was forcing its ideology on the students and that it was pursuing a centralized educational policy. Although 'one people-ism' faded away, the Student National Protection Corps persisted unchanged.

At the time of its establishment, the Rhee regime's educational policy was set as 'democratic and nationalist education', 'unification of the people's thought', 'anti-Communist spirit' and 'a skill for everyone' as it sought to unify the people behind its anti-Communist doctrine. After the outbreak of the Korean War, the regime intensified its anti-Communist education under the name of national defence education. In February 1951, the Rhee regime announced its 'special principles for wartime education', proclaiming its pursuit of moral, technical and national defence education and calling for 'fostering the belief of certain victory over Communism, clarifying perceptions of the wartime situation and of international collective security, and providing guidance for living in wartime'.

The Rhee regime also revised the school system, abolishing the six year middle school and replacing it with a three year middle school and a three year high school in March 1951. This was implemented despite opposition saying that the change would introduce yet another round of entrance examinations as students sought to advance from middle to high school, that it would cause schools to focus on preparing their students for examinations and that it would double the financial burden on parents.

Although the education law provided the legal basis for a system of educational autonomy, its implementation was delayed due to the Korean War and it wasn't until June 1952 that city and district educational committees were established in the area south of the Han River. The district educational committees were established at the county level and were under the control of provincial governors, the Minister of Education and the Minister of Internal Affairs, and were composed of county chiefs and members selected from the county seat and each township. The superintendents of education, who were district administrators, were nominated by the district committees but the nominations had to be approved by the provincial governor and the Minister of Education, with final appointments being made by the president. The city educational committees were also made up ten persons chosen by the mayors and the city councils and also had superintendents of education. The provincial educational committees were made up of one person from each district and city educational committee along with three persons appointed by the governor, but real educational authority was in the hands of provincial educational and social bureau chiefs and the educational committees only acted as advisory boards.

The educational autonomy system was intended to free education from centralization and put it under local control, to make it independent of regular administration and put it under professional administration, and to exclude bureaucratic control and make it more democratic. However, under the Syngman Rhee regime it resulted in a compromise between central and local control, in the incomplete separation of regular and professional administration, in a compromise between bureaucratic and civilian control and in the failure to exclude totally non-professional management. Whereas the city educational committees exercised actual administrative control, the provincial and central educational committees were not even able to fulfil their roles as advisory boards and the county-based district committees had an undefined role as decision-making bodies. Furthermore, the educational autonomy system was severely under-funded. Together these problems made it difficult to get out from being under centralized and bureaucratic control.

Even though the free compulsory elementary school education called for by the constitution was not thoroughly implemented, continuing policy efforts were made to achieve that goal and budgets were gradually increased. By 1960, the Ministry of Education's budget had grown to 15.2% of the total and the share of the Ministry's budget allocated to free compulsory education had reached 80.9%.

The school population had also increased greatly. The number of elementary schools expanded by 62.3% from 2,834 in 1945 to 4,602 in 1960, whereas the number of students increased 260% from 1,366,024 to 3,597,627. During the same period, the number of schools increased eleven-fold from 97 to 1,053. The number of high schools, including both liberal arts and vocational schools, nearly tripled from 224 in 1945 to 640 in 1960, while the number of high school students grew 310% from 84,363 to 263,563. The number of colleges and universities expanded 330% from 19 to 63 and the number of college students increased twelve-fold from 7,819 to 97,819.

The factors behind the rapid growth in the school population include the explosion of pent-up demand from the colonial period, the post-liberation implementation of open educational policies to meet the demand, the growth in the school-age population, the demise of the old colonial era view that college education was only for the ruling class and the bourgeoisie, deferment of military service for students during and after the Korean War, and difficulty in finding employment, especially for those with only elementary, middle school and high school educations. However, the rate of growth in the number of students far exceeded the rate of growth in the number of schools. The consequence was a decline in the quality of education, particularly in higher education.

THE POST-19-APRIL MOVEMENT FOR ACADEMIC DEMOCRATIZATION

The 19 April movement, which arose as a movement for democracy in opposition to the dictatorial politics and corruption of the Syngman Rhee regime, immediately turned its attention to the elimination of non-democratic elements that had taken root in academia during the Rhee years. There were continuous demonstrations against schools and school foundations as the situation grew more complicated. The academic democratization movement began with the elimination of educational figures who had been involved in the corruption and election irregularities of the Rhee regime.

The students' strong demands were supported by the caretaker government of Hŏ Chŏng, which on 26 May 1960 promulgated its 'emergency measure for academic normalcy'. This measure provided for the punishment according to law of educational bureaucrats and the withdrawal of government approval of the appointments of deans, presidents, principles and board members of private schools who fell into the following categories: one, 'those educators or ordinary citizens who, by having actively participated in the 15 March election irregularities, are shunned by ordinary citizens'; two, 'those who used their connections with the old government to engage in autocratic, corrupt or illegal actions in educational administration in order to gain personal power and wealth, and those who disrupted academic order and brought shame to the world of education'; and three, 'those who through impure motives instigated actions by students or colleagues that disrupted academic order and those who abandoned or neglected their duties'.

The post-19-April movement for academic democratization also demanded the dissolution of the Student National Protection Corps, which had been undemocratic, top-down, bureaucratic and politically abused, and its replacement with autonomous student body associations. The Hŏ Chŏng government also supported the students on this issue and promulgated its 'abolition of the regulations pertaining to the Student National Protection Corps' on 10 May 1960. This was followed by the formation at schools, of all levels, of student associations as executive bodies and student assemblies as legislative bodies, which in turn led to the 9 September 1960 establishment of the General Federation of Korean College Students. This latter became the matrix for student participation in the post-19-April democracy and national liberation movements.

The academic democratization movement led the Chang Myŏn regime to reduce centralization of educational administration and delegate the power to appoint educational officials and to approve foundations operating kindergartens, elementary schools, middle schools and high schools to local governments. The Chang regime also established a 'council on autonomous educational institutions' to strengthen educational autonomy and also activated the central educational committee that had almost never met during the Rhee era.

A crucial issue of the post-19-April academic democratization movement was the question of teacher's union organizations. There had already been controversy between teachers and school foundations over this problem in 1959 before the fall of Syngman Rhee and after 19 April a strong movement to form a teachers' labour union arose among those teachers who had rejected the Korean Education Association. The movement began with the formation of a middle and high school teachers' labour union in Taegu on 6 May 1960 and rapidly spread to other areas. Before long, over 300 representatives from schools of all levels, including college professors, gathered at Seoul National University on 22 May to form the Federation of Korean Teachers' Labour Unions with a programme that called for a struggle to raise the economic position of teachers, the freedom and democratization of schools, and for contributing to world peace through the construction of a democratic state. Subsequently federations were established in each province to confront the Korean Education Association. The movement was most active in South Kyŏngsang Province, where over 90% of all teachers joined teachers' labour unions, and North Kyŏngsang Province, where over 70% joined. Both the Hŏ Chŏng caretaker government and the Chang Myŏn regime were consistent in refusing to recognize the teachers' unions and a group of legislators presented legislation to outlaw teachers' unions. This failed, however, due to fierce opposition from teachers' labour unions.

The Chang Myŏn regime sought to deal with the teachers' labour union movement by drafting legislation that would have recognized teachers' organizations and their right to engage in collective bargaining, but that denied their right to collective action. However, this was opposed by the Korean Education Association on the grounds that it would promote divisions among teachers. The teachers' labour unions also opposed it because it required official approval for the formation of organizations, did not allow for labour disputes, and did not recognize collective bargaining rights for teachers in public schools. The legislation never made it to the National Assembly floor.

The Federation of Korean Teachers' Labour Unions opened a national congress of representatives opposed to the illegalization of teachers' labour unions on 18 October 1960 where over 400 representatives expressed their opposition to the National Assembly and the Ministry of Education. The Ministry of Education also refused to recognize the teachers' labour union movement in a statement that said: 'Lowering teachers to the level of labourers is an insult to a sacred profession. For that reason, while we allow organizing, we cannot approve of allowing teachers to engage in labour disputes.' Despite its rejection by the Chang regime, the teachers' labour union movement continued, adopting resolutions demanding the withdrawal of the regime's 'temporary special anti-Communist law' and its 'law restricting large demonstration' and responding positively to the proposal for talks between north and south Korean students. After the 16 May 1961 military *coup*, however, this movement was completely outlawed and many of its participants were oppressed. Only the Korean Education Association remained.

As soon as the 19 April democracy movement succeeded in ousting Syngman Rhee's dictatorial regime, it immediately linked up with the academic democratization movement. There was some short-term chaos in the process of eliminating the undemocratic elements that had accumulated in a society that had long been oppressed but now was suddenly free. Nonetheless, the post-19-April academic democratization movement centred on the dissolution of the Student National Protection Corps and the teachers' labour union movement formed one chapter in the democracy movement in south Korea after 1945.

THE PARK CHUNG HEE REGIME'S EDUCATIONAL POLICY

The educational principles and the education policy direction of the nearly twenty-year long Park Chung Hee regime are characterized by the National Charter of Education promulgated on 5 December 1968. The National Charter of Education is replete with such terms as 'pioneering spirit', 'co-operative spirit', 'citizens' spirit', 'revival of the nation', 'anti-Communist democratic spirit', 'shared prosperity of humankind', 'public profit and order', 'the future of the reunified fatherland', and 'development of capabilities'.

The National Charter of Education, which was drafted by Park, who had received a normal school education under the Japanese, and other Japanese-trained scholars, was reminiscent of the Imperial Rescript on Education of militarist Japan and was criticized for its excessive emphasis on the state and the nation. The Charter brought the intensification of Park's autonomy education, security system education, and the New Village Movement's education for collaboration between industry and academia.

Park's autonomy education was based on two goals. One was the 'liquidation' of the vestiges of Japanese colonial rule and the other was establishing the legitimacy of the Park regime in the confrontation between north and south. Thus the regime pushed its idea of 'history with nationality', established a committee for strengthening education in Korean history in 1972, and required that all history textbooks be approved by the government in 1973. The regime also strengthened its 'national ethics' education based on anti-Communism and morality, an aspect that it emphasized even more after the declaration of the Yushin system.

The Park regime reorganized the Student National Protection Corps that had been dissolved after 19 April in order to implement military education. In the early-1970s the regime proclaimed a national emergency at the time of the north-south Red Cross talks in order to deal with the movement for academic democratization and strengthened its security education system. Its educational guidelines set forth the following directions for education:

'We will strengthen security system education in all areas of school training so that all teachers and students will apply themselves to their studies diligently with a new awareness and determination regarding the national emergency situation and we will fulfil our role as leaders to establish a new value system for the completion of the historic tasks of overcoming the national emergency and achieving the revival of the nation.'

The 1 February 1962 'special temporary law on education' promulgated after the 16 May military coup incorporated the autonomous education system into the regular administrative system, thus bringing it to a temporary end until it was revived two years later. The revived system, however, was not implemented at the city and county level but only at the provincial level where the educational committee, which included the governor, were all appointees. The superintendents of education were appointed through the committees' recommendations. In short, the 'autonomous education system' had very little autonomy.

One major change under the Park regime was the restructuring of entrance examinations at each level of the educational system. Middle school entrance examinations were changed from the system where each school had its own examination to a state-administered examination system and then in 1971 to a residential area school group system by which admissions were determined by a lottery instead of examinations. This change promised to do away with the excessive competition for middle school admissions and the abuses of such extra-curricular education as private tutoring and examination preparation academies. On the other hand, there were concerns about the differences in school facilities and student preparation between more affluent and less affluent neighborhoods leading to general decline in the quality of education.

In the case of high schools, the regime implemented a programme of consolidated preliminary examinations followed by a lottery system. This was implemented first in Seoul and Pusan, where the competition for admission to the best high schools was most severe and later expanded to some provincial cities. But the lack of appropriate policies to deal with differences in school facilities and students' abilities and differences in the quality of teaching meant that this effort to standardize high school education could not be implemented throughout the whole country.

With regard to colleges and universities, in 1961 the Park regime implemented a 'special law for bachelor's degree qualifying examinations', but it ended after two years. It then implemented in 1969 a preliminary examination system that limited the number of passers to double the number of students to be admitted according to the quota system and required that scores in the preliminary examinations be reflected in part in the final scores each college or university calculated on its final entrance examinations. The preliminary examination system was intended to deal with excessive competition for university admissions and to keep universities from admitting students beyond their assigned quotas, but at the same time it also reduced universities' autonomy in selecting their students.

The Park Chung Hee regime's educational policy was primarily focused on the strengthening of national autonomy education and security education and emphasized Korean history, ethics, anti-Communism and military training. Student movements in opposition to the regularization of south Korean-Japanese relations in 1965, to electoral irregularities in 1967, to the amendment of the constitution in 1969, the strengthening of military training in 1971 and the establishment of the Yushin system in 1972 resulted in repeated instances of classes being cancelled, of schools being temporarily closed, and of early winter and summer vacations.

Under the Yushin system, great emphasis was put on Yushin education, New Village education, and Confucian loyalty/filial piety education as the state sought unilaterally to force its ideology on the students. It was under such conditions that Professors Sŏng Naehun (1926–90) and Song Kisuk and twelve professors of South Chŏlla National University published 'our educational indices' that criticized the National Charter of Education, which can be seen as the foundation of Yushin education, challenged the Yushin educational system, and called for 'true democratic education and true human education. All were dismissed from their positions and jailed.

EDUCATIONAL POLICIES OF THE CHUN AND ROH REGIMES AND THE NATIONAL TEACHERS' UNION

The educational policy implemented during the Chun Doo Hwan regime and the early years of the Roh Tae Woo regime can be broken down into two periods before and after the establishment of the 'educational reform council' on 7 March 1985. During these two periods, the fundamental basis and goal of educational policy was the 'strengthening of citizen spirit education', but differences can be drawn between the two periods in terms of educational plans and measures. The educational policy of the first period was determined by the 1980 '30 July educational measures' taken by the committee for the establishment of legislation to protect the state. On the other hand, the educational policy of the second period, unlike that of the first five years of the Chun regime, focused on producing a national consciousness and labour force capable of dealing with rapidly changing economic conditions.

The Chun Doo Hwan regime, which came to power through the 12 December incident, the 17 May expansion of martial law, the suppression of the Kwangju *minjung* resistance and the establishment of the State Protection Emergency Measures Committee, faced two difficult problems. One was overcoming its lack of legitimacy and the other was overcoming the severe economic downturn of the late-1970s and early-1980s. Thus all policies focused on creating legitimacy for the regime. In educational policy, this took the form of Chun's citizen spirit education.

Citizen spirit education was declared to be 'education for forming and putting into practice the basic value system required in the lives of the citizens for the maintenance and prosperity of the national and state community'. It was systematized as a concept that included education for reunification and security, economic education, New Village Movement education, and social purification education and was implemented not only in schools but throughout society at large.

Economic education had the goals of easing the people's concerns over the economic inequality that had arisen during the rapid economic development of the 1960s and 1970s and of developing the consciousness necessary to deal with rapidly changing economic conditions. Another purpose was to develop a systematic ideological critique of the workers' movement to gain their fair share.

Although citizen spirit education was supposed to be done on the basis of the voluntary participation of the people, in fact it was carried out with the strong backing of the government and was slanted toward promoting government policies. In the case of education in schools, Minister of Education Yi Kyuho oversaw the strengthening of ideological critique education by making 'citizens' ethics' a required course at all four-year colleges and universities. At the same time, a 'nine item citizen spirit education' programme was implemented in all elementary, middle and high schools in an intensive effort to implant the regime's values in students' minds.

The content of the '30 July educational measures' can be summarized as revisions of the college entrance examination system and the so-called measures to normalize education. The revisions of the entrance examination system included abolishing the final examinations held by each university and requiring that consideration be given to high school work, and replacing the entrance quota system with a graduation quota system. The abolition of university-based examinations meant that students were to be selected on the basis of their scores in the national standard college entrance qualifying examination and their high school work. This was done in hopes of reducing excessive private tutoring and of standardizing high school education which had increasingly focused on preparing students for college entrance examinations. The graduation quota system that was enforced beginning in 1981 was evaluated by the Ministry of Education as a measure to foster an atmosphere of diligent study and to cope with the chronic unrest on college campuses. It was also seen, however, as an attempt by the government to establish control over the college admissions process and ran into strong opposition.

At that time, 15% of south Korea's total 9,800,000 elementary, middle and high school students were getting extra-curricular private tutoring and 26% of liberal arts high schools were being tutored privately in preparation for college entrance examinations. The total amount spent annually by parents on private tutoring was 327,500,000,000 *wŏn*, an amount that was equal to 30% of the entire budget of the Ministry of Education. The so-called measures to standardize education included a harsh prohibition of extra-curricular classes at private academies and private tutoring along with a reduction in the number of courses students were required to take in the schools. The prohibition of private tutoring was a measure that sought to win the support of the people for the regime by injecting state power to force the standardization of an extraordinarily abnormal educational situation. Without rectifying the root causes, however, such as the differences in pay according to levels of education and the monopolistic economic structure, these measures constituted nothing but a superficial reform that could not hope to resolve the educational irregularities that were part of the social pathology of south Korea.

The measures to revise the curriculum were introduced with the goal of promoting 'whole person education' but in the end they only resulted in changing the location of extra-curricular classes from private academies to after-hours supplementary courses at schools and to the so-called 'television extra-curricular courses' on educational television. The measures were criticized at the time as constituting strong government intervention in school curricula.

At the heart of the Chun regime's educational policy of the early-1980s was an attempt to broaden the regime's base of support among the people by relieving to some degree the accumulated social and economic equalities through theoretically egalitarian educational reforms. However, the regime soon immediately found itself forced to abandon the graduation quota system and unable to enforce the prohibition of extra-curricular private lessons because of dwindling support from the people. This meant that the regime had no choice but to search for a new direction in its educational policies.

The rapidly changing world situation in the late-1980s produced an educational reform movement along with demands from the economic sector to find solutions for south Korea's weakening international competitiveness. On top of that, there was a great deal of discontent with and mistrust of government policies among the people and rising demands for educational reform among teachers, led largely by the National Teachers' Labour Union. The educational policy of the early-1980s was focused primarily on the attainment of urgent political goals; while political goals remained important in the late-1980s, demands from the economic sector forced the regime to move in the direction of establishing concrete policies that embodied those demands.

The pursuit of diversity and excellence in education became the main thrust of educational policy in the late-1980s. In particular, the pursuit of excellence in education was a reflection of the shift from labour-intensive industries of the 1960s and 1970s to advanced technological industries that required highly trained personnel. This effort first got underway in the early-1980s with the October 1982 plan to develop science and technology that provided assistance for basic science education, established science high schools and implemented a programme of special training for gifted students. On the other hand, the pursuit of diversification and excellence meant the weakening of the government's uniform management of education and the introduction of discriminatory educational policies that went against the principle of equal access to education.

In addition, the 1980s saw the 5 December 1981 creation of an education tax, the passage of such legislative measures as the law to promote the education of preschool children and the law for social education both passed on 31 December 1982, as well as the creation of open universities and schools operated by industrial firms. Amidst all this, however, one particularly noteworthy thing was the 29 May 1989 formation of the National Teachers' Labour Union by teachers demanding 'true education'.

Strong control by the Chun regime which had come to power by suppressing the Kwangju *minjung* protest led to a period of relative quiet in the democratization movement during the early-1980s, and the educational sector was no exception. In the late-1980s, however, fervour for democratization began to rise again. This was reflected in the educational sector by the publication in 1985 of the magazine *Minjung kyoyuk* (*Minjung* education) by a group of committed teachers. Although Kim Chin'gyŏng and the other teachers who led the publication of this magazine were arrested and dismissed from their teaching posts, after the 10 June democratization movement the National Association of Teachers for the Promotion of Democratic Education was formed and led the struggle for the reform of bad education laws. This association carried out a petition movement for the reform of education law and held a 20 November 1988 national teachers' assembly in Yŏŭido Square attended by over 13,000 teachers. On 19 February 1989, a meeting of association representatives adopted a resolution to form a teachers' labour union to press for guarantees of the three rights of labour.

They overcame government suppression to form on 29 May 1989 the National Teachers' Labour Union, the first of its kind since the teachers' labour unions had been disbanded at the time of the 16 May 1961 military *coup*. The National Teachers' Labour Union immediately opened up fifteen city and provincial offices and over 600 local branches with more than 20,000 union members.

The National Teachers' Labour Union's programme called for the following four things: first, the establishment of autonomy and professionalism in education and the implementation of democratic education; second, improvement of educational conditions and improvement in the social and economic position of teachers; third, the realization of national, democratic and human education to enable students to live autonomous lives as democratic citizens; and fourth, solidarity with other teachers' organizations and other organizations that love freedom, peace and democracy. The Roh regime, however, arrested 60 union members and forced over 1,500 union members from their jobs, including 1,074 who were dismissed, 383 who were removed from the classroom and 13 who were suspended. Even after the rise of the civilian government under Kim Young Sam, the National Teachers' Labour Union has not been legalized and the teachers have not yet been restored to their positions.

REFERENCES

Han'guk kyoyuk simnyŏnsa kanhaenghoe, *Han'guk kyoyuk simnyŏnsa* (History of ten years of education in the Republic of Korea), P'ungmunsa, 1960.

O Ch'ŏnsŏk, *Han'guk sin kyoyuksa* (New history of education in Korea), Hyŏndae kyoyuk ch'ongsŏ ch'ulp'ansa, 1964.

Kuksa p'yŏnch'an wiwŏnhoe, *Charyo taeha min'guk sa* (Materials on the history of the Republic of Korea), 1970.

Tonga ilbosa, *Kaehang 100nyŏn yŏnp'yo/charyo chip* (Chronology and materials for 100 years of open ports), Seoul, 1976.

Han'guk kyoyuk kaebarwŏn, *Han'guk kyoyuk chŏngch'aek ŭi inyŏm* (Principles of Korean educational policies), 1987.

Han'guk kyoyuk yŏn'guso, *Han'guk kyoyuk ŭi sŏnggyŏk kwa kyojigwŏn nojo undong* (The nature of Korean education and the teachers' labour union movement), P'urŭn namu, 1990.

SECTION TWO
The Labour Movement under the Division System

THE US MILITARY GOVERNMENT LABOUR POLICY AND THE LABOUR MOVEMENT

The Korean Peninsula that emerged from under harsh Japanese colonial rule was faced with serious social and economic problems, including a contraction in production, inflation, a decline in workers' real wages and an increase in unemployment. Industrial productivity of south Korea alone had been at 527,935,000 *wŏn* in 1939 but declined to 152,192,000 in 1946, a decrease of 71.2%. At the time of liberation, southern Korea had only fertilizer and cement plants and a few military production facilities in the machinery sector, along with a few large-scale cotton and wool spinning and weaving plants. All production oriented towards Japan came to half and those factories reverted to US military government management under which they were largely neglected.

In the midst of this contraction in production, prices climbed rapidly. Using August 1945 as a base index of 100 *wŏn*, prices in 1947 rose to 2,295; if we use 1936 as the base, prices rose to 40,203. Factors behind this severe inflation included relaxation of wartime controls after Japan's defeat, a consequent surge in speculative activity, the Government-General's excessive release of Bank of Chosen notes and its release of foodstuff collection funds at the time of Japan's surrender, the US military government's excessive issuance of currency, the temporary cessation of productive activity and population growth due to the arrival in south Korea of people fleeing the north and people returning from overseas.

At the same time, the contraction in production and the increase in population caused a rise in unemployment. As seen in Table 1, the number of industrial firms decreased from 10,065 to 4,500 between 1943 and March 1947 while the number of employed workers also shrank from 255,398 to 139,979 during the same period. The unemployment rate was made even worse by the influx of people from north Korea and overseas.

The total number of unemployed in south Korea as of November 1946 was calculated at 1,112,000 persons. Of those, 57.8% were unemployed due to war damage and 42.2% due to plants being shut down or operations curtailed. Inflation and unemployment naturally resulted in a reduction in workers' real wages. Table 2, using 1936 as a base index of 100, shows that wholesale prices climbed to 58,305 by 1947 while workers' real wages declined to 29.3 in the same period.

The labour policies put forth by the various political parties in the national liberation movement front of the colonial period contained various provisions for the protection of workers. The Korean

Table 1: Industrial firms (five or more employees) and workers in south Korea

Industry type	Number of firms			Number of workers		
	1943	1947	% Decline	1943	1947	% Decline
Metals	426	262	36.9	12,578	6,118	51.4
Machines	944	874	7.4	27,331	20,510	25.0
Chemicals	681	582	14.5	22,869	21,457	6.2
Gas, Electricity, Water	70	32	52.8	2,864	1,927	32.7
Ceramics, Pottery	1,172	700	40.3	20,616	10,686	48.2
Weaving	1,683	537	68.1	61,210	37,353	39.0
Lumber, Wood Products	1,359	542	60.1	14,598	11,315	22.5
Food Processing	1,704	643	62.3	19,854	12,506	37.0
Printing	420	143	65.9	7,370	2,655	63.7
Construction	997	90	91.0	53,680	6,297	88.3
Other	619	95	84.6	12,423	3,155	74.6
Totals:	10,065	4,500	55.3	255,393	133,979	47.5

Source: Kim Nakchung, *Han'guk nodong undongsa–haebang hu p'yŏn* p. 52.

Table 2: Trends in real wages after liberation

Month and Year	Wholesale prices	Nominal wages	Real wages
1937	116.61	120.12	103.0
1940	180.01	145.72	80.9
1943	215.09	199.80	92.8
1944	241.12	224.51	93.1
Dec. 1945	4,359.20	2,724.50	62.5
July 1946	12,806.60	6,996.40	54.6
Jan. 1947	29,261.00	11,450.90	39.1
July 1947	38,797.30	15,666.10	40.3
Dec. 1947	58,305.20	17,088.30	29.3

Source: Kim Nakchung, *Han'guk nodong undongsa–haebang hu p'yŏn* p. 52.

Independence Party called for the 'establishment of factory and labour protection laws to ensure the improvements of workers' lives', while the Korean National Revolution Party declared it would 'guarantee the freedom of labour movements'. The Interim Government's programme called for the 'prohibition of night work by older workers, child workers, and female workers and of work that was inappropriate for the ages of the workers, or work that was done in inappropriate places and times'. The Interim Government also suggested the establishment of labour protection laws, an eight-hour work day, freedom for labour movements, and protection of old, young and female workers.

Given the contraction in production, the inflation, the decline in real wages and the increase in unemployment following liberation in August 1945, it is not certain what kind of labour policies could have been implemented by a government made up of national liberation movement forces, but the US military government's labour policy was manifested in such measures as the 30 October 1945 'regulations on the control of excess profits', the 12 December 'labour regulation committee law', the 23 July 1946 'law regarding public policy on the labour problem and establishment of a Ministry of Labour', an 18 September 1945 'child labour law', and an 11 November 1946 'law on maximum working hours'.

The 'regulations on the control of excess profits' was a measure to protect labour rights and to prevent excess profits on daily necessities. A central labour committee and provincial labour committees were established in each province on 12 December 1948 in order to carry out this measure. The central committee was made up of five Koreans and seven Americans and was charged with handling labour disputes involving two or more provinces, while the provincial committees were responsible for disputes within their own provinces. The frequency of labour disputes led the US military government to upgrade the labour section of the mining and industry bureau to the status of a labour bureau.

The US military government sought to regulate the working hours, working conditions, health and sanitation, recreational facilities and minimum wages of child workers through its 'child labour law', but the law had little effect on improving the working conditions of the estimated 800,000 child workers in south Korea. Later, on 8 April 1947, it was amended by a 'juvenile labour protection law' passed by the interim legislature. This law prohibited children from doing dangerous jobs or overly heavy work and prescribed punishment for the employers and parents of children under 12 years of age. In reality, however, this was a law in name only and had little practical effect.

The 'law on maximum working hours' set standard working hours at 48 hours per week with a maximum limit of 60 hours. It provided for time-and-a-half overtime pay for hours exceeding 48 and established penalties for violators. An investigation by the US military government during November and December 1947 found no fewer than 157 violations, but the business owners were not punished. Those 157 cases were only a small fraction of actual violations.

The active labour movement of the 1920s contracted under strong Japanese suppression in the 1930s, but after liberation in 1945 the lifting of restrictions on political activity and the US military government's abolition of the peace preservation law, the political criminal punishment law and the preliminary detention law on 9 October 1945, along with inflation, the decrease in real wages and rising unemployment brought the labour movement back to life. By November 1945, over 1,000 labour unions are estimated to have been formed throughout the country.

The first nation-wide labour union federation was the left-wing National Council of Korean Labour Unions. The National Council was formed on 5 November 1945 as a federation of 1,194 labour unions, including 13 industry unions in mining and other sectors and had a total of over 500,000 members. The National Council declared that it would 'participate actively in the formation of a national unification front government that is based in progressive democracy and excludes national traitors and pro-Japanese collaborators'. It set forth a 'practical programme' that called for 'co-operating with conscientious national capitalists to construct industry and overcome shortage panics and pernicious inflation'. The National Council also presented a 19-point 'programme for general action' that included such things as the establishment of a minimum wage system, an eight-hour work day, one day off per week, one month's paid annual vacation, the prohibition of child workers under age fourteen, and paid leave of two months before and after giving birth for women workers.

In the declaration issued at its formation meeting, the National Council stated that 'we must also fight against the tendency toward leftist infantilism that is divorced from the masses, ignores the struggle for the daily interests of the workers and attempts to lead them only to the political struggle, and we must emphasize that at the current stage there is strong tendency toward extreme leftist sectarianism'. The National Council thus made it clear that it rejected extreme leftism and the main goal of its movement was not to become a political movement but pursue the economic interests of the workers.

The right-wing labour movement, which had lost the industrial unions to the National Council, got its start through the anti-Communist youth movement. The National Youth League for the Promotion of Korean Independence, formed as a federation of the Buddhist Youth Association, the Protestant Youth Association, and the National Party's Youth Division on 21 November 1945, established a labour department and began to organize unions in some factories. During the struggle against trusteeship, it was decided that an independent labour union was necessary, leading eventually to the formation of the Association of Korean Labour Unions for the Promotion of Independence on 10 March 1946. The Association, which set forth a programme calling for the 'establishment of state based on the principles of democracy and new nationalism', for 'friendship between management and labour that regrets neither blood nor sweat', and the 'unification of the national labour front', was at its inception formed out of an anti-Communist youth group and not of workers or workers' organizations, and it had very few workers under its umbrella. But with the strong backing of right-wing political organizations, it infiltrated labour unions belonging to the National Council of Korean Labour Unions and set up Association chapters opposed to the National Council.

The labour organizations of the US military government period, which were split between the National Council and the Association, held

separate May Day celebrations in 1946. The rift between the two continued to grow until the National Council was eventually outlawed,
leaving the Association of Korean Labour Unions for the Promotion of
Independence as the main labour movement organization.

The first nation-wide general strike led by the National Council was
the 13 September 1946 'September general strike' carried out by the
Korean Railroad Labour Union, which demanded the provision of
lunchtime meals, the replacement of the daily wage system with a
monthly salary system and the provision of food rations. Once the US
military government rejected these demands, railroad workers throughout the whole country went on strike. The US military government
mobilized the police, right-wing youth organizations and the Korean
National Labour Union Association for the Promotion of Independence
to take over the strike headquarters and arrest over 1,200 striking
workers. The Association then issued the exact same demands, which the
US military government accepted, thus bringing the strike to an end. The
September general strike marked the beginning of successive strikes led
by the National Council. In response to the bloody suppression of the
October *minjung* uprising of 1 October 1946 in which workers, students
and ordinary citizens joined forces to attack police offices and which
then spread to surrounding areas in North Kyŏngsang Province, Chŏlla
Province and Kangwŏn Provinces, in March of the following year the
National Council issued demands for the punishment of police officials,
the democratization of the police force, the prevention of terror, the prevention of unemployment, the freeing of imprisoned left-wing persons
and guarantees of livelihood. The National Council then went into a
nation-wide strike that resulted in the arrest of 2,000 workers by the end
of the month.

When the US took the Korean question to the United Nations in
August 1947, it outlawed the National Council and arrested large
numbers of persons belonging to left-wing socialist organizations.
Nonetheless, there was yet another general strike on 7 February 1948
in opposition to the coming to Korea of the United Nations Temporary
Commission on Korea. According to police reports, there were '70
instances of rioting, 103 demonstrations, 204 instances of arson, 50
strikes and 34 cases of boycotting classes'.

Although the National Council of Korean Labour Unions declared at
its inception that it rejected political struggle and extreme leftist
methods, it supported the Korean People's Republic set up by the
Committee for the Preparation of Korean Independence, it supported the
movement in favour of trusteeship, and once the 'September general
strike' made clear the hostile nature of its relations with the US military government, it turned into a political movement. On the other
hand, the Association of Korean Labour Unions for the Promotion of
Independence made its anti-Communist, anti-trusteeship political line
clear from the very beginning. Neither side limited itself just to the
labour movement.

THE SYNGMAN RHEE REGIME'S LABOUR POLICY AND THE LABOUR MOVEMENT

The constitution under which the Rhee regime took power specified in its seventeenth article that 'all the citizens have the rights and duties of labour', and 'female and child labour receive special protections'. The eighteenth article stated: 'The freedom of workers to associate and to engage in collective bargaining and collective actions are guaranteed within the limits of the law. Workers in for-profit enterprises have the right to participate in the sharing of profits as determined by law.'

The passage of labour relations laws as prescribed by these articles of the constitution was delayed by the Korean War until 1953 when a labour union law with the goals of 'guaranteeing the rights of labour to free association and to collective bargaining and collective action and maintaining the working conditions of workers so as to enhance their social and economic position and contribute to the development of the national economy', and a labour dispute resolution law with the goals of 'guaranteeing the free rights of workers to collective action and the maintenance of industrial peace through the fair resolution of labour disputes', were enacted. To these were added a labour council law 'for the development of the national economy and the democratization of labour administration' and a labour standards law for 'guaranteeing the basic livelihood of workers and promoting the balanced development of the national economy by establishing standards for working conditions'. Thus four basic labour relations laws were finally enacted.

The Association of Korean Labour Unions for the Promotion of Independence participated actively in the 10 May 1948 elections for the establishment of a separate government in the south and made major contributions to the founding of the government of the Republic of Korea. After the government took office, it changed its name to the Association of Korean Labour Unions. Before long, however, the Association found itself in confrontation with Syngman Rhee over the issue of labour unions for government employees. The Railroad League of the Association fought against the state employee law that prohibited government employees from forming labour unions and maintained itself as a union. The workers at the government-owned Korean Electric Corporation also overcame government and management interference to form a labour union. At the time of the 1952 'Pusan political disturbance', Syngman Rhee drove those who opposed him out of the Korean National Labour Union Association and turned it over to forces that supported his re-election, in effect making the Association an extension of Rhee's Liberal Party and turning it into a political tool. The consequence was the transformation of the Association into a space for ugly factional struggles and competition to demonstrate loyalty to the regime.

The seventh national representatives' congress of the Association held in 1954 adopted a resolution that contained a provision declaring 'absolute support for the foreign policy of his excellency President

Syngman Rhee'. When Syngman Rhee, who had forced through a revision of the constitution allowing him to run for a third term, leaked a story that he might not run for president, the Federation mobilized carts drawn by horses and bulls for street parades expressing its 'ardent wish' that he run again for the presidency.

On the other hand, a group of labour union leaders critical of the corruption and factional struggles of the government stooges at the top of the Federation began a movement to create a separate national labour union federation. Eventually, 32 representatives of 24 of the country's 37 labour union alliances gathered to form a 'committee to prepare for the establishment of a Korean Confederation of Trade Unions' on 11 August 1959. These representatives set forth a programme calling for three things: one, 'struggling to protect workers rights and interests and to promote their welfare through a free and democratic labour movement', two, 'contributing to the development of a healthy national economy and the construction of an egalitarian society with equality between labour and capital through a democratic labour movement', and three, 'contributing to the establishment of national sovereignty and world peace aligning with the world labour movement through democratic labour'. It was able to overcome persistent efforts at disruption by the Korean National Labour Union Association to convene a secret meeting of 21 representatives from 14 labour alliances to form a new confederation and begin activities when the 19 April revolution opened up new possibilities for the labour movement.

There were numerous labour disputes after the establishment of the Syngman Rhee regime, including the struggle of the Railroad League of the Korean National Labour Union Association to maintain itself as a labour union and the movement for the formation of a labour union at the Korean Electric Corporation. There were also large-scale labour movements during the Korean War, such as the labour dispute at the Pusan Chosŏn Spinning and Weaving Company and the strike by dock workers in Pusan. The 1951 strike at the Pusan Chosŏn Spinning and Weaving Company, which was formerly a Japanese-owned firm, demanded the dismissal of the president that had been forced on the company by the government, guarantees of a free labour movement and protection of workers' human rights. The labour dispute continued for about three months, during which time there were such actions as one in which over 1,000 female workers demonstrated in front of the wartime National Assembly building in Pusan. In the end, however, a combination of the Rhee regime's merciless suppression and the passive stance of the Korean National Labour Union Association led to about 1,000 workers being dismissed and another 500 quitting, bringing the dispute to an end.

The wartime dock workers strike in Pusan began with a demand by the Freedom League, which was the Federation's alliance of nation-wide dock workers' labour unions, for a 280% increase in wages. Large numbers of the refugees who had flowed into Pusan looked for work at the docks unloading military supplies. The monthly income of these day labourers was less than 12,000 *wŏn* per month, barely more than the 11,500 *wŏn* needed to buy one *mal* (20 litres) of rice. They went on strike on 17 July 1952 after the US military ignored their demand for higher wages. Caught off guard, the US military raised the wages of day labourers 200% and those of contractor workers 100%, bringing the strike to an end.

Even though some degree of recovery from wartime destruction was attained during the post-war years, life continued to be hard for workers. A 1957 Ministry of Health and Social Affairs investigation of 37,909 workers at 101 businesses throughout the country, revealed that their average monthly income was 20,153 *hwan* while the average amount needed for minimal monthly living expenses was 40,509 *hwan*. Even after adding in other miscellaneous sources of income, the average worker's total monthly income was still 13,178 *hwan*, or 32.5%, in the red.

Low pay and bad working conditions led to continuing strike actions during the immediate post-war years. The second half of 1954 alone saw several major strikes, including the December strike by over 7,000 workers at the state-owned Taehan Coal Corporation demanding the payment of wages that had been delayed during the war, the August strike by 12,000 employees of US military bases in Pusan demanding a pay increase and the application of Korea's labour standards law, the August strike by 17,000 workers working at the docks unloading imported fertilizer demanding higher wages, and a September automobile workers strike in Seoul that succeeded in its demands for an eight-hour work day and the conclusion of a collective bargaining agreement.

Disputes and strikes also arose continuously during the second half of the 1950s when the Rhee regime was strengthening it dictatorship. Some of the larger ones from 1956 included the dispute by the workers of Taehan Spinning and Weaving in Taegu in protest of unfair firings and demanding a collective bargaining agreement, the dispute by the Coal and Mining Workers Union Alliance that succeeded in its demand for higher wages, and the dispute by Samch'ŏk Cement workers whose demonstrations succeeded in getting the payment of back wages. The following years saw continuing labour disputes, such as the 1958 dispute by 4,000 workers at the Namsŏn Electric Company for the payment of compensation, the 1958 dispute by over 6,000 workers at the Taehan Shipbuilding Company for the payment of back wages, the 1959 dispute by 36,500 members of the National Alliance of Textile Workers' Unions for a reduction in work hours, the 1959 dispute by over 5,000 dock workers in Pusan demanding a raise in pay, and the 1959 dispute against the state-owned Taehan Coal Corporation demanding higher wages by 8,700 workers of the Coal and Mining Workers Union Alliance.

Despite the transformation of the Korean National Labour Union Association into a stooge for the government, workers in its affiliated organizations carried out continuous disputes and strikes. There were some successes, but there were also many cases of failure, such as when the Taehan Spinning and Weaving Company ignored a resolution by the National Assembly and brought in the police to break up the strike.

The year 1959 – the year just before the overthrow of the Rhee regime – saw the largest number of labour disputes with the largest number of participants since the government was first established in 1948. This was one factor behind the downfall of the dictatorial regime.

THE '19 APRIL SPACE' AND THE LABOUR MOVEMENT

Although there were frequent labour disputes and strikes during the final years of the Rhee regime, they were not enough by themselves to bring down the regime. Nonetheless, as soon as the Rhee regime fell, there was a strong struggle by workers against the Korean National Labour Union Association, which had played an important role in the election irregularities. The result was a change in the executive board of the Association and some degree of democratization of labour unions.

The movement for the democratization of labour unions began in the Pusan Dock Workers Union, then spread throughout the entire country's labour unions, including the Inch'ŏn Free Workers Union, the Railroad Workers Union, the Seoul Electric Company Union and the Textile Workers Union. The workers held demonstrations to force union leaders to resign, chose new leaders and made some progress in the democratization of their unions. This movement did not result in the reorganization of all labour unions but nonetheless brought a rapid enhancement of workers' democratic consciousness.

The Korean National Labour Union Association, in order to maintain its existence, severed its connections with all political parties. It also called on 23 April 1960 for the resignation of vice-president elect Yi Kibung and of all National Assembly members in an effort to support Syngman Rhee. The Confederation of Korean Trade Unions, which had overcome government suppression to form itself near the end of the Rhee regime, issued a statement denouncing starvation wages and the failure to pay back wages. It also demanded the resignation of the leadership of the Korean National Labour Union Association, the resignation of all labour leaders who had collaborated with business owners, the democratic reorganization of labour unions, the cessation of police interference with the labour movement, and the resignation of government officials responsible for the administration of labour affairs.

The Korean Confederation of Trade Unions expanded its organization after 19 April, reorganizing and incorporating 170 union locals and adding 160,000 new members. On the other hand, a movement arose to consolidate the Korean National Labour Union Association and the Confederation of Korean Trade Unions. A gathering of representatives of these two organizations and 723 independent labour union representatives was held on 25 November 1960 to establish the Federation of Korean Labour Unions.

The Federation of Korean Labour Unions set forth a basic programme calling for struggle to protect workers' human rights and to enhance their social and economic position through a democratic labour movement, for the reconstruction of the industrial economy through a raising of productivity, for the construction of an egalitarian society with equality between management and labour, for the realization of complete state freedom though the establishment of civil rights, and for contribution to world peace through links with international free labour movement organizations. It also set forth a 21-point action programme calling for an eight-hour working day, the establishment of collective bargaining rights, the establishment of the right to strike, the implementation of a minimum wage system, and for the implementation of social insurance and unemployment insurance. In addition, it pointed the way for a new direction in the labour movement by adopting a collective leadership operational committee system. The new Federation, however, was dissolved after the 16 May 1961 military *coup*.

The labour movement became suddenly very active after the 19 April revolution, inspired by the general atmosphere of social freedom and the growth of the workers' democratic consciousness. As seen in Table 3 below, the number of labour disputes grew from 45 in 1957 to 227 in 1960, the year that the Rhee regime was overthrown, while the number of participants grew from 9,394 to 64,335 in the same period.

Furthermore, the number of labour disputes rose to over 282 in the twelve months following 19 April, of which 19% were strikes. This contrasts with the average annual number of 41 disputes, of which 7% were strikes, for the years between 1953 and 1959, and indicates the extent to which the labour movement became active after 19 April.

Important labour disputes of the Chang Myŏn era included the January 1961 strike by the maritime workers union which demanded the immediate conclusion of collective bargaining, a 30% increase in wages, an increase in stipends for duty outside Korea and the payment of overtime wages as specified by law; and the strikes by female workers demanding wage increases and an eight-hour working day at such textile firms as Hŭnghan Spinning and Weaving (May 1960), Kyŏngsŏng Spinning and Weaving (September 1960) and Cheil Wool (June 1960).

One characteristic of the labour movement under the Chang regime was the strengthening of activity to organize government employees and intellectuals. The struggle to organize government employees focused on the unions at the Korean National Railroad Company, the Government Monopoly Office and the Bureau of Communications that had been forced to endure severe repression under the Rhee regime. In the case of the railroad union, the members went on strike demanding increases in basic pay and allowances for dangerous duty and travel, revisions in work hours, and the establishment of a separate pay system. The government agreed to all their demands except for the increase in basic pay. The union then resolved to carry out a staged strike beginning with a temporary communications stoppage, to be followed by the refusal to sell tickets, the suspension of fuel supplies to engines, the suspension of station signals and finally a full-blown strike. The strike came to an end when the government agreed to a 30% increase in basic pay.

Table 3: Trends in employment and labour disputes

Year	Employed		Unemployed		Labour disputes			
	Number	Index	Number	Index	Incidents	Index	Participants	Index
1957	8,076,000	100	277,000	100	45	100	9,394	100
1958	8,748,000	108	344,000	121	41	91	10,031	107
1959	8,768,000	109	347,000	125	95	211	49,813	530
1960	8,521,000	106	434,000	157	277	504	64,335	685

Source: Kim Nakchung, *Han'guk nodong undongsa–haebang hu p'yŏn*, p. 294.

The Government Monopoly Office workers engaged in a work slow-down that succeeded in their demands for pay raises, payment of technical stipends and awards to encourage productivity, and a revision of their collective bargaining agreement. The communications labour union also demanded pay raises, the payment of stipends as provided by law, the total implementation of legally established holidays and days off, and the total implementation of a vacation system. It decided to strike on the basis of a vote by the membership and succeeded in attaining its demands.

Developments worthy of note in the effort to organize intellectuals include both the previously discussed teachers' union movement and the formation and activities of bank labour unions. A number of banks fell under *chaebŏl* ownership as a result of their conversion to civilian management under the Rhee regime and those banks became the source of supply for the Rhee regime's political funds. This situation led to a labour union movement to protect the interests of bank employees and to democratize financial institutions.

The creation of a labour union at the Chohŭng Bank led to the formation of labour unions at other banks, including the Korea Industrial Bank, the Cheil Bank, the Hanil Bank and the Seoul Bank. These unions eventually came together to form a national federation of bank employee unions on 23 July 1960. The federation, which set forth a programme calling for the protection of bank employees' interests through the rejection of inappropriate outside interference, the normalization of the unhealthy situation of secretive competition and the normal development of the national economy through the democratization of finances, succeeding in attaining an agreement for collective bargaining.

A labour union was also formed at the Agriculture Bank, which had been established with funds from the peasants and from such agricultural organizations as the Peasant Union Co-operative, and demanded an increase in wages and the conclusion of a collective bargaining agreement. When the bank suppressed the union's leaders, the bank's branch offices in Pusan went on strike but many employees soon began to cross the picket lines. In the face of public opinion holding that it was not right for Agricultural Bank workers, whose income was much higher than the peasants they were supposed to serve, to go on strike for higher wages, union branches in South Kyŏngsang Province and Seoul announced their dissolution. This shows one aspect of the labour union movement among intellectual workers.

LABOUR POLICY IN THE YEARS OF ECONOMIC GROWTH AND THE LABOUR MOVEMENT

After the 16 May *coup*, the military regime announced as its fifth decree a 19 May 'special statement on the recovery of economic order' that prohibited all labour disputes. Furthermore, in its sixth degree of 23 May, the Supreme Council for National Reconstruction dissolved all political parties and social organizations. This meant the dissolution of labour organizations throughout the country, including the Federation of Korean Labour Unions and the arrest of many union leaders.

The Supreme Council for National Reconstruction promulgated its 'law on temporary measures to deal with the organized activities of labour' on 3 August 1981 permitting labour union activity. On the next day, it appointed a number of men to be responsible for organizing industry unions and launched a 'committee for the reconstruction of Korean labour organizations'. That committee then appointed organizational committees for the formation of labour unions in fifteen industries, and hastily convened a congress of labour unions from thirteen industries (it excluded dock worker and printing worker unions) to form the Federation of Korean Trade Unions on 29 August 1960.

The Federation of Korean Trade Unions set forth a programme promising to work for 'democratic national reunification by strengthening the anti-Communist system and establishing an autonomous economy', for 'protecting the basic rights of workers and raise their living standards through strong solidarity' and for 'the development of a democratic labour movement through political neutrality and financial self-sufficiency'. It also expressed its total support for the '16 May military revolution' and issued resolutions for the active introduction of foreign capital, for repeal of the order prohibiting labour disputes, and for the implementation of a minimum wage system and a social security system.

Members of the pre-16-May Federation of Korean Labour Unions stepped forth to challenge the establishment of the Federation of Korean Trade Unions on the grounds that 'the reconstruction of labour unions must be done on a democratic and self-regulating basis'. Once political activity was allowed in 1963, old Federation of Korean Labour Union elements proposed to file a suit seeking 'confirmation of the invalidity of the resolutions of the founding congress of the Federation of Korean Trade Unions', and gathered 300 representatives from labour unions of each industry, including railroads, mines and foreign organs, to hold a congress to prepare for a separate 'General Association of Korean Labour Unions' on 17 February 1963.

They then began full-scale organization activities at the grassroots level and confronted the Federation of Korean Trade Unions with such slogans as 'eradicate government sponsored trade unions' and 'establish the right to labour disputes'. But the military regime, which had announced its procedures for 'turning the government over to civilians', revised the labour union law to require labour unions to get government authorization and refused to recognize 'organizations that inhibited the regular operation of existing labour unions', thereby outlawing those unions affiliated with the General Association of Korean Labour Unions.

On the other hand, there was a movement to establish a workers' political party in anticipation of the transfer of power to civilian authority. It was clear that the Federation of Korean Trade Unions would not be able maintain political neutrality, leading some labour forces to conclude that it would be better to form a workers' political party in order to realize the protection of workers' rights through the National Assembly. Labour union chairs from eight industrial unions, including the mine workers' union, formed a committee for the establishment of the Democratic Workers' Party and issued a statement of intent, but interference from the government and the Federation of Korean Trade Unions prevented the launching of the party.

The economic development policies of the Park Chung Hee regime in the 1960s brought certain changes to the lives of workers. First, the rapid dissolution of the peasant stratum and the consequent increase in the number of persons who left the villages to seek work resulted in growth in the amount of low-wage labour available for the mining and industrial sectors. Whereas persons engaged in agricultural, forestry and fishing accounted for 63.1% of the workforce in 1963, by 1971 their share had shrunk to 48.4%, while the proportion of the workforce engaged in mining and manufacturing grew from 8.7% to 14.2% during the same period.

The people who abandoned the rural villages during the process of economic growth became a source of cheap labour for the manufacturing sector, resulting in an overall decline in the living standards of workers. The proportion of income accounted for by employed persons was 38.7% in 1959 but fell annually to a low of 28.8% in 1964 before finally barely climbing back up to the 1959 level by 1968.

Furthermore, as can be seen in Table 4 below, the average wage of workers in the manufacturing sector fell far short of urban household expenses. It was not even enough to cover food, much less housing, light and heat, clothing, and other sundry expenses. In addition, there was no improvement in working conditions. For example, average daily working hours for female workers in 1969 totaled 11.1 hours. Women working six hours constituted 13.7% of the total, women working eight hours 17.9%, women working ten hours 17.9%, women working 12 hours 29.9%, women working 13 hours 15.2% and women working seventeen hours 0.4%.

Industrial injuries and occupational diseases increased sharply, from 1,189 victims in 1964 to 38,872 in 1969. An August to December 1970 survey of 75 workplaces in the Yŏngdŭngp'o district of Seoul revealed that 78.7% of the workers surveyed were suffering from occupational diseases.

The increase in the overall number of workers also brought an increase in the number of organized workers. When workers once again started to organize following the military government's August 1963 promulgation of the law allowing organized labour activity, there were 96,831 members of 172 locals in 14 industrial unions. By the end of 1971, the number of organized workers had increased five-fold to 493,711 members of 437 locals in 17 industrial unions. Despite the rapid increase in union membership during the 1960s, it was still far below that of other countries. Furthermore the rate of increase dropped following the promulgation of the state protection law in 1972.

Table 4: Average monthly wages and urban household expenses
(in *wŏn*)

Year	Wages	Urban household expenses	Expenditures for foodstuffs
1961	2,610		
1962	2,780		
1963	3,180		
1964	3,880	8,620	5,130
1965	4,600	9,780	5,550
1966	5,420	13,560	6,580
1967	6,640	20,620	9,180
1968	8,400	23,190	9,840
1969	11,270	26,070	10,670
1970	14,150	29,950	12,120

Source: Han'guk nodong chohap ch'ong yŏnmaeng, *Han'guk nodong chohap undongsa*, p. 563.

Of an estimated 1970 total of 3,780,000 employed persons, only 496,000, or 12.4%, were organized. By contrast, 34.5% of Japanese workers, 48% of British workers and 35.4% of west German workers were organized in 1970, and 29.4% of US workers were organized as of 1967. One of the reasons for the low rate of organization in south Korea was that many workers were employed in difficult to organize small factories while large enterprises either prevented the formation of unions or engaged in actions to destroy them after they had been formed. There were also legal restrictions against organizing government employees and teachers.

Even under such difficult conditions, there were continuous labour disputes throughout the 1960s. Even during the first two years after the 16 May military *coup* when labour unions had been dissolved and labour disputes were prohibited, there were continuing protests, petitions and complaints seeking the formation of unions, pay increases and improvement of working conditions. In 1963, the year when martial law was lifted, there were 89 labour disputes involving 168,843 workers.

From 1963 until the time when a national emergency was declared and the state protection law put into effect in late-1971, there was an annual average of 103 labour disputes involving an average of 154,288 participants. There were large-scale disputes in the mid-1960s in the textile, metal and chemical industries that produced most of the country's exports. In the early-1970s there were active bottom-up movements among the base-level unorganized workers who had been excluded from the export-led growth policy. An important example was the self-immolation Chŏn T'aeil, a sewing worker at the Ch'ŏnggye market in Seoul.

As shown in Table 5 below, demands for pay increases constituted the lion's share of labour dispute demands at 67.3%. This was followed by demands for workers' rights, such as the forming of unions and collective bargaining rights. This reflects the reality of the low wages paid to workers during the years of fast economic growth and also tells of enterprise opposition to the formation of labour unions and enterprise attempts to make unions management puppets.

LABOUR POLICY AND THE LABOUR MOVEMENT UNDER THE YUSHIN SYSTEM

In response to growing labour resistance, the Park Chung Hee regime declared its 1971 emergency situation and promulgated a 'law for special measures for the protection of the state' (state protection law) that greatly restricted the collective bargaining rights and collective action rights that were guaranteed by the constitution. Labour unions no longer had the right to implement labour disputes on their own and had to have all disputes and negotiations mediated by relevant government officials.

Suppression of all social movements, including the labour movement was intensified under the Yushin system. Nonetheless, workers' resistance and the labour movement continued to develop even under such harsh suppression. The forces that led the labour movement in the 1970s were not the existing labour organizations but new 'democratic labour unions'. Some representative examples include the Ch'ŏnggye Clothing Workers' Union, the Tongil Textile Workers' Union, the Wŏnp'ung Wool Union, the Control Data Union, the Pando Company Union, and the YH Union. These unions carried out continuous efforts to improve working conditions even in the face of the regime's suppression. They implemented democratic principles in their internal organization and began to put roots down in the working place. The union executives gained support by being faithful to the wishes of the rank-and-file members and raised the consciousness of the workers through educational and team activities. Through team activities, the unions educated workers in the labour problem, strengthened their organizations and were able to carry out bold collective action for the improvement of working conditions even under the 'state protection law'.

The democratic labour unions carried out their collective actions through intensive preparations to realize their demands, improve working conditions and gain the trust of their members while on the other hand raising general social awareness of the labour problem. Typical examples of labour actions that heightened political and social concern over the labour problem included the Ch'ŏnggye Clothing Workers' Union struggle to establish itself and to get classrooms for its members, the Tongil Textile Workers' Union struggle to protect itself and to get dismissed members rehired and the occupying of the National Assembly building by members of the YH Union.

Table 5: Trends in numbers and demands of labour disputes

Year	Disputes	Participants	Major demands (as % of total)					
			Wage hikes	Allowances	Opposition to dismissal	Working hours	Workers' rights	Other
1963	89	168,843	58.4	7.9	3.4	1.1	22.5	–
1964	126	207,406	73.3	6.7	4.8	0.9	12.4	–
1965	113	103,707	61.9	7.2	8.2	2.1	14.4	–
1966	117	145,168	69.2	9.6	0.9	3.8	13.5	3.0
1967	105	150,535	80.0	3.9	–	0.9	14.3	0.9
1968	112	265,941	54.3	5.3	6.2	–	22.3	1.9
1969	70	108,248	70.0	2.9	2.9	–	22.8	1.4
1970	88	182,808	70.0	–	2.5	–	25.0	2.5
1971	101	115,943	68.3	5.0	2.0	–	18.0	5.9

Source: Han'guk nodong chohap ch'ong yŏnmaeng, *Han'guk nodong chohap undongsa*, p. 567.

Chŏn T'aeil's self-immolation became the occasion for intellectuals and religious figures to begin actively participating in the labour movement. The Urban Industrial Mission Church and the Association of Catholic Working Youth were formed at the end of the 1950s for the purpose of proselytizing among workers, but both began to contribute seriously to the labour movement in the 1970s. The labour night school movement by intellectuals and students also expanded significantly in the second half of the 1970s and contributed greatly to enhancing the consciousness of workers.

The efforts of the Urban Industrial Mission Church and the Association of Catholic Working Youth to recruit workers for their classes on the labour problem, to support the improvement of working conditions and to bring the labour problem to the attention of the general public were particularly important. These organizations actively supported the formation, education and collective action of democratic labour unions and played a major role in the struggle for the implementation of an eight-hour working day. In the circumstances where the Federation of Korean Trade Unions and individual industrial unions had become supporters of the government, the Urban Industrial Mission Church and the Association of Catholic Working Youth were virtually the only places where individual company unions and branches could find real support.

The activation of the democratic labour union movement brought continuous growth in the overall labour movement. As seen in Table 6, the total number of labour union members grew from 497,000 in 1970 to over 1,000,000 by 1979 while the number of union locals grew from 3,063 to 4,394 during the same period. Although the number of disputes did not grow much beyond 100, it is enough to tell us that even under the state security law that made it impossible to carry out legal disputes, workers' resistance was never extinguished.

Table 6. Trends in numbers of labour unions, membership and disputes

Year	Number of unions	Number of members	Number of disputes
1971	3,061	497,000	101
1972	2,961	515,000	0
1973	2,865	548,000	0
1974	3,352	656,000	0
1975	3,585	750,000	133
1976	3,854	846,000	110
1977	4,042	955,000	96
1978	4,305	1,055,000	102
1979	4,394	1,088,000	105

Source: Han'guk nodong yŏn'guwŏn, *Imgŭm kwallyŏn t'onggye charyo chip,* pp. 153–155.

After the assassination of Park Chung Hee on 26 October 1979 brought the fall of the Yushin regime and a relative relaxation of controls on the labour movement, there was an eruption of activity by workers, who had long been suffering from low wages and long working hours. Disputes arose at many companies and the number of disputes in 1980 increased to 407, four times that of the previous year. Particularly fierce strikes and demonstrations continued at large-scale enterprises. In April 1980 the workers at the Sabuk Coal Mine in Kangwŏn Province went on strike demanding pay raises and the withdrawal of the pro-company union. Residents in neighbouring areas joined in support of the strike and it developed into a large regional joint protest. The town of Sabuk itself was occupied by the workers for several days. In addition, workers at such large-scale manufacturing concerns as Inch'ŏn Iron, Tongguk Steel and Wŏnjin Rayon also engaged in aggressive strikes. The movement to demand the removal of pro-government and pro-business unions and the democratization of labour unions at the local, regional and even national (Federation of Korean Trade Unions) levels spread rapidly. Such activity was brought to halt, however, once the 'new military' of Chun Doo Hwan and the Army Security Command proclaimed the expansion of martial law on 17 May 1980.

THE LABOUR MOVEMENT UNDER THE CHUN DOO HWAN REGIME

The suppression of labour by the Chun Doo Hwan regime, which came to power through the 12 December incident, the expansion of martial law and the suppression of the Kwangju *minjung* resistance, was even more severe than that of Park Chung Hee. Right after expanding martial law, the Chun regime removed many labour leaders and dissolved many regional associations in the name of 'purification', a move that constituted a particularly harsh blow to the workers of small enterprises. In December 1980, the Chun regime carried out a major revision of labour laws that strengthened institutional limitations on the labour movement.

The main thrust of Chun's reform of the labour laws was to make all labour unions into single company unions. The conditions for establishing labour unions were strengthened to make it more difficult and closed union shops were made illegal. While strengthening the ability of government agencies to intervene in labour unions, the regime also added new provisions prohibiting the intervention of third parties in an effort to stop intellectuals from participating in the labour movement. Restrictions against disputes were also strengthened. Disputes were prohibited at government agencies, autonomous regional organizations, state-run enterprises and defence industry firms. The cooling off period for disputes was also extended. Binding arbitration was expanded from nonprofit organizations to general businesses, making it possible for the government to halt all disputes.

The Chun regime's suppression of the labour movement broke up the democratic labour unions that began growing in the late-1970s.

In January 1981, the regime ordered the dissolution of the Ch'ŏnggye Clothing Workers' Union and sent the police in to occupy its headquarters. The union's members occupied the office of the Asian and American Free Labour Institute (AAFLI) in protest, but they were dispersed by the police and eleven of their number was arrested. The regime subsequently also disbanded the Pando Company Union and the Control Data Union. The Wŏnp'ung Wool Union, which held out longest, was finally broken up by its own union members at government and management instigation in September 1982 and replaced by a pro-government and pro-management union.

The breakup of the democratic labour unions by the government made workers realize that the labour movement could not be separated from the political movement. Furthermore, after the suppression of the Kwangju *minjung* resistance, many intellectuals and students entered the labour force as workers, threw themselves into the labour movement and contributed greatly to raising workers' awareness of their rights.

Once the oppressive rule of the Chun regime began to ease somewhat in 1984, the labour movement once again became active. A taxi drivers' strike arose in Taegu and quickly spread to other cities throughout the country, including Pusan, Masan and Taejŏn. Furthermore, new democratic labour unions were formed at such companies as Dae Woo Apparel, Hyosŏng Products, Sŏnil Textiles and Karibong Electronics, picking up where the late-1970s democratic labour unions had left off. But the government refused to authorize these new style unions, making it difficult to attain a broad reconstruction of the democratic labour union movement.

Nonetheless, a number of legally authorized unions realized that the limitations of the 1970s democratic union movement lay in their focus on economic issues and their relative lack of interest in union solidarity. These unions then began to engage in elementary political education and efforts to achieve solidarity and strengthened their organizational power. A consequence of this was the activation of movements on site by workers themselves independent of direct guidance or instruction from union headquarters. There was a strike at Dae Woo Motors led by workers with college student backgrounds and there were collective actions for union democratization at Changsŏng Mining, Haet'ae Confections, T'ongil Industries and Hanil Stainless Steel.

This brought a re-intensification of suppression by the Chun regime, resulting in the June 1985 arrest of the leaders of the Dae Woo Apparel union, which was at the centre of the democratic labour union movement, on charges of violating the labour dispute law. Union members occupied the factory building in protest. The labour unions at Hyosŏng Products, Sŏnil Textiles, Karibong Electronics and the Puhŭng Company, along with unions at such Kuro Industrial Complex companies as Sejin Electronics, Romk'oria, Namsŏng Electrical and T'ongil Industries, entered into a solidarity strike in support of the Dae Woo Apparel union workers, but it was broken up by police and management. The arrest of over 30 union members and the firing of over 1,000 resulted in another dissolution of the democratic labour union movement. Nonetheless, this was important as the first attempt in a long time at a full-scale solidarity struggle.

In the mid-1980s semi-legal labour organizations were organized in addition to the regular labour unions and made contributions to the development of the labour movement. Such organizations as the Korean Workers Welfare Association (March 1984) and the Korean Christian Workers Alliance (February 1985) were created by former democratic labour union leaders. Unlike the Urban Industrial Mission Church of the 1970s, these organizations were led by the workers themselves – that is they were not simple support organizations but entities of the labour movement itself.

After the breakup of the solidarity strike at the Kuro Industrial Complex, strong arguments were made that the labour union must overcome unionism and transform itself into a social reform movement and illegal and secret labour movement organizations different from ordinary labour unions came into being. A representative example was the Seoul Labour Movement Alliance. The Seoul Labour Movement Alliance described itself as a mass political organization and established political agitation and political struggle for social reform to be its most important tasks. It also called for nonco-operative methods in economic struggles.

The formation of the Seoul Labour Movement Alliance sparked the creation of similar regional organizations, such as the Inch'ŏn Area Workers' League and the Anyang Area Committee for the Three Rights of Labour. These organizations supported the workers' struggle to improve working conditions while carrying out activities to enhance the workers' political consciousness. But these organizations' activities were largely limited to former college students and some workers with heightened consciousness and did not enjoy the broad participation of the working class. That was because these organizations over-emphasized the political struggle, did not pay proper heed to the resolution of the workers' urgent demands, and devoted themselves to leadership struggles divorced from the workers' needs. In addition they were criticized for not having clear political lines and gradually began to lose influence. Other ideas about the line that the labour movement should take were presented and other secret organizations were formed, but because of severe government suppression they were not able to penetrate into the workplaces.

THE 10 JUNE DEMOCRATIZATION MOVEMENT AND THE LABOUR MOVEMENT

After the 10 June democratization movement forced the Chun Doo Hwan regime to make its 29 June statement, there was an easing of political oppression and the long suppressed demands of the workers exploded. That led to the so-called 'July and August struggle' of 1987 which was the largest labour dispute since liberation in 1945. The July and August struggle began at the Hyundai complex in Ulsan. When labour unions were formed in the various Hyundai affiliates there, Hyundai Automobiles and Hyundai Heavy Industries, the two main affiliates, created pro-management unions in an attempt to block the formation of democratic labour unions, leading to a strike by workers.

The Hyundai strike quickly spread to other enterprises in the Ulsan area, then to other industrial areas in South Kyŏngsang Province such as Pusan, Masan and Ch'angwŏn, and before long throughout the whole country. There were over 400 disputes under way each day in mid-August and the number increased to nearly 500 after 20 August, reaching a peak of 743 on 27 August. The striking workers demanded various improvements in working conditions and struggled particularly hard for the formation of democratic labour unions. The strikes were not limited to manufacturing – mine workers and transportation workers also engaged in strikes and serious demonstrations.

Once the labour disputes began to spread, the Korean Employers Federation released a list of 34 instances of labour disputes that 'violated human morality' and this was given wide exposure in the media. The government then returned to its policy of oppression and sent the police into the sites of major disputes such as Hyundai Heavy Industries and Dae Woo Automobiles to detain and arrest large numbers of workers. This resulted in a cooling of disputes and there were no more large-scale disputes after 15 September. During the period of the July and August struggle, there was a total of 3,337 labour disputes. The fact that there were disputes at 75.5% of all big enterprises with over 1,000 employees shows that the workers' resistance was broadly based. Furthermore, this period saw the creation of a large number of democratic labour unions that formed the foundation for later labour movement development.

The labour movement began to develop in new directions during the July and August struggle. First, the movement was led by the working masses themselves. Unions were formed by workers at each workplace, were operated in a democratic way and sought to achieve their demands through collective action. This meant that the labour movement had now established itself as a major social force and could exercise major influence on society as a whole. This was reflected in and reinforced by the growth in the number of labour unions. Whereas there were 2,742 labour unions in June of 1987, by the end of 1989 the number of unions had grown to 7,861. During the same period, the number of union members nearly doubled from roughly 1,000,000 to over 1,900,000. Labour unions were formed in 59.4% of businesses with 300–499 employees, 77% of businesses with 500–999 employees and 79.2% in businesses with over 1,000 employees. Furthermore, progress in the democratization of labour unions meant that almost all the old pro-management and pro-government unions had disappeared.

The second new change of the July-August struggle period was the spread of unions to white collar workers. Although there had been a brief period after 19 April 1960 when attempts were made to organize white collar workers, they did not succeed. After the 10 June democratization movement, however, numerous labour unions appeared in financial institutions, mass media firms, hospitals, universities and government investment organs. In addition, teachers at schools of all levels struggled against interference from the government, from the conservative camp and from the privileged elements of society to form the National Teachers Labour Union and join in the labour movement. In addition to the white collar unions' demands for better pay and better working conditions, the mass media labour unions issued demands for the institutionalization of fair reporting and the National Teachers Labour Union made its call for 'true education' to stand at the front of the struggle for democratization.

The third change to come out of the July-August struggle was the creation of a new 'democratic' national labour organization separate from the old Federation of Korean Trade Unions. First, there was the 1987 formation of regional labour union associations led by the new democratic labour unions that had come into being after the 10 June democratization movement and other older unions that had democratized themselves. Unlike the labour unions of the Federation of Korean Trade Unions, these new regional labour union associations took a very clear stance in their relations with management, implemented democratic operational practices within their unions, and began to establish themselves in such locales as Masan and Ch'angwŏn. After a certain period of preparation, the regional labour union associations formed the Korean Confederation of Trade Unions under the chairmanship of Tan Pyŏngho in January 1990. The Korean Confederation of Trade Unions presented itself as following the traditions of the democratic labour union movement that began in the 1970s. It declared that it would 'overcome the co-operative and undemocratic labour unions of the Federation of Korean Trade Unions to develop an autonomous and democratic labour movement', and that 'it would struggle in solidarity with various democratic forces to attain economic and social reform and to advance the cause of the independent, democratic and peaceful reunification of the fatherland'.

The Korean Confederation of Trade Unions subsequently led a nationwide solidarity struggle for wage increases, actively supported the collective actions of individual branches and led a general strike on May Day. It also joined the 'national alliance', a *minjung* organization, and participated in the political struggle for democratization. But it was not particularly successful in expanding the number of unions under its umbrella because of active suppression by the government. Thus it was not able to become anything beyond the status of a militant minority within the overall labour movement. Although many large enterprise labour unions sympathized with the Korean Confederation of Trade Unions, they were concerned about management's reaction and thus did not join the Confederation, meaning that there were real limits to the Confederation's ability to expand its influence.

The white collar unions also formed separate occupational unions away from the Federation of Korean Trade Unions. They created nation-wide organizations such as the Federation of Office and Financial Workers, the Federation of Hospital Workers, the Federation of Professional and Technicians, and the Federation of Broadcast and Print Media Workers and formed a nation-wide Occupational Union Association Council. The Council did not succeed in its attempt to merge with the Korean Confederation of Trade Unions, but it agreed with many of the Confederation's goals and engaged in many activities in support of the overall advancement of the labour movement.

On the other hand, the Federation of Korean Trade Unions, stimulated by the nation-wide expansion of democratic labour unions, held a large-scale meeting at which it expressed its strong opposition to certain government proposals. The Federation, however, had real limits in its ability to side with the workers against government suppression of the labour movement.

The labour movement which was activated by the 10 June democratization movement began to contract as a result of renewed government suppression in 1989. The number of collective actions decreased sharply from 1,873 in 1988 and 1,616 in 1989 to 322 in 1990, and 234 in 1991. The 'no work, no pay' policy of government and management was fulfilled. The labour movement fought strongly against, but failed to prevent, the 1992 implementation of the aggregate wage system. Solidarity activities among labour unions also decreased, and even though there was growing awareness of the need to overcome the company union system, in reality the company union system grew stronger. The number of union members belonging to the Confederation of Korean Trade Unions continued to decline to the extent that some of its unions were no longer able to function. Participation by members of company unions locally also weakened, so that management was in a position to anticipate support from union members for the moderate, management-labour co-operation line.

On the other hand, even after 1990, labour union elections at major enterprises generally continued to choose workers who called for democratic labour unions, making it possible to maintain some momentum toward a democratic labour movement. This can be seen in the strikes by individual unions at Hyundai Heavy Industries and the government-owned Korean Broadcasting System calling for an end to government suppression.

REFERENCES

Kim Yunhwan, Kim Nakchung, *Han'guk nodong undong sa* (History of the Korean labour movement), Seoul: Ilchokak, 1975.

Han'guk nodong chohap ch'ongyŏnmaeng, *Han'guk nodong chohap undong sa* (History of the Korean labour union movement), 1979.

Kim Nakchung, *Han'guk nodong undong sa–haebanghu p'yŏn* (History of the Korean labour movement after liberation), Seoul: Ch'ongsa, 1982.

Han'guk kidokkyo kyohoe hyŏbŭihoe, *1970nyŏndae nodong hyŏnjang kwa chŭngŏn* (Testimony on the workplace of the 1970s), Seoul: P'ulpit, 1984.

Kim Kŭmsu, Pak Hyŏnch'ae oe, *Han'guk nodong undong non* (Theories on the Korean labour movement), Miraesa, 1985.

Yi Yŏngmin, *Hyŏn tan'gye han'guk nodong undong ŭi kwaje* (Tasks of the Korean labour movement at the current stage), Chuksan, 1988.

Han'guk sahoe yŏn'guso, *Nodong chohap chojik yŏn'gu* (Studies in the organization of labour unions), Paeksan sŏdang, 1989.

Han'guk yŏksa yŏn'guhoe hyŏndaesa yŏn'guban, *Han'guk hyondae sa 4* (Contemporary Korean history, volume 4), Seoul: P'ulpit, 1991.

SECTION THREE

The Cultural Movement of the Era of Division

THE DIVISION OF THE CULTURAL WORLD

National cultural activities, which had been mostly stagnant throughout the colonial era and especially in the period of wars of aggression near the end, took on new life after the defeat of Japan and many new cultural organizations of various kinds were formed. But these new organizations almost immediately split along left- and right-wing lines, bringing a division in the world of culture and art. This meant a 50% reduction in the capacity for cultural reconstruction and confusion over the direction in which such reconstruction should proceed.

In the case of literary circles, initially writers from the KAPF (Korean Proletariat Artists Federation) group and some writers from the 'pure literature' group joined to form the Headquarters for the Construction of Korean Literature while another KAPF-led group formed a Proletarian Literature League. Subsequently these two organizations merged to form the Korean Writers League with Hong Myŏnghŭi as chair and Yi T'aejun (1904–?) and Yi Pyŏnggi (1891–1968) as vice-chairs on 16 December 1945.

A right-wing writers' association known as the Central Cultural Association was also formed. This association then developed into the All-Korea Writers' Association with Chŏng Inbo as chair, and Pak Chonghwa (1901–81) and Sŏl Ŭisik as vice-chairs, established on 13 March 1946. A vanguard organization with an even stronger right-wing slant, the Korean Youth Writers' Association under Kim Tongni as chair, was created on 4 April 1946.

In the case of the arts, a Headquarters for the Construction of Korean Art of an unclear nature that covered such fields as Eastern painting, Western painting, sculpture, industrial art, children's art and propaganda art was formed on 18 August 1945. Once, however, the left-wing Proletarian Art League was formed on 20 September, the Headquarters for the Construction of Korean Art was disbanded. The Proletarian Art League subsequently led to the formation of the Korean Artists' League which then merged with a different organization, the Korean Plastic Arts League, to create the Korean Arts League under the chairmanship of Kil Chinsŏp. On the other hand, after the dissolution of the Headquarters for the Construction of Korean Art, a right-wing art organization known as the Korean Artists' Association was established with Ko Ûidong (1886–1965) as chair. The two organizations existed in confrontation with each other until the Korean Arts League was purged after the formation of the Syngman Rhee government in 1948.

Drama circles formed a Headquarters for the Construction of Korean Drama that, like the Headquarters for the Construction of Korean Art, did not have a sharp distinction between left and right. The left-wing also formed its Proletarian Drama League. The left-wing elements inside the Headquarters for the Construction of Korean Drama subsequently joined with the Proletarian Drama League to form the Korean Drama League, set forth a programme calling for the liquidation of remaining Japanese elements and old feudal elements, for the rejection of fascism, the establishment of a progressive national theatre, and alliance with progressive international drama groups. It also established such affiliated drama groups as the Korean Drama Theatre group and took the initiative in the world of drama right after liberation. On the other hand, right-wing elements that left the Headquarters for the Construction of Korean Drama such as Yu Ch'isin (1905–74) led the formation of the Dramatic Arts Association in 1947, an organization oriented towards pure drama and pure art. Most left-wing dramatists went north after the establishment of the Syngman Rhee regime, leaving the Dramatic Arts Association to take the lead in the world of drama.

A Headquarters for the Construction of Korean Music was also established immediately after liberation, as was a left-wing Proletarian Musicians League. The two organizations soon merged into the Korean Musicians' Association headed by Yi Seyŏng. Right-wing musicians formed a Concert Music Association under Hyŏn Chemyŏng (1902–60) along with another organization known as the Korean Musicians' Association. Motion picture circles also progressed through a Headquarters for the Construction of Korean Cinema and a Proletarian Cinema League before forming the Korean Cinema League under An Chonghwa (1902–66) as chair of its central executive committee. The Korean Cinema League had a number of subsidiary organizations for such things as production, promotion, technology and research, and also had provincial organizations.

The separate establishment of these cultural organizations meant that general associations would also be separately established. First, there was the 18 August 1945 creation of the Central Association for the Construction of Korean Culture as a general association for the various construction headquarters for literature, art and music. This Central Association, whose programme called for the liberation of culture, the construction of culture and the formation of a united front, was the first general association of artists formed after liberation and the left/right distinctions of its constituent organizations was not clear. However, the almost immediate establishment of the various proletarian cultural leagues led to the 31 September 1945 formation of the Proletarian Arts League. At this time, the left-wing forces were also divided between those who saw the historical stage of the 'liberation space' as that of the socialist revolution and those who saw it as that of the bourgeois revolution. Such a division also existed in the cultural and artistic movement, where there developed a tendency toward extreme leftism. On the other hand, efforts to overcome the methodological confusion in the national cultural movement led to the merging of the Central Association for the Construction of Korean Culture and the Proletarian Arts League to form the General League of Korean Cultural Organizations on 24 February 1946.

The General League of Korean Cultural Organizations was made up of a wide range of organizations. It included thirteen academic associations, such as the Korean Academy and the Korean Scientists' League formed right after liberation and the Chindan Society that had been formed during the colonial period. It also embraced nine artistic organizations, such as the Korean Writers' League, Musicians' League and Dramatists' League that had been created out of the merger of organizations belonging to the Central Association for the Construction of Korean Culture and the Proletarian Arts League, and 25 other cultural organizations such as the Korean Reporters' Association, the Korean Educators' Association and the Korean Physical Education Association.

The General League set forth a programme that called for the construction of a democratic national culture by perpetuating appropriate aspects of the Korean cultural heritage while absorbing general world culture, by the introduction of and research into advanced science and the establishment of scientific theory, by the democratic education and scientific enlightenment of the people, and by the rejection of undemocratic and unscientific tendencies. The General League made its political line clear when it announced its support of the Democratic National Front established as a united front organization for left-wing political, social and cultural organizations. This action led right-wing elements to establish a separate new general association known as the National Federation of Cultural Organizations on 13 February 1947.

The National Federation of Cultural Organizations, which was made up of 33 right-wing cultural organizations such as the Korean Writers' Association, the Korean Artists Association and the Korean Musicians' Association, set forth a programme calling for the eradication of all roadblocks on the way to liberation and the promotion of independence, for the creation of a national culture out of the ideals of world culture and the enhancement of the self-respect of all the small nations throughout the world, and for protection of the dignity of cultural treasures and the individuality of artists.

Post-liberation literary circles can be broken down into four groups, two left wing and two right wing. The two left-wing groups included the writers affiliated with the Proletarian Literature League who can be seen as writers of class literature and the writers of the Headquarters for the Construction of Literature who can be seen as forming the left wing of the national literature faction. The two right-wing groups included the writers affiliated with the Korean Writers' Association who can be seen as forming the right wing of the national literature faction and the writers of the Korean Youth Writers' Association who can be seen as belonging to the pure literature faction.

Although there was room for finding common theoretical ground between the writers of the left and right wings of the national literature faction, the process of the division of the nation left no place for national literature theory. On the contrary, theories of class literature and pure literature and eventually anti-Communist literary theory became dominant. Other artistic fields followed the same general path as the division system solidified in the world of culture.

19 APRIL, 16 MAY AND LITERARY ACTIVITIES

During the process of the establishment of separate states, left-wing writers in the south generally went north, while right-wing writers in the north generally went south, making clear the division among writers. The division was further intensified by the Korean War.

After the outbreak of the war, cultural and artistic figures in south Korea formed such organizations as the National Emergency Propaganda Brigade and the Brigade of Artists to Save the Nation attached to the military office of morale or formed separate organizations of army, marine corps, and air force writers and composers. They produced the *Chŏnsŏn munhak (Frontline Magazine)* through which they produced writings intended to promote the moral of the soldiers or wrote and composed military songs. They also held a Congress of Cultural Leaders for a Decisive War to Save the Nation.

The cultural circles did their part in intensifying the division system during the war and in the process became virtually inseparable from the division system itself, with the result that they also played a decisive role in support of the post-war dictatorship. After the disaster in which Koreans killed other Koreans, cultural circles fell into a post-war slump of decadence, hedonism and severe pessimism. Even as they drew further and further away from opening a new path for national culture and from solving the national problem, they were drawn into the corruption and dictatorship of the Syngman Rhee regime.

The pure literature magazine *Hyŏndae munhak (Modern Literature)* was established and came to lead the world of literary endeavour. On the other hand, the government promulgated a system of registration for cultural figures, opened an academy for scholarship and an academy for the arts on 30 July 1954, and held meetings of anti-Communist intellectuals and exhibits of anti-Communist art. With the strengthening of the Rhee dictatorship, a group of thugs organized the Corps of Anti-Communist Artists and produced such things as the movie *The Young Syngman Rhee and the Independence Club* to be used in elections. A 'Congress of Artists to Welcome the Candidacy of Dr. Syngman Rhee and Mr. Yi Kibung' was held while some writers took turns writing *Yi Kibung, the man* to praise Yi Kibung and support his election campaign.

Although the general trend throughout cultural and artistic circles in the 1950s was oriented towards pure literature and anti-Communist art and supported the Rhee dictatorship, the magazine *Sasanggye* (*World of Thought*), which began publication in April 1953, began to instil a more critical consciousness toward the Rhee regime among its readers. Near the end of the Rhee regime, literature written to expose social ills and works written to give voice to the pain of national division began to appear despite the strong influence of existentialism in south Korean literary circles.

The 1956 poem *Hyujŏnsŏn* (*Cease-fire line*) by Im Pongu searches for the 'beautiful path' even as it is filled with pain from the war and fear of the fresh outbreak of hostilities.

> Oh, that chilling scene of two sides staring at each other,
> What has become of the beautiful spirit of Koguryŏ and tales of Silla?
> The sky occupied by all those stars is, in the end, just one.
>
> . . .
>
> What meaning can be found here for our faces fearful of some unspoken dread?
>
> . . .
>
> Gruesome wind that must blow like the tongue of a poisonous snake,
> Will you have us endure yet another winter's misery like that you already know?
> How much longer must the innocent flowers live where they are now?
> Is this all there is to the beautiful path?

The 19 April Revolution, which arose at the time when protest literature was just beginning to challenge the dominance of pure literature and anti-Communist literature, had a huge influence on literature and the arts. To begin with, the National Federation of Cultural Organizations and the Corps of Anti-Communist Artists which had filled the roles of puppet organizations for the Rhee dictatorship were disbanded. A new national literature-oriented Post-War Writers' Association that called for the 'rejection of the objective limitations imposed by the dictatorial regime and the self-justified actions of literary politicians and the more active writing of works for the establishment of national literature' was formed. Furthermore, there was a flood of works that sung the praises of the 19 April movement and of democracy. This was the awakening of the literary world which had been mired in symbolism, surrealism and existentialism during the Rhee years.

The following poem by an elementary student became widely known.

> That unforgettable day, April 19,
>
> . . .
>
> On the way home from school,
> Bullets flew through the air
> And blood covered the streets.
> The lonely discarded book bag
> Was as heavy as it could be.
> I know, yes, we all know
> Even if mom and dad say nothing
> Why our brothers and sisters were bleeding.

As seen in the following poem by Pak Tujin, the entire literary world became a space of 'participation' that sung the praises of freedom and democracy.

> True democracy in government,
> True freedom of thought,
> True parity in the economy,
> True equality in human rights.
> Our goal is victory for the Fatherland,
> Our goal is the greatest victory,
> Our goals are the victory of humankind,
> Justice, humanity, freedom, equality, love.
> Until we attain our revolution
> For the victory of the people,
> We cannot yet
> Lower our picket signs.
> We cannot yet
> Stop shouting our blood.
> We cannot yet
> Stop our progress
> On the road of blood and fire.
> Oh, revolution!

However, this new movement among cultural and artistic circles came to an end with the 16 May 1961 military *coup*. The new military government issued an edict ordering the dissolution, along with all social organizations, of all cultural and artistic organizations. The military government also formed a new General Federation of Korean Artistic and Cultural Organizations to take the place of the Rhee regime's National Federation of Cultural Organizations in January 1962.

Although the cultural world contracted once again after the military *coup*, the tendency of literary activity towards exposing wrongdoing and towards criticism of the system became more active as a result of such things as economic development, the agreement normalizing relations between Korea and Japan, the dispatch of troops to Vietnam and the amendment of the constitution to allow Park Chung Hee to run for a third term as president. Furthermore, there was an expanding awareness of the social nature of literature and an increasing historical consciousness in literary activities. The following poem by Sin Tongmun shows Korea to be a fearsome, frustrating, anguishing, unjust and tragic fatherland.

> A quiet rear area,
> A warm village path,
> No war, no enemy,
> Just the sound of army boots,
> Passing in the night,
> Does it not scare you?
> Oh, my fatherland.
> 'Advance' and 'retreat',
> Heavier than chains,
> Commands back and forth,
> Are you not stifled?
> Oh, my fatherland.
> They block our innocent,
> Eyes, ears, and mouths,
> And sign their refrain,
> Just follow after us!
> Are you not enraged?
> Oh, my fatherland.

Nam Chŏnghyŏn's novel, *Punji* (*Land of Excrement*) that was published around the same time resulted in the author being arrested under the anti-Communist law on charges of being anti-Japanese, anti-American and anti-government.

The literary world, whose social and historical consciousness had been elevated through the 19 April revolution and the 16 May military *coup*, now found itself faced with another debate between the advocates of the so-called pure literature and the advocates of committed literature. After experiencing 19 April and 16 May, one part of the literary world once again sought security in naturalism, surrealism and modernism, argued that 'art had already achieved its goals in and of itself', and opposed the participation of literature in reality. On the other hand, however, other writers contended that literature can achieve its true value only when it deals with the realities of the national problem and its historical reflection and contributes to the establishment of true national subjectivity. Kim Ujong, a critic of pure literature, reviled its advocates:

'We can understand the nature of pure literature when we realize that its advocates in the colonial period were the only ones who avoided the oppression of the Japanese police to preserve themselves safely.

Those who closed their ears to the sad cries of the *minjung*, spent their time in debauchery and proclaimed themselves to have been washed clean by the waves, were they not the pure literature people?'

The literary world of the Syngman Rhee era, which was dominated by pure literature and anti-Communist literature theorists, encountered a change with the rise of committed literature theory after 19 April. It was divided after 16 May into those who sought to maintain committed literature and those who retreated back to pure literature. Nonetheless, the committed literature theory that arose in the 1960s continued to advance and eventually developed into the national literature theory.

THE DEVELOPMENT OF NATIONAL LITERATURE THEORY

The so-called national (*kungmin*) literature movement of the 1920s, which could not deal directly with the realities of the national problem under colonial rule and turned to a kind of antiquarianism before it began to fall apart in the 1930s, managed to persist up to liberation in 1945, but was rendered irrelevant by a new national (*minjok*) literature debate that arose immediately after liberation. The national literature theory of the leftist writers centred on the Korean Writers' League argued for a while that the task of national literature was the erection of a democratic government that had as its goals the national independence and national liberation and gave precedence to national literature over class literature by arguing that the 'the essence of national literature is not in the question of nation versus class but rather in the question of nation versus anti-nation'.

However, the strengthening of right-wing literary activity resulted in an emphasis on the methodological differences between left- and right-wing theories and the deepening of the Cold War confrontation led the left-wing national literature theorists to proclaim that national literature theory was based 'not on the ideals of the bourgeoisie but on the ideals of the workers and peasants'. On the other hand, the right wing's All-Korea Writers' Association presented a founding statement of principles that called for 'the truest and most democratic view of the state and view of the world that respects human rights, protects freedom, destroys class divisions and the gap between rich and poor', the 'reconstruction of the fatherland, whose history had been disrupted, on the basis of the ideal of the nation-state' and the 'construction of a true democratic culture that had become the ideal of politically oriented life after experiencing life-or-death struggles'. This was the presentation of a national literature theory that served the construction of a democratic nation-state and that was virtually identical to that first set forth by the Korean Writers' League.

This kind of national literature theory was all but eradicated during the process of the establishment of separate states and the national bloodletting of the Korean War. Post-war literary theory was either bound up in the pure literature theory that was totally alienated from the problems of political, economic and social realities or, in the case of those writers who had some degree of concern about national realities, was limited to anti-Communist literary theory. The Park Chung Hee regime, concerned about the weakness of its legitimacy, emphasized national autonomy (*chuch'e sŏng*) and pursued a restorationist cultural policy of preserving and restoring traditional culture.

The Park regime's restorationist policy notwithstanding, the 1970s saw the reappearance of a national literature theory inspired by the growth of *minjung* consciousness through the experiences of the post-19-April democracy and national reunification movements and the 4 July 1972 north-south joint statement. The national literature theory of this period developed on the basis of a critique of real political, economic and social problems, on the practices of the democratization movement, on the national reunification problem, and on an understanding of the problems of and solidarity with the countries of the Third World.

The national literature movement of the 1970s, which was developed largely through the pages of the quarterly *Creation and Critique (Ch'angjak kwa pip'yŏng)* founded in 1966, went beyond the protest literature and committed literature of the early-1960s to systematize and put into practice national literature theory. The national literature of this time was defined as 'literature that arose during the process of overcoming feudalism and developed as a subject of the national liberation movement and depicts the desperate experiences of the *minjung* who form a solid base of the national and democratic capacities of our time', and as 'literature that unifies within itself the anti-feudal modern consciousness and the anti-imperialist nation consciousness that are the highest values of national history' (Yŏm Muung). This constituted affirmation that national literature was literature that depicted the realities of the lives of the *minjung* who had emerged as the historical subject responsible for carrying out the historical tasks of overcoming feudalism and imperialism that were directly related to the modern Korean national movement and national liberation movement.

This national literature theory spread to the national cultural movement and developed an even closer linkage with the national historical task of the division period, as seen in the following declaration:

The mission entrusted to our national cultural movement is to grasp concretely the situation of our national reunification-oriented *minjung* movement, to lead it to the proper path, and to ensure its proper practice. In order to achieve this, our national cultural movement must participate in the practice of the struggle demanding the restoration of basic civil rights and improvement in the living conditions of the working masses and must make efforts to promote the national literature and national artistic movements, to analyse and criticise comprador culture, and to create non-institutional media and education.

Furthermore, the national cultural movement declared that it must link itself with the human liberation movement in order to reject fascism, statism and racial discrimination, and must link itself with the practices of the human rights movement and the national unification movement in order to realize the greatest task of the national history of the division era, the democratic reunification of Korea; also the 'national literature movement must make clear that it is part of the most progressive literary movement of the world, the literature of the Third World' (Paek Nakch'ŏng).

The 1970s establishment of national literature theory was accompanied by its sublimation in literary works and its application in practical action. In his 1967 poem *Cast off the Shell*, Sin Tonghyŏp (1930–69) emphasized that the true seed of the nation was the forces oriented toward national reunification.

Go away, you outer shell.
April leaves only the seed,
The shell must go away.
The shell must go away.
At the ferry of the Tonghak years, only the clamour remains,
The shell has gone away.
One more time, once again,
The shell must go away.
In this place two hearts that have brought themselves so far,
Asadal and Asanyŏ stand before the wedding hall of neutrality,
Show their shyness,
And bow to each other.
The shell must go away.
From Halla to Paektu,
The fragrant earth shall remain,
The iron of war must go away.

In addition, Kim Chiha's poem *Ojŏk* (*The five bandits*), Hwang Sŏgyŏng's novel *Kaekchi* (*A foreign land*) and Sin Kyŏngnim's poem *Nongmu* (*Peasant dance*) exposed corruption and depicted the growth of workers' consciousness and decried the miseries of peasant life.

Furthermore, writers' opposition to Park Chung Hee's Yusin system found immediate expression in action. The 'declaration for free media practice' that was issued by reporters at the *Tong ilbo* newspaper on 24 October 1947 and spread to the entire media provided the occasion for over 100 writers to form the 'Association of Writers Association for Free Practice' on 18 November 1974. The Association demanded the release of intellectuals, religious leaders and students who had been detained by emergency measures and also demanded freedom of the press, freedom of publication, freedom of assembly, freedom of association, freedom of religion and freedom of expression, and the revision of labour laws along democratic lines. It also continued the anti-dictatorship struggle while sublimating the problems of democracy and national reunification it the works of its members.

This can be seen in the following poem by Ko Ûn.

> Looking at the flowers and water in this remote place,
> I found resolve walking mountain paths in Kangwŏn,
> Nothing has meaning without north-south reunificiation.
> The democracy we have so craved has no meaning,
> The only true meaning is the meaning of reunification.
> The man who turns back submissively before a country bull,
> Will hope in his dreams tonight under the light of torches
> For a life in a country, our country, made whole.
> No, we must not end our days in a land of two pieces,
> Our land is not two pieces where we sleep and eat,
> They say tomorrow is the day of reunification.
> Tomorrow is always the day of reunification.
> I will climb to the top of Ch'ŏngbong, to the heavens,
> And I will cut off my head to see the Diamond Mountains.

The national literature movement of the 1970s can be said to have progressed along three major directions. The first was the active effort to establish the theory of national literature itself. The second was the depiction of the national and historical tasks in its works to a much greater degree than ever before. The third was the way in which writers practised and put into action the theory of national literature.

THE DEEPENING OF NATIONAL LITERATURE THEORY

The national literature circles suffered a severe blow with the establishment of the Chun Doo Hwan regime at the beginning of the 1980s. The quarterly journals that had led the national literature movement in the 1970s, *Creation and Critique* and *Literature and Intellect* (*Munhak kwa chisŏng*), were shut down by the Chun regime on 31 July 1980. Nonetheless, the quarterly *Practical Literature* (*Silch'ŏn munhak*) continued to be published and such irregular publications as *The Poetry of May* (*Owŏl si*), *Poetry and Economy* (*Si wa kyŏngje*) and *The Literature of Life* (*Salm ŭi munhak*), known collectively as '*muk'u*' were published actively, opening the so-called '*muk'u*' period. This movement overcame suppression by the military dictatorship to spread widely among the nationally-oriented and *minjung*-oriented movements.

The Association of Writers for Free Practice lapsed into activity for a while under the suppression of the Chun regime in the early-1980s but it revived itself by linking up with the new generation of young writers who made their appearance through *muk'u* activities. The Association of Writers for Free Practice announced their 1 August 1985 'declaration of 401 writers for freedom in writing and expression' and their February 1987 '1987 declaration of writers for free practice', thus providing a sharp contrast with the General Association of Artists and the Korean Writers' Association that supported the Chun Doo Hwan regime. The Association of Writers for Free Practice subsequently changed its name to the Association of Writers of National Literature under the chairmanship of Kim Chŏnghan on 19 September 1987 and reorganized and expanded its organization to develop into a large-scale organization with over 700 members.

The 1980s also saw, in addition to the literary sector, major development in *minjung* arts. The so-called *munhwap'ae* movement that arose in the 1970s to revive and creatively adapt traditional *minjung* arts developed in the early-1980s into the '*Minjung* Art Association Collective', the first-ever *minjung* art movement organization, in April 1980. This was followed by a newly active 'small theatre' movement, leading eventually to the 14 April 1984 formation of the Association of *Minjung* Cultural Movements. The activities of the Association of *Minjung* Cultural Movements were closely tied to the actively discussed social reform theories of the time, leading it to give greater importance to the issues of the *minjung* nature and the class nature of its activities. As a result, it changed its name to the 'Alliance of *Minjung* Cultural Movements' in 1986. Subsequently, with the activation of the *minjung* and labour movements in the second half of the 1980s, it merged in 1989 with the Institute of Literature and Art of the new generation of scholars of literature and art to form the 'Alliance of Workers Culture and Art Movements' that set up the goals of avoiding getting caught up in issues relating to the current consciousness of workers and the current problems of the labour movement and focusing instead on artistic activities to foster a more fundamental class consciousness and to contribute to a more fundamental social reform movement.

This period also saw the formation of the National Association of Workers' Cultural Movement Organizations as a body that focused primarily on the workplace and on activist-centred movements that were oriented toward a cultural movement based on the lives of the *minjung*, and the Seoul Association of Workers' Cultural and Artistic Organizations that was oriented toward the production of propaganda materials on the problems faced by the labour movement.

The art sector already had some continuing efforts beginning in the 1970s to tie art activities to the realities of the nation and the *minjung*. The development of the national democratic movement in the 1980s brought about the need for propaganda and agitation through audio-visual materials, resulting in the active participation of some progressive artists. These elements engaged in the activation of such groups as Reality and Statement or Imsul nyŏn while sponsoring such theme exhibitions as the *Spirit of the Times* and the *Exhibition of the Forty-year History of Liberation*. These organizations and activities provided the base for the 22 November 1985 creation of the National Art Association.

This was followed by the formation of an organization of drama professionals known as the National Association of Drama Movements and the 23 December 1988 creation of the General Federation of Korean

National Artists as a general mass organization of cultural and artistic figures that had a base organization made up of committees for literature, drama, cinema, shamanic rites, architecture, art, music, dance and photography. The General Federation of Korean National Artists had Cho Sŏngguk, Ko Ŭn and Kim Yunsu as co-chairs and was the first general federation of progressive cultural and artistic figures since the outbreak of the Korean War. The General Federation led such activities as the issuance of statements targeted on the government and the issuance of statements by cultural and literary figures on the current situation. It also engaged in such activities as attaining solidarity with the entire national and *minjung* movements, the sponsoring of large-scale performances, the analysis and criticism of the government's artistic policies, and solidarity with foreign *minjung* movements.

The 1980s, a decade that started with the Kwangju *minjung* resistance, saw emphasis on such things as the *minjung*-ness and the working class and socialist factionalism of literature and was criticized for the lack of a thorough *minjung*-ness in its national literature theory. In its initial issue, the *muk'u* magazine *Literary and Artistic Movement* (*Munhak yesul undong*) criticized Paek Nakch'ŏng and other representative national literature theorists of the 1970s for their inability to transcend the limits of the petit bourgeoisie and presented an argument for a '*minjung* national literature theory' that called for close ties with the *minjung* movement and the transfer of leadership of the movement from intellectuals to the *minjung* proletariat.

In response, Cho Chŏnghwan presented a critique of 1970s national literature theory that recognized its ideological totality and objectivity but contended that its abstract understanding of *minjung*-ness and its lack of a class perspective meant that it could only develop into recognition of bourgeois hegemony. He set forth a new concept of 'democratic national literature' that fulfilled the partisan nature and the leadership of the working class, the most democratic social class.

With the upsurge in the *minjung* movement and the search for diversification of the social reform movement in the second half of the 1980s, national literature transcended the stage of theoretical attack and defence to assay a new search for a new diversification of the ideals of the literature movement. Also, a new 'workers liberation literature' arose that denied the validity of the national literature framework itself while there also appeared a 'national liberation literature' theory that was influenced by north Korea's *chuch'e* (*juche*) ideology and a 'labour liberation art' theory that criticized the partisan nature of worker's liberation literature for being subjective.

Nonetheless, these debates did not go to the stage of abandoning the progressive and scientific nature of national literature. On the contrary, through this process of debate, the original *minjung* orientation of national literature theory was scientifically strengthened and its perception of the special nature of a divided nation was intensified to allow it to increase its acceptance of partisanship. During the 1980s, national literature theory developed to a new level through its negotiations with *minjung* literature theory and socialist literature theory.

The 1980s search for new literature theory based on class perception produced advances in the literary depiction of *minjung* realities, particularly of the lives of the working class and of the working class movement. This period saw the appearance of such poets and novelists of working class origins as Pak Nohae, Paek Musan, Chŏng Hwajin and Pang Hyŏngsŏk. Pak Nohae wrote simple and unaffected poems showing a fierce determination to overcome the realities of class confrontation based on the oppression and inequality suffered by the working class. His poem *Grave of Hands (Son mudŏm)* cried out:

> On this children's day for once,
> I must grab the hands of wife and son,
> And go to Children's Land Park.
> The hand of my laughing friend Chŏng
> Has flown away.
>
> . . .
>
> The still pulsating hand caught in the machine,
> I draw it from the oily glove,
> I am at a loss for words as I look at
> The hand of thirty-six years of working man's grief.
>
> . . .
>
> Chŏng's hand held to my chest
> Grows cold and gray.
> We wash the hand in soju,
> And bury it on the sunny side of the factory wall.
> We will bury
> Those yellow hands of exploitation,
> And those white hands that never work,
> Dissipating themselves in the prosperity of a fatherland,
> Built on the blood and sweat of the workers.
> We will cut them off bit by bit with a press,
> And we will bury them in our tears of resentment.
> Until the working hands
> Come back to life with happy gesture,
> We will bury them and bury them again.

His poetry went beyond the simple shocking description of the site of class confrontation to observe sharply with the eyes of an 'awakened workers' the contradictions hidden in that reality and open up new territory for national literature. Chŏng Hwajin and Pang Hyŏngsŏk have also been evaluated as providing sophisticated depictions of the realities of labour based on their own experiences as workers. During these years, intellectual writers also began to focus on the realities of labour. On the

other hand, the works of poets and writers of base class origins were criticized for 'focusing on the efforts of the workers to liberate themselves
and for not reaching the mature stage of awareness and practice that
embraces the *minjung* and national problems'.

In reflecting on the failure of the Kwangju *minjung* resistance, the
general *minjung* and national movements of the 1980s deepened their
awareness of the imperialist nature of the United States and anti-
American perceptions and activities began to increase. This trend was
clearly manifested in literary activities. Many poets and novelists
renewed their awareness of the United States as the cause of the reality
of national division. The poet Kim Namju, who had spent years in prison
under the Park Chung Hee regime due to the 'south Korea national liberation front incident', depicted these sentiments in his poem *Massacre
1 (Haksal 1)*.

> This country of ours,
> Of small body like my sister,
> Of long waist like my woman,
>
> . . .
>
> Who split you into north and south?
> Who turned my village and my city
> Into Asuras of agonizing cries?
> Who put iron barbs instead of flowers
> in the wound of my bent back?
>
> . . .
>
> It was America
> That speaks of love for freedom and peace
> While manipulating from behind
> The strings of the puppet
> That massacres by plan
> The *minjung* who struggle
> For liberation and independence
> Of their Fatherland.
>
> . . .
>
> Look at the heart of my Fatherland
> Turned into a beehive
> By the bullets you have sold
> Look at the bloody hair
> Of a maiden who was killed.
> Look at the stomach of a woman with child
> Slit open by the sword
> Look at the clear eyes
> Of the massacred children.

The anti-Communist ideology that had been strengthened by the Korean War was finally beginning to be overcome in the 1980s. This made it possible for literary works, which had dealt with the division problem in the 1970s, to now depict contemporary history from a more objective standpoint. Cho Chŏngnae's novel *T'aebaek Mountains* (*T'aebaek sanmaek*) stepped outside anti-Communist ideology to describe the fierce class struggles and anti-imperialist struggles and the process of national division in a way that resounded throughout the country. On the other hand, such poets as Ko Ûn and Sin Kyŏngnnim, who had been active since the 1970s, continued to write vigorously in the 1980s. In particular, Ko Ûn's poetry collections *A Genealogy for All* (*Manin po*), *Mount Paektu* (*Paektusan*), and *Star of the Fatherland* (*Choguk ŭi pyŏl*) were appraised as having opened up new vistas in the national literature movement.

Nonetheless, the class perspective attained in the national literature of the 1980s still faces the tasks of overcoming its early narrowness to achieve a new reflection of the national reality 'through the eyes of an awakened working class' as a true ideological medium of the nation and the *minjung*. When that task is fulfilled amid the changing international and domestic situation of the 1990s, national literature will have attained the true fruit it has been working toward since the 1970s.

REFERENCES

Han'guk munin hyŏphoe, *Haebang munhak isimnyŏn* (Twenty years of liberation literature), Chŏngŭmsa, 1971.

Im Hŏnyŏng, *Munhak nonchaeng chip* (Collection of literary debates), T'aegŭk ch'ulp'ansa, 1976.

Paek Nakch'ŏng, *Minjok munhak kwa segye munhak* (National literature and world literature), Ch'angjak kwa pip'yŏngsa, 1979.

Paek Nakch'ŏng, *In'gan haebang ŭi nolli rŭl ch'ajasŏ* (In search of a logic of human liberation), Sininsa, 1979.

Yŏm Muung, *Minjung sidae ŭi munhak* (Literature of the *minjung* era), Ch'angjak kwa pip'yŏngsa, 1979.

Ku Chungsŏ, *Pundan sidae ŭi munhak* (Literature of the division era), Chŏnyewŏn, 1982.

Ch'oe Wŏnsik, *Minjok munhak ŭi nolli* (Logic of national literature), Ch'angjak kwa pip'yŏngsa, 1982.

Index